McGraw Hill Education create™

Annual Editions: Race and Ethnic Relations, 19e

by John A. Kromkowski
Catholic University of America

create™

http://create.mcgraw-hill.com

ISBN-10: 0078136113 ISBN-13: 9780078136115

Contents

Preface

This collection is a contemporary guide to public attention to race and ethnicity. Beginning with the decade that preceded the Civil Rights and Immigration Laws of the mid-1960s, America began the search for answers to a variety of dilemmas in the post-WWII era. Among the most notable intellectual expressions of that search was ***Beyond the Melting Pot (1963).*** This edition is issued on the fiftieth anniversary of Moynihan and Glazer's pioneering work. Their book prompted the development of new explanations of public affairs and added race and ethnicity as dimensions and variables. The ethnic factor could no longer be ignored or neglected. This collection provides examples of the uniquely American experience of governing race and ethnic relations.

Race and ethnicity are neither primordial nor fixed, especially in large immigrant receiving and mobile countries such as America. In America race and ethnicity are significantly, if not essentially contextual. They are shaped initially by familial and neighborhood experiences. This collection documents the creation of ethnic and racial distinctions in law, methods of data collection and policy regimes and social practices that intersect to construct ethnic identities and organizations.

This collection illustrates how agents of change employ creativity and imagination into the articulation of ethnic and racial relations. Contemporary experiences of diversity in America have been structured by our past and embedded with patterns constituted by its reception of immigrants. Diversity has been influenced by wars, conquests and dominations, and by legal remedies to overcome exclusion. Race and ethnic relations are related to public policies of metropolitan-urbanization, central-city isolation, immigration and refugees, changes in the workforce, globalization, violence and war, and the ongoing attention to disparities of ethnic and racial privilege.

New perspectives on race and ethnic relations aspire to overcome dichotomous mentalities. They invoke the moral imagination of the human rights and cultural rights movements. While new they are rooted in the American promise of liberty and justice for all. This aspiration drives immigrants as they adopt the American creed and search beyond withered cultural icons and the dichotomous logic of divisiveness. This re-interpretive project has fostered the recognition and celebration of a more complex matrix of ethnicities. The appreciation of various ethnic cultures and the legal defense of such claims to identity constitute a new approach to public affairs that balances citizenships and cultural democracy in American.

Several learning features are included to aid students and expand critical thinking about each article topic. *Learning Outcomes accompany each article* and outline the key concepts that students should focus on as they are reading the material. *Critical Thinking* questions, located at the end of each article, allow students to test their understanding of the key points of the article. A *Topic Guide* assists students in finding other articles on a given subject within this edition, while a list of recommended *Internet References at the end of each article* guides them to sources of additional information. Finally, a *Correlation Guide* to major textbooks is also included.

Editor

John A. Kromkowski is president of the National Center for Urban Ethnic Affairs (NCUEA) and Associate Professor in the Department of Politics at The Catholic University of America in Washington DC. Kromkowski is the Associate Director of The Council for Research in Values and Philosophy (CRVP) and a fellow of CUA Institute for Policy Research. He is the author and editor of scores of books, convener of an annual international, multiethnic forum and scholarly seminars whose findings are published in the series titled Cultural Heritage and Contemporary Change, accessible at CRVP.Org. Kromkowski has devoted years of public service and advocacy on the Boards of Nonprofit Organizations and advisory panels of local, state and national governments.

Academic Advisory Board

Members of the Academic Advisory Board are instrumental in the final selection of articles for the *Annual Editions series.* Their review of articles for content, level, and appropriateness provides critical direction to the editors and staff. We think you will find their careful consideration well reflected in this volume.

Correlation Guide

The *Annual Editions* series provides students with convenient, inexpensive access to current, carefully selected articles from the public press. ***Annual Editions: Race and Ethnic Relations, 19/e*** is an easy-to-use reader that presents articles on important topics such as *demography, immigration, local experiences,* and many more. For more information on other McGraw-Hill Create™ titles and collections, visit www.mcgrawhillcreate.com.

This convenient guide matches the units in ***Annual Editions: Race and Ethnic Relations, 19/e*** with the corresponding chapters in two of our best-selling McGraw-Hill Sociology textbooks by Aguirre/Turner and Kottak/Kozaitis.

***Annual Editions: Race and Ethnic Relations*, 19/e**	***American Ethnicity*, 7/e by Aguirre/Turner**	***On Being Different*, 4/e by Kottak/Kozaitis**
Unit 1: Contemporary Experiences: Persons and Places, Identities and Communities	**Chapter 4:** White Ethnic Americans **Chapter 5:** African Americans **Chapter 6:** Native Americans **Chapter 7:** Latinos **Chapter 8:** Asian and Pacific Island Americans **Chapter 9:** Arab Americans	**Chapter 4:** The Multicultural Society **Chapter 14:** Places and Spaces
Unit 2: Immigration: The Origin of Diversity, the Political Constructions of Disparities and the Development of Pluralism	**Chapter 1:** Ethnicity and Ethnic Relations	
Unit 3: Indigenous Ethnic Groups: The Native Americans	**Chapter 1:** Ethnicity and Ethnic Relations **Chapter 2:** Explaining Ethnic Relations	**Chapter 13:** Class **Chapter 14:** Places and Spaces
Unit 4: African Americans	**Chapter 6:** Native Americans	**Chapter 3:** Globalization and Identity
Unit 5: Hispanic/Latino/a Americans	**Chapter 5:** African Americans	**Chapter 5:** Ethnicity **Chapter 8:** Race: Its Social Construction **Chapter 15:** Linguistic Diversity
Unit 6: Asian Americans	**Chapter 7:** Latinos	**Chapter 5:** Ethnicity
Unit 7: Euro/Mediterranean Ethnic Americans	**Chapter 8:** Asian and Pacific Island Americans	**Chapter 5:** Ethnicity
Unit 8: Contemporary Dilemmas and Contentions: The Search for Convergent Issues and Common Values	**Chapter 4:** White Ethnic Americans **Chapter 9:** Arab Americans	**Chapter 5:** Ethnicity
Unit 9: New Horizons and the Recovery of Insight: Understanding Cultural Pluralism	**Chapter 1:** Ethnicity and Ethnic Relations **Chapter 2:** Explaining Ethnic Relations	**Chapter 4:** The Multicultural Society **Chapter 4:** The Multicultural Society **Chapter 17:** Conclusion

Topic Guide

This topic guide suggests how the selections in this book relate to the subjects covered in your course.

All the articles that relate to each topic are listed below the bold-faced terms.

Unit 1

UNIT

Prepared by: John A. Kromkowski, *Catholic University of America*

Contemporary Experiences: Persons and Places, Identities and Communities

Attention to contemporary local and personal experiences is the foundation of understanding race and ethnic relations. In large immigrant receiving and mobile countries such as America, ethnicity and race are best viewed as a process that is driven by place and time. This is not to say that local knowledge is the only way of exploring this feature of human behavior and social existence. Contemporary American pluralism and ethnic and racial identities are woven into large-scale processes of social construction and the production of complex relationships. In modern and postmodern countries ethnicity and race intersect a variety of cultures. In large countries this process is significantly shaped by the place of settlement and neither entirely dependent on one's origin nor on one's descendants. In large immigrant receiving countries ethnicities are ever intertwined into dense networks that vary from place to place. New ethnic groups are engaged with persons and organizations that have emigrated from the same regions of the world and settled during earlier periods. But the clustering of all ethnic populations many generations removed from immigration constitute sets of local contexts that produce remarkably different patterns of race and ethnic relations. Thus localism is a feature of race and ethnic relations experienced in specific lived communities and the bonds of shared values and traditions that are formative of personal consciousness and group identity.

Newspapers and magazines frequently profile ethnic groups and such research typically presents a case study of local ethnicities. This evidence of ethnic experiences found in many thousands of weekly profiles of ethnics, immigrants, and enclave populations are a major contemporary and accessible source of information about ethnic organizations and practices. Relying on local newspapers and magazines for access to distinctive locations and their particular qualities are a good research strategy. In composite, these findings are the pieces of pluralism that constitute metropolitan areas, states, small towns and neighborhoods. This approach to American urban ethnicities that are becoming part of the American reality explores local expressions of social fabric and the values rooted in rural traditions of other countries. These materials acquaint us with local articulations of human variety. Such local knowledge is nearly experiential and serves as a corrective to generalizations about ethnic groups.

The challenges and opportunities of contemporary race and ethnic relations in America are shaped within the framework of large-scale social, political, economic, and cultural institutions. Contemporary trends that include current opinions and attitudes, are influenced by significant events and communications, as well as imaginative portrayals at times called "literary ethnicity." Such social processes are woven into a porous configuration of local, regional, and national relationships. Viewed from this perspective, a significant facet of what constitutes the American reality is derived from localized demography. To adopt this perspective requires attention to the variety of populations, their settlement patterns, and the movement and succession of groups and cultures from the old neighborhoods to new neighborhoods. This social and analytical approach invites the observer to examine the American reality as a dynamic process involving the shifting clustering of racial and ethnic groups and their renegotiation of relationships in new places, in new ways, and with new opportunities and challenges that are endemic to American pluralism.

Reading articles that recount experiences of ethnic populations in specific situations and places is a way of engaging portrayal of unresolved dilemmas related to American pluralism. Ethnic clustering was driven in part by the "creative destructiveness" of economic growth and the bonds of group affinity—their choices, opportunities, and challenges experienced in both turbulent group relations and the hopeful processes of recovering viable urban communities. The pivotal significance of terrorism on immigration is particularly salient for the entire country. Yet the process of forging new relations among communities reveals the development of new strategies and the formation of shared values derived from various traditions and articulated as each group negotiates the pathway from immigrant to ethnic American. Thus "becoming American" occurs in the ongoing process of addressing challenges and opportunities.

This shift in consciousness regarding race and ethnic relations as well as the technological capacity, information and data explosion, produces new models and explanations of society and culture and further increases awareness of ethnicity and race. Modern ethnicities and races are not simply primordial givens. On the contrary, they are dynamic and changing cultural forms. They are fashioned from relationships among persons and in the constitutions of groups, and they are significantly, if not essentially, shaped by the willful orchestration of leaders intent on explanations and action within social, economic, and cultural institutions.

Reading articles that address the particularities of places rivets our attention on the importance of local knowledge, the qualities of enclave cultures, and the attendant challenges. Such background is foundational for our ability to explore larger scale dimensions of race and ethnic relations and other forces that shaped cultural patterns. The particular social history of a region clearly shapes its self-articulation. A new overarching synthesis founded in the appreciation of American ethnic and religious pluralism must stand the test of social and political realism and the various crises of the moment. Divisive strategies of ethnic group relations and the global challenge is to fashion an even wider horizon of a inclusive ethno-religious synthesis. The refashioning of ethnic and racial relationships in support of peaceful resolution of differences and pan-ethnic participation in citizenship require strategies of convergence and inclusion. Christians, Jews, Muslims and the religiously unaffiliated must discover or create pluralistic forms of group relations and use a new politics of values and the appropriation of deeper reasons for convergence among people and traditions. Such a search for order awaits imaginative leaders who cast new forms of social processes to renew religious, ethnic, and cultural modes of conveying meaning to persons that are attentive to collective legacies without divisiveness. Even more such an effort requires the confirmation of the integrity of American political institutions and the attendant conferral of legitimacy to the political sphere as a parallel form of social-economic order within which cultural, ethnic and religious and economic relationships may flourish.

Article

Prepared by: John A. Kromkowski, *Catholic University of America*

Judge Upholds Most of Arizona Law Banning Ethnic Studies

LINDSEY COLLOM

Learning Outcomes

After reading this article, you will be able to:

- Identify the reasons for legal control of school curriculum in Arizona.
- Describe the concern of those that support ethnic studies in school.

State officials have won a significant legal battle in a long-running saga over a controversial Tucson schools ethnic-studies program, with a federal judge ruling that a law designed to ban it is constitutional.

Authorities instrumental in the law's passage said Monday that they feel vindicated in their efforts to ban what they deemed to be racially divisive courses in public schools.

Arizona Attorney General Tom Horne, who helped craft the law and personally argued the case in Tucson, called the decision "a victory for ensuring that public education is not held captive to radical, political elements and that students treat each other as individuals—not on the basis of the race they were bom into."

The challenge to the new state law was initially launched in 2010 by teachers of the Tucson Unified School District's Mexican-American studies program, which offered a slate of history, government and literature classes at four high schools. They had claimed the law infringed the constitutional rights of Hispanic teachers and students to free speech and equal protection.

The program was discontinued by the Tucson Unified School District's governing board in January 2012 after an administrative law judge determined that the program presented material in a "biased, political and emotionally charged manner."

Proponents of the curriculum said the classes connected students—including those with Native American, Mexican-American, Asian-American and African-American heritages —to their cultural past and their roles in American history. District data showed that students who took the courses performed better on standardized tests.

A former student of the program intervened to carry the case on the teachers' behalf when they were dismissed as plaintiffs.

Judge A. Wallace Tashima. in a ruling released Friday, said objections to the law did not "meet the high threshold to establish a constitutional violation."

But Tashima said a subsection that prohibits courses designed for a particular ethnic group is "unconstitutionally vague" and could have a chilling effect on "legitimate and objective ethnic studies courses." The judge declined to issue a permanent injunction on that portion of the law and said the court has jurisdiction on any future proceedings, if warranted.

The state law, which took effect in January 2011, prohibits Arizona school districts and charter schools from offering classes that promote overthrowing the U.S. government, promote resentment for a certain race or class of people, are geared for students of a particular ethnic background, or advocate ethnic solidarity instead of recognizing students as individuals.

TUSD was not a party to the case, but spokeswoman Cara Rene said Monday that the ruling allows the district to move forward with curriculum requirements of a recently finalized desegregation plan. The plan was the outgrowth of a 40-year-old case in which several families had accused the district of discrimination.

Critical Thinking

1. Why is banning ethnic studies an important issue in Arizona?
2. Is learning an ethnic tradition achieved in school or in an ethnic family and community?

Create Central

www.mhhe.com/createcentral

Internet References

American Indian Ritual Object Repatriation Foundation
www.repatriationfoundation.on.org

Center for Research in Ethnic Relations
www.warwickac.ukllaclsoc/CRER_RC

Diversity.com
www.diversity.com

Social Science Information Gateway
http://sosig.esrc.bris.ac.uk

Sociosite
www.sociosite.net

Yale University Guide to American Ethnic Studies
www.library.yale.edulrsc/ethniclintemet html

Article

Prepared by: John A. Kromkowski, *Catholic University of America*

Chicago and the Irish

TOM DEIGNAN

Learning Outcomes

After reading this article, you will be able to:

- Describe Chicago and the Irish Americans in Chicago.
- List and explain the most important aspects of Irish American participation in the development of Chicago.
- Explain why Mrs. O'Leary's cow is part of ethnic history.

Before he was the trailblazing Democratic nominee for president, Barack Obama was an ambitious young politician who learned a valuable lesson thanks to the Chicago Irish.

The year was 1999. Obama, a state senator, announced he was going to challenge Congressman Bobby L. Rush, a legend in the working-class African-American wards of Chicago's South Side. Decades earlier, the South Side was heavily Irish. It was the world that James T. Farrell recreated in his famous Studs Lonigan trilogy of novels from the 1930s.

In fact, for all the changes in Chicago, the same rules have always applied when it comes to politics: you have to pay your dues before you challenge a veteran.

Meanwhile, though it's true that the district that Obama hoped to win was 65 percent black, it also had "several relatively affluent Irish-American neighborhoods," as *The New York Times* noted recently.

Obama (himself Irish on his mother's side) was ultimately trounced in the South Side race, and learned that when it came to Windy City politics, he still had some dues to pay.

Obama's loss illustrates key facts about the Chicago Irish experience. First, the Irish have been playing a crucial political role in Chicago for over 150 years. Furthermore, the Irish have always had to build coalitions among other racial, ethnic and religious groups. Often, they did so successfully, though other times, the result was tension and violence.

Either way, from Studs Lonigan, Michael Flatley and Mrs. O'Leary's infamous cow to Comiskey Park and O'Hare International Airport, the Irish have left a deep impression upon Chicago.

"City on the Prairie"

Unlike Boston, New York or Philadelphia, Chicago was not settled until the 1800s. So the Chicago Irish did not face the worst kind of anti-Catholic, anti-Irish bigotry from established, native-born elites. This also allowed early Irish immigrants to, in a sense, get in on the ground floor of Chicago.

"For the Irish, Chicago's emergence as the nascent city on the prairie was timely," writes John Gerard McLaughlin in his book *Irish Chicago*. "The construction of the Illinois and Michigan Canal, which would connect the Great Lakes to the Mississippi River, began in 1836, drawing Irish laborers. . . . The completion of the canal in 1848 coincided with the mass emigration from Ireland caused by the Great Famine."

Kerry native Dr. William Bradford was among the earliest boosters of Chicago and the opportunities presented by the canal's construction. Bradford, a physician, was also one of Chicago's earliest successful real estate speculators.

Canal work brought hordes of additional laborers—as well as class tension and cries for unionization. It also meant that when the Great Hunger struck Ireland, some Chicago laborers were able to send money, food and other materials back to Ireland.

"Depraved, Debased, Worthless"

Although Chicago was spared the anti-Irish violence of other large American cities, there was no lack of rabid anti-Irish sentiment. The *Chicago Tribune,* edited by Joseph Medill (a descendant of Scotch-Irish Presbyterians), regularly dismissed the Irish as lazy and shiftless.

"Who does not know that the most depraved, debased, worthless and irredeemable drunkards and sots which curse the community are Irish Catholics?" the *Tribune* sneered. This came even as Irish laborers worked feverishly to complete Chicago's stately St. Patrick's church at Adams and Desplaines Streets in the mid-1850s.

Besides Dr. Bradford, another example of Chicago's Irish rising class was Cork native James Lane. In this city which would lead the nation in meat production, Lane is said to have opened Chicago's first meat market in 1836. He marched in the city's first St. Patrick's Day parade in 1843—and was still doing so five decades later, in the 1890s.

Meanwhile, decades before Jane Addams and Hull House became synonymous with Chicago charity, Carlow native Agatha O'Brien and nuns from the Mercy Sisters worked in hospitals, schools and asylums caring for victims of cholera and other diseases.

By the 1870s, the Irish-born population of Chicago was approaching 70,000—over 25 percent of the people. Then came a calamity which transformed the city forever.

The Great Fire

According to legend, the Great Chicago Fire was started by Mrs. O'Leary's cow. The immigrant family was ultimately exonerated, but the O'Learys were subjected to awful harassment. The fire scorched large swaths of Chicago, including a dressmaking business owned by Cork native and future labor leader Mary Harris "Mother" Jones, who entered the labor movement soon after the fire. The newly rebuilt city saw further upward mobility for the Irish.

A priest at St. John's parish on the South Side, Father Woldron, watched "in sorrow as hundreds of beloved families surrendered their humble homes and moved."

By the 1880s, 30 percent of Chicago's police force and other civil service jobs were held by Irish Americans. Many of Chicago's Irish Americans now earned enough money to move to neighborhoods such as Englewood, where (much to the dismay of local Protestants) they laid foundations for working- or middle-class parishes such as St. Bernard's.

Politics, Labor and Religion

The Irish, as they did in many other cities, proved adept at politics, as well as parish life.

Again, Chicago is unique in that, while the Irish were the largest immigrant minority group in other large cities, they were just one of many in Chicago. Germans, Poles, Jews and other Eastern Europeans flocked to Chicago in large numbers.

"Second generation Chicago Irishmen assumed the role of buffers between the strange speaking newcomers and the native, older residents," Paul M. Green has written.

Affairs in Ireland were also profoundly important to the Chicago Irish. The revolutionary group Clan na Gael had a strong presence in the city, where support was strong for controversial measures such as the London bombing campaign of the 1880s, meant to draw attention to the cause of freedom for Ireland. This became a tougher stance to defend, however, in the wake of the infamous Haymarket Square bombing of 1886, when Irish nationalists in Chicago struggled to draw distinctions between anti-British nationalism and homegrown American anarchism.

Meanwhile, Irish pride in Chicago was not merely confined to the continued struggle against the British.

According to Ellen Skerrit: "Since the 1890s, the city's Irish have played a leading role in the cultural revival of traditional music and dance."

Cork native Francis O'Neill, a police chief, was one of the driving forces behind reviving traditional Irish music in the Chicago area.

Meanwhile, as Charles Fanning has noted, Chicago writer Finley Peter Dunne created one of the great voices in American letters at the turn of the century: Mr. Dooley, the saloon keeper/philosopher with the exaggerated brogue who was beloved by millions in nationwide newspapers and books.

Finally, early 1900s labor leaders included Margaret Haley, president of the Chicago Teachers Federation, and John Fitzpatrick, leader of Chicago's Federation of Labor.

Gangsters and "Studs"

There was also a dark side to Chicago Irish life, painted most memorably in the 1930s Studs Lonigan trilogy of novels by James T. Farrell. Particularly disturbing is the racism, violence and narrow-mindedness we see among Studs, his family and friends. It should be added, however, that Farrell also wrote another series of novels about a youth named Danny O'Neill, who escaped Chicago and chased his dreams. Chicago groups such as the Catholic Interracial Council also showed that some Chicago Irish were promoters of racial justice.

Meanwhile, by the 1920s, though many Chicago Irish moved into the American mainstream, another group chose a very different path. This was evident on the morning of February 14, 1929—Valentine's Day—when two men dressed as police officers ushered six gangsters into a garage on Chicago's North Side. A hail of bullets followed.

The famous massacre had been ordered by Al Capone. He was gunning for Bugs Moran, but the Irish crime boss had escaped. The St. Valentine's Day massacre was the culmination of Irish-Italian turf wars which dominated the 1920s. Prohibition, and competition over the sale of illegal booze, led to these gang wars, and Chicago was the center of Irish organized crime. (Jimmy Cagney's electrifying film *The Public Enemy*, from 1931, was set in the Windy City.)

Deanie O'Banion was the era's most prominent Irish gangster. He grew up in a notorious neighborhood known as Little Hell. Even when he became a full-time murderer, O'Banion sported a rosary in his pocket and a carnation in his jacket. In fact, O'Banion so loved flowers that he opened a flower shop on North State Street, which was where he was killed in 1924, after he had swindled members of Capone's crew.

The Daley Dynasty

All in all, Chicago has had a dozen Irish mayors. Early city leaders include John Comiskey (father of White Sox baseball owner Charles Comiskey), John Coughlin, "Foxy" Ed Cullerton and Johnny Powers. Later, in 1979, Irish-American Jane Byrne was the first woman to serve as Chicago mayor.

The most powerful Irish-American mayor ever was Richard J. Daley, who ran Chicago for over 20 years, beginning with his 1955 election. Daley was a humble, devout Catholic who raised his family not far from the South Side Irish enclave where he grew up. As a multi-ethnic town, Chicago required a mayor who knew how to reward all ethnic groups, a task which Daley mastered.

Daley became such a key figure in the Democratic Party that he was known as a "president-maker," whose support was needed to nominate any White House candidate.

Daley's image was tarnished by the violent events of the 1968 Chicago Democratic convention. But in the mayoral election of 1971, Daley received nearly 60 percent of the vote. He died while in office in 1976. Fittingly, his son, Richard M. Daley, was later elected Chicago mayor in 1989.

The New Chicago Irish

By the 1980s, many Chicago Irish had been in the city three or four generations. But a whole new wave of immigrants then arrived, escaping an Ireland which was still struggling economically.

These immigrants breathed new life into Chicago's Irish-American life and culture. A daughter of immigrants, Liz Carroll is a Chicago native who is one of today's top Irish fiddlers. Then, of course, there is *Riverdance* star Michael Flatley. A native of the South Side, Flatley reinvented Irish dance and brought it to the international masses.

Dance is not something we would expect to arise from the streets once stalked by Studs Lonigan and his band of roughs. But history shows us that, when it comes to the Chicago Irish, there is one thing you should expect: the unexpected.

Critical Thinking

1. In what respects are Irish Americans in Chicago different from Irish Americans in Boston and New York?
2. From among the central five elements of this narrative, which are essential to our understanding of this ethnic group?

Create Central

www.mhhe.com/createcentral

Internet References

The American Irish Historical Society
www.aihs.org

The Ancient Order of Hibernians
www.aoh.org

Article

Prepared by: John A. Kromkowski, *Catholic University of America*

Jewish and Muslim, Bonding Over Dieting

A Bridge-Building Idea From Israel Has Its American Debut

DINA KRAFT

Learning Outcomes

After reading this article, you will be able to:

- Know what is the function and role of an organizer.
- Know under what conditions health, food and esteem become bonding forces.

Brookline, Mass.—Your mother-in-law fixes you a plate of food. Does she determine what you eat, and how much?

So went the question, part of a nutrition-themed game inspired by "Family Feud," during a meeting of a women's weight-loss group here the other night.

Charlotte Badler, 23, lunged forward to answer.

"What if you asked if you could wrap up the rest of it for tomorrow?" she offered, and then addressed an imaginary mother-in-law: "Because I would *love* to take it to lunch at work tomorrow."

"I love it," cheered her teammate, Adebola Yakubu-Owolewa, 29. The two leaned in for a high-five.

Ms. Badler is Jewish; Ms. Yakubu-Owolewa is Muslim. They and eight other women—five Muslims and five Jews—meet on Tuesday evenings at a Boston-area high school for lessons and activities around healthy eating and self-esteem. The group is the United States introduction of Slim Peace, a nonprofit organization that brings Israeli and Palestinian women together around the universal theme of weight-loss support.

Yael Luttwak, a documentary filmmaker, founded the first group during the second Palestinian uprising, more than a decade ago, hitting upon a formula of using women struggling with their weight as a tool for Israeli and Palestinian connection. She was in a Weight Watchers group in Tel Aviv and wondered if the leaders at the time, Ariel Sharon, Israel's prime minister, and Yasir Arafat, the Palestinian Authority president, might be more likely to talk peace if they tried to lose weight together.

When Ms. Luttwak, who made a documentary film about the first Slim Peace group, visited American Jewish communities to talk about her work, they told her they had problems in their own communities with anti-Muslim sentiment and anti-Israel sentiment, and it occurred to her that the Slim Peace model could be brought here. After a talk and screening of her film in Boston, she was approached by Emma Samuels, who said that she would like to help start such a group here and that she had just the partner to run it with: Aminah Herzig, a close friend and fellow dietitian who is Muslim. They now lead the Boston group, facilitating conversations on healthy eating and cultural differences.

The plan is to expand Slim Peace to four other American cities—Chicago, Cleveland, Detroit and Washington—all of which have significant Muslim and Jewish populations. Groups are open to members of other faiths, and in Detroit, for example, the organization will be reaching out to the city's large Arab-American Christian community.

"We are not a peace-dialogue group and not a conflict-resolution group," said Ms. Luttwak, 40, who now lives in Washington. "But we are bringing dialogue and exposure."

Mrs. Herzig and Mrs. Samuels said they were surprised by how quickly the women's questions to each other revolved around their backgrounds and communities.

"They were hungry for that," Mrs. Samuels said. "Here we were talking about fiber, dairy and water intake, and they wanted to talk about religion."

Mrs. Herzig, 30, and Mrs. Samuels, 37, confide in each other about work and motherhood and take turns bringing dinner on Slim Peace nights. For the recent session, Mrs. Samuels brought steamed broccoli and chickpeas in a curry sauce atop a bed of baby kale.

The women swapped strategies for coping with cravings for food they find hardest to resist.

"I find it semihelpful to go to a substitute like an 80-calorie cookie bar," said Debra Wekstein, a 45-year-old lawyer who is Jewish.

Hafsa Salim's eyes widened under her brown hijab as she asked: "Do you really just eat one of those?"

"Yes," Ms. Wekstein said. "I buy the ones that are individually wrapped."

Mrs. Salim, 28, a part-time human resources manager, has become close to a Jewish member of the group, Julie Bailit, 41, who works at a health care consulting firm. Each has invited the other to worship services, and they check in between meetings.

Recently Mrs. Bailit was having a stressful day, and it was Mrs. Salim she reached out to, dashing off an e-mail, to which Mrs. Salim sent an empathic response.

Mrs. Salim's skirt skims the ground, and she covers her hair in public. "When people see me they think I'm superreligious, but I have my struggles," she said. "I feel I'm put on this pedestal, and it's hard to live up to that."

Mrs. Bailit told the group: "I had never spent any time with any Muslim people before this group. I feel like my whole life is Jewish." She went on: "I'm really invested in my synagogue. I send my kids to a Jewish school. I hunger for diversity."

Ms. Wekstein told of a Christian friend who asked if she was afraid attending these sessions. She replied that she was not. The friend, Ms. Wekstein recounted, went on, "But you would be more afraid if it was meeting with their husbands."

"Yet another stereotype of Muslim men being violent," said Anne Myers, 23, a Harvard divinity student who converted to Islam. "I hear it so many times, but it does not hurt any less."

They discussed the popular assumption that Muslims and Jews are incapable of getting along.

"It's insulting," Ms. Myers said. "It's not correct. I wish people didn't think that way."

They will continue to meet for monthly dinners at one another's homes and possibly, for workout sessions once their initial program ends. A recent meeting closed with each woman choosing one word to express how they were feeling. Words like "moved," "joy" and "grateful" filled the quiet room.

"Sameach," announced Ms. Yakubu-Owolewa, her face lit by a wide smile. "It means 'happy' in Hebrew."

Critical Thinking

1. Who organized this meeting? Why was it organized?
2. What is the meaning of convergence?

Create Central

www.mhhe.com/createcentral

Internet References

The Anti Defamation League
www.ADC.org

The Jewish American Committee
www.ajc.org

The Jewish American Congress
www.Ajcongress.org

Article

Prepared by: John A. Kromkowski, *Catholic University of America*

New African Immigrants

Data gathered from 2010 US Census, American Community Survey and migration policy institute indicate that about two million African-born live in the United States; of which 53 percent are 44 years and under. They are highly educated, very religiously attuned and have strong family orientation. Increasingly, they are making the transition from legal permanent residents and acquiring status as American citizens. Yet this status does not readily translate into a sense of belonging due to constraints that are both external and internal to the African community. Many live in the space between; shuttling between two continents; remaining as sojourners in the American society and the Church, while their American-born or American-raised children struggle to find a niche. They form many national and numerous ethnic-based associations in an effort to maintain an identity within their new environment, and as a forum for addressing issues that confront them. Although these organizations provide members a sense of continuity and belonging within the narrow context, they are a source of dissipation of resources, both human and financial; constituting a hindrance to the African-born quest for visibility within the larger context. The situation calls for a paradigm shift within the African community; for a different pastoral approach to the presence of the African-born and the gifts they bring to the Church. More specifically, it challenges African-born Catholics to see beyond their narrowly defined context of identity, to pull their resources together, and to identify with and engage the broader society so they can better address issues that affect them. Doing so will better position them to transmit their values to their children and provide a forum to inculcate in them a genuine sense of belonging to the Church family in the United States.

ANIEDI OKURE

Learning Outcomes

After reading this article, you will be able to:

- Know what the central challenges are that are faced by immigrants.
- Know what sources of information describe the relationship of new immigrants to others.

The African Born in the United States

Race classification is a complex issue. While this is not a central concern of this work, it touches on it in relation to the discourse on the identity of the African born in the United States. The focus however, is to engage the issues of visibility of the African born in the American society and within the Church community, and how the African born find a welcome in both the society and the Church. The reader will notice that the discussion on acculturation of the African born does not engage at length mitigating factors that lie outside the African born community. It mentions them in passing and focuses rather on ways the African born could maintain visibility and belonging to both the Church and the American society.

Characteristics of African-Born in the United States

Data gathered from US Census,[1] American Community Survey, Migration Policy Institute[2] indicate that about two million African-born live in the United States. Figures from African community leaders are much higher.[3] The median age of the all African born is 36.1 years. They are slightly younger compared with the overall foreign-born population with a median age of 37.5 years.[4] In all, 53 percent of the African born in the US are 44 years and under. More than half reside in seven states: New York, California, Texas, Maryland, Virginia, New Jersey and Massachusetts. Between 2000 and 2012, about 600,000 African born gained Legal Permanent Resident status (LPR); of which 94,711 obtained LPR in 2007 alone. Within the same period more than 36,000 were admitted on F-1 (student) and J-1 (professional) Visas.[5]

Census figures of the African born vary between the official (census bureau) and other sources. These discrepancies are largely due to who gets counted for what purpose. The first is that many African-born, especially those whose immigration status has expired, generally do not get counted in the official census. The second is that when the census bureau says the African-born, it means just that; namely those who were born in Africa and are now living in the United States legally or are naturalized US citizens. However, many African-born heads of households would generally count their American-born children as African born. We see in this instance that while an African-born couple with four children might think they are six Africans in the household, the census bureau counts two.

The African born are spread out in major metro areas: DC, New York, Atlanta, Houston, Los Angeles, and Boston. They live in inner cities on first arrival and move into the suburbs later as they get better jobs and settle to raise families. They find the suburbs better environments for raising a family. This has consequences for the African community. They are dispersed all around. They are less likely to live in segregated areas so there are no large clusters of African-born communities; a factor contributing to their invisibility.

Other Category of African-Born: Priests and Religious

Presently, there are about 900 priests and 1,200 African sisters in the United States. They too are recent arrivals. A majority arrived since 1990. The number is growing. They are engaged in diverse ministries; in chaplaincies, parish ministry & education. About 5% serve African-born Catholic communities. Most serve the US born Catholic communities in parishes; hospital chaplaincies; prison ministries; military chaplaincy. They are part of the Church in the US; even in rural Midwest in Iowa. There is growing number in ordination classes; including those joining US based religious communities such as the Josephites.

African born sisters are engaged mainly in primary and secondary education, health care ministry and social work. They work for the vulnerable members of the society; they are an integral part of the Church family in the United States.

Compared to other immigrants, the educational status of the African-born in the United States is impressive. Some 48.9% hold a college diploma; about 20% have graduate degrees, 26% have less than college diploma (associate degree, registered nurses, etc.). 7.6% of African born in the 2010 census indicated they were not fluent in English.[6] These statistics show that African-born Catholics have some common denominators that should serve as strong basis for working together and building a strong community: (1) they share the status of foreign born, (2) they have a common language—English/French. Even most French speaking Africans also speak English and more especially (3) they have a common faith and, with the exception of the Ge'ez (Ethiopia & Eritrea), and Coptic (Egypt), they have a common rite—the Latin rite.

Living in Two Homes

The African-born tries to keep home tradition alive in many ways, including food which is used to maintain social relations. Many Africans come to the United States with the hope of returning within a few years to their home country. However, for most, the "few years" turn into 15, 20, 30 years and counting. In the meantime, they have investments here in the form of American-born children, homes they have purchased and are financing, social networks, citizenship and job. They have invested into the US economy for a long time by way of taxes and social security contributions.

In the meantime their long absence from their home country means diminishing connections even when they visit regularly. The visits lasts only a short time. They have less social capital in their country of birth and more social capital in the United States. Yet most have not taken the necessary steps to anchor themselves within the American society and the Church, and take advantage of their social location. Many still see themselves as "immigrants"; a mentality that contributes to accepting their location on the fringes of the American society and culture. Some of this mentality is also carried into the Church community.

As indicated earlier, there are elements within the American society and in the Church that contribute to this feeling; elements that are beyond the control of the African born. However, the interest here is on factors that are internal to African-born community, things that lie within their control, and, consequently, things that they can change.

Identity Challenge to the African Born

Among the more than 40 million "blacks" in the United States, about 8 percent—3.4 million are foreign born, almost evenly split between Africa and the Caribbean.[7] The way African born and indeed all immigrants define their identities affects how they interact with the larger society and with the Church. Prior to arrival in the United States, the African born was identified by nationality and ethnicity. Upon arrival in the United States, they are categorized within the American mix (Black/African American). The African born ceases to be Nigerian, Tanzanian, Kenyan, Cameroonian, Ethiopian, Congolese, Eritrean, Ghanaian, etc. They ceased to be classified based on native language and ethnicity. They are now black or African American. Feeling somewhat threatened by this new and broad identity category; a category that effectively renders their treasured identity null and void, many African born resort to, and emphasize even their narrower ethnic identity over their broader national identity and seek recognition within this narrower comfort zone. This can be counterproductive especially if such narrowly circumscribed identity reference generates undue in-group sympathies and can slow down if not impede acculturation and integration into the broader society. Social identity theory maintains that strong in-group sympathies can give rise to out-group antipathies which in turn can fuel intolerance and conflict.[8] While intolerance on the part of a minority group can at best be symbolic vis-à-vis the larger group, the adverse effects on the minority in-group can be far reaching. It can fuel isolationist fears of the other's culture and a hindrance to genuine integration. The lesson from the Tutsis and the Hutus in Rwanda highlights this problem in a larger scale.[9]

Regardless of whether or not the African born chose to identify within the broader category of **black/African American,** they are nonetheless identified as such by the American public and the salience of stereotypes associated with blacks continue to impinge on their lives.[10] Like other blacks, the African born is saddled on a daily basis with finding ways to address and negotiate American society's assumptions about them.

Belonging to the American Society

The African born population struggles to belong to the American society. Even naturalized citizens have constant reminders: (a) they cannot be president, although this is applicable to all foreign born (b) their striking intonation makes them distinguished, (c) the constant questions: "Where are you from?" How long are you here for? When are you going back?—Elements that continue to place them outside the inner circle of society, even if mentally. While these are general questions that the foreign born are asked, the foreign born of African descent seem to bear the brunt of it. He or she is asked far more frequently than other foreign born living in the United States. From a cultural standpoint, such questions imply "you are not welcome here" for long.

Response by African-Born

In the light of the "alienating" atmosphere, some African born resurrect and hang onto the home culture and seek out a "welcoming" environment, including other non-catholic Christian churches even if that implies being an occasional participant. They resort to traditional associations. Again, such recourse to reinforce one's identity is not exclusive to the African born; it applies generally to uprooted people. In all, the African born finds that although they are members of the church family, that they are permanent residents and even citizens of the United States, their entitlements and rights can only go so far; there is a glass ceiling.

Reinforcement of Culture

There is no single African born identity. The African born tend to reproduce and reinvent themselves[11] once in the United States. One finds various national and ethnic based organizations across the country, including numerous non-profit organizations started by African born groups or individuals. A consequence of this multiplication is the dissipation of energy and resources among African born. But let us not misread this as advocating for the melting pot theory or the call by some integrationists for the annulment of the immigrant identity and recreating a new one that is fashioned the American way. Even in a true melting pot with a symphony of taste, individual constituting ingredients can still be identified.

Religion and Social Network

The African-born are very religiously attuned. For most, churches are not only religious institutions; they also serve civic centers and forum of socialization.[12] They serve as central networks that provide services such as counseling, shelter, employment resources, financial assistance, health services, real estate tips, etc.[13] These are central to persevering ethnic identity. Some African born have also started to create their own church congregations with loose denominational affiliation. The new trend in African communities includes creating separate churches where African born can worship as African congregation, some with Pan African flavor such as the Bethel Church in Silver Spring, Maryland whose services are rendered in English and French. Others consist only of nationals from the country of origin. This allows for worship in the languages of the ethnic composition of the congregation.[14]

Implications of Identity Re-Enforcement

The energy vested by the African born to create and invest in the micro-identity marker often seems counterproductive. The American society sees and identifies them in the context of black identity and attributes to them the general markers associated with this group. Yet the social arrangements within the African born community tend to ignore this categorization. Instead, one sees a continuous emphasis on, and engagement in the narrower identity circle and consequently in (a) Spreading thin of meager resources which otherwise could have been pulled together for a broader cause, and better service to the community; (b) Group fragmentation by resorting to close-knit organizations which is often limited to a very small geographic region. These close-knit kindred groups serve as important safety anchors, and do give a shot in the arm, in regard to a sense of belonging. However, overconcentration in these groups often isolates the African born from the larger context and slows their integration. The longer they keep together the harder it is to integrate with others. Sometimes, the resistance to integration is driven by concerns among the long standing "officials of the group" and their place in the merger should they occur.

African Born and Church Family in the US

The dynamics described in the context of the general society applies to the African born within the church community. They participate or better, attend church activities but many generally feel as guests. How does this come about? The reasons will be explained later but for now, suffice it to say that the observation is not indictment on the host community or on the African born but a simple acknowledgement the fact.

Church as Family

Most Africans see the Church as a family. The family is the fundamental unit of belonging; a place where every member calls home; a place where one would normally expect an unconditional acceptance and a sense of security. The family is the fundamental unit of identity. Within the family, members stand together shoulder to shoulder, the uniqueness of individuals are acknowledged and each is expected to assume responsibilities unique to his or her place in the family as older members and newer members.

An important aspect of the family is its role as the primary unit of socialization. Older members socialize new members into the family so that they can assume responsibility and carry on the family name and tradition within the larger context of society. The socialization process is crucial for the continuance of the family. It is an important undertaking and requires patience, dedication, commitment of time, and investment of resources; knowing that it will pay off in the long run. The family lives on through the next generation; the generation we leave behind.

Another aspect of the family is that it is the place where we learn the basic process of relationship—that for the family to function properly, we must imbibe the principle of give and take. As new members arrive, older members of the family adjust to accommodate the new ones. An important lesson the new members learn quickly is that the world does not revolve around them. There is a give and take relationship. The family of God is the greatest family one can ever have.

When African Bishops gathered for the 1994 Synod of Bishops, they adopted the theme: *Church* as *God's Family.*[15] For the Bishops, this was the most appropriate guiding principle for evangelization. Just as it is the fundamental unit of society, the Christian family is the primordial unit of the church, or as the Second Vatican Council puts it, the family is the domestic church.[16] The Bishops noted that the image of the Church as family calls attention to the rich concept of solidarity and complementality. It emphasizes warmth in human relationships, acceptance, dialogue, trust, and a helping hand when needed.

The bishops pointed out that *building up the Church as Family* avoids all ethnocentrism and excessive particularism. Seeing the Church as a Family tries instead to encourage reconciliation and true communion between different ethnic groups. It favors solidarity and the sharing of personnel and resources among the particular Churches, without undue ethnic considerations.[17] The Second Vatican Council's Dogmatic Constitution *Lumen Gentium* points out that "the Church is a sign of intimate union with God and of the unity of all mankind."[18]

New Paradigm for Building the Family of God

The US bishops have noted that "The Church of the twenty-first century will be, as it has always been, a Church of many cultures, languages, and traditions, yet simultaneously one, as God is one—Father, Son and Holy Spirit—unity in diversity."[19] The 21st century ushers in an era of world shrinking and calls for a paradigm shift in how we define and operate as a family of God. Today's high-tech media environment imposes on us new sets of challenges. Communication systems and means of transportation have reached an unprecedented height, such that distances that took months to cover a century ago are now covered in hours. In my last trip from Nigeria to the United States, for example, I had dinner in Lagos, breakfast in Paris, and lunch in Washington DC—all within sixteen hours.

Advances in technology, which has accelerated the phenomenon of globalization, spurred the intermingling of peoples, and call into question previously established boundaries and categorization of peoples, particularly nation-state, race, citizenship and nationality. Today the concept of "global citizens" emerging out of the Article 2 of the universal declaration of Human Rights,[20] multi-heritage and multi-racial individuals are part of our common discourse. This fast growing demographic challenges the traditional understanding of race and ethnicity.

Recently I came across a young lady from Mexico who is married to a Nigerian. Her mother is Chinese; her father Mexican. Her paternal grandmother is from Portugal. Their children will have ancestry from Africa, Latin America, Asia and Europe. What will be the racial, ethnic and cultural heritage of these children? While this may not be the norm, the future will certainly be seeing more of such families.

Responding to the signs of the time, multinational corporations have devised new ways of corporate presence and a paradigm shift on how business is conducted. American Express, for example, operates a twenty-four hour customer service. But how are customers attended to? From where are the customers getting their service? If you call American Express customer service department at 10:00 pm Eastern Standard Time in the United States, your customer service will be provided from Asia, most likely from New Delhi, India. Most probably, the customer service consultant in India is not sitting in the office to render the service but in a computer room in the comfort of his or her home.

We see mergers within the corporate world. Unlikely bedfellows get together to maximize their presence or for the sake of survival. It seems that the corporate world is living out the gospel of unity for the sake of the dollar and profit while the family of God, whose vocation is specifically to cultivate oneness in Christ, is falling behind. Jesus prayed that we may be one, just as he and the Father are one (John 17:22). The apostle Paul reminds us that in Christ Jesus, there is no slave or free born, Jew or Greek, male or female (Romans 10:12). How can we live out this vocation within the Church Family in the United States? What new paradigm is needed to bring together persons of different cultural backgrounds in the larger context of the Church family in the United States not as "separate but equal" but truly as a family of God?

The Second Vatican Council proclaims that the Church can learn from the world. The Vatican has taken the lead in learning from the world—modern communications, reaching out to the Society of Pius the X, building coalition with Anglicans, setting up a website and using modern means of communication to advance its ministry of evangelization. It is therefore appropriate to learn from modern forms of mergers, and training in cross cultural sensitivity and communication to enhance the work of evangelization and building one community from a diversity of cultures.

Borrowing a Leaf from a Mega Parish in Nigeria

St. Dominic parish in Lagos, Nigeria has about twenty thousand (20,000) parishioners. Many are not located within the geographic boundaries of the parish; they come from all over Lagos. The parish community is a mosaic of Nigeria's cultural and ethnic diversity. People from the East and West, middle belt, North and South come together and work together as a family; they have a common focus; they see themselves first and foremost as Catholics belonging to St. Dominic's parish. They take pride in belonging. Such a disposition pushes ethnic and linguistic differences into the background. Does this mean they have forgotten about or annulled their ethnic identities? Certainly not! Rather, they have brought their respective identities to fashion a much larger identity that is richer and more inclusive. The result is a vibrant faith community that continues to attract new members.

Catholic Christians need to learn how to work together; to see the Church family of God in the larger context; a context that transcends individual national and ethnic boundaries. This would be a true reading of the signs of the time in a world that is becoming more complex with among other things, increasing numbers of multi-racial individuals[21] and dual citizens which by themselves continue to challenge the traditional understanding of race and ethnicity; citizenship and nationality, and calls for redefining one's self in a given environment. Catholic Christians need to learn to read the signs of the time.

A Way Forward

African born Catholics retain a strong fidelity to the Church. They identify closely with the Church's teaching on marriage and family. Their rate of church attendance is much higher than that of American born Catholics. However, the participation of African born in parish life in the United States is generally limited to attendance at sacramental celebrations. Many are not incorporated as an integral part of the ecclesial community and thus few play a role within the Church; granted that they are limited as to the role they can play within the Church.

Given the American ethos of a self-made individual, the African born might be served better by applying President John Kennedy's famous inaugural statement which is restated and substituted here: "Ask not what the Church can do for you; rather ask what you can do for the Church" and of course with the understanding that there are limitations. There are instances where some African born have offered to be of service within the Church but were politely denied. There is a perception by some African born that the parish is self sufficient and therefore do not feel the need to support the church beyond the contributions to the Sunday collection. There is need to change this mentality and strive for self reliance. It seems that the onus of integration rests more on African born Catholics. They need to work harder at becoming an integral part of the Church so they can bring their gifts to enrich the Church Family of God in the United States.

Notes

1. The basic data is from 2010 US Census www.census.gov/2010census/data/
2. www.migrationpolicy.org/
3. The discrepancy is due to who gets included/excluded by the Census Bureau of which I shall explain shortly.
4. US Census 2010 www.census.gov/prod/2012pubs/acs-19.pdf Accessed March 20, 2013. See David Dixon (2006) *"Characteristics of the African Born in the United States,"* Migration Policy Institute;
5. Davidson (2006) op. cit.
6. US Census 2010; see: David Dixon (2006), The African born in the US, Migration Policy Institute (www.migrationinformation.org/usfocus/display.cfm?ID=366#13)
7. US Census 2010, See David Dixon (2006), The African born in the US, Migration Policy Institute
8. Gibson study of ethnic Groups in South Africa seems to suggest that this is not necessarily the case. See: James L. Gibson (2006) Do Strong Group Identities Fuel Intolerance? Evidence from South African Case; *Political Psychology* Vol. 27 No 5; 665–705
9. See Susan Fiske (2011) *Envy UP, Scorn Down: How Status Divides us,* New York, Russell Sage Foundation
10. The issue of identity is often misunderstood by those outside the "black" community and even by those within the "black" community. Negative media images of Africa on the one hand and hip-hop culture and the negative projection of images of African America youth, especially the projection of young women by rap music video generate mutual caution in regard to "belonging" within the community. See Fiske, op cit
11. Jacob Olupona and Regina Geminacni ed. (2007), *African Immigrant Religions in America,* New York University Press
12. Michael W. Foley and Dean R. Hoge (2007) *Religion and the New Immigrants: How Faith Communities Form Our Newest Citizens,* New York, Oxford University Press
13. Olupona & Geminacni (2007), *African Immigrant Religions in America,* New York University Press
14. Olupona & Geminacni *op. cit.*
15. John Paul II (1994) *Ecclesia In Africa* Post-Synodal Apostolic Exhortation
16. *Ecclesia in Africa* §80
17. *Ecclesia in Africa* §63
18. *Lumen Gentium* Dogmatic Constitution On The Church, Promulgated By Paul VI on November 21, 1964 §1
19. Welcoming the Stranger Among Us: Unity In Diversity A Statement of the U.S. Catholic Bishops, Issued November 15, 2000 by the NCCB/USCC
20. See UN declaration of Human Rights www.un.org/en/documents/udhr/index.shtml#a2 Article 2: "Everyone is entitled to all the rights and freedoms set forth in this Declaration, without distinction of any kind, such as race, colour, sex, language, religion, political or other opinion, national or social origin, property, birth or other status. Furthermore, no distinction shall be made on the basis of the political, jurisdictional or international status of the country or territory to which a person belongs, whether it be independent, trust, non-self-governing or under any other limitation of sovereignty.
21. According to the 2010 Census, 1 in 12 marriages in United States are multi-cultural, accounting for 4.8 million interracial marriages. In 2010 15% of all new marriages were between persons of different race or ethnicity. Within the same period 9 million Americans or 3% of the US population identified themselves as multi-racial. For the US population under 18 years the percentage is 5.6. See: David Dixon (2006), *The African born in the US,* Migration Policy Institute; Wendy Wang (2012), "The Rise of Intermarriage Rates, Characteristics Vary by Race and Gender" From: www.pewsocialtrends.org/2012/02/16/the-rise-of-intermarriage/ Accessed March 20, 2013

Critical Thinking

1. What data sources were used in this article?
2. What challenges do immigrants from Africa face?

Create Central

www.mhhe.com/createcentral

Internet References

The International Center for Migration, Ethnicity, and Citizenship
www.newschool.edu/icmec

Library of Congress
www.loc.gov

National Catholic Bishops Conference
www.USCCB.org

Social Science Information Gateway
http://sosig.esrc.bris.ac.uk

Sociosite
www.sociosite.net

Article

Prepared by: John A. Kromkowski, *Catholic University of America*

Prince William's Struggle Offers Mixed Lessons for Immigration Reform

PAMELA CONSTABLE AND TARA BAHRAMPOUR

Learning Outcomes

After reading this article, you will be able to:

- Explain whether or not communities need organizers to resolve conflicts and tensions among groups.
- List and describe specific aspects of the Washington Metropolitan area that are attractive.

Five years ago, as Prince William County police began reporting illegal immigrants to federal officials, Edilio Morales tried to lie low. The Guatemalan warehouse worker avoided hitching rides with other undocumented friends and started bicycling to church. Several times, he said, the police stopped him and asked him for identification but let him go after he took out his Bible.

About the same time, Steve Thomas was getting fed up. One house on his street was home to four immigrant families, who were running an illegal laundry and day-care center. As operations chairman of Help Save Manassas, a group that aimed to remove illegal immigrants from the area, Thomas ardently endorsed the new police mandate.

Today, Morales's fear has abated, and so has Thomas's frustration.

Thomas says the rental houses on his street in Manassas no longer have multiple families and neighbors have resolved their differences. "I've actually become pretty good friends with some of the people who were on the other side of the issue," he said.

Morales, 44, who stopped to chat recently while browsing among guavas and chilies in a Woodbridge supermarket, no longer looks over his shoulder. "We are not afraid of the police anymore," he said. "My family is all here, and I have a good job. I have faith that Mr. Obama will fulfill his promise so I can be legal, too."

Prince William has changed dramatically since 2007, when officials, responding to a massive influx of poor and often undocumented Hispanics, passed an unusually tough ordinance aimed at driving them out. The action helped spur similar efforts in Arizona and Alabama, spread panic among Latinos and created emotional confrontations that tore at the fabric of this Northern Virginia county of 400,000.

Today, as Congress struggles with how to handle the nation's 11 million illegal immigrants, Prince William's remarkable journey offers a lesson in compromise. The county ultimately paired tougher enforcement regulations with a more inclusive and tolerant approach, a combination that in many ways reflects the current bipartisan proposal.

After a contentious trial run, the initial law was softened. Meanwhile, zoning codes were toughened, reducing overcrowding and other problems that had accompanied the immigrant wave.

Prince William has emerged as a more tolerant mosaic. The immigrant population has remained steady at about 20 percent, and the mix still includes many illegal immigrants, but some have become legal residents and U.S. citizens by now.

"At the time of the anti-immigrant bill, even U.S. citizens felt unwanted. Now the fear is leaving and people are getting back to business," said Carlos Castro, 50, a naturalized U.S. citizen from El Salvador who owns several supermarkets in Prince William. "Despite all the suffering and anguish, our community is stronger and others are more accepting of us."

Tension and Polarization

The 2007 ordinance transformed the county into an ideological war zone, sparking boycotts and threats and emptying out entire residential streets.

Proponents of the the law said it was necessary to reduce the problems of crime, residential overcrowding and overburdened social services they said had resulted from the flow of illegal immigrants moving in due to the then-booming economy.

"It got worse and worse," said Corey Stewart, chairman of the the Board of County Supervisors and a leading proponent of the ordinance. "We had police on the street telling us they had picked up suspects they presumed were illegal immigrants and sent to jail, and they would see them again in the community, and that was frustrating to them."

The law called for police to question people they suspected of being in the country illegally. It also denied services to elderly, homeless, or drug-addicted illegal immigrants. In addition, the county had joined a federal program, known as 287 (G), that established formal cooperation between local law enforcement and the Immigration and Customs Enforcement agency.

Immigrants and their advocates called the ordinance unconstitutional and predicted it would lead to racial profiling. Latinos here illegally became nervous about driving, going to the hospital or even walking down the street.

Fears of deportation, combined with the nationwide economic downturn, prompted between 2,000 and 6,000 immigrants to leave, according to a later study by the University of Virginia. Legal immigrants, too, reported being asked to show proof of residency for basic services.

"This was a very polarized community, and there were unrealistic expectations on all sides," said Charlie Deane, who was county police chief when the measure was approved.

At the height of the tensions, activists reported receiving threats. Elena Schlossberg, a mother of two who opposed the law, got intimidating e-mails. "People hated you that didn't even know you, and wished horrible things upon you," she recalled.

After the county board voted unanimously to fund the new police program, stunned immigrants began to pack their belongings.

Meanwhile, county police, worried that the law would overturn years of building good community relations, embarked on a public information blitz, attending community meetings and circulating brochures in Spanish that pledged not to arrest people "based on their racial appearance" and promised to protect crime victims from being deported.

Finally, in 2008, amid growing controversy over its legality, the ordinance was modified. Police were directed to question all criminal suspects about their immigration status—but only after an arrest.

"Within weeks of changing the policy," said board member Marty Nohe, "it ceased to be the prime thing people talked about."

No Easy Solutions

On a recent snowy evening in February, every chair in the Union Hispana, a financial services office in Manassas, was taken by Latinos waiting for help with their tax returns. Some were illegal immigrants, but all had arrived with pay stubs, taxpayer ID cards and a desire to solidify their place in American society.

"Our family is doing okay, but our dream is to be 100 percent legal," said Miguel Serrano, 34, a landscaper from Guatemala. "We have three kids and a house now, but my wife does not have papers, and we always worry about what would happen if she got sent home. But now that Mr. Obama has a second term, we are praying that he can resolve our problems once and for all."

While some illegal immigrants said they were more focused on being safe from deportation than on becoming U.S. citizens, several recently naturalized citizens expressed a newfound sense of belonging in Prince William, a former farming county that has been transformed by townhouse developments, strip malls and multi-lane parkways.

"Before, we were a meek minority with limited English. Now we are voters," said Julio Piñeda, 42, a stocky maintenance worker who was shopping for cactus pads in a Woodbridge market while mariachi music blared overhead. Two decades ago, he was an undocumented refugee from El Salvador; today he is a confident American citizen who proudly declared he had voted for Obama.

As memories of Prince William's divisive battles recede, many non-immigrants say the issue of illegal immigration has faded.

At the food court in the Potomac Mills shopping center in Woodbridge, college student Kendra Miles, 19, said that when she moved to the area five years ago, she often heard people complain about immigrants "hanging out on the streets." Today, she said, "I think they're just part of the culture."

Robert Weiss, 55, who owns an equipment-repair business, was eating at a nearby table. He said he had supported the original law but now favors offering illegal immigrants a path to citizenship—as long as they don't jump ahead of legal immigrants who have been waiting their turn.

"It can't be an easy solution," Weiss said, adding that it would be wrong to reward those who broke U.S. immigration laws.

Some of the concerns about illegal immigrants still linger. At a smoke-filled billiard parlor in Woodbridge, Jan Hayes, a 30-year-old restaurant cook, said he feared his job would be taken by an illegal immigrant willing to work for lower wages. "They're kind of taking over," he said.

But Barbara Parsels, a floral designer from Manassas, said she felt the influx of immigrant labor had played a positive role in the county's economic progress.

"I'm all for strengthening our borders and checking ID, so I think that's all good," Parsels said. "But for the people who are already here and working to be able to get a way to stay? I think that's good too."

These days, many in Prince William look at the burgeoning national debate on immigration and recognize the arc of their own journey—the heated rhetoric, the hurt feelings, the clashes of ideology, and the eventual agreement to search for common ground.

With the softening of the original law and the reduction in social problems since then, both sides have claimed a measure of victory.

"The number of illegal aliens seems to be lower than it was," said Greg Letiecq, who headed Help Save Manassas and was one of the law's most vocal proponents. "Day laborer activity has decreased, and residential overcrowding . . . seems to be almost entirely abated."

Stewart, who is currently running for Virginia lieutenant governor, said he intends to keep the issue alive in the race. Both he and Letiecq blasted moderate Republicans who have endorsed a bipartisan proposal for a path to legalization for those now here illegally.

But other county Republicans say they support the proposal. Thomas says he likes what he is hearing from U.S. Sen. Marco

Rubio (Fla.) and hopes a path to citizenship can be achieved in a measured way.

"I think folks realize that you can't keep having the same debate year after year," he said. "The demographics are changing. . . . We've got to figure out a way to assimilate these folks."

The study by the University of Virginia, commissioned by the county, found that while in 2007 and 2008 Hispanics in Prince William reported a plunge in their quality of life and their level of trust in police, these measures have since bounced back. Levels for other groups remained relatively steady. The study noted that immigrants make up only a small percentage of those arrested for serious crimes.

Police officials in Prince William argue that it was outreach and empathy, not force and fear, that enabled them to weed out serious lawbreakers without losing the confidence of most Latinos. (The department ended its affiliation with the federal ICE program last year.)

"We tried to calm these fears and explain exactly what we would and would not do," Deane said. "As a result, we were able to regain the Hispanic community's trust and build respect on both sides."

Thomas, who also chairs the City of Manassas Republican Committee, said that as the conversation has moved on to the national arena, "I think that folks on my side of the debate are a little bit more open. . . . The citizens that were involved on the other side, they're our neighbors. They're not bad people, they just disagree."

Schlossberg, the activist who once received threatening e-mails, said she hopes the lessons of her community will be reflected on the national stage.

"I think what you see is the country going the way of Prince William County, where things got really heated, and I think even the people who believed immigration should be dealt with started getting uncomfortable with all the rhetoric," she said.

"There is a sense that we engaged in a nasty debate, and sanity won."

Critical Thinking

1. What evidence is there of replicating the experiences of immigrants settling in Washington D.C.?
2. Explain the sources of tensions and ways of resolving them.

Create Central

www.mhhe.com/createcentral

Internet References

The International Center for Migration, Ethnicity, and Citizenship
www.newschool.edu/icmec

Library of Congress
www.loc.gov

Social Science Information Gateway
http://sosig.esrc.bris.ac.uk

Sociosite
www.sociosite.net

Article

Prepared by: John A. Kromkowski, *Catholic University of America*

Towson Community Frustrated with Negative Attention over Racial Issues

Hundreds attend unity rally

CARRIE WELLS

Learning Outcomes

After reading this article, you will be able to:

- Describe what universities should do about the activities of off-campus groups?
- Define the boundaries of tolerance.

Hundreds of students, alumni and professors at Towson University gathered Tuesday to declare that the school stands for tolerance and diversity, and that a student who has attracted international news coverage for advocating racial segregation does not represent them.

Some of those attending the student-planned rally said they were deeply frustrated and angry with news media attention to student Matthew Heimbach's White Student Union and the nighttime patrols that he said are aimed at fighting crime.

As they marched through Towson's campus, they sought to portray an image of inclusion and tolerance—one they say is far more representative of the majority of the university.

"It's very obvious to Towson students that it's a handful of students" who are bringing negative attention, said Becky Wiacek, a 20-year-old sophomore. "We want to make that apparent."

"I think that we're portrayed outside as divided, but this rally shows that we're united more than ever," said her friend and fellow Student Government Association member, Kurt Anderson, 19.

The controversy began in early March when Heimbach and another man, Scott Terry, who is not a Towson student but says he is part of the White Student Union, drew attention for racially charged comments at the Conservative Political Action Conference. Terry suggested segregating black Republicans from the rest of the party.

A short time later, they were back in the news with plans for nighttime patrols to watch for crime, with claims that black-on-white crime was spiking.

Towson, one of the largest public universities in Maryland, has said that despite an increase in enrollment, crime is down significantly on campus.

The school's administrators have tried to distance the school's image from Heimbach, while acknowledging they cannot interfere with his right to free speech. His group is not formally recognized by the university, since officials say they have neither the required faculty sponsor nor enough students who want to join. Two-thirds of Towson students are white.

"There is no White Student Union," Towson President Maravene Loeschke said after addressing students at the rally. "We don't like it. It's not us."

Mark Potok, a senior fellow with the Southern Poverty Law Center—which recently identified the White Student Union as a hate group—said such groups on college campuses are uncommon.

Heimbach, along with others on several college campuses nationwide, started chapters of a group called Youth for Western Civilization a couple of years ago. But that group fell apart on Towson's campus and on others as evidence of racism emerged, Potok said.

"I'm sure this is a mortal embarrassment to the administrators," Potok said of Towson. "No school wants to get the reputation as a home for racists."

Student Stephen Middleton, 23, told the crowd at the rally that he visited a store recently, and as he was leaving, a stranger spotted his Towson attire and told him to look out for himself on campus.

"Rather than thanking him for his concern, I was frustrated," said Middleton, who is black. "Frustrated because of the fact that it made me realize for some people, one bad thing can overshadow so much good."

As students dispersed after the rally, Heimbach appeared, standing in the middle of a group of students and debating whether the white race was under "genocide."

Heimbach, 21, promotes racial segregation. He says his views are based on the Bible—not on hate.

"It's not just about race, it's about culture and Christianity and race," he said. "The idea is that God separated us for a reason. People label that as white supremacy but it's not."

Administrators said they are concerned that potential students would be discouraged from applying because of the controversy over Heimbach's statements. They think Heimbach believes what he says but also revels in the publicity he draws.

Heimbach denies that he is a provocateur.

"I think he's trying to push a certain mindset that has lost its cachet and popularity," said Victor Collins, an assistant vice president who oversees diversity efforts. "He seems mired in a bygone era."

In his age group, Heimbach's views are unusual. In a survey of racial attitudes among the Millennial generation in 2010, Pew Research Center found about 9 of 10 were accepting of interracial marriage, far more so than in older generations. Pew also found that a majority of Millennials say that at least some of their friends are of a different race, while older Americans are less likely to have cross-racial friendships.

Still, students said it was obvious that racism is a concern, which is why they attended the unity rally.

"Segregation is more of a class issue now," said Brandon Thomas, a graduate student from Tennessee. "But it's definitely still here—racism and all those 'isms.' That's why I'm here, to show support against all those things."

Potok, of the Southern Poverty Law Center, said that universities should address the issue of racism head on, and that rallies like the one Towson held can help the campus return to a feeling of normalcy.

"The worst thing the school can do is pretend it's not happening," he said. "That really does give aid and comfort to the racists."

Heimbach, who grew up in Montgomery County, says he had liberal opinions until about the age of 15, when he got into the writings of Pat Buchanan, the conservative former presidential candidate. He said he believes that the white race and culture is under attack by immigration and race mixing.

After he graduates in May with a degree in U.S. history, Heimbach said he plans to look at graduate schools or perhaps join the priesthood.

Heimbach said a few in his group did a patrol Sunday night "without much fanfare," and did a few last semester, too. He said they did not see any crime on Sunday.

University officials distributed pamphlets to news media representatives Tuesday containing the school's official response to the controversy. In it are pictures of students holding signs saying "#TUstands4" ideals such as courage, justice and integrity.

Students at the rally spoke favorably of Towson's president, who has also been in the news recently after the governor and comptroller criticized her decision to eliminate two men's sports teams. The governor this week announced funding and a plan to save the baseball team.

Loeschke grinned as students spoke of their love and respect for her.

Addressing students, Loeschke said she had never been more proud of them.

"No one told you to have this event," she said. "It captures every core value we have on this campus."

Critical Thinking

1. Explain the origins of the problems on this campus.
2. Are there similar situations on other campuses? What is the best leadership style for administrators and students confronted with extremism and group conflict?

Create Central

www.mhhe.com/createcentral

Internet References

American Civil Liberties Union (ACLU)
www.aclu.org

Human Rights Web
www.hrweb.org

Sociosite
www.sociosite.net

Baltimore Sun Media Group reporter Jon Meoli contributed to this article.

Unit 2

UNIT

Prepared by: John A. Kromkowski, *Catholic University of America*

Immigration: The Origin of Diversity, the Political Constructions of Disparities and the Development of Pluralism

The political construction of disparities, immigration and the formation of ethnic groups are the origins of ethnic and race relations. American diversity is embedded in the history and demography of America. Attention to the ongoing process of peopling America and the key interventions of government that at its outset established and more than a century later disestablished the policy regime regarding race and ethnicity. Although ethnic variety was certainly a feature of colonial America, the U.S. Constitution is not focused on ethnic pluralism. The public sentiments of the founders suggested that the American idea was directed toward the creation of a new form of human order. They defined themselves not by "emigration from," but rather by "immigration to" America. Of course, aspirations and vision are more easily written than practiced. Reality and imagination clashed in the experiences of indigenous populations and the legalization of slavery. For these ethnicities and races, the American promise of dignity and freedom would be denied, deferred and at least legally begin only centuries later.

Curiously the founding worldview and sentiments are expressed in Voltaire's *Candide,* the devilishly funny, picaresque novel and Enlightenment critique of Europe. Voltaire, a contemporary of Benjamin Franklin, provided a total critique of the pre-enlightenment human condition. He proclaimed a new gospel of independence and freedom with revolutionary devotion to the avoidance of cities, a national governments and armies. He announced an era of liberty driven by the commandment to settle for a small-scale, decent private life and to work at 'cultivating one's garden'. His literary window onto a founding dimension of the American mind illustrates the linkage between imagination, policy and reality. Of course, the processes of social formation of large-scale countries and the impacts of immigration and urbanization do not follow imaginary templates. And the magical incantations do transform reality. Reflections on the founding are relevant because they point to the ideological origins of the founders and their interest in republican citizenship and forecast the first act of the Congress that defined exclusiveness and limits to citizenship. The founders conspicuously compromised the claims of The Declaration of Independence of unalienable rights fought for fourteen years before the ratification of the U.S. Constitution, which denied democratic republicanism and instituted a peculiar form of constitutional status for African slaves and indigenous populations.

The action of Congress, the Executive Branch and the Supreme Court to redress the complex relationship between our constitutional system and the social and political facts of diversity has been an ongoing drama of governance of a pluralistic society toward "equal justice under the law" for all persons in all states. Moreover, the history of American immigration legislation reveals an ambiguous legacy and fundamental ambiguity as well as ambivalence toward the role of government and best pathways toward 'equal justice' for all. Diaspora as a concept provides a frame within which the clarification of the origins of diversity, disparities and political development can be broached. The constitutional framework and the social and economic process driven by a consumer market and the freedom it demands have created an attractive ferment that is mirrored in the rise and fall of political forces that seek to influence the definition of citizenship and the constitutional and political-social meanings of ethnicity and race.

This drama of definition finds contemporary Supreme Court challenges to voter rights and other aspects of civil rights consensus embodied in the landmark actions of the Supreme Court. Advocates of immigration reform and control have turned to State legislatures to address their concerns. Such local and disparate laws will inevitably require the Supreme Court and Congress to clarify the civil rights and civil liberties criteria related to race and ethnicity in public affairs. Such expressions of popular ferment are played out in elections and referenda. The movement of public sentiment reflects the tension between the will of the people in particular states and the rule and supremacy of national law and equal protection and due process. The mediation between laws and popular expression at the political nexus of state and federal legitimacy is a challenging and contentious aspect of race and ethnic relations.

The specific dynamics of group isolation and integration point to the complexity generated by public policy in large-scale countries. Multiple racial and ethnic identity were measured for the first time in the 2000 U.S. Census. The politics of demography has been enabled by the plentitude of data and the social imagination of community leaders, as well as specific disparities among populations—their size, scale, and scope—and the range of governmental policies determine race and ethnic relations. The U.S Census has unveiled complex features of the American reality and our grasp of demography has enabled us to distinguish the imaginative from the real and thus to know: the variety and specificity of populations, the scale and region of demographic patterns and the historically embedded characteristics of dominant cultures and their interaction with minority groups.

The particular demography of a region clearly shapes regional cultures, but demography alone cannot express the ongoing presence of the past and reveal its impact on current approaches to race relations. In the 1990 Census the south and west were the only regions of the United States that had measurable respondents that indicated "white" as an ancestry or ethnicity. The south had by far the largest percentage and absolute number of persons reporting "United States" as their ethnicity, race or ancestry. Unlike other regions with large immigrant populations and descendants of nineteenth-century immigrants, over 15 percent of the population of the south provided no answer to the ancestry question on the 1990 Census. The ongoing process of peopling America and the remarkably "lumpy" distribution of geographic patterns in various states and regions are important for race and ethnic relations. The persistence of ethnic identification and the arrival of new immigrants are measured in these data and can now be accessed and systematically analyzed. The specific dynamics of group isolation and integration point to the complexity generated by public policy and to differential outcomes among racial and ethnic groups and thus our distance from liberty and justice for all.

Article

Prepared by: John A. Kromkowski, *Catholic University of America*

Racial Restrictions in the Law of Citizenship

IAN F. HANEY LÓPEZ

Learning Outcomes

After reading this article, you will be able to:

- Explain the relations between the U.S. Congress, racial prejudice, and citizenship.
- Discuss the ways in which birthright, citizenship, and naturalization intersect with the development of race and gender in the development and change of the U.S. Constitution?
- Explain the ways that knowing the historical origin of government policy influences our understanding of current policy, debates, and directions?

The racial composition of the U.S. citizenry reflects in part the accident of world migration patterns. More than this, however, it reflects the conscious design of U.S. immigration and naturalization laws.

Federal law restricted immigration to this country on the basis of race for nearly one hundred years, roughly from the Chinese exclusion laws of the 1880s until the end of the national origin quotas in 1965.[1] The history of this discrimination can briefly be traced. Nativist sentiment against Irish and German Catholics on the East Coast and against Chinese and Mexicans on the West Coast, which had been doused by the Civil War, reignited during the economic slump of the 1870s. Though most of the nativist efforts failed to gain congressional sanction, Congress in 1882 passed the Chinese Exclusion Act, which suspended the immigration of Chinese laborers for ten years.[2] The Act was expanded to exclude all Chinese in 1884, and was eventually implemented indefinitely.[3] In 1917, Congress created "an Asiatic barred zone," excluding all persons from Asia.[4] During this same period, the Senate passed a bill to exclude "all members of the African or black race." This effort was defeated in the House only after intensive lobbying by the NAACP.[5] Efforts to exclude the supposedly racially undesirable southern and eastern Europeans were more successful. In 1921, Congress established a temporary quota system designed "to confine immigration as much as possible to western and northern European stock," making this bar permanent three years later in the National Origin Act of 1924.[6] With the onset of the Depression, attention shifted to Mexican immigrants. Although no law explicitly targeted this group, federal immigration officials began a series of round-ups and mass deportations of people of Mexican descent under the general rubric of a "repatriation campaign." Approximately 500,000 people were forcibly returned to Mexico during the Depression, more than half of them U.S. citizens.[7] This pattern was repeated in the 1950s, when Attorney General Herbert Brownell launched a program to expel Mexicans. This effort, dubbed "Operation Wetback," indiscriminately deported more than one million citizens and noncitizens in 1954 alone.[8]

Racial restrictions on immigration were not significantly dismantled until 1965, when Congress in a major overhaul of immigration law abolished both the national origin system and the Asiatic Barred Zone.[9] Even so, purposeful racial discrimination in immigration law by Congress remains constitutionally permissible, since the case that upheld the Chinese Exclusion Act to this day remains good law.[10] Moreover, arguably racial discrimination in immigration law continues. For example, Congress has enacted special provisions to encourage Irish immigration, while refusing to ameliorate the backlog of would-be immigrants from the Philippines, India, South Korea, China, and Hong Kong, backlogs created in part through a century of racial exclusion.[11] The history of racial discrimination in U.S. immigration law is a long and continuing one.

As discriminatory as the laws of immigration have been, the laws of citizenship betray an even more dismal record of racial exclusion. From this country's inception, the laws regulating who was or could become a citizen were tainted by racial prejudice. Birthright citizenship, the automatic acquisition of citizenship by virtue of birth, was tied to race until 1940. Naturalized citizenship, the acquisition of citizenship by any means other than through birth, was conditioned on race until 1952. Like immigration laws, the laws of birthright citizenship and naturalization shaped the racial character of the United States.

Birthright Citizenship

Most persons acquire citizenship by birth rather than through naturalization. During the 1990s, for example, naturalization will account for only 7.5 percent of the increase in the U.S. citizen population.[12] At the time of the prerequisite cases, the proportion of persons gaining citizenship through naturalization was probably somewhat higher, given the higher ratio of immigrants to total population, but still far smaller than the number of people gaining citizenship by birth. In order to situate the prerequisite laws, therefore, it is useful first to review the history of racial discrimination in the laws of birthright citizenship.

The U.S. Constitution as ratified did not define the citizenry, probably because it was assumed that the English common law rule of *jus soli* would continue.[13] Under *jus soli,* citizenship accrues to "all" born within a nation's jurisdiction. Despite the seeming breadth of this doctrine, the word "all" is qualified because for the first one hundred years and more of this country's history it did not fully encompass racial minorities. This is the import of the *Dred Scott* decision.[14] Scott, an enslaved man, sought to use the federal courts to sue for his freedom. However, access to the courts was predicated on citizenship. Dismissing his claim, the United States Supreme Court in the person of Chief Justice Roger Taney declared in 1857 that Scott and all other Blacks, free and enslaved, were not and could never be citizens because they were "a subordinate and inferior class of beings." The decision protected the slave-holding South and infuriated much of the North, further dividing a country already fractured around the issues of slavery and the power of the national government. *Dred Scott* was invalidated after the Civil War by the Civil Rights Act of 1866, which declared that "All persons born . . . in the United States and not subject to any foreign power, excluding Indians not taxed, are declared to be citizens of the United States."[15] *Jus soli* subsequently became part of the organic law of the land in the form of the Fourteenth Amendment: "All persons born or naturalized in the United States, and subject to the jurisdiction thereof, are citizens of the United States and of the state wherein they reside."[16]

Despite the broad language of the Fourteenth Amendment—though in keeping with the words of the 1866 act—some racial minorities remained outside the bounds of *jus soli* even after its constitutional enactment. In particular, questions persisted about the citizenship status of children born in the United States to noncitizen parents, and about the status of Native Americans. The Supreme Court did not decide the status of the former until 1898, when it ruled in *U.S. v. Wong Kim Ark* that native-born children of aliens, even those permanently barred by race from acquiring citizenship, were birthright citizens of the United States.[17] On the citizenship of the latter, the Supreme Court answered negatively in 1884, holding in *Elk v. Wilkins* that Native Americans owed allegiance to their tribe and so did not acquire citizenship upon birth.[18] Congress responded by granting Native Americans citizenship in piecemeal fashion, often tribe by tribe. Not until 1924 did Congress pass an act conferring citizenship on all Native Americans in the United States.[19] Even then, however, questions arose regarding the citizenship of those born in the United States after the effective date of the 1924 act. These questions were finally resolved, and *jus soli* fully applied, under the Nationality Act of 1940, which specifically bestowed citizenship on all those born in the United States "to a member of an Indian, Eskimo, Aleutian, or other aboriginal tribe."[20] Thus, the basic law of citizenship, that a person born here is a citizen here, did not include all racial minorities until 1940.

Unfortunately, the impulse to restrict birthright citizenship by race is far from dead in this country. Apparently, California Governor Pete Wilson and many others seek a return to the times when citizenship depended on racial proxies such as immigrant status. Wilson has called for a federal constitutional amendment that would prevent the American-born children of undocumented persons from receiving birthright citizenship.[21] His call has not been ignored: thirteen members of Congress recently sponsored a constitutional amendment that would repeal the existing Citizenship Clause of the Fourteenth Amendment and replace it with a provision that "All persons born in the United States . . . of mothers who are citizens or legal residents of the United States . . . are citizens of the United States."[22] Apparently, such a change is supported by 49 percent of Americans.[23] In addition to explicitly discriminating against fathers by eliminating their right to confer citizenship through parentage, this proposal implicitly discriminates along racial lines. The effort to deny citizenship to children born here to undocumented immigrants seems to be motivated not by an abstract concern over the political status of the parents, but by racial animosity against Asians and Latinos, those commonly seen as comprising the vast bulk of undocumented migrants. Bill Ong Hing writes, "The discussion of who is and who is not American, who can and cannot become American, goes beyond the technicalities of citizenship and residency requirements; it strikes at the very heart of our nation's long and troubled legacy of race relations.[24] As this troubled legacy reveals, the triumph over racial discrimination in the laws of citizenship and alienage came slowly and only recently. In the campaign for the "control of our borders," we are once again debating the citizenship of the native-born and the merits of *Dred Scott.*[25]

Naturalization

Although the Constitution did not originally define the citizenry, it explicitly gave Congress the authority to establish the criteria for granting citizenship after birth. Article I grants Congress the power "To establish a uniform Rule of Naturalization."[26] From the start, Congress exercised this power in a manner that burdened naturalization laws with racial restrictions that tracked those in the law of birthright citizenship. In 1790, only a few months after ratification of the Constitution, Congress limited naturalization to "any alien, being a free white person who shall have resided within the limits and under the jurisdiction of the United States for a term of two years."[27] This clause mirrored not only the de facto laws of birthright citizenship, but also the racially restrictive naturalization laws of several states. At least three states had previously limited citizenship to "white persons": Virginia in 1779, South Carolina in 1784, and Georgia in 1785.[28] Though there would be many subsequent changes in the requirements for federal naturalization, racial identity endured as a bedrock requirement for the next

162 years. In every naturalization act from 1790 until 1952, Congress included the "white person" prerequisite.[29]

The history of racial prerequisites to naturalization can be divided into two periods of approximately eighty years each. The first period extended from 1790 to 1870, when only Whites were able to naturalize. In the wake of the Civil War, the "white person" restriction on naturalization came under serious attack as part of the effort to expunge *Dred Scott.* Some congressmen, Charles Sumner chief among them, argued that racial barriers to naturalization should be struck altogether. However, racial prejudice against Native Americans and Asians forestalled the complete elimination of the racial prerequisites. During congressional debates, one senator argued against conferring "the rank, privileges, and immunities of citizenship upon the cruel savages who destroyed [Minnesota's] peaceful settlements and massacred the people with circumstances of atrocity too horrible to relate."[30] Another senator wondered "whether this door [of citizenship] shall now be thrown open to the Asiatic population," warning that to do so would spell for the Pacific coast "an end to republican government there, because it is very well ascertained that those people have no appreciation of that form of government; it seems to be obnoxious to their very nature; they seem to be incapable either of understanding or carrying it out."[31] Sentiments such as these ensured that even after the Civil War, bars against Native American and Asian naturalization would continue.[32] Congress opted to maintain the "white person" prerequisite, but to extend the right to naturalize to "persons of African nativity, or African descent."[33] After 1870, Blacks as well as Whites could naturalize, but not others.

During the second period, from 1870 until the last of the prerequisite laws were abolished in 1952, the White-Black dichotomy in American race relations dominated naturalization law. During this period, Whites and Blacks were eligible for citizenship, but others, particularly those from Asia, were not. Indeed, increasing antipathy toward Asians on the West Coast resulted in an explicit disqualification of Chinese persons from naturalization in 1882.[34] The prohibition of Chinese naturalization, the only U.S. law ever to exclude by name a particular nationality from citizenship, was coupled with the ban on Chinese immigration discussed previously. The Supreme Court readily upheld the bar, writing that "Chinese persons not born in this country have never been recognized as citizens of the United States, nor authorized to become such under the naturalization laws."[35] While Blacks were permitted to naturalize beginning in 1870, the Chinese and most "other non-Whites" would have to wait until the 1940s for the right to naturalize.[36]

World War II forced a domestic reconsideration of the racism integral to U.S. naturalization law. In 1935, Hitler's Germany limited citizenship to members of the Aryan race, making Germany the only country other than the United States with a racial restriction on naturalization.[37] The fact of this bad company was not lost on those administering our naturalization laws. "When Earl G. Harrison in 1944 resigned as United States Commissioner of Immigration and Naturalization, he said that the only country in the world, outside the United States, that observes racial discrimination in matters relating to naturalization was Nazi Germany, 'and we all agree that this is not very desirable company.'"[38] Furthermore, the United States was open to charges of hypocrisy for banning from naturalization the nationals of many of its Asian allies. During the war, the United States seemed through some of its laws and social practices to embrace the same racism it was fighting. Both fronts of the war exposed profound inconsistencies between U.S. naturalization law and broader social ideals. These considerations, among others, led Congress to begin a process of piecemeal reform in the laws governing citizenship.

In 1940, Congress opened naturalization to "descendants of races indigenous to the Western Hemisphere."[39] Apparently, this "additional limitation was designed 'to more fully cement' the ties of Pan-Americanism" at a time of impending crisis.[40] In 1943, Congress replaced the prohibition on the naturalization of Chinese persons with a provision explicitly granting them this boon.[41] In 1946, it opened up naturalization to persons from the Philippines and India as well.[42] Thus, at the end of the war, our naturalization law looked like this:

The right to become a naturalized citizen under the provisions of this Act shall extend only to—

1. white persons, persons of African nativity or descent, and persons of races indigenous to the continents of North or South America or adjacent islands and Filipino persons or persons of Filipino descent;
2. persons who possess, either singly or in combination, a preponderance of blood of one or more of the classes specified in clause (1);
3. Chinese persons or persons of Chinese descent; and persons of races indigenous to India; and
4. persons who possess, either singly or in combination, a preponderance of blood of one or more of the classes specified in clause (3) or, either singly or in combination, as much as one-half blood of those classes and some additional blood of one of the classes specified in clause (1).[43]

This incremental retreat from a "Whites only" conception of citizenship made the arbitrariness of U.S. naturalization law increasingly obvious. For example, under the above statute, the right to acquire citizenship depended for some on blood-quantum distinctions based on descent from peoples indigenous to islands adjacent to the Americas. In 1952, Congress moved towards wholesale reform, overhauling the naturalization statute to read simply that "[t]he right of a person to become a naturalized citizen of the United States shall not be denied or abridged because of race or sex or because such person is married."[44] Thus, in 1952, racial bars on naturalization came to an official end.[45]

Notice the mention of gender in the statutory language ending racial restrictions in naturalization. The issue of women and citizenship can only be touched on here, but deserves significant study in its own right.[46] As the language of the 1952 Act implies, eligibility for naturalization once depended on a woman's marital status. Congress in 1855 declared that a foreign woman automatically acquired citizenship upon marriage to a U.S. citizen, or upon the naturalization of her alien husband.[47] This provision built upon the supposition that a woman's social and political status flowed from her husband. As an 1895 treatise on naturalization put it, "A woman partakes of her husband's nationality; her nationality is merged in that of her husband; her political status follows that of her husband."[48] A wife's acquisition of citizenship, however, remained subject to her individual qualification for naturalization—that is, on whether she was a "white person."[49] Thus, the Supreme Court held in 1868 that only "white women" could gain citizenship by marrying a citizen.[50] Racial restrictions further complicated matters for noncitizen women in that naturalization was denied to those married to a man racially ineligible for citizenship, irrespective of the woman's own qualifications, racial or otherwise.[51] The automatic naturalization of a woman upon her marriage to a citizen or upon the naturalization of her husband ended in 1922.[52]

The citizenship of American-born women was also affected by the interplay of gender and racial restrictions. Even though under English common law a woman's nationality was unaffected by marriage, many courts in this country stripped women who married noncitizens of their U.S. citizenship.[53] Congress recognized and mandated this practice in 1907, legislating that an American woman's marriage to an alien terminated her citizenship.[54] Under considerable pressure, Congress partially repealed this act in 1922.[55] However, the 1922 act continued to require the expatriation of any woman who married a foreigner racially barred from citizenship, flatly declaring that "any woman citizen who marries an alien ineligible to citizenship shall cease to be a citizen."[56] Until Congress repealed this provision in 1931,[57] marriage to a non-White alien by an American woman was akin to treason against this country: either of these acts justified the stripping of citizenship from someone American by birth. Indeed, a woman's marriage to a non-White foreigner was perhaps a worse crime, for while a traitor lost his citizenship only after trial, the woman lost hers automatically.[58] The laws governing the racial composition of this country's citizenry came inseverably bound up with and exacerbated by sexism. It is in this context of combined racial and gender prejudice that we should understand the absence of any women among the petitioners named in the prerequisite cases: it is not that women were unaffected by the racial bars, but that they were doubly bound by them, restricted both as individuals, and as less than individuals (that is, as wives).

Notes

1. U.S. COMMISSION ON CIVIL RIGHTS, THE TARNISHED GOLDEN DOOR: CIVIL RIGHTS ISSUES IN IMMIGRATION 1–12 (1990).
2. Chinese Exclusion Act, ch. 126, 22 Stat. 58 (1882). *See generally* Harold Hongju Koh, *Bitter Fruit of the Asian Immigration Cases,* 6 CONSTITUTION 69 (1994). For a sobering account of the many lynchings of Chinese in the western United States during this period, *see* John R. Wunder, *Anti-Chinese Violence in the American West, 1850–1910,* LAW FOR THE ELEPHANT, LAW FOR THE BEAVER: ESSAYS IN THE LEGAL HISTORY OF THE NORTH AMERICAN WEST 212 (John McLaren, Hamar Foster, and Chet Orloff eds., 1992). Charles McClain, Jr., discusses the historical origins of anti-Chinese prejudice and the legal responses undertaken by that community on the West Coast. Charles McClain, Jr., *The Chinese Struggle for Civil Rights in Nineteenth Century America: The First Phase, 1850–1870,* 72 CAL. L. REV. 529 (1984). For a discussion of contemporary racial violence against Asian Americans, *see* Note, *Racial Violence against Asian Americans,* 106 HARV. L. REV. 1926 (1993); Robert Chang, *Toward an Asian American Legal Scholarship: Critical Race Theory, Post-Structuralism, and Narrative Space,* 81 CAL. L. REV. 1241, 1251–58 (1993).
3. Act of July 9, 1884, ch. 220, 23 Stat. 115; Act of May 5, 1892, ch. 60, 27 Stat. 25; Act of April 29, 1902, ch. 641, 32 Stat. 176; Act of April 27, 1904, ch. 1630, 33 Stat. 428.
4. Act of Feb. 5, 1917, ch. 29, 39 Stat. 874.
5. U.S. COMMISSION ON CIVIL RIGHTS, *supra,* at 9.
6. *Id. See* Act of May 19, 1921, ch. 8, 42 Stat. 5; Act of May 26, 1924, ch. 190, 43 Stat. 153.
7. U.S. COMMISSION ON CIVIL RIGHTS, *supra,* at 10.
8. *Id.* at 11. *See generally* JUAN RAMON GARCIA, OPERATION WETBACK: THE MASS DEPORTATION OF MEXICAN UNDOCUMENTED WORKERS IN 1954 (1980).
9. Act of Oct. 2, 1965, 79 Stat. 911.
10. Chae Chan Ping v. United States, 130 U.S. 581 (1889). The Court reasoned in part that if "the government of the United States, through its legislative department, considers the presence of foreigners of a different race in this country, who will not assimilate with us, to be dangerous to its peace and security, their exclusion is not to be stayed." For a critique of this deplorable result, *see* Louis Henkin, *The Constitution and United States Sovereignty: A Century of Chinese Exclusion and Its Progeny,* 100 HARV. L. REV. 853 (1987).
11. For efforts to encourage Irish immigration, *see, e.g., Immigration Act of 1990, § 131, 104 Stat. 4978 (codified as amended at 8 U.S.C. § 1153 (c) [1994]). Bill Ong Hing argues that Congress continues to discriminate against Asians. "Through an examination of past exclusion laws, previous legislation, and the specific provisions of the Immigration Act of 1990, the conclusion can be drawn that Congress never intended to make up for nearly 80 years of Asian exclusion, and that a conscious hostility towards persons of Asian descent continues to pervade Congressional circles." Bill Ong Hing,* Asian Americans and Present U.S. Immigration Policies: A Legacy of Asian Exclusion, *ASIAN AMERICANS AND THE SUPREME COURT: A DOCUMENTARY HISTORY 1106, 1107 (Hyung-Chan Kim ed., 1992).*
12. Louis DeSipio and Harry Pachon, Making Americans: Administrative Discretion and Americanization, *12 CHICANO-LATINO L. REV. 52, 53 (1992).*
13. CHARLES GORDON AND STANLEY MAILMAN, IMMIGRATION LAW AND PROCEDURE § 92.03[1][b] (rev. ed. 1992).
14. Dred Scott v. Sandford, 60 U.S. (19 How.) 393 (1857). For an insightful discussion of the role of *Dred Scott* in the development of American citizenship, see *JAMES KETTNER, THE DEVELOPMENT OF AMERICAN CITIZENSHIP, 1608–1870, at 300–333 (1978);* see also *KENNETH L. KARST, BELONGING TO AMERICA: EQUAL CITIZENSHIP AND THE CONSTITUTION 43–61 (1989).*
15. Civil Rights Act of 1866, ch. 31, 14 Stat. 27.
16. U.S. Const. amend. XIV.

17. 169 U.S. 649 (1898).
18. 112 U.S. 94 (1884).
19. Act of June 2, 1924, ch. 233, 43 Stat. 253.
20. Nationality Act of 1940, § 201(b), 54 Stat. 1138. See generally *GORDON AND MAILMAN, supra, at § 92.03[3][e].*
21. Pete Wilson, Crack Down on Illegals, *USA TODAY, Aug. 20, 1993, at 12A.*
22. H. R. J. Res. 129, 103d Cong., 1st Sess. (1993). An earlier, scholarly call to revamp the Fourteenth Amendment can be found in PETER SCHUCK and ROGER SMITH, CITIZENSHIP WITHOUT CONSENT: ILLEGAL ALIENS IN THE AMERICAN POLITY (1985).
23. Koh, *supra, at 69–70.*
24. Bill Ong Hing, Beyond the Rhetoric of Assimilation and Cultural Pluralism: Addressing the Tension of Separatism and Conflict in an Immigration-Driven Multiracial Society, *81 CAL. L. REV. 863, 866 (1993).*
25. Gerald Neuman warns against amending the Citizenship Clause. Gerald Neuman, Back to *Dred Scott? 24 SAN DIEGO L. REV. 485, 500 (1987).* See also *Note,* The Birthright Citizenship Amendment: A Threat to Equality, *107 HARV. L. REV. 1026 (1994).*
26. U.S. Const. art. I, sec. 8, cl. 4.
27. Act of March 26, 1790, ch. 3, 1 Stat. 103.
28. KETTNER, *supra, at 215–16.*
29. One exception exists. In revisions undertaken in 1870, the "white person" limitation was omitted. However, this omission is regarded as accidental, and the prerequisite was reinserted in 1875 by "an act to correct errors and to supply omissions in the Revised Statutes of the United States." Act of Feb. 18, 1875, ch. 80, 18 Stat. 318. See *In re Ah Yup, 1 F.Cas. 223 (C.C.D.Cal. 1878) ("Upon revision of the statutes, the revisors, probably inadvertently, as Congress did not contemplate a change of the laws in force, omitted the words 'white persons.' ").*
30. Statement of Senator Hendricks, 59 CONG. GLOBE, 42nd Cong., 1st Sess. 2939 (1866). See also *John Guendelsberger,* Access to Citizenship for Children Born Within the State to Foreign Parents, *40 AM. J. COMP. L. 379, 407–9 (1992).*
31. Statement of Senator Cowan, 57 CONG. GLOBE, 42nd Cong., 1st Sess. 499 (1866). For a discussion of the role of anti-Asian prejudice in the laws governing naturalization, see generally *Elizabeth Hull,* Naturalization and Denaturalization, *ASIAN AMERICANS AND THE SUPREME COURT: A DOCUMENTARY HISTORY 403 (Hyung-Chan Kim ed., 1992).*
32. The Senate rejected an amendment that would have allowed Chinese persons to naturalize. The proposed amendment read: "That the naturalization laws are hereby extended to aliens of African nativity, and to persons of African descent, and to persons born in the Chinese empire." BILL ONG HING, MAKING AND REMAKING ASIAN AMERICA THROUGH IMMIGRATION POLICY, 1850–1990, at 239 n.34 (1993).
33. Act of July 14, 1870, ch. 255, § 7, 16 Stat. 254.
34. Chinese Exclusion Act, ch. 126, § 14, 22 Stat. 58 (1882).
35. Fong Yue Ting v. United States, 149 U.S. 698, 716 (1893).
36. Neil Gotanda contends that separate racial ideologies function with respect to "other non-Whites," meaning non-Black racial minorities such as Asians, Native Americans, and Latinos. Neil Gotanda, "Other Non-Whites" in American Legal History: A Review of *Justice at War, 85 COLUM. L. REV. 1186 (1985). Gotanda explicitly identifies the operation of this separate ideology in the Supreme Court's jurisprudence regarding Asians and citizenship. Neil Gotanda,* Asian American Rights and the "Miss Saigon Syndrome," *ASIAN AMERICANS AND THE SUPREME COURT: A DOCUMENTARY HISTORY 1087, 1096–97 (Hyung-Chan Kim ed., 1992).*
37. Charles Gordon, The Racial Barrier to American Citizenship, *93 U. PA. L. REV. 237, 252 (1945).*
38. MILTON KONVITZ, THE ALIEN AND THE ASIATIC IN AMERICAN LAW 80–81 (1946) (citation omitted).
39. Act of Oct. 14, 1940, ch. 876, § 303, 54 Stat. 1140.
40. Note, The Nationality Act of 1940, *54 HARV. L. REV. 860, 865 n.40 (1941).*
41. Act of Dec. 17, 1943, ch. 344, 3, 57 Stat. 600.
42. Act of July 2, 1946, ch. 534, 60 Stat. 416.
43. Id.
44. Immigration and Nationality Act of 1952, ch. 2, § 311, 66 Stat. 239 (codified as amended at 8 U.S.C. 1422 [1988]).
45. Arguably, the continued substantial exclusion of Asians from immigration not remedied until 1965, rendered their eligibility for naturalization relatively meaningless. "[T]he national quota system for admitting immigrants which was built into the 1952 Act gave the grant of eligibility a hollow ring." Chin Kim and Bok Lim Kim, Asian Immigrants in American Law: A Look at the Past and the Challenge Which Remains, *26 AM. U. L. REV. 373, 390 (1977).*
46. *See generally Ursula Vogel,* Is Citizenship Gender-Specific? *THE FRONTIERS OF CITIZENSHIP 58 (Ursula Vogel and Michael Moran eds., 1991).*
47. Act of Feb. 10, 1855, ch. 71, § 2, 10 Stat. 604. Because gender-based laws in the area of citizenship were motivated by the idea that a woman's citizenship should follow that of her husband, no naturalization law has explicitly targeted unmarried women. GORDON AND MAILMAN, *supra, at § 95.03[6] ("An unmarried woman has never been statutorily* barred from naturalization.").
48. PRENTISS WEBSTER, LAW OF NATURALIZATION IN THE UNITED STATES OF AMERICA AND OTHER COUNTRIES 80 (1895).
49. Act of Feb. 10, 1855, ch. 71, § 2, 10 Stat. 604.
50. Kelly v. Owen, 74 U.S. 496, 498 (1868).
51. GORDON AND MAILMAN, *supra* at § 95.03[6].
52. Act of Sept. 22, 1922, ch. 411, § 2, 42 Stat. 1021.
53. GORDON AND MAILMAN, *supra* at § 100.03[4][m].
54. Act of March 2, 1907, ch. 2534, § 3, 34 Stat. 1228. This act was upheld in MacKenzie v. Hare, 239 U.S. 299 (1915) (expatriating a U.S.-born woman upon her marriage to a British citizen).
55. Act of Sept. 22, 1922, ch. 411, § 3, 42 Stat. 1021.
56. *Id.* The Act also stated that "[n]o woman whose husband is not eligible to citizenship shall be naturalized during the continuance of the marriage."
57. Act of March 3, 1931, ch. 442, § 4(a), 46 Stat. 1511.
58. The loss of birthright citizenship was particularly harsh for those women whose race made them unable to regain citizenship through naturalization, especially after 1924, when the immigration laws of this country barred entry to any alien ineligible to citizenship. Immigration Act of 1924, ch. 190, § 13(c), 43 Stat. 162. *See, e.g.,* Ex parte (Ng) Fung Sing, 6 F.2d 670 (W. D. Wash. 1925). In that case, a U.S. birthright citizen

of Chinese descent was expatriated because of her marriage to a Chinese citizen, and was subsequently refused admittance to the United States as an alien ineligible to citizenship.

Critical Thinking

1. Explain the relationship between the U.S. Congress and racial prejudice and citizenship.
2. What does this article about American history have meaning for current events and contemporary society?
3. In what ways has birthright citizenship and naturalization intersected with race and gender in the development of the American Constitution?

Create Central

www.mhhe.com/createcentral

Internet References

Library of Congress
www.loc.gov

Social Science Information Gateway
http://sosig.esrc.bris.ac.uk

Sociosite
www.sociosite.net

Supreme Court/Legal Information Institute
http://supct.law.cornell.edu/supct/index.html

Article

Prepared by: John A. Kromkowski, *Catholic University of America*

Dred Scott v. Sandford

December term 1856.

Learning Outcomes

After reading this article, you will be able to:

- Explain the strengths and weaknesses of the Congressional and Supreme Court in the process of governance.
- Explain the various roles and functions of the court in American political change.
- Discuss the current and past meaning of "the people of the United States."

Mr. Chief Justice Taney delivered the opinion of the court.

This case has been twice argued. After the argument at the last term, differences of opinion were found to exist among the members of the court; and as the questions in controversy are of the highest importance, and the court was at that time much pressed by the ordinary business of the term, it was deemed advisable to continue the case, and direct a re-argument on some of the points, in order that we might have an opportunity of giving to the whole subject a more deliberate consideration. It has accordingly been again argued by counsel, and considered by the court; and I now proceed to deliver its opinion.

There are two leading questions presented by the record:

1. Had the Circuit Court of the United States jurisdiction to hear and determine the case between these parties? And
2. If it had jurisdiction, is the judgment it has given erroneous or not?

The plaintiff in error, who was also the plaintiff in the court below, was, with his wife and children, held as slaves by the defendant, in the State of Missouri; and he brought this action in the Circuit Court of the United States for that district, to assert the title of himself and his family to freedom.

The declaration is in the form usually adopted in that State to try questions of this description, and contains the averment necessary to give the court jurisdiction; that he and the defendant are citizens of different States; that is, that he is a citizen of Missouri, and the defendant a citizen of New York.

The defendant pleaded in abatement to the jurisdiction of the court, that the plaintiff was not a citizen of the State of Missouri, as alleged in his declaration, being a negro of African descent, whose ancestors were of pure African blood, and who were brought into this country and sold as slaves.

To this plea the plaintiff demurred, and the defendant joined in demurrer. The court overruled the plea, and gave judgment that the defendant should answer over. And he thereupon put in sundry pleas in bar, upon which issues were joined; and at the trial the verdict and judgment were in his favor. Whereupon the plaintiff brought this writ of error.

Before we speak of the pleas in bar, it will be proper to dispose of the questions which have arisen on the plea in abatement.

That plea denies the right of the plaintiff to sue in a court of the United States, for the reasons therein stated.

If the question raised by it is legally before us, and the court should be of opinion that the facts stated in it disqualify the plaintiff from becoming a citizen, in the sense in which that word is used in the Constitution of the United States, then the judgment of the Circuit Court is erroneous, and must be reversed.

It is suggested, however, that this plea is not before us; and that as the judgment in the court below on this plea was in favor of the plaintiff, he does not seek to reverse it, or bring it before the court for revision by his writ of error; and also that the defendant waived this defence by pleading over, and thereby admitted the jurisdiction of the court.

But, in making this objection, we think the peculiar and limited jurisdiction of courts of the United States has not been adverted to. This peculiar and limited jurisdiction has made it necessary, in these courts, to adopt different rules and principles of pleading, so far as jurisdiction is concerned, from those which regulate courts of common law in England, and in the different States of the Union which have adopted the common-law rules.

In these last-mentioned courts, where their character and rank are analogous to that of a Circuit Court of the United States; in other words, where they are what the law terms courts of general jurisdiction; they are presumed to have jurisdiction, unless the contrary appears. No averment in the pleadings of the plaintiff is necessary, in order to give jurisdiction. If the defendant objects to it, he must plead it specially, and unless the fact on which he relies is found to be true by a jury, or admitted to be true by the plaintiff, the jurisdiction cannot be disputed in an appellate court.

Now, it is not necessary to inquire whether in courts of that description a party who pleads over in bar, when a plea to the jurisdiction has been ruled against him, does or does not waive his plea; nor whether upon a judgment in his favor on the pleas in bar, and a writ of error brought by the plaintiff, the question upon the plea in abatement would be open for revision in the appellate court. Cases that may have been decided in such courts, or rules that may have been laid down by common-law pleaders, can have no influence in the decision in this court. Because, under the Constitution and laws of the United States, the rules which govern the pleadings in its courts, in questions of jurisdiction, stand on different principles and are regulated by different laws.

This difference arises, as we have said, from the peculiar character of the Government of the United States. For although it is sovereign and supreme in its appropriate sphere of action, yet it does not possess all the powers which usually belong to the sovereignty of a nation. Certain specified powers, enumerated in the Constitution, have been conferred upon it; and neither the legislative, executive, nor judicial departments of the Government can lawfully exercise any authority beyond the limits marked out by the Constitution. And in regulating the judicial department, the cases in which the courts of the United States shall have jurisdiction are particularly and specifically enumerated and defined; and they are not authorized to take cognizance of any case which does not come within the description therein specified. Hence, when a plaintiff sues in a court of the United States, it is necessary that he should show, in his pleading, that the suit he brings is within the jurisdiction of the court, and that he is entitled to sue there. And if he omits to do this, and should, by any oversight of the Circuit Court, obtain a judgment in his favor, the judgment would be reversed in the appellate court for want of jurisdiction in the court below. The jurisdiction would not be presumed, as in the case of a common-law English or State court, unless the contrary appeared. But the record, when it comes before the appellate court, must show, affirmatively, that the inferior court had authority under the Constitution, to hear and determine the case. And if the plaintiff claims a right to sue in a Circuit Court of the United States, under that provision of the Constitution which gives jurisdiction in controversies between citizens of different States, he must distinctly aver in his pleading that they are citizens of different States; and he cannot maintain his suit without showing that fact in the pleadings.

This point was decided in the case of *Bingham v. Cabot,* (in 3 Dall., 382,) and ever since adhered to by the court. And in *Jackson v. Ashton,* (8 Pet., 148,) it was held that the objection to which it was open could not be waived by the opposite party because consent of parties could not give jurisdiction.

It is needless to accumulate cases on this subject. Those already referred to, and the cases of *Capron v. Van Noorden,* (in 2 Cr., 126) and *Montalet v. Murray,* (4 Cr., 46,) are sufficient to show the rule of which we have spoken. The case of *Capron v. Van Noorden* strikingly illustrates the difference between a common-law court and a court of the United States.

If, however, the fact of citizenship is averred in the declaration, and the defendant does not deny it, and put it in issue by plea in abatement, he cannot offer evidence at the trial to disprove it, and consequently cannot avail himself of the objection in the appellate court, unless the defect should be apparent in some other part of the record. For if there is no plea in abatement, and the want of jurisdiction does not appear in any other part of the transcript brought up by the writ of error, the undisputed averment of citizenship in the declaration must be taken in this court to be true. In this case, the citizenship is averred, but it is denied by the defendant in the manner required by the rules of pleading, and the fact upon which the denial is based is admitted by the demurrer. And, if the plea and demurrer, and judgment of the court below upon it, are before us upon this record, the question to be decided is, whether the facts stated in the plea are sufficient to show that the plaintiff is not entitled to sue as a citizen in a court of the United States. . . .

We think they are before us. The plea in abatement and the judgment of the court upon it, are a part of the judicial proceedings in the Circuit Court, and are there recorded as such; and a writ of error always brings up to the superior court the whole record of the proceedings in the court below. And in the case of the *United States v. Smith,* (11 Wheat., 172) this court said, that the case being brought up by writ of error, the whole record was under the consideration of this court. And this being the case in the present instance, the plea in abatement is necessarily under consideration; and it becomes, therefore, our duty to decide whether the facts stated in the plea are or are not sufficient to show that the plaintiff is not entitled to sue as a citizen in a court of the United States.

This is certainly a very serious question, and one that now for the first time has been brought for decision before this court. But it is brought here by those who have a right to bring it, and it is our duty to meet it and decide it.

The question is simply this: Can a negro, whose ancestors were imported into this country, and sold as slaves, become a member of the political community formed and brought into existence by the Constitution of the United States, and as such become entitled to all the rights, and privileges, and immunities, guarantied by that instrument to the citizen? One of which rights is the privilege of suing in a court of the United States in the cases specified in the Constitution.

It will be observed, that the plea applies to that class of persons only whose ancestors were negroes of the African race, and imported into this country, and sold and held as slaves. The only matter in issue before the court, therefore, is, whether the descendants of such slaves, when they shall be emancipated, or who are born of parents who had become free before their birth, are citizens of a State, in the sense in which the word citizen is used in the Constitution of the United States. And this being the only matter in dispute on the pleadings, the court must be understood as speaking in this opinion of that class only, that is, of those persons who are the descendants of Africans who were imported into this country, and sold as slaves.

The situation of this population was altogether unlike that of the Indian race. The latter, it is true, formed no part of the colonial communities, and never amalgamated with them in social connections or in government. But although they were uncivilized, they were yet a free and independent people, associated together in nations or tribes, and governed by their own laws. Many of these political communities were situated in territories to which the white race claimed the ultimate right of dominion. But that claim was acknowledged to be subject to the right of the Indians to occupy it as long as they thought proper, and neither the English nor colonial Governments claimed or exercised any dominion over the tribe or nation by whom it was occupied, nor claimed the right to the possession of the territory, until the tribe or nation consented to cede it. These Indian Governments were regarded and treated as foreign Governments, as must so as if an ocean had separated the red man from the white; and their freedom has constantly been acknowledged, from the time of the first emigration to the English colonies to the present day, by the different Governments which succeeded each other. Treaties have been negotiated with them, and their alliance sought for in war; and the people who compose these Indian political communities have always been treated as foreigners not living under our Government. It is true that the course of events has brought the Indian tribes within the limits of the United States under subjection to the white race; and it has been found necessary, for their sake as well as our own, to regard them as in a state of pupilage, and to legislate to a certain extent over them and the territory they occupy. But they may, without doubt, like the subjects of any other foreign Government, be naturalized by the authority of Congress, and become citizens of a State, and of the United States; and if an individual should leave his nation or tribe, and take up his abode among the white population, he would be entitled to all the rights and privileges which would belong to an emigrant from any other foreign people.

We proceed to examine the case as presented by the pleadings.

The words "people of the United States" and "citizens" are synonymous terms, and mean the same thing. They both describe the political body who, according to our republican institutions, form the sovereignty and who hold the power and conduct the Government through their representatives. They are what we familiarly call the "sovereign people," and every citizen is one of this people, and a constituent member of this sovereignty. The question before us is, whether the class of persons described in the plea in abatement compose a portion of this people, and are constituent members of this sovereignty? We think they are not, and that they are not included, and were not intended to be included, under the word "citizens" in the Constitution, and can therefore claim none of the rights and privileges which that instrument provides for and secures to citizens of the United States. On the contrary, they were at that time considered as a subordinate and inferior class of beings, who had been subjugated by the dominant race, and, whether emancipated or not, yet remained subject to their authority, and had no rights or privileges but such as those who held the power and the Government might choose to grant them.

It is not the province of the court to decide upon the justice or injustice, the policy or impolicy, of these laws. The decision of that question belonged to the political or law-making power; to those who formed the sovereignty and framed the Constitution. The duty of the court is, to interpret the instrument they have framed, with the best lights we can obtain on the subject, and to administer it as we find it, according to its true intent and meaning when it was adopted.

In discussing this question, we must not confound the rights of citizenship which a State may confer within its own limits, and the rights of citizenship as a member of the Union. It does not by any means follow, because he has all the rights and privileges of a citizen of a State, that he must be a citizen of the United States. He may have all of the rights and privileges of the citizen of a State, and yet not be entitled to the rights and privileges of a citizen in any other State. For, previous to the adoption of the Constitution of the United States, every State had the undoubted right to confer on whomsoever it pleased the character of citizen, and to endow him with all its rights. But this character of course was confined to the boundaries of the State, and gave him no rights or privileges in other States beyond those secured to him by the laws of nations and the comity of States. Nor have the several States surrendered the power of conferring these rights and privileges by adopting the Constitution of the United States. Each State may still confer them upon an alien, or any one it thinks proper, or upon any class or description of persons; yet he would not be a citizen in the sense in which that word is used in the Constitution of the United States, nor entitled to sue as such in one of its courts, nor to the privileges and immunities of a citizen in the other States. The rights which he would acquire would be restricted to the State which gave them. The Constitution has conferred on Congress the right to establish a uniform rule of naturalization, and this right is evidently exclusive, and has always been held by this court to be so. Consequently, no State, since the adoption of the Constitution, can by naturalizing an alien invest him with the rights and privileges secured to a citizen of a State under the Federal Government, although, so far as the State alone was concerned, he would undoubtedly be entitled to the rights of a citizen, and clothed with all the rights and immunities which the Constitution and laws of the State attached to that character.

It is very clear, therefore, that no State can, by any act or law of its own, passed since the adoption of the Constitution, introduce a new member into the political community created by the Constitution of the United States. It cannot make him a member of this community by making him a member of its own. And for the same reason it cannot introduce any person, or description of persons, who were not intended to be embraced in this new political family which the Constitution brought into existence, but were intended to be excluded from it.

The question then arises, whether the provisions of the Constitution, in relation to the personal rights and privileges to which the citizen of a State should be entitled, embraced the negro African race, at that time in this country or who might afterwards be imported, who had then or should afterwards be made free in any State; and to put it in the power of a single State to make him a citizen of the United States, and endue him with the full rights of citizenship in every other State without their consent? Does the Constitution of the United States act upon him whenever he shall be made free under the laws of a State, and raised there to the rank of a citizen, and immediately clothe him with all the privileges of a citizen in every other State, and in its own courts?

The courts think the affirmative of these propositions cannot be maintained. And if it cannot, the plaintiff in error could not be a citizen of the State of Missouri, within the meaning of the Constitution of the United States, and, consequently, was not entitled to sue in its courts.

It is true, every person, and every class and description of persons, who were at the time of the adoption of the Constitution recognised as citizens in the several States, became also citizens of this new political body; but none other; it was formed by them, and for them and their posterity, but for no one else. And the personal rights and privileges guarantied to citizens of this new sovereignty were intended to embrace those only who were then members of the several State communities, or who should afterwards by birthright or otherwise become members, according to the provisions of the Constitution and the principles on which it was founded. It was the union of those who were at that time members of distinct and separate political communities into one political family, whose power, for certain specified purposes, was to extend over the whole territory of the United States. And it gave to each citizen rights and privileges outside of his State which he did not before possess, and placed him in every other State upon a perfect equality with its own citizens as to rights of person and rights of property; it made him a citizen of the United States.

It becomes necessary, therefore, to determine who were citizens of the several States when the Constitution was adopted. And in order to do this, we must recur to the Governments and institutions of the thirteen colonies, when they separated from Great Britain and formed new sovereignties, and took their places in the family of independent nations. We must inquire who, at that time, were recognised as the people or citizens of a State, whose rights and liberties had been outraged by the English Government; and who declared their independence, and assumed the powers of Government to defend their rights by force of arms.

In the opinion of the court, the legislation and histories of the times, and the language used in the Declaration of Independence, show, that neither the class of persons who had been imported as slaves, nor their descendants, whether they had become free or not, were then acknowledged as a part of the people, nor intended to be included in the general words used in that memorable instrument. . . .

Critical Thinking

1. What are the questions at issue in *Dred Scott v. Sandford?*
2. Explain in what ways does the Court view "the Indian race," "Negroes of African blood," and "people of the United States"?

Create Central

www.mhhe.com/createcentral

Internet References

Supreme Court/Legal Information Institute
http://supct.law.cornell.edu/supct/index.html

U.S. Census Bureau
www.census.gov

U.S. Supreme Court Reports
http://bulk.resource.orglcourts.gov/c/US

Supreme Court of the United States, 1856.

Article

Prepared by: John A. Kromkowski, *Catholic University of America*

Brown et al. v. Board of Education of Topeka et al.

347 U.S. 483 (1954).

Learning Outcomes

After reading this article, you will be able to:

- Explain the relationship between ending racial segregation in schools and housing policy.
- List the benefits associated with diversity.
- Explain the relationship of income, education and the cost of housing and the relevance of your findings for race and ethnic relations.

Mr. Chief Justice Warren delivered the opinion of the Court.

These cases come to us from the States of Kansas, South Carolina, Virginia, and Delaware. They are premised on different facts and different local conditions, but a common legal question justifies their consideration together in this consolidated opinion.[1]

In each of the cases, minors of the Negro race, through their legal representatives, seek the aid of the courts in obtaining admission to the public schools of their community on a nonsegregated basis. In each instance, they had been denied admission to schools attended by white children under laws requiring or permitting segregation according to race. This segregation was alleged to deprive the plaintiffs of the equal protection of the laws under the Fourteenth Amendment. In each of the cases other than the Delaware case, a three-judge federal district court denied relief to the plaintiffs on the so-called "separate but equal" doctrine announced by this Court in *Plessy v. Ferguson,* 163 U.S. 537. Under that doctrine, equality of treatment is accorded when the races are provided substantially equal facilities, even though these facilities be separate. In the Delaware case, the Supreme Court of Delaware adhered to that doctrine, but ordered that the plaintiffs be admitted to the white schools because of their superiority to the Negro schools.

The plaintiffs contend that segregated public schools are not "equal" and cannot be made "equal," and that hence they are deprived of the equal protection of the laws. Because of the obvious importance of the question presented, the Court took jurisdiction.[2] Argument was heard in the 1952 Term, and reargument was heard this Term on certain questions propounded by the Court.[3]

Reargument was largely devoted to the circumstances surrounding the adoption of the Fourteenth Amendment in 1868. It covered exhaustively consideration of the Amendment in Congress, ratification by the states, then existing practices in racial segregation, and the views of proponents and opponents of the Amendment. This discussion and our own investigation convince us that, although these sources cast some light, it is not enough to resolve the problem with which we are faced. At best, they are inconclusive. The most avid proponents of the post–War Amendments undoubtedly intended them to remove all legal distinctions among "all persons born or naturalized in the United States." Their opponents, just as certainly, were antagonistic to both the letter and the spirit of the Amendments and wished them to have the most limited effect. What others in Congress and the state legislatures had in mind cannot be determined with any degree of certainty.

An additional reason for the inconclusive nature of the Amendment's history, with respect to segregated schools, is the status of public education at that time.[4] In the South, the movement toward free common schools, supported by general taxation, had not yet taken hold. Education of white children was largely in the hands of private groups. Education of Negroes was almost nonexistent, and practically all of the race were illiterate. In fact, any education of Negroes was forbidden by law in some states. Today, in contrast, many Negroes have achieved outstanding success in the arts and sciences as well as in the business and professional world. It is true that public school education at the time of the Amendment had advanced further in the North, but the effect of the Amendment on northern States was generally ignored in the congressional debates. Even in the North, the conditions of public education did not approximate those existing today. The curriculum was usually rudimentary; ungraded schools were common in rural areas; the school term was but three months a year in many states; and compulsory school attendance was virtually unknown. As a consequence, it is not surprising that there should be so little in the history of the Fourteenth Amendment relating to its intended effect on public education.

In the first cases in this Court construing the Fourteenth Amendment, decided shortly after its adoption, the Court interpreted it as proscribing all state-imposed discriminations against the Negro race.[5] The doctrine of "separate but equal" did not make its appearance in this Court until 1896 in the case of *Plessy v. Ferguson, supra,* involving not education but transportation.[6] American courts have since labored with the doctrine for over half a century. In this Court, there have been six cases involving the "separate but equal" doctrine in the field of public education.[7] In *Cumming v. County Board of Education,* 175 U.S. 528, and *Gong Lum v. Rice,* 275 U.S. 78, the validity of the doctrine itself was not challenged.[8] In more recent cases, all on the graduate school level, inequality was found in that specific benefits enjoyed by white students were denied to Negro students of the same educational qualifications. *Missouri ex rel. Gaines v. Canada,* 305 U.S. 337; *Sipuel v. Oklahoma,* 332 U.S. 631; *Sweatt v. Painter,* 339 U.S. 629; *McLaurin v. Oklahoma State Regents,* 339 U.S. 637. In none of these cases was it necessary to reexamine the doctrine to grant relief to the Negro plaintiff. And in *Sweatt v. Painter, supra,* the Court expressly reserved decision on the question whether *Plessy v. Ferguson* should be held inapplicable to public education.

In the instant cases, that question is directly presented. Here, unlike *Sweatt v. Painter,* there are findings below that the Negro and white schools involved have been equalized, or are being equalized, with respect to buildings, curricula, qualifications and salaries of teachers, and other "tangible" factors.[9] Our decision, therefore, cannot turn on merely a comparison of these tangible factors in the Negro and white schools involved in each of the cases. We must look instead to the effect of segregation itself on public education.

In approaching this problem, we cannot turn the clock back to 1868 when the Amendment was adopted, or even to 1896 when *Plessy v. Ferguson* was written. We must consider public education in the light of its full development and its present place in American life throughout the Nation. Only in this way can it be determined if segregation in public schools deprives these plaintiffs of the equal protection of the laws.

Today, education is perhaps the most important function of state and local governments. Compulsory school attendance laws and the great expenditures for education both demonstrate our recognition of the importance of education to our democratic society. It is required in the performance of our most basic public responsibilities, even service in the armed forces. It is the very foundation of good citizenship. Today it is a principal instrument in awakening the child to cultural values, in preparing him for later professional training, and in helping him to adjust normally to his environment. In these days, it is doubtful that any child may reasonably be expected to succeed in life if he is denied the opportunity of an education. Such an opportunity, where the state has undertaken to provide it, is a right which must be made available to all on equal terms.

We come then to the question presented: Does segregation of children in public schools solely on the basis of race, even though the physical facilities and other "tangible" factors may be equal, deprive the children of the minority group of equal educational opportunities? We believe that it does.

In *Sweatt v. Painter, supra,* in finding that a segregated law school for Negroes could not provide them equal educational opportunities, this Court relied in large part on "those qualities which are incapable of objective measurement but which make for greatness in a law school." In *McLaurin v. Oklahoma State Regents, supra,* the Court, in requiring that a Negro admitted to a white graduate school be treated like all other students, again resorted to intangible considerations: ". . . his ability to study, to engage in discussions and exchange views with other students, and, in general, to learn his profession." Such considerations apply with added force to children in grade and high schools. To separate them from others of similar age and qualifications solely because of their race generates a feeling of inferiority as to their status in the community that may affect their hearts and minds in a way unlikely ever to be undone. The effect of this separation on their educational opportunities was well stated by a finding in the Kansas case by a court which nevertheless felt compelled to rule against the Negro plaintiffs:

> "Segregation of white and colored children in public schools has a detrimental effect upon the colored children. The impact is greater when it has the sanction of the law; for the policy of separating the races is usually interpreted as denoting the inferiority of the negro group. A sense of inferiority affects the motivation of a child to learn. Segregation with the sanction of law, therefore, has a tendency to [retard] the educational and mental development of negro children and to deprive them of some of the benefits they would receive in a racial[ly] integrated school system."[10]

Whatever may have been the extent of psychological knowledge at the time of *Plessy v. Ferguson,* this finding is amply supported by modern authority.[11] Any language in *Plessy v. Ferguson* contrary to this finding is rejected.

We conclude that in the field of public education the doctrine of "separate but equal" has no place. Separate educational facilities are inherently unequal. Therefore, we hold that the plaintiffs and others similarly situated for whom the actions have been brought are, by reason of the segregation complained of, deprived of the equal protection of the laws guaranteed by the Fourteenth Amendment. This disposition makes unnecessary any discussion whether such segregation also violates the Due Process Clause of the Fourteenth Amendment.[12]

Because these are class actions, because of the wide applicability of this decision, and because of the great variety of local conditions, the formulation of decrees in these cases presents problems of considerable complexity. On reargument, the consideration of appropriate relief was necessarily subordinated to the primary question—the constitutionality of segregation in public education. We have now announced that such segregation is a denial of the equal protection of the laws. In order that we may have the full assistance of the parties in formulating decrees, the cases will be restored to the docket, and the parties are requested to present further argument on Questions 4 and 5 previously propounded by the Court for the reargument this Term.[13] The Attorney General of the United States is again invited to participate. The Attorneys General of the states requiring or permitting segregation in public education will also be permitted to appear as *amici curiae* upon request to do so by September 15, 1954, and submission of briefs by October 1, 1954.[14]

It is so ordered.

Notes

1. In the Kansas case, *Brown v. Board of Education,* the plaintiffs are Negro children of elementary school age residing in Topeka. They brought this action in the United States District Court for the District of Kansas to enjoin enforcement of a Kansas statute which permits, but does not require, cities of more than 15,000 population to maintain separate school facilities for Negro and white students. Kan. Gen. Stat. §72–1724 (1949). Pursuant to that authority, the Topeka Board of Education elected to establish segregated elementary schools. Other public schools in the community, however, are operated on a nonsegregated basis.

   In the South Carolina case, *Briggs v. Elliott,* the plaintiffs are Negro children of both elementary and high school age residing in Clarendon County. They brought this action in the United States District Court for the Eastern District of South Carolina to enjoin enforcement of provisions in the state constitution and statutory code which require the segregation of Negroes and whites in public schools. . . .

   In the Virginia case, *Davis v. County School Board,* the plaintiffs are Negro children of high school age residing in Prince Edward County. They brought this action in the United States District Court for the Eastern District of Virginia to enjoin enforcement of provisions in the state constitution and statutory code which require the segregation of Negroes and whites in public schools. . . .

   In the Delaware case, *Gebhart v. Belton,* the plaintiffs are Negro children of both elementary and high school age residing in New Castle county. They brought this action in the Delaware Court of Chancery to enjoin enforcement of provisions in the state constitution and statutory code which require the segregation of Negroes and whites in public schools. . . .
2. technical footnote deleted.
3. technical footnote deleted.
4. technical footnote deleted.
5. technical footnote deleted.
6. technical footnote deleted.
7. technical footnote deleted.
8. technical footnote deleted.
9. technical footnote deleted.
10. technical footnote deleted.
11. K. B. Clark, Effect of Prejudice and Discrimination on Personality Development (Midcentury White House Conference on Children and Youth, 1950); Witmer and Kotinsky, Personality in the Making (1952), c. VI; Deutscher and Chein, The Psychological Effects of Enforced Segregation: A Survey of Social Science Opinion, 26 *J. Psychol.* 259 (1948); Chein, What Are the Psychological Effects of Segregation Under Conditions of Equal Facilities?, 3 *Int. J. Opinion and Attitude Res.* 229 (1949); Brameld, Educational Costs, in Discrimination and National Welfare (MacIver, ed., 1949), 44–48; Frazier, The Negro in the United States (1949), 674–681. And see generally Myrdal, An American Dilemma (1944).
12. technical footnote deleted.
13. technical footnote deleted.
14. technical footnote deleted.

Critical Thinking

1. In retrospect, does ending racial segregation in schools without ending segregation in housing seem to be the fundamental constraint on the success desired and the type of fairness and equal protection sought by the Supreme Court in this case?
2. What are *de jure* and *de facto* forms or types of racial segregation?

Create Central

www.mhhe.com/createcentral

Internet References

Supreme Court/Legal Information Institute
http://supct.law.cornell.edu/supct/index.html

U.S. Census Bureau
www.census.gov

U.S. Supreme Court Reports
http://bulk.resource.orglcourts.gov/c/US

Supreme Court of the United States, 1954.

Article

Prepared by: John A. Kromkowski, *Catholic University of America*

Historical Discrimination in the Immigration Laws

Learning Outcomes

After reading this article, you will be able to:

- Relate the history of immigration to the current debate on immigration reform.
- Discuss the implications, costs and benefits of unregulated immigration.
- Explain how people's attitudes about immigration differ in various parts of the country.

The Early Years

During the formative years of this country's growth, immigration was encouraged with little restraint. Any restrictions on immigration in the 1700s were the result of selection standards established by each colonial settlement. The only Federal regulation of immigration in this period lasted only 2 years and came from the Alien Act of 1798, which gave the President the authority to expel aliens who posed a threat to national security.[1]

Immigrants from northern and western Europe began to trickle into the country as a result of the faltering economic conditions within their own countries. In Germany, unfavorable economic prospects in industry and trade, combined with political unrest, drove many of its nationals to seek opportunities to ply their trades here.[2] In Ireland, the problems of the economy, compounded by several successive potato crop failures in the 1840s, sent thousands of Irish to seaports where ships bound for the United States were docked.[3] For other European nationals, the emigration from their native countries received impetus not only from adverse economic conditions at home but also from favorable stories of free land and good wages in America.[4]

The Nativist Movements

As a result of the large numbers of Catholics who emigrated from Europe, a nativist movement began in the 1830s.[5] It advocated immigration restriction to prevent further arrivals of Catholics into this country. Anti-Catholicism was a very popular theme, and many Catholics and Catholic institutions suffered violent attacks from nativist sympathizers. The movement, however, did not gain great political strength and its goal of curbing immigration did not materialize.

Immigrants in the mid-19th century did not come only from northern and western Europe. In China, political unrest and the decline in agricultural productivity spawned the immigration of Chinese to American shores.[6] The numbers of Chinese immigrants steadily increased after the so-called Opium War, due not only to the Chinese economy, but also to the widespread stories of available employment, good wages, and the discovery of gold at Sutter's Mill, which filtered in through arrivals from the Western nations.[7]

The nativist movement of the 1830s resurfaced in the late 1840s and developed into a political party, the Know-Nothing Party.[8] Its western adherents added an anti-Chinese theme to the eastern anti-Catholic sentiment.[9] But once again, the nativist movement, while acquiring local political strength, failed in its attempts to enact legislation curbing immigration. On the local level, however, the cry of "America for Americans" often led to discriminatory State statutes that penalized certain racially identifiable groups.[10] As an example, California adopted licensing statutes for foreign miners and fishermen, which were almost exclusively enforced against Chinese.[11]

In the mid-1850s, the Know-Nothing Party lost steam as a result of a division over the question of slavery, the most important issue of that time.[12] The nativist movement and antiforeign sentiment receded because of the slavery issue and the Civil War. It maintained this secondary role until the Panic of 1873 struck.

Chinese Exclusion

The depression economy of the 1870s was blamed on aliens who were accused of driving wages to a substandard level as well as taking away jobs that "belonged" to white Americans. While the economic charges were not totally without basis, reality shows that most aliens did not compete with white labor for "desirable" white jobs. Instead, aliens usually were relegated to the most menial employment.[13]

The primary target was the Chinese, whose high racial visibility, coupled with cultural dissimilarity and lack of political power, made them more than an adequate scapegoat for the economic problems of the 1870s.[14] Newspapers adopted the exhortations of labor leaders, blaming the Chinese for the economic plight of the working class. Workers released their frustrations and anger on the Chinese, particularly in the West.[15] Finally, politicians succumbed to the growing cry for exclusion of Chinese.

Congress responded by passing the Chinese Exclusion Act of 1882.[16] That act suspended immigration of Chinese laborers for 10 years, except for those who were in the country on November 17, 1880. Those who were not lawfully entitled to reside in the United States were subject to deportation. Chinese immigrants were also prohibited from obtaining United States citizenship after the effective date of the act.

The 1882 act was amended in 1884 to cover all subjects of China and Chinese who resided in any other foreign country.[17] Then in 1888, another act was enacted that extended the suspension of immigration for all Chinese except Chinese officials, merchants, students, teachers, and travelers for pleasure.[18] Supplemental legislation to that act also prohibited Chinese laborers from reentering the country, as provided for in the 1882 act, unless they reentered prior to the effective date of the legislation.[19]

Senator Matthew C. Butler of South Carolina summed up the congressional efforts to exclude Chinese by stating:

> [I]t seems to me that this whole Chinese business has been a matter of political advantage, and we have not been governed by that deliberation which it would seem to me the gravity of the question requires. In other words, there is a very important Presidential election pending. One House of Congress passes an act driving these poor devils into the Pacific Ocean, and the other House comes up and says, "Yes, we will drive them further into the Pacific Ocean, notwithstanding the treaties between the two governments."[20]

Nevertheless, the Chinese exclusion law was extended in 1892[21] and 1902,[22] and in 1904 it was extended indefinitely.[23]

Although challenged by American residents of Chinese ancestry, the provisions of these exclusion acts were usually upheld by judicial decisions. For example, the 1892 act[24] mandated that Chinese laborers obtain certificates of residency within 1 year after the passage of the act or face deportation. In order to obtain the certificate, the testimony of one credible white witness was required to establish that the Chinese laborer was an American resident prior to the passage of the act. That requirement was upheld by the United States Supreme Court in *Fong Yue Ting v. United States.*[25]

Literacy Tests and the Asiatic Barred Zone

The racial nature of immigration laws clearly manifested itself in further restrictions on prospective immigrants who were either from Asian countries or of Asian descent. In addition to extending the statutory life of the Chinese exclusion law, the 1902 act also applied that law to American territorial possessions, thereby prohibiting not only the immigration of noncitizen Chinese laborers from "such island territory to the mainland territory," but also "from one portion of the island territory of the United States to another portion of said island territory."[26] Soon after, Japanese were restricted from free immigration to the United States by the "Gentleman's Agreement" negotiated between the respective governments in 1907.[27] Additional evidence would be provided by the prohibition of immigration from countries in the Asia-Pacific Triangle as established by the Immigration Act of 1917.[28]

During this period, congressional attempts were also made to prevent blacks from immigrating to this country. In 1915 an amendment to exclude "all members of the African or black race" from admission to the United States was introduced in the Senate during its deliberations on a proposed immigration bill.[29] The Senate approved the amendment on a 29 to 25 vote,[30] but it was later defeated in the House by a 253 to 74 vote,[31] after intensive lobbying by the NAACP.[32]

In 1917 Congress codified existing immigration laws in the Immigration Act of that year.[33] That act retained all the prior grounds for inadmissibility and added illiterates to the list of those ineligible to immigrate, as a response to the influx of immigrants from southern and eastern Europe. Because of a fear that American standards would be lowered by these new immigrants who were believed to be racially "unassimilable" and illiterate, any alien who was over 16 and could not read was excluded. The other important feature of this statute was the creation of the Asia-Pacific Triangle, an Asiatic barred zone, designed to exclude Asians completely from immigration to the United States. The only exemptions from this zone were from an area that included Persia and parts of Afghanistan and Russia.

The 1917 immigration law reflected the movement of American immigration policy toward the curbing of free immigration. Free immigration, particularly from nations that were culturally dissimilar to the northern and western European background of most Americans, was popularly believed to be the root of both the economic problems and the social problems confronting this country.

The National Origins Quota System

Four years later, Congress created a temporary quota law that limited the number of aliens of any nationality who could immigrate to 3 percent of the United States residents of that nationality living in the country in 1910.[34] The total annual immigration allowable in any one year was set at 350,000. Western Hemisphere aliens were exempt from the quota if their country of origin was an independent nation and the alien had resided there at least 1 year.

The clear intent of the 1921 quota law was to confine immigration as much as possible to western and northern European stock. As the minority report noted:

> The obvious purpose of this discrimination is the adoption of an unfounded anthropological theory that the nations which are favored are the progeny of fictitious and hitherto unsuspected Nordic ancestors, while those discriminated against are not classified as belonging to that mythical ancestral stock. No scientific evidence worthy of consideration was introduced to substantiate this pseudoscientific proposition. It is pure fiction and the creation of a journalistic imagination. . . .

The majority report insinuates that some of those who have come from foreign countries are non-assimilable or slow of assimilation. No facts are offered in support of such a statement. The preponderance of testimony adduced before the committee is to the contrary.[35]

Notwithstanding these objections, Congress made the temporary quota a permanent one with the enactment of the 1924 National Origins Act.[36] A ceiling of 150,000 immigrants per year was imposed. Quotas for each nationality group were 2 percent of the total members of that nationality residing in the United States according to the 1890 census.[37] Again, Western Hemisphere aliens were exempt from the quotas (thus, classified as "nonquota" immigrants). Any prospective immigrant was required to obtain a sponsor in this country and to obtain a visa from an American consulate office abroad. Entering the country without a visa and in violation of the law subjected the entrant to deportation without regard to the time of entry (no statute of limitation). Another provision, prohibiting the immigration of aliens ineligible for citizenship, completely closed the door on Japanese immigration, since the Supreme Court had ruled that Japanese were ineligible to become naturalized citizens.[38] Prior to the 1924 act, Japanese immigration had been subjected to "voluntary" restraint by the Gentleman's Agreement negotiated between the Japanese Government and President Theodore Roosevelt.

In addition to its expressed discriminatory provisions, the 1924 law was also criticized as discriminatory against blacks in general and against black West Indians in particular.[39]

The Mexican "Repatriation" Campaign

Although Mexican Americans have a long history of residence within present United States territory,[40] Mexican immigration to this country is of relatively recent vintage.[41] Mexican citizens began immigrating to this country in significant numbers after 1909 because of economic conditions as well as the violence and political upheaval of the Mexican Revolution.[42] These refugees were welcomed by Americans, for they helped to alleviate the labor shortage caused by the First World War.[43] The spirit of acceptance lasted only a short time, however.

Spurred by the economic distress of the Great Depression, Federal immigration officials expelled hundreds of thousands of persons of Mexican descent from this country through increased Border Patrol raids and other immigration law enforcement techniques.[44] To mollify public objection to the mass expulsions, this program was called the "repatriation" campaign. Approximately 500,000 persons were "repatriated" to Mexico, with more than half of them being United States citizens.[45]

Erosion of Certain Discriminatory Barriers

Prior to the next recodification of the immigration laws, there were several congressional enactments that cut away at the discriminatory barriers established by the national origins system. In 1943 the Chinese Exclusion Act was repealed, allowing a quota of 105 Chinese to immigrate annually to this country and declaring Chinese eligible for naturalization.[46] The War Brides Act of 1945[47] permitted the immigration of 118,000 spouses and children of military servicemen. In 1946 Congress enacted legislation granting eligibility for naturalization to Pilipinos[48] and to races indigenous to India.[49] A Presidential proclamation in that same year increased the Pilipino quota from 50 to 100.[50] In 1948 the Displaced Persons Act provided for the entry of approximately 400,000 refugees from Germany, Italy, and Austria (an additional 214,000 refugees were later admitted to the United States).[51]

The McCarran-Walter Act of 1952

The McCarran-Walter Act of 1952,[52] the basic law in effect today, codified the immigration laws under a single statute. It established three principles for immigration policy:

1. the reunification of families,
2. the protection of the domestic labor force, and
3. the immigration of persons with needed skills.

However, it retained the concept of the national origins system, as well as unrestricted immigration from the Western Hemisphere. An important provision of the statute removed the bar to immigration and citizenship for races that had been denied those privileges prior to that time. Asian countries, nevertheless, were still discriminated against, for prospective immigrants whose ancestry was one-half of any Far Eastern race were chargeable to minimal quotas for that nation, regardless of the birthplace of the immigrant.

"Operation Wetback"

Soon after the repatriation campaigns of the 1930s, the United States entered the Second World War. Mobilization for the war effort produced a labor shortage that resulted in a shift in American attitudes toward immigration from Mexico. Once again Mexican nationals were welcomed with open arms. However, this "open arms" policy was just as short lived as before.

In the 1950s many Americans were alarmed by the number of immigrants from Mexico. As a result, then United States Attorney General Herbert Brownell, Jr., launched "Operation Wetback," to expel Mexicans from this country. Among those caught up in the expulsion campaign were American citizens of Mexican descent who were forced to leave the country of their birth. To ensure the effectiveness of the expulsion process, many of those apprehended were denied a hearing to assert their constitutional rights and to present evidence that would have prevented their deportation. More than 1 million persons of Mexican descent were expelled from this country in 1954 at the height of "Operation Wetback."[53]

The 1965 Amendments

The national origins immigration quota system generated opposition from the time of its inception, condemned for its attempts to maintain the existing racial composition of the United States. Finally, in 1965, amendments to the McCarran-Walter Act abolished the national origins system as well as the Asiatic barred zone.[54] Nevertheless, numerical restrictions were still imposed to limit annual immigration. The Eastern Hemisphere was subject to an overall limitation of 170,000 and a limit of 20,000 per country. Further, colonial territories were limited to 1 percent of the total available to the mother country (later raised to 3 percent or 600 immigrants in the 1976 amendments). The Western Hemisphere, for the first time, was subject to an overall limitation of 120,000 annually, although no individual per country limits were imposed. In place of the national origins system, Congress created a seven category preference system giving immigration priority to relatives of United States residents and immigrants with needed talents or skills.[55] The 20,000 limitation per country and the colonial limitations, as well as the preference for relatives of Americans preferred under the former selections process, have been referred to by critics as "the last vestiges of the national origins system" because they perpetuate the racial discrimination produced by the national origins system.

Restricting Mexican Immigration

After 1965 the economic conditions in the United States changed. With the economic crunch felt by many Americans, the cry for more restrictive immigration laws resurfaced. The difference from the 19th century situation is that the brunt of the attacks is now focused on Mexicans, not Chinese. High "guesstimates" of the number of undocumented Mexican aliens entering the United States, many of which originated from Immigration and Naturalization Service sources, have been the subject of press coverage.[56]

As a partial response to the demand for "stemming the tide" of Mexican immigration, Congress amended the Immigration and Nationality Act in 1976,[57] imposing the seven category preference system and the 20,000 numerical limitation per country on Western Hemisphere nations. Legal immigration from Mexico, which had been more than 40,000[58] people per year, with a waiting list 2 years long, was thus cut by over 50 percent.

Recent Revisions of the Immigrant Quota System

Although the annual per-country limitations have remained intact, Congress did amend the Immigration and Nationality Act in 1978 to eliminate the hemispheric quotas of 170,000 for Eastern Hemisphere countries and 120,000 for Western Hemisphere countries. Those hemispheric ceilings were replaced with an overall annual worldwide ceiling of 290,000.[59]

In 1980 the immigrant quota system was further revised by the enactment of the Refugee Act. In addition to broadening the definition of refugee, that statute eliminated the seventh preference visa category by establishing a separate worldwide ceiling for refugee admissions to this country. It also reduced the annual worldwide ceiling for the remaining six preference categories to 270,000 visas, and it increased the number of visas allocated to the second preference to 26 percent.[60]

Notes

1. Ch. 58, 1 Stat. 570 (1798).
2. Carl Wittke, *We Who Built America* (rev. 1964), p. 67.
3. Ibid., pp. 129–33.
4. Ibid., pp. 101–10.
5. Ibid., pp. 491–97.
6. Li Chien-nung, *The Political History of China, 1840–1928* (1956), pp. 48–49; Stanford Lyman, *Chinese Americans* (1974), pp. 4–5.
7. Mary Roberts Coolidge, *Chinese Immigration* (1909), pp. 16–17.
8. Wittke, *We Who Built America,* pp. 497–510.
9. Coolidge, *Chinese Immigration,* p. 58.
10. Ibid., pp. 69–82. Some municipalities also adopted ordinances that discriminated against Chinese. As an example, a San Francisco municipal ordinance, subsequently held unconstitutional in Yick Wo v. Hopkins, 118 U.S. 356 (1886), was enacted regulating the operation of public laundries but in practice was enforced almost exclusively against Chinese.
11. Ibid., pp. 33–38, 69–74.
12. Wittke, *We Who Built America,* pp. 509–10.
13. As one author noted, "[b]efore the late 1870s the Chinese engaged only in such work as white laborers refused to perform. Thus the Chinese not only were noninjurious competitors but in effect were benefactors to the white laborer." S.W. Kung, *Chinese in American Life: Some Aspects of Their History, Status, Problems, and Contributions* (1962), p. 68.
14. Carey McWilliams, *Brothers Under the Skin* (rev. 1951), pp. 101–03.
15. Coolidge, *Chinese Immigration,* p. 188.
16. Ch. 126, 22 Stat. 58 (1882).
17. Ch. 220, 23 Stat. 115 (1884).
18. Ch. 1015, 25 Stat. 476 (1888).
19. Ch. 1064, 25 Stat. 504 (1888).
20. 19 Cong. Rec. 8218 (1888).
21. Ch. 60, 27 Stat. 25 (1892).
22. Ch. 641, 32 Stat. 176 (1902).
23. Ch. 1630, 33 Stat. 428. (1904).
24. Ch. 60, 27 Stat. 25 (1892).
25. 149 U.S. 698 (1893).
26. Ch. 641, 32 Stat. 176 (1902).
27. The Gentleman's Agreement of 1907, U.S. Department of State, *Papers Relating to the Foreign Relations of the United States 1924* (1939), vol. 2, p. 339.
28. Ch. 29, 39 Stat. 874 (1917).
29. 52 Cong. Rec. 805 (1914).
30. *Id.* at 807.
31. *Id.* at 1138–39.
32. See *Crisis,* vol. 9 (February 1915), p. 190.
33. Ch. 29, 39 Stat. 874 (1917).
34. Ch. 8, 42 Stat. 5 (1921).
35. As reprinted in the legislative history of the INA [1952] U.S. Code Cong. and Ad. News 1653, 1668.
36. Ch. 190, 43 Stat. 153 (1924).

37. That act provided, however, that:

    The annual quota of any nationality for the fiscal year beginning July 1, 1927, and for each fiscal year thereafter, shall be a number which bears the same ratio to 150,000 as the number of inhabitants in continental United States in 1920 having that national origin (ascertained as hereinafter provided in this section) bears to the number of inhabitants in continental United States in 1920, but the minimum quota of any nationality shall be 100.

    Ch. 190, 43 Stat. 153, 159, § 11(b).
38. Early congressional enactments restricted eligibility for naturalization to free white persons (ch. 3, 1 Stat. 103 (1790)) and to persons of African nativity or descent (Rev. Stat. §2169 (1875)). But when Congress passed the Naturalization Act of June 29, 1906 (ch. 3592, 34 Stat. 596), persons of Japanese ancestry began submitting petitions to become naturalized citizens under the procedures established by that act. The Supreme Court, however, held that the 1906 act was limited by the prior congressional enactments and thus Japanese were ineligible for naturalization. Ozawa v. United States, 260 U.S. 178 (1922).
39. "West Indian Immigration and the American Negro," *Opportunity,* October 1924, pp. 298–99.
40. Under the Treaty of Guadalupe Hidalgo, many Mexican citizens became United States citizens after the annexation of territory by the United States following the Mexican War. Leo Grebler, Joan W. Moore, and Ralph C. Guzman, *The Mexican American People* (1970), pp. 40–41. The Treaty of Guadalupe Hidalgo is reprinted in Wayne Moquin, *A Documentary History of the Mexican Americans* (1971), p. 183.
41. Grebler, Moore, and Guzman, *The Mexican Americans People,* pp. 62–63.
42. Ibid.
43. Ibid., p. 64.
44. Ibid., pp. 523–26.
45. Moquin, *A Documentary History of the Mexican Americans,* p. 294.
46. Ch. 344, 57 Stat. 600 (1943).
47. Ch. 591, 59 Stat. 659 (1945).
48. 60 Stat. 1353.
49. Ch. 534, 60 Stat. 416 (1946).
50. Presidential Proclamation No. 2696, [1946] U.S. Code Cong. and Ad. News 1732.
51. Ch. 647, 62 Stat. 1009 (1948).
52. Ch. 477, 66 Stat. 163 (1952).
53. Grebler, Moore, and Guzman, *The Mexican American People,* pp. 521–22. Mark A. Chamberlin *et al.,* eds., "Our Badge of Infamy: A Petition to the United Nations on the Treatment of the Mexican Immigrant," in *The Mexican American and the Law* (1974 ed.), pp. 31–34.
54. Pub. L. No. 89–236, 79 Stat. 911 (1965).
55. The 1965 amendments to the Immigration and Nationality Act provided the following seven category preference system:

    First preference: unmarried sons and daughters of U.S. citizens. (20 percent)

    Second preference: spouses and unmarried sons and daughters of lawful resident aliens. (20 percent plus any visas not required for first preference)

    Third preference: members of the professions and scientists and artists of exceptional ability and their spouses and children. (10 percent)

    Fourth preference: married sons and daughters of U.S. citizens and their spouses and children. (10 percent plus any visas not required for first three preferences)

    Fifth preference: brothers and sisters of U.S. citizens and their spouses and children. (24 percent plus any visas not required for first four preferences)

    Sixth preference: skilled and unskilled workers in occupations for which labor is in short supply in this country, and their spouses and children. (10 percent)

    Seventh preference: refugees. (6 percent)

    Spouses and minor children of American citizens are exempt from the preference system.
56. "6–8 million," *New West Magazine,* May 23, 1977; "4–12 million," *Los Angeles Times,* Aug. 7, 1977.
57. Pub. L. No. 94–571, 90 Stat. 2703 (1976).
58. In 1976 there were 57,863 immigrants from Mexico; in 1975, 62,205. U.S., Immigration and Naturalization Service, *Annual Report 1976,* p. 89.
59. Pub. L. No. 95–412, 92 Stat. 907 (1978).
60. Refugee Act of 1980, Pub. L. No. 96–212 (to be codified in scattered sections of 8 U.S.C.). The Refugee Act also increased the allocation of refugee visas to 50,000 annually for the first three fiscal years under the statute and provided that the number of refugee admissions in the following years would be determined by the President after consultation with Congress.

Critical Thinking

1. From among the various historical actions taken to regulate immigration, select three that are particularly hard to understand?
2. What is "Operation Wetback?"
3. What is the National Origins Quota System?

Create Central

www.mhhe.com/createcentral

Internet References

Diversity.com
www.diversity.com

Library of Congress
www.loc.gov

Social Science Information Gateway
http://sosig.esrc.bris.ac.uk

Sociosite
www.sociosite.net

U.S. Census Bureau
www.census.gov

From *The Tarnished Golden Door,* September 1980. Published by United States Commission on Civil Rights.

Article

Prepared by: John A. Kromkowski, *Catholic University of America*

The American Community Survey: The New Dimensions of Race and Ethnicity in America

John David Kromkowski

Learning Outcomes

After reading this article, you will be able to:

- Explain the various implications of data collection by the U.S. Census.
- List and discuss the benefits of easy access to information about the distribution and concentration of ethnic populations, as well as the various social and economic indicators.

Beginning in 1980, most ethnic and ancestry information was collected by the US Census Bureau from the 'Long Form' of the Decennial Enumeration of the Population of the The United States, when the "Ancestry Question" was added to the Census. The record of data collection regarding race, "ethnic," and color (bracketing the distinction between native or foreign-born) can be viewed in the US Census forms excerpts regarding classifications of race or color from 1790–2010. However, for the first time since 1940, the 2010 Census was short-form-only census. This is because the decennial long form has been replaced by the American Community Survey (ACS). The ACS is a nationwide, continuous survey designed to provide reliable and timely demographic, housing, social, and economic data every year.

Demographers and other data users have long viewed the collection interval of ten years between censuses as a severe constraint to understanding change in modem America. In 1995, the US Census Bureau began to address such limitations and to devise new approaches to generating national data that would more rapidly update information requirements of our contemporary society and economy and to measure the accelerating rates of social change and mobility. The mission, goal and objective was to institute a new data collection process for obtaining demographic, housing, social, and economic information previously obtained from the 'Long Form' of the Decennial Census. Congress authorized the American Community Survey (ACS) and testing of the American Community Survey began in 1996. The ACS program began producing test data in 2000. In addition to the data base derived decennial censuses, the American Community Survey introduced an ongoing data collection process and the production of accurate and statistically sound surveys. The U.S. Census Bureau sends questionnaires to approximately 250,000 addresses monthly (or 3 million per year). The Bureau regularly gathers information previously contained only in the Long Form of the decennial census. This effort is the largest data collection project, except for the decennial census that the Census Bureau administers. The ACS will replace the long form in 2010 and thereafter by collecting long-form-type information throughout the decade rather than only once every 10 years.

Recently, the data produced by ACS has become available online via the Census Bureau web site. (See http://census.gov/acs/www/) The array of information available is stunning in its scope. A researcher can download data for over 7000 geographic units and over 175 ethnicities and develop cross-tabs and do statistical tests for a variety of general, social, economic and housing variables related to specific ethnicities. For any selected population group, data is available for hundreds of variables that are grouped under the following thirty-two major headings: total number of races reported, sex and age, relationship, households by type, marital status, school enrollment, educational attainment, fertility, responsibility for grandchildren under 18 years, veteran status, disability status, residence 1 year ago, place of birth, citizenship status and year of entry, world region of birth of foreign born, language spoken at home and ability to speak english, employment status, commuting to work, occupation, industry class of worker, income in the past 12 months, poverty rates for families and people for whom poverty status is determined, housing tenure, units in structure, year structure built, vehicles available, house heating fuel, selected housing characteristics, selected monthly owner costs as a percentage of household income in the past 12 months, owner characteristics, gross rent as a percentage of household income in the past 12 months, and gross rent. By 2002, the data collected by the sampling was encompassing enough to make national estimates. Because it includes the Ancestry Question, the Hispanic Origin Question as well as the "race" question, it is an increasingly important tool for a demographic understanding of race and ethnicity in America. The available data also provides sufficient information to obtain standard errors. As a result, doing statistical tests to determine significance is not difficult. The determination of statistical significance takes into account the difference between the two estimates as well as the standard errors of both estimates.

In broadest outline, what the data reveal is that America is diverse and that statistically meaningful distinctions continue to exist and to evolve in what can be characterized as remarkable "lumpy" society and a geographically clustering of ethnicities which can not be described by concepts such as integration and segregation. To understand population clustering of this sort and at this magnitude demands more detailed analysis of ethnic and race patterns along with other economic and social indicators. Why do differences remain and are they meaningful or merely statistical artifacts? Do we actually understand the analytical tools necessary for dealing with "big data"? See the American Factfinder website of the Census Bureau and tool to analyze data for example at http://www.nctr.usf.edu/abstracts/abs77802.htm.

Even the evolution of the kind of language we use reveals the cracks and faults with the concept of race. Two examples, may provide a starting point for discussion. In 2013, the U.S. Census Bureau announced that it was ending the use of "Negro" on its surveys and forms after more than 100 years of use. The government had considered ending usage of the word "Negro" for the 2010 Census but ultimately decided against it. The bureau reasoned that there was still a segment of the U.S. population that personally identified with the term. Most of them were older blacks living in the Southern states. But the description has come to be viewed as outdated and even offensive by many people in the black community, officials say, so the bureau will reduce the options to "black" or "African-American." The agency will include the new language next year in its annual American Community Survey. Also revealing, however, is the multitude of responses to the 2010 "race question" under "Some Other Race." Nearly 16 million Americans chose "some other race" alone and 21.7 million people chose it in combination with another response. These self reported responses include many of the ancestry groups identified in the Ancestry Question of the American Community Survey, for example - Polish, Italian, Irish, etc. Is it time to dump the race question and simply gather data through the ancestry question? If not, what are the reasons?

2010

→ **NOTE: Please answer BOTH Question 5 about Hispanic origin and Question 6 about race. For this census, Hispanic origins are not races.**

5. Is this person of Hispanic, Latino, or Spanish origin?

☐ **No,** not of Hispanic, Latino, or Spanish origin
☐ Yes, Mexican, Mexican Am., Chicano
☐ Yes, Puerto Rican
☐ Yes, Cuban
☐ Yes, another Hispanic, Latino, or Spanish origin — *Print origin, for example Argentinean, Colombian, Dominican, Nicaraguan, Salvadoran, Spaniard, and so on.*

6. What is this person's race? *Mark X one or more boxes.*

☐ White
☐ Black, African Am., or Negro
☐ American Indian or Alaska Native — *Print name of enrolled or Principal tribe.*

☐ Asian Indian ☐ Japanese ☐ Native Hawaiian
☐ Chinese ☐ Korean ☐ Guamanian or Chamorro
☐ Filipino ☐ Vietnamese ☐ Samoan
☐ Other Asian — *Print race, for example, Hmong, Laotian, Thai, Pakistani, Cambodian, and so on.*
☐ Other Pacific Islander — *Print race, for example, Fijan, Tongan, and so on.*

☐ Some other race — *Print race.*

2000

→ **NOTE: Please answer BOTH Questions 7 and 8.**

7. **Is person 1 Spanish/Hispanic/Latino?** *Mark* ☒ *the* ***"No"*** *box if* ***not*** *Spanish/Hispanic/Latino.*
   - ☐ No, not Spanish/Hispanic/Latino
   - ☐ Yes, Puerto Rican
   - ☐ Yes, Mexican, Mexican Am., Chicano
   - ☐ Yes, Cuban
   - ☐ Yes, other Spanish/Hispanic/Latino — *Print group.*

8. **What is Person 1's race?** ***Mark*** ☒ ***one or more races*** *to indicate what this person considers himself/herself to be.*
   - ☐ White
   - ☐ Black, African Am., or Negro
   - ☐ American Indian or Alaska Native — *Print name of enrolled or principal tribe.*
   - ☐ Asian Indian
   - ☐ Japanese
   - ☐ Native Hawaiian
   - ☐ Chinese
   - ☐ Korean
   - ☐ Guamanian or Chamorro
   - ☐ Filipino
   - ☐ Vietnamese
   - ☐ Samoan
   - ☐ Other Asian — *Print race.*
   - ☐ Other Pacific Islander — *Print race.*
   - ☐ Some other race — *Print race*

1990

4. Race Fill ONE circle for the race that the person considers himself/herself to be. If Indian (Amer.), print the name of the enrolled or principal tribe. → If Other Asian or Pacific Islander (API) print one group, for example: Hraong, Rjan, Laodan, Thai, Tongan, Paidsanl, Cambodan, and so on. → If Other race, print race. →	○ White ○ Black or Negro ○ Indian (Amer.) (Print the name of the enrolled or principal tribe.) ○ Eskimo ○ Aleut <u>Asian or Pacific Islander (API)</u> ○ Chinese ○ Japanese ○ Filipino ○ Asian Indian ○ Hawaiian ○ Samoan ○ Korean ○ Guamanian ○ Vietnamese ○ Other API ○ Other race (Print race)
7. Is this person of Spanish/Hispanic origin? Fill ONE circle for each person. If Yes, other Spanish/Hispanic, print one group, →	○ No (not Spanish/Hispanic) ○ Yes, Mexican, Mexican-Am, Chicago ○ Yes, Pardo Rican ○ Yes, Cuban ○ Yes, other Spanish/Hispanic (Print one group, for example: Argentinian, Colombian, Dominican, Nicaraguan, Salvadoran, Sparland and so on.)

1980

4. Is this person – *Fill one circle.*	O White O Black or Negro O Japanese O Chinese O Filipino O Korean O Vietnamese O Indian (Amer.) *Print tribe*	O Asian Indian O Hawaiian O Guamanian O Samoan O Eskimo O Aleut O Other – *Specify*
7. Is this person of Spanish/ Hispanic origin or descent? *Fill one circle.*	O No (not Spanish/Hispanic) O Yes, Mexican, Mexican-Amer., Chicano O Yes, Puerto Rican O Yes, Cuban O Yes, other Spanish/Hispanic	

1970

4. COLOR OR RACE

Fill one circle.

If "Indian (American)," also give tribe.

If "Other," also give race.

O White	O Japanese	O Hawaiian
	O Chinese	O Korean
O Negro or Black	O Filipino	O Other – *Print race*
O Indian (Amer.) *Print tribe* →		

1960

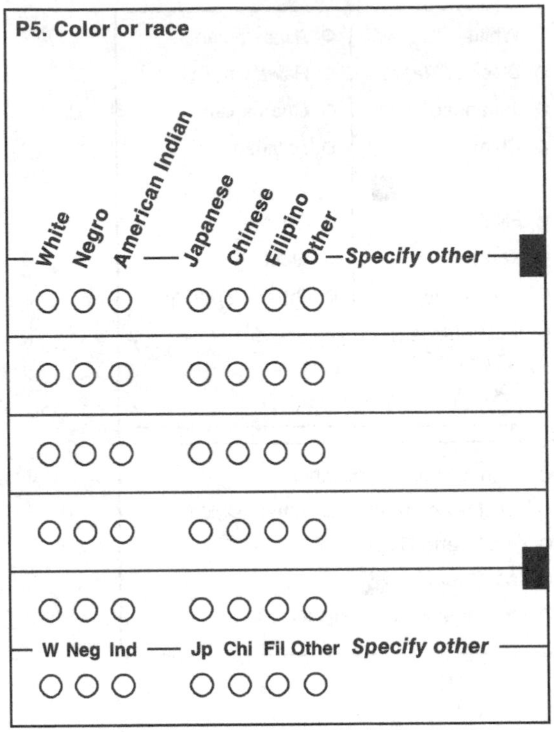

P5. Color or race

White / Negro / American Indian / Japanese / Chinese / Filipino / Other — *Specify other*

W Neg Ind — Jp Chi Fil Other *Specify other*

1950

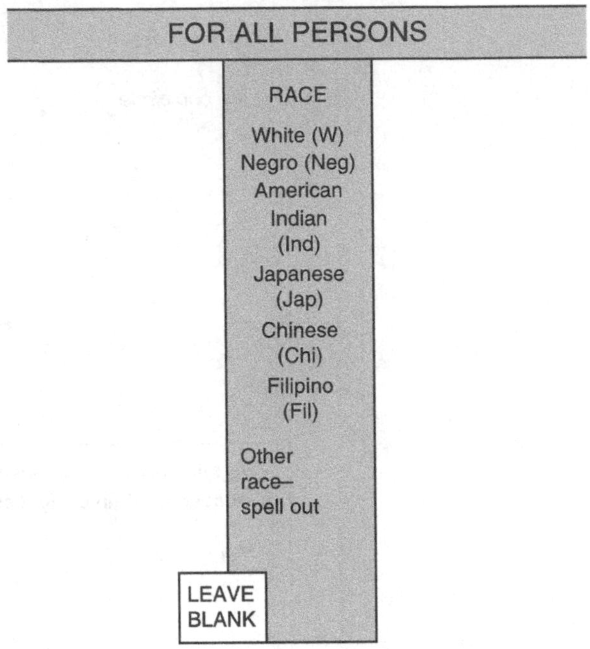

FOR ALL PERSONS

RACE

White (W)
Negro (Neg)
American Indian (Ind)
Japanese (Jap)
Chinese (Chi)
Filipino (Fil)
Other race—spell out

LEAVE BLANK

1940

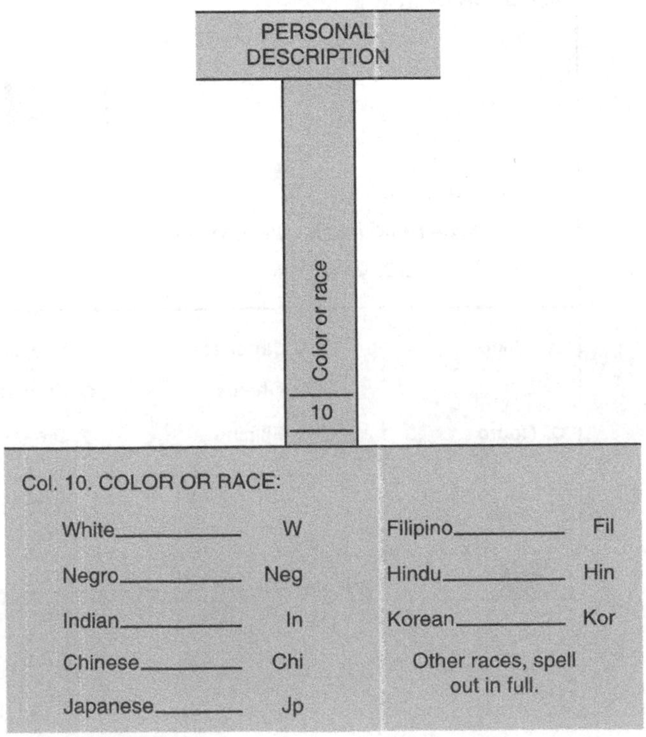

PERSONAL DESCRIPTION

Color or race

10

Col. 10. COLOR OR RACE:

White	W	Filipino	Fil
Negro	Neg	Hindu	Hin
Indian	In	Korean	Kor
Chinese	Chi	Other races, spell out in full.	
Japanese	Jp		

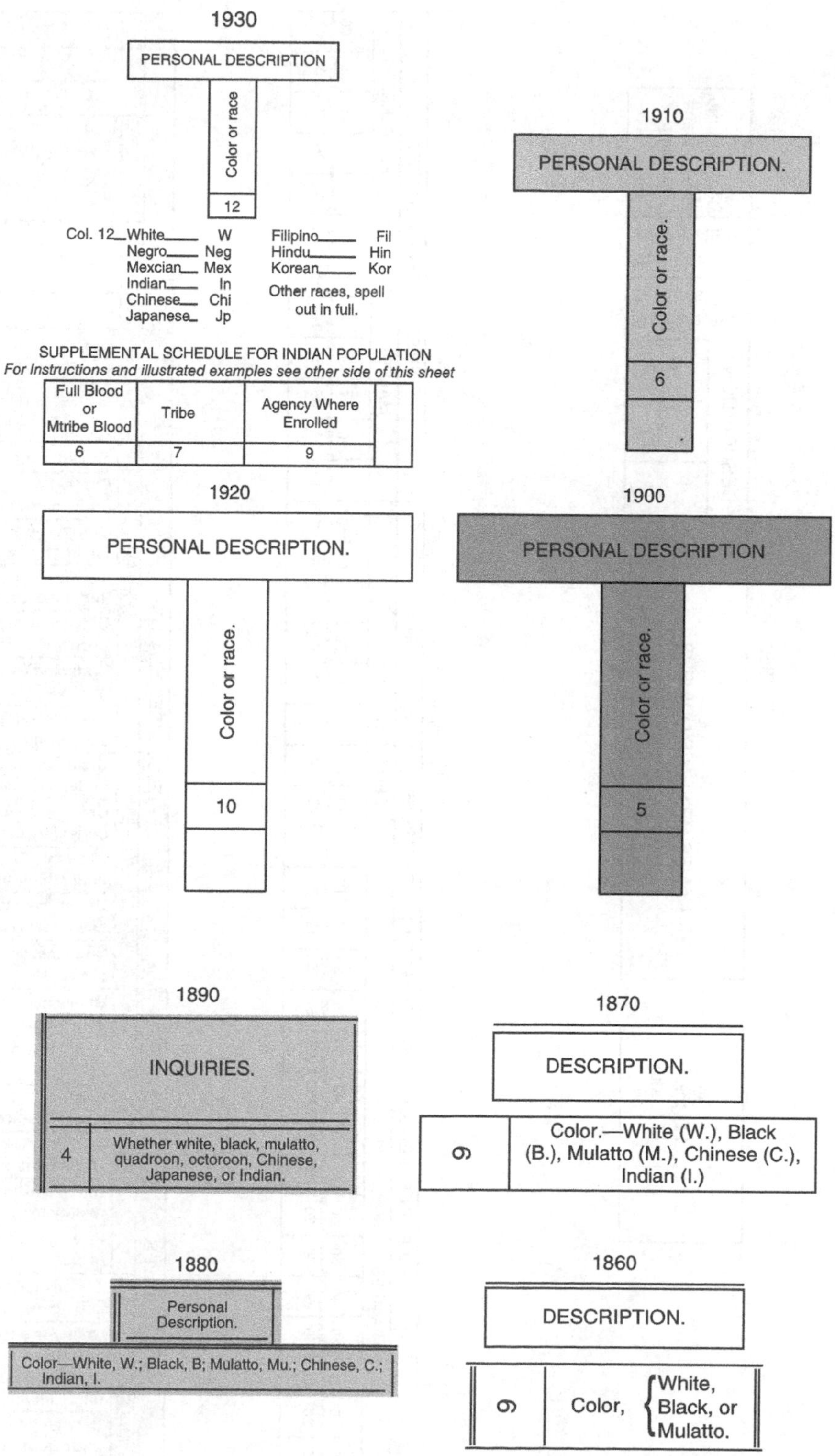
1930
PERSONAL DESCRIPTION
Color or race
12
Col. 12 White W Negro Neg Mexcian Mex Indian In Chinese Chi Japanese Jp
Filipino Fil Hindu Hin Korean Kor
Other races, spell out in full.
SUPPLEMENTAL SCHEDULE FOR INDIAN POPULATION
For Instructions and illustrated examples see other side of this sheet
Full Blood or Mtribe Blood
Tribe
Agency Where Enrolled
6
7
9
1910
PERSONAL DESCRIPTION.
Color or race.
6
1920
PERSONAL DESCRIPTION.
Color or race.
10
1900
PERSONAL DESCRIPTION
Color or race.
5
1890
INQUIRIES.
4
Whether white, black, mulatto, quadroon, octoroon, Chinese, Japanese, or Indian.
1870
DESCRIPTION.
6
Color.—White (W.), Black (B.), Mulatto (M.), Chinese (C.), Indian (I.)
1880
Personal Description.
Color—White, W.; Black, B; Mulatto, Mu.; Chinese, C.; Indian, I.
1860
DESCRIPTION.
6
Color, White, Black, or Mulatto.

1850

Color, { White, Black, or Mulatto.

NAMES OF SLAVE OWNERS.	Number of Slave.	DESCRIPTION.			Fugitives from the State.	Number manumitted.	Deaf & dumb, blind, insane, or idiotic.
		Age.	Sex.	Color.			

1840

FREE WHITE PERSONS, INCLUDING HEADS OF FAMILIES.																										FREE COLORED PERSONS.											
MALES.													FEMALES.													MALES.						FEMALES.					
Under 5	5 & under 10	10 & under 15	15 & under 20	20 & under 30	30 & under 40	40 & under 50	50 & under 60	60 & under 70	70 & under 80	80 & under 90	90 & under 100	100 and upwards.	Under 5	5 & under 10	10 & under 15	15 & under 20	20 & under 30	30 & under 40	40 & under 50	50 & under 60	60 & under 70	70 & under 80	80 & under 90	90 & under 100	100 and upwards.	Under 10	10 & under 24	24 & under 36	36 & under 55	55 & under 100	100 and upwards.	Under 10	10 & under 24	24 & under 36	36 & under 55	55 & under 100	100 and upwards.

1830

SLAVES.												FREE COLORED PERSONS.												TOTAL	
MALES						FEMALES						MALES						FEMALES							
Under ten years of age.	Of ten and under twenty-four.	Of twenty-four and under thirty-six.	Of thirty-six and under fifty-five.	Of fifty-five and under one hundred.	Of one hundred and upwards.	Under ten years of age.	Of ten and under twenty-four.	Of twenty-four and under thirty-six.	Of thirty-six and under fifty-five.	Of fifty-five and under one hundred.	Of one hundred and upwards.	Under ten years of age.	Of ten and under twenty-four.	Of twenty-four and under thirty-six.	Of thirty-six and under fifty-five.	Of fifty-five and under one hundred.	Of one hundred and upwards.	Under ten years of age.	Of ten and under twenty-four.	Of twenty-four and under thirty-six.	Of thirty-six and under fifty-five.	Of fifty-five and under one hundred.	Of one hundred and upwards.		Ms not clear
under 10	10 to 24	24 to 35	35 to 55	55 to 100	100, Inc	under 10	10 to 24	24 to 35	35 to 55	55 to 100	100, Inc	under 10	10 to 24	24 to 35	35 to 55	55 to 100	100, Inc	under 10	10 to 24	24 to 35	35 to 55	55 to 100	100, Inc		

1820

Names of heads of families & Names of men of 21 years of age	Free White Males						Free White Females					Naturalised	Agricultural	Commercial	Manufactures	Free persons of soulder	Males of the age of 21 year & upwards	Remarks (33)
Delaware Co. Indiana. 1820.	under 10	Over 10 & under 16	Over 16 & under 18	Over 16 & under 26	Over 26 & under 44	Over 44 & upwards	Under 10	Over 10 & under 16	Over 16 & under 26	Over 26 & under 45	all over 45 years							
Benjamine-Cutbirth	2	—	—	3	—	/	—	2	/	—	/	—	4	—	—	—	2	

1810

FREE WHITE MALES.					FREE WHITE FEMALES.					All other free persons, except Indians, not taxed.	Slaves.
Under ten years of age	Of ten years, and under sixteen.	Of sixteen, and under twenty-six, including heads of families.	Of twenty-six, and under forty-five, including heads of families.	Of forty-five and upwards, including head of families.	Under ten years of age.	Of ten years, and under sixteen.	Of sixteen, and under twenty-six, including heads of families.	Of twenty-six, and under forty-five, including heads of families.	Of forty-five and upwards, including head of families.		
to 10.	to 16.	to 26.	to 45.	45 & c.	to 10.	to 16.	to 26.	to 45.	45 & c.		

1800

Free White Males					*Free White Females*					*All other free persons except Indians not taxed*	*Slaves*
to 10	*10–16*	*16–26*	*26–45*	*45 &*	*to 10*	*10–16*	*16–26*	*26–45*	*45 &*		
264	*195*	*152*	*163*	*101*	*233*	*149*	*146*	*166*	*96*	*3*	*36*

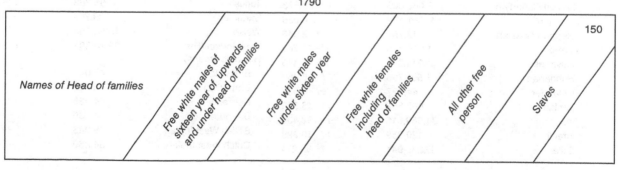

1790

Names of Head of families	*Free white males of sixteen year of upwards and under head of families*	*Free white males under sixteen year*	*Free white females including head of families*	*All other free person*	*Slaves*	150

2010 American Community Survey 1-Year Estimates - Ancestry

Ancestry	Estimate	Margin of Error
Total:	309,349,689	*****
Afghan	79,775	+/−10,244
Albanian	193,813	+/−14,737
Alsatian	9,537	+/−1,490
American	19,975,875	+/−105,096
Arab:	1,646,371	+/−36,587
Egyptian	190,078	+/−14,249
Iraqi	105,981	+/−13,195
Jordanian	61,664	+/−8,585
Lebanese	501,988	+/−14,992
Moroccan	82,073	+/−8,848
Palestinian	93,438	+/−11,185
Syrian	148,214	+/−10,956
Arab	290,893	+/−18,004
Other Arab	223,020	+/−15,403
Armenian	474,559	+/−18,151
Assyrian/Chaldean/Syriac	106,298	+/−9,274
Australian	93,063	+/−6,325
Austrian	722,282	+/−16,851
Basque	53,052	+/−5,677
Belgian	360,912	+/−12,022
Brazilian	361,814	+/−16,826
British	1,181,340	+/−19,681
Bulgarian	95,568	+/−8,384
Cajun	103,091	+/−6,726
Canadian	717,390	+/−17,498
Carpatho Rusyn	8,934	+/−1,570
Celtic	50,919	+/−4,476
Croatian	411,427	+/−13,210
Cypriot	6,388	+/−1,597
Czech	1,525,187	+/−25,310
Czechoslovakian	304,020	+/−9,162
Danish	1,375,506	+/−24,059
Dutch	4,645,131	+/−40,097
Eastern European	489,534	+/−15,228
English	25,926,451	+/−117,804
Estonian	30,641	+/−4,238
European	3,616,843	+/−44,797
Finnish	647,697	+/−15,866
French (except Basque)	8,761,496	+/−55,528
French Canadian	2,042,808	+/−28,673
German	47,901,779	+/−110,936
German Russian	18,752	+/−2,946
Greek	1,315,775	+/−29,760
Guyanese	214,315	+/−14,116
Hungarian	1,501,736	+/−28,060
Icelander	44,027	+/−3,947
Iranian	463,552	+/−18,925
Irish	34,669,616	+/−132,430
Israeli	129,359	+/−10,929
Italian	17,235,941	+/−89,274
Latvian	84,664	+/−5,919
Lithuanian	660,071	+/−18,202
Luxemburger	40,975	+/−2,958
Macedonian	61,287	+/−7,220
Maltese	35,103	+/−4,237
New Zealander	19,961	+/−2,644
Northern European	282,953	+/−13,422
Norwegian	4,470,081	+/−44,484
Pennsylvania German	332,341	+/−13,407
Polish	9,569,207	+/−81,176
Portuguese	1,405,909	+/−27,954
Romanian	447,293	+/−14,196
Russian	2,971,599	+/−42,579
Scandinavian	570,696	+/−15,941
Scotch-Irish	3,257,161	+/−37,878
Scottish	5,460,679	+/−50,422
Serbian	187,739	+/−9,494
Slavic	136,636	+/−6,696
Slovak	762,030	+/−17,141
Slovene	171,923	+/−7,828
Soviet Union	1,749	+/−683
Subsaharan African:	2,789,129	+/−44,560
Cape Verdean	95,003	+/−8,865
Ethiopian	201,707	+/−15,456
Ghanaian	91,322	+/−8,350
Kenyan	51,749	+/−6,951
Liberian	51,296	+/−7,467
Nigerian	259,058	+/−17,258
Senegalese	11,369	+/−3,194
Sierra Leonean	16,929	+/−4,726
Somalian	120,102	+/−10,979
South African	57,327	+/−6,817
Sudanese	42,147	+/−6,603
Ugandan	12,549	+/−3,711
Zimbabwean	7,323	+/−2,525
African	1,676,413	+/−35,051
Other Subsaharan African	143,867	+/−10,966
Swedish	4,088,555	+/−36,876
Swiss	961,380	+/−20,027
Turkish	195,283	+/−10,380
Ukrainian	939,746	+/−23,848
Welsh	1,793,356	+/−25,237
West Indian (Except Hispanic groups)	2,624,392	+/−41,889
Bahamian	48,043	+/−6,299
Barbadian	58,215	+/−5,870
Belizean	54,925	+/−7,492
Bermudan	4,730	+/−1,096
British West Indian	88,043	+/−7,258
Dutch West Indian	54,260	+/−4,886

Ancestry	Estimate	Margin of Error
Haitian	881,488	+/−31,399
Jamaican	965,355	+/−27,254
Trinidadian & Tobagonian	197,520	+/−10,996
U.S. Virgin Islander	11,674	+/−2,496
West Indian	299,010	+/−15,401
Other West Indian	7,969	+/−1,884
Yugoslavian	326,576	+/−19,510
Other groups	120,017,996	+/−141,232
Unclassified or not reported	36,730,332	+/−134,914

Data are based on a sample and are subject to sampling variability. The degree of uncertainty for an estimate arising from sampling variability is represented through the use of a margin of error. The value shown here is the 90 percent margin of error. The margin of error can be interpreted roughly as providing a 90 percent probability that the interval defined by the estimate minus the margin of error and the estimate plus the margin of error (the lower and upper confidence bounds) contains the true value. In addition to sampling variability, the ACS estimates are subject to nonsampling error (for a discussion of nonsampling variability, see Accuracy of the Data). The effect of nonsampling error is not represented in these tables.

Starting in 2008, the Scotch-Irish category does not include Irish-Scotch. People who reported Irish-Scotch ancestry are classified under "Other groups," whereas in 2007 and earlier they were classified as Scotch-Irish.

The American Community Survey (ACS) implemented a variety of new race and ethnicity coding changes in 2010 to be consistent with the 2010 decennial census coding rules. Any changes in ancestry estimates for 2010 and beyond should be used with caution. For more information on these changes, please see "Coding Changes to the American Community Survey Between 2009 and 2010 and Their Potential Effect on the Estimates of Ancestry Groups" on the Ethnicity and Ancestry Branch website at http://www.census.gov/population/www/ancestry/.

S0201: Selected Population Profile in the United States of Groups with Over 1,000,000

2009–2011 American Community Survey 3-Year Estimates

Subject	White	Black or African American	Chinese	Filipino	Japanese	Korean	Vietnamese
TOTAL POPULATION	236,382,436	41,941,857	4,104,990	3,396,753	1,315,737	1,725,771	1,803,143
SEX AND AGE							
Median age (years)	39.2	30.9	35.0	33.7	37.5	33.1	34.3
HOUSEHOLDS BY TYPE							
Family households	66.0%	63.5%	70.1%	76.4%	60.0%	66.9%	80.3%
Married-couple family	51.6%	28.0%	57.1%	56.5%	46.8%	53.3%	60.6%
Female householder, no husband present, family	10.2%	29.4%	8.6%	14.8%	9.3%	9.8%	12.5%
Nonfamily households	34.0%	36.5%	29.9%	23.6%	40.0%	33.1%	19.7%
Average family size	3.11	3.42	3.39	3.76	3.09	3.22	3.91
SCHOOL ENROLLMENT							
Percent enrolled in college or graduate school	25.1%	21.4%	40.6%	29.4%	30.8%	39.6%	32.3%
Female 3 years and over enrolled in school	30,178,920	7,278,719	702,941	530,816	197,348	296,966	286,370
EDUCATIONAL ATTAINMENT							

(continued)

Subject	White	Black or African American	Chinese	Filipino	Japanese	Korean	Vietnamese
Less than high school diploma	12.3%	17.9%	17.9%	7.6%	5.0%	7.8%	30.0%
High school graduate (includes equivalency)	28.8%	31.2%	15.4%	16.1%	19.7%	18.6%	21.4%
Some college or associate's degree	29.4%	32.6%	15.7%	30.4%	28.9%	21.5%	22.9%
Bachelor's degree	18.6%	11.9%	25.4%	37.5%	30.8%	34.0%	18.7%
Graduate or professional degree	10.9%	6.4%	25.6%	8.4%	15.6%	18.0%	7.0%
RESPONSIBILITY FOR GRAND-CHILDREN UNDER 18 YEARS							
Living with grandchild(ren)	3.1%	6.1%	5.3%	7.1%	2.6%	2.9%	7.1%
RESIDENCE 1 YEAR AGO							
Same house	85.7%	80.5%	83.6%	84.3%	85.4%	80.2%	86.1%
PLACE OF BIRTH, CITIZENSHIP STATUS AND YEAR OF ENTRY							
Native	216,551,848	38,426,311	1,604,582	1,629,780	978,754	633,051	651,600
Foreign born	19,830,588	3,515,546	2,500,408	1,766,973	336,983	1,092,720	1,151,543
Foreign born; naturalized U.S. citizen	8,372,013	1,763,870	1,489,082	1,143,860	106,611	609,658	852,147
Foreign born; not a U.S. citizen	11,458,575	1,751,676	1,011,326	623,113	230,372	483,062	299,396
Population born outside the United States	19,830,588	3,515,546	2,500,408	1,766,973	336,983	1,092,720	1,151,543
LANGUAGE SPOKEN AT HOME AND ABILITY TO SPEAK ENGLISH							
English only	84.9%	91.4%	25.3%	44.3%	66.3%	29.6%	15.4%
Language other than English	15.1%	8.6%	74.7%	55.7%	33.7%	70.4%	84.6%
Speak English less than "very well"	6.1%	3.0%	41.1%	18.2%	15.7%	39.6%	51.0%
EMPLOYMENT STATUS							
Unemployed	5.8%	10.7%	5.0%	6.1%	4.2%	4.8%	6.4%
CLASS OF WORKER							
Self-employed workers in own not incorporated business	6.7%	3.6%	5.5%	3.2%	6.1%	10.3%	8.7%
INCOME							
Median household income (dollars)	54,387	34,826	67,118	77,147	67,620	52,674	54,525
Median income (dollars)	33,370	26,012	45,112	52,895	50,071	35,223	35,152
Per capita income (dollars)	29,408	17,688	30,217	26,219	32,322	26,115	20,996
POVERTY RATES							
All families	8.7%	23.0%	10.2%	5.4%	4.8%	11.8%	13.4%
Married-couple family	4.7%	8.0%	8.1%	2.7%	2.7%	8.9%	10.9%
Female householder, no husband present, family	26.4%	37.1%	21.6%	14.6%	15.3%	26.7%	25.6%

S0201: Selected Population Profile in the United States of Groups with Over 1,000,000

2009–2011 American Community Survey 3-Year Estimates

	Mexican	Puerto Rican	Cuban	Dominican	British	Czech	Danish
TOTAL POPULATION	32,869,887	4,749,070	1,829,495	1,485,465	1,181,125	1,543,514	1,394,031
SEX AND AGE							
Median age (years)	25.6	28.3	40.3	29.3	46.2	42.3	46.0
HOUSEHOLDS BY TYPE							
Family households	80.8%	70.0%	69.1%	79.1%	62.8%	62.9%	64.3%
Married-couple family	52.1%	36.5%	48.3%	34.8%	53.9%	52.1%	54.0%
Female householder, no husband present, family	19.2%	26.7%	14.9%	35.6%	6.4%	7.7%	7.6%
Nonfamily households	19.2%	30.0%	30.9%	20.9%	37.2%	37.1%	35.7%
Average family size	4.14	3.44	3.44	3.71	2.92	2.93	2.95
SCHOOL ENROLLMENT							
Percent enrolled in college or graduate school	14.4%	17.3%	27.4%	21.7%	38.9%	30.0%	30.0%
Female 3 years and over enrolled in school	5,514,839	801,842	226,358	244,553	130,089	194,893	165,135
EDUCATIONAL ATTAINMENT							
Less than high school diploma	43.4%	25.6%	23.5%	34.6%	3.1%	4.7%	3.8%
High school graduate (includes equivalency)	26.3%	29.6%	28.4%	25.8%	14.5%	24.6%	21.5%
Some college or associate's degree	20.9%	28.8%	24.1%	24.5%	27.9%	31.3%	34.5%
Bachelor's degree	6.8%	10.8%	15.0%	10.6%	30.0%	24.9%	25.1%
Graduate or professional degree	2.6%	5.3%	9.0%	4.5%	24.6%	14.5%	15.2%
RESPONSIBILITY FOR GRANDCHILDREN UNDER 18 YEARS							
Living with grandchild(ren)	8.5%	5.9%	5.4%	8.5%	1.7%	1.6%	2.1%
RESIDENCE 1 YEAR AGO							
Same house	82.2%	80.3%	84.9%	83.1%	86.4%	87.2%	87.2%
PLACE OF BIRTH, CITIZENSHIP STATUS AND YEAR OF ENTRY							
Native	21,214,207	4,696,856	763,195	644,015	973,584	1,506,509	1,357,362
Foreign born	11,655,680	52,214	1,066,300	841,450	207,541	37,005	36,669
Foreign born; naturalized U.S. citizen	2,705,102	24,637	598,124	398,826	86,387	22,756	15,824
Foreign born; not a U.S. citizen	8,950,578	27,577	468,176	442,624	121,154	14,249	20,845
Population born outside the United States	11,655,680	52,214	1,066,300	841,450	207,541	37,005	36,669

(continued)

	Mexican	Puerto Rican	Cuban	Dominican	British	Czech	Danish
LANGUAGE SPOKEN AT HOME AND ABILITY TO SPEAK ENGLISH							
English only	24.7%	35.6%	18.2%	9.2%	95.9%	95.1%	95.6%
Language other than English	75.3%	64.4%	81.8%	90.8%	4.1%	4.9%	4.4%
Speak English less than "very well"	35.7%	18.4%	40.9%	45.2%	0.5%	0.9%	0.5%
EMPLOYMENT STATUS							
Unemployed	8.3%	9.6%	7.9%	9.6%	4.5%	4.9%	4.6%
CLASS OF WORKER							
Self-employed workers in own not incorporated business	6.1%	3.0%	6.9%	5.8%	7.6%	7.0%	8.3%
INCOME							
Median household income (dollars)	40,060	37,668	41,191	34,575	72,668	62,578	62,295
Median income (dollars)	24,209	22,572	30,524	23,130	48,357	42,024	45,043
Per capita income (dollars)	13,740	17,372	22,692	15,268	46,444	35,481	35,921
POVERTY RATES							
All families	24.0%	23.5%	13.9%	26.2%	3.7%	4.1%	4.4%
Married-couple family	17.6%	9.2%	9.8%	12.8%	2.1%	2.1%	2.5%
Female householder, no husband present, family	42.1%	43.1%	27.0%	40.9%	15.6%	17.0%	16.3%

S0201: Selected Population Profile in the United States of Groups with Over 1,000,000

2009–2011 American Community Survey 3-Year Estimates

	Greek	Hungarian	Irish	Italian	Norwegian	Polish	Portuguese
TOTAL POPULATION	1,311,844	1,484,821	35,186,074	17,488,984	4,491,712	9,660,864	1,420,978
SEX AND AGE							
Median age (years)	37.2	44.0	39.0	35.9	40.8	39.6	37.6
HOUSEHOLDS BY TYPE							
Family households	63.1%	62.2%	63.8%	64.3%	64.3%	63.4%	67.4%
Married-couple family	49.6%	50.8%	49.4%	50.2%	52.9%	51.2%	51.2%
Female householder, no husband present, family	9.3%	8.3%	10.6%	10.1%	8.1%	8.7%	11.9%
Nonfamily households	36.9%	37.8%	36.2%	35.7%	35.7%	36.6%	32.6%
Average family size	3.11	2.98	3.06	3.10	2.95	3.02	3.20
SCHOOL ENROLLMENT							
Percent enrolled in college or graduate school	29.7%	30.1%	26.2%	27.2%	27.3%	28.7%	25.1%

(continued)

	Greek	Hungarian	Irish	Italian	Norwegian	Polish	Portuguese
Female 3 years and over enrolled in school	190,604	180,496	4,773,621	2,589,185	580,916	1,291,236	194,149
EDUCATIONAL ATTAINMENT							
Less than high school diploma	9.7%	5.9%	7.5%	7.6%	4.4%	6.2%	17.1%
High school graduate (includes equivalency)	22.5%	25.7%	27.1%	27.9%	24.2%	27.2%	29.4%
Some college or associate's degree	27.7%	28.9%	32.7%	30.0%	34.6%	29.7%	30.0%
Bachelor's degree	24.1%	22.8%	20.7%	21.6%	24.1%	22.4%	15.6%
Graduate or professional degree	16.1%	16.6%	12.0%	12.9%	12.6%	14.6%	7.8%
RESPONSIBILITY FOR GRANDCHILDREN UNDER 18 YEARS							
Living with grandchild(ren)	2.0%	1.8%	2.7%	2.1%	1.8%	1.9%	3.2%
RESIDENCE 1 YEAR AGO							
Same house	86.4%	87.7%	85.4%	86.3%	86.2%	87.8%	85.9%
PLACE OF BIRTH, CITIZENSHIP STATUS AND YEAR OF ENTRY							
Native	1,152,953	1,382,912	34,935,046	16,948,324	4,454,898	9,155,031	1,160,439
Foreign born	158,891	101,909	251,028	540,660	36,814	505,833	260,539
Foreign born; naturalized U.S. citizen	123,796	74,794	148,144	354,800	18,161	320,307	155,378
Foreign born; not a U.S. citizen	35,095	27,115	102,884	185,860	18,653	185,526	105,161
Population born outside the United States	158,891	101,909	251,028	540,660	36,814	505,833	260,539
LANGUAGE SPOKEN AT HOME AND ABILITY TO SPEAK ENGLISH							
English only	74.1%	89.5%	97.6%	93.0%	97.0%	91.6%	73.7%
Language other than English	25.9%	10.5%	2.4%	7.0%	3.0%	8.4%	26.3%
Speak English less than "very well"	6.3%	2.9%	0.3%	1.7%	0.4%	2.9%	9.7%
EMPLOYMENT STATUS							
Unemployed	6.1%	5.7%	6.2%	6.3%	5.1%	6.0%	7.1%
CLASS OF WORKER							
Self-employed workers in own not incorporated business	7.1%	6.7%	6.0%	5.9%	7.2%	5.8%	7.0%
INCOME							
Median household income (dollars)	63,099	61,458	58,311	63,934	61,310	63,016	59,587
Median income (dollars)	41,335	41,272	36,626	39,461	38,870	41,302	37,032
Per capita income (dollars)	34,207	37,211	31,411	32,637	33,300	34,465	29,137
POVERTY RATES							
All families	6.3%	5.6%	6.9%	6.3%	5.1%	5.0%	7.7%
Married-couple family	3.2%	3.4%	3.1%	2.8%	2.5%	2.5%	3.7%
Female householder, no husband present, family	21.3%	17.6%	22.5%	21.3%	19.4%	18.4%	22.9%

S0201: Selected Population Profile in the United States of Groups with Over 1,000,000

2009–2011 American Community Survey 3-Year Estimates

	Russian	Scotch-Irish	Scottish	Swedish	American
TOTAL POPULATION	3,027,065	3,308,414	5,562,022	4,128,135	20,875,080
SEX AND AGE					
Median age (years)	43.1	50.9	45.4	43.8	40.4
HOUSEHOLDS BY TYPE					
Family households	60.7%	61.1%	64.8%	63.6%	67.1%
Married-couple family	50.4%	50.0%	54.2%	52.4%	52.3%
Female householder, no husband present, family	7.4%	7.9%	7.1%	8.3%	10.8%
Nonfamily households	39.3%	38.9%	35.2%	36.4%	32.9%
Average family size	2.92	2.80	2.94	2.95	2.98
SCHOOL ENROLLMENT					
Percent enrolled in college or graduate school	30.1%	31.3%	33.2%	28.0%	19.8%
Female 3 years and over enrolled in school	384,415	325,628	602,549	516,287	2,672,602
EDUCATIONAL ATTAINMENT					
Less than high school diploma	3.7%	4.8%	4.2%	4.3%	14.4%
High school graduate (includes equivalency)	15.2%	21.5%	20.2%	22.8%	36.9%
Some college or associate's degree	23.8%	32.9%	32.9%	33.2%	28.2%
Bachelor's degree	29.0%	24.3%	26.0%	25.3%	13.6%
Graduate or professional degree	28.2%	16.5%	16.7%	14.4%	6.8%
RESPONSIBILITY FOR GRANDCHILDREN UNDER 18 YEARS					
Living with grandchild(ren)	1.6%	2.3%	2.1%	2.1%	3.3%
RESIDENCE 1 YEAR AGO					
Same house	87.1%	88.2%	86.3%	86.8%	87.7%
PLACE OF BIRTH, CITIZENSHIP STATUS AND YEAR OF ENTRY					
Native	2,506,790	3,289,164	5,413,743	4,075,464	20,822,902
Foreign born	520,275	19,250	148,279	52,671	52,178
Foreign born; naturalized U.S. citizen	351,786	10,238	75,477	23,208	40,640
Foreign born; not a U.S. citizen	168,489	9,012	72,802	29,463	11,538
Population born outside the United States	520,275	19,250	148,279	52,671	52,178

(continued)

	Russian	Scotch-Irish	Scottish	Swedish	American
LANGUAGE SPOKEN AT HOME AND ABILITY TO SPEAK ENGLISH					
English only	79.7%	97.7%	97.3%	96.6%	96.9%
Language other than English	20.3%	2.3%	2.7%	3.4%	3.1%
Speak English less than "very well"	8.2%	0.3%	0.3%	0.4%	0.6%
EMPLOYMENT STATUS					
Unemployed	5.4%	4.9%	5.2%	5.0%	5.7%
CLASS OF WORKER					
Self-employed workers in own not incorporated business	9.6%	7.8%	7.5%	7.5%	6.5%
INCOME					
Median household income (dollars)	71,644	56,675	63,843	61,607	47,334
Median income (dollars)	45,995	42,643	42,187	41,936	30,073
Per capita income (dollars)	47,673	35,978	39,257	34,817	24,800
POVERTY RATES					
All families	5.2%	4.5%	4.6%	4.7%	9.7%
Married-couple family	3.1%	2.3%	2.6%	2.3%	5.2%
Female householder, no husband present, family	17.1%	15.9%	16.9%	18.2%	28.8%

Critical Thinking

1. Do you agree with the way data is collected by the U.S. Census?
2. In what ways is having all the ethnic data available in the U.S. Census helpful to seekers?

Create Central

www.mhhe.com/createcentral

Internet References

Library of Congress
www.loc.gov

Social Science Information Gateway
http://sosig.esrc.bris.ac.uk

Sociosite
www.sociosite.net

U. S. Bureau of Citizenship and Immigration Services
www.USCIS.gov/portaffsftefuscis

Article

Prepared by: John A. Kromkowski, *Catholic University of America*

Still Unmelted after All These Years[1]

JOHN DAVID KROMKOWSKI

Learning Outcomes

After reading this article, you will be able to:

- Discuss the implication of population differences in the various regions of America.
- Explain the different purposes of State boundaries and regional clusters.

Are Polish Americans or Italian Americans or African Americans uniformly distributed through the United States? No; in fact, America is stunningly "unmelted." Just look. MAPS 1-4 Distribution by State of Polish, Italian, Irish, and "American."

A bowl of raw meat and uncooked potatoes, celery, carrots and onions is not per se appetizing. But even in a well simmered and tasty soup or stew, you can tell by looking that there are carrots, potatoes, celery, onions and meat. So let's not despair. Let's investigate.

The Ancestry Question on the US Census has produced a stunning array of information about how Americans self-describe themselves. The self-describing aspect of the US Census, especially The Ancestry Question is an highly important feature of data collection in a pluralistic democracy. Unlike the Race Question on the US Census which was constitutionally and historically imposed and rooted in pseudo-scientific and political assumptions of exclusion, the Ancestry Question emerged from a more current understanding[2] of ethnicity and its organic character and growth through the self-determined iterations rooted in the person, family, household and neighborhoods that constitute the American experience of immigration, urbanization and the attendant cultural pluralism of democratization and freedom fostered by a wide range of forces that accompanied American political development especially for the past seven decades. These social economic, political, and personal dynamics make the demography of ethnicity in America seem messy. Indeed, the ostensible messiness of immigration, the articulation of ancestry and identity rooted in ethnicity may well explain the slow evolutionary process and the significant impediments to collection of demographic information. Uniform data would be achieved by replacing the variety of Race and Ethnic Origin Questions associated with Hispanic, Asian, Indigenous

Legend

Data Classes
Percent
0.0–2.5
2.7–5.2
6.7–9.3

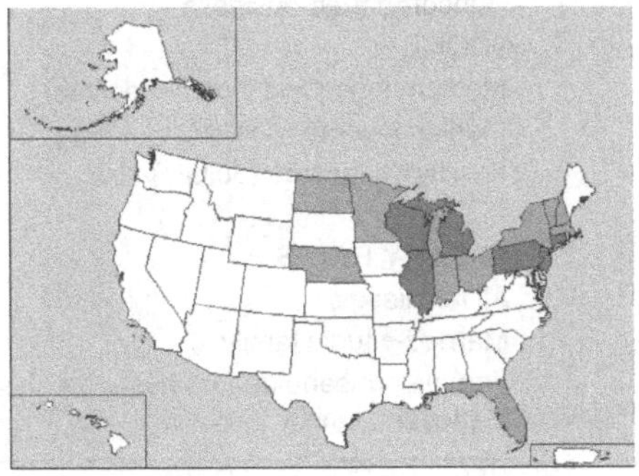

TM-PCT037. Percent of Persons of Polish Ancestry: 2000.
Universe: Total population.
Data Set: Census 2000 Summary File 3 (SF 3)—Sample Data United States by State.
Source: U.S. Census Bureau, Census 2000 Summary File 3, Matrices P1, and PCT18.

Legend

Data Classes
Percent
0.2–3.9
4.3–9.3
11.6–19.0

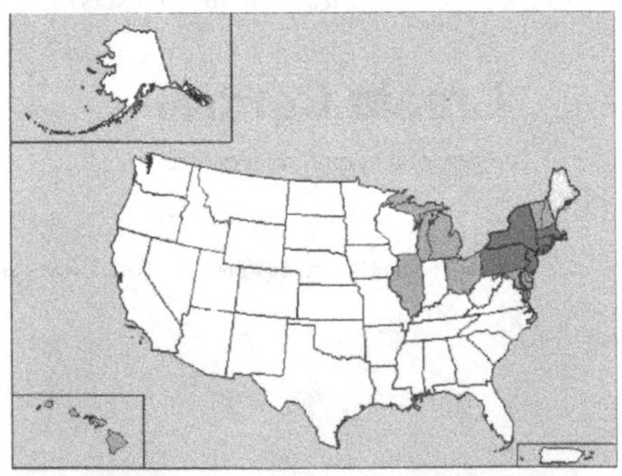

TM-PCT034. Percent of Persons of Italian Ancestry: 2000.
Universe: Total population.
Data Set: Census 2000 Summary File 3 (SF 3)—Sample Data United States by State.
Source: U.S. Census Bureau, Census 2000 Summary File 3, Matrices P1, and PCT18.

Peoples with a single Ancestry question and the tabulation of the multiple responses that are clearly evident in America. Nonetheless, now that Ancestry data has been collected for the last three Censuses and the computer driven computational revolution is firmly in place, demographic analysis can employ standard protocols and verifiable methods that enable

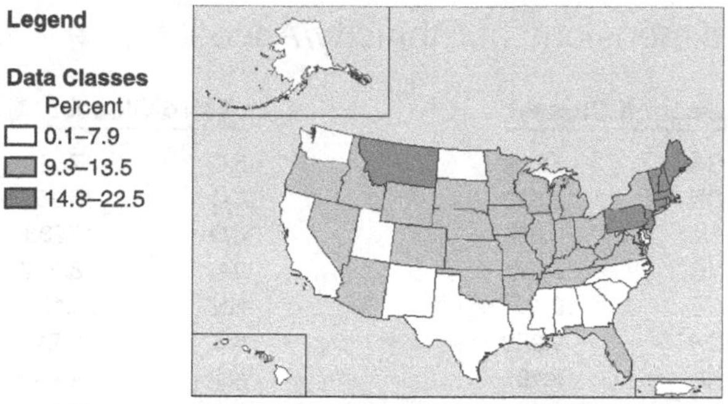

TM-PCT033. Percent of Persons of Irish Ancestry: 2000.
Universe: Total population.
Data Set: Census 2000 Summary File 3(SF 3)—Sample Data United States by State.

Source: U.S. Census Bureau, Census 2000 Summary File 3, Matrices P1, and PCT18.

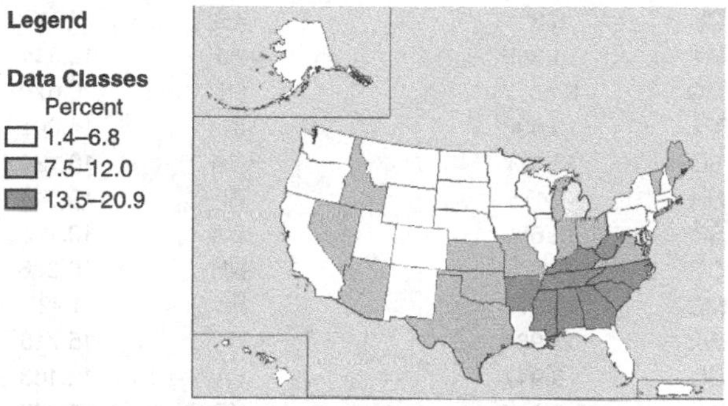

TM-PCT047. Percent of Persons of United States or American Ancestry: 2000.
Universe: Total population.
Date Set: Census 2000 Summary File 3 (SF 3)—Sample Data United States by State.

Source: U.S. Census Bureau, Census 2000 Summary File 3, Matrices P1, and PCT18.

a fresh look at the data and thus establish connections, patterns and places and further discussion, interpretations and a scientific understanding of American pluralism.

This article investigates one such method: State Similarity Scores. A Similarity Score investigates the "distance" between States. Consider three cities: Baltimore, MD; Washington, DC and Chicago, IL. Baltimore is about a 40 mile drive from Washington. The driving distance between Washington and Chicago is roughly 710 miles. Chicago is 720 miles from Baltimore on the interstates. Knowing these distances, we can conceive of the triangle that these cities form and how they are geographically related.

In the two dimensional space of a map, a computer can now easily crunch out distances from a simple formula derived from Phythagoras.

$$\text{Distance}^2 = a^2 + b^2 \text{ or}$$
$$\text{Distance} = \sqrt{(a^2 + b^2)}$$

For example, using latitude and longitude to get the distance between Chicago and Baltimore, we find the difference between Chicago's latitude and Baltimore's latitude and the difference between Chicago's longitude and Baltimore's longitude.

$$a = \text{Lat}_{\text{Chicago}} - \text{Lat}_{\text{Baltimore}} \text{ and } b = \text{Long}_{\text{Chicago}} - \text{Long}_{\text{Baltimore}}$$

$$\text{So, Distance} = \sqrt{\begin{aligned}&(\text{Lat}_{\text{Chicago}} - \text{Lat}_{\text{Baltimore}})^2\\ &+ (\text{Long}_{\text{Chicago}} - \text{Long}_{\text{Baltimore}})^2\end{aligned}}$$

In three dimensions, we'd add c^2, to handle perhaps altitude for Google Earth. The theorem isn't limited to our spatial definition of distance. It can apply to any orthogonal dimensions: space, time, movie tastes, colors, temperatures, and even ancestry responses. There is no limit to the number of variables. The focus, however, of this research is race, ethnicity and ancestry data form the US Census 2000. Appropriately, this type of investigation is also known as Nearest Neighbor Analysis. To find out how closely related any two states in terms of ethnicity, our equation would look like this:

$$\text{Distance} = \sqrt{\begin{aligned}&(\text{Ancestry1}_{\text{State 1}} - \text{Ancestry1}_{\text{State 2}})^2\\ &+ (\text{Ancestry2}_{\text{State 1}} - \text{Ancestry2}_{\text{State 2}})^2\\ &+ \cdots + (\text{Ancestry N}_{\text{State 1}} - \text{Ancestry N}_{\text{State 2}})^2\end{aligned}}$$

For this paper I used 56 of the largest ethnicities[3] as orthogonal dimensions: Asian Indian, Asian Multiple Response, American Indian, "American", Arab, Austrian, Black or African American, Belgian, British, Canadian, Chinese, Cuban, Czech, Czechoslovakian, Danish, Dutch, English, Finnish, French excluding Basque, Filipino, French Canadian, German, Greek, Guamanian and/or Chamorrian, Jamaican, Japanese, Korean, Hawaiian, Hispanic or Latino Other, Hungarian, Irish, Lithuanian, Mexican, Native Not Specified, Norwegian, "Others", Other Asian, Other Pacific Islander, Puerto Rican, Polish, Portuguese, Russian, Samoan, Scandinavian, "Scotch Irish", Scottish, Slovak, Slovene, "Some Other Race", Sub Saharan African, Swedish, Ukrainian, Vietnamese, Welsh, and West Indian.[4]

For any two states, we can calculate a measure of similarity. A measure of 0, would mean that the two states are identical, i.e. they have exactly the same percentage of Polish American, Italian Americans, Irish Americans, African Americans, etc. The largest "distance" between two states was between DC and North Dakota at 91.429. The closest "distance" between two states was between Tennessee and Arkansas 3.720. Table 1 shows each state's "nearest cultural neighbors" and the "distance" metric.

If we look at only the closest connection for each of state, some distinct networks or groupings emerge. The largest of these clusters happens to correspond roughly to "The South."

Table 1 Nearest Neighbors along 56 dimensions of Ethnicity/Ancest

	First Closest		Second Closest		Third Closest	
AL	SC	5.947	GA	7.213	NC	7.639
AK	WA	12.354	OK	12.893	CO	15.157
AZ	NV	9.405	TX	16.69	CO	17.233
AR	TN	3.720	NC	7.809	VA	8.382
CA	TX	10.344	AZ	19.1	NM	21.128
CO	WA	9.759	OR	9.958	KS	12.213
CT	MA	11.011	RI	14.181	NJ	14.499
DC	MS	33.68	LA	37.691	GA	40.758
DE	VA	10.625	MI	12.782	NJ	12.936
FL	NY	10.115	VA	10.430	NJ	11.253
GA	SC	4.179	AL	7.213	MS	9.648
HI	CA	47.499	NM	49.38	TX	51.121
ID	OR	7.619	WY	9.058	WA	10.961
IL	NJ	13.474	MI	13.955	DE	14.214
IN	MO	5.327	OH	6.3	KS	7.847
IA	NE	8.916	MT	13.289	WI	13.514
KS	IN	7.847	MO	8.337	OR	8.670
KY	WV	6.661	TN	13.896	IN	14.001
LA	MS	12.163	SC	13.077	GA	13.124
ME	VT	4.781	NH	7.475	RI	19.544
MD	VA	12.451	SC	12.606	GA	13.117
MA	RI	7.942	CT	11.011	NH	16.286
MI	OH	10.340	MO	10.977	PA	11.927
MN	SD	11.895	WI	13.981	IA	15.716
MS	GA	9.648	SC	9.947	LA	12.163
MO	OH	4.801	IN	5.327	KS	8.337
MT	WY	9.427	IA	13.289	OR	14.668
NE	IA	8.916	WI	11.648	WY	15.914
NV	AZ	9.405	CO	13.675	IL	14.786
NH	VT	4.607	ME	7.475	MA	16.286
NJ	NY	6.026	FL	11.253	DE	12.936
NM	CA	21.128	TX	23.53	AZ	27.923
NY	NJ	6.026	FL	10.115	DE	14.651
NC	VA	5.9	AL	7.639	AR	7.809
ND	SD	17.030	MN	17.407	WI	24.532
OH	MO	4.801	IN	6.3	PA	6.692
OK	AR	12.557	AK	12.893	FL	14.080
OR	WA	4.784	ID	7.619	KS	8.670
PA	OH	6.692	MO	10.27	IN	10.718
RI	MA	7.942	CT	14.181	NH	16.638
SC	GA	4.179	AL	5.947	NC	9.094
SD	MN	11.895	WI	14.146	IA	14.527
TN	AR	3.720	NC	9.043	VA	9.934
TX	CA	10.344	AZ	16.69	NV	18.018
UT	ID	14.655	OR	20.362	WA	21.495
VT	NH	4.607	ME	4.781	MA	17.455
VA	NC	5.9	AR	8.382	TN	9.934
WA	OR	4.784	CO	9.759	KS	10.921
WV	KY	6.661	IN	14.056	MO	17.644
WI	NE	11.648	IA	13.514	MN	13.981
WY	OR	8.960	ID	9.058	MT	9.427

DC-MS-GA-SC-AL-NC-AR-TN
LA | *VA OK*
MD DE

Other networks also emerged, when considering only the first closest connection:

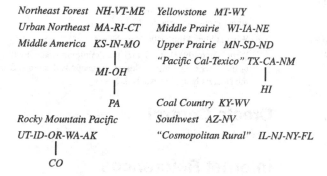

Northeast Forest NH-VT-ME
Urban Northeast MA-RI-CT
Middle America KS-IN-MO
|
MI-OH
|
PA

Rocky Mountain Pacific
UT-ID-OR-WA-AK
|
CO

Yellowstone MT-WY
Middle Prairie WI-IA-NE
Upper Prairie MN-SD-ND
"Pacific Cal-Texico" TX-CA-NM
|
HI

Coal Country KY-WV
Southwest AZ-NV
"Cosmopolitan Rural" IL-NJ-NY-FL

We can also connect all of the States with the minimum possible distance among states, i.e a "minimum spanning tree," as follows:

NE Forest
| *(NH-MA)*
Urban NE
| *(CT-NJ)*
Cosmo Rural — (IL-MI) — Mid Amer. — (MI-DE) — South — (TN-KY) — Coal Courntry
| *(OK-AK)*
Pac Cal Texico — (AZ-TX) — Southwest — (NV-CO) — Rocky Mt. Pac.
| *(ID-WY)*
Yellowstone
| *(MT-IA)*
Upper Prairie — (SD-WI) — Middle Prairie

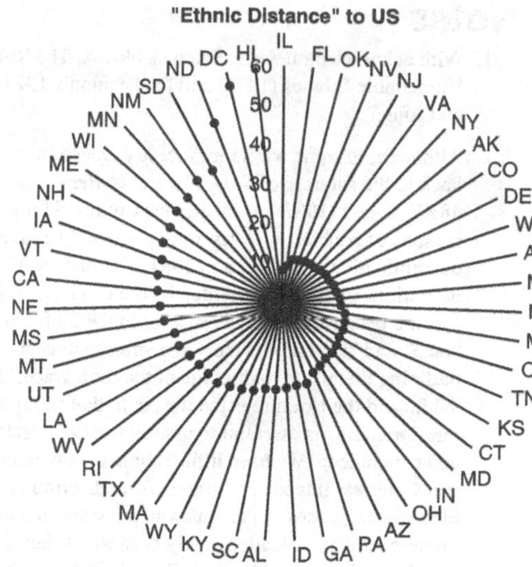

Figure 1 "Ethnic Distance" to US.

Finally, we can also measure the distance of each State to the United States as a whole. Illinois and Florida are very similar to the entire US, while North Dakota, DC and Hawaii are furthest in "distance" from the US in our 56 dimensional ethnic space. See Figure 1.

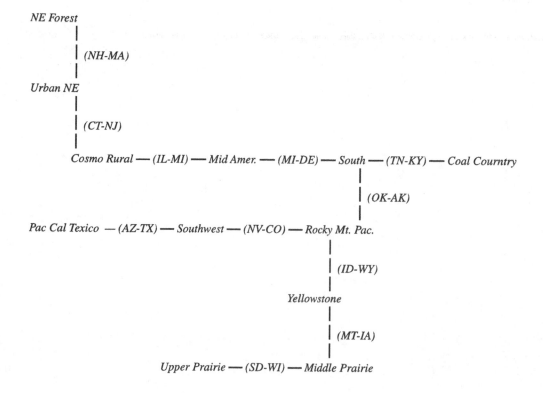

Notes

1. With acknowledgments to Michael Novak, The Rise of the Unmeltable Ethnics (1972) and Paul Simon's 1975 album and song.
2. Although, in some ways the Ancestry Question is arguably back to the future. See *Saint Francis College v. al-Khazraji,* 481 U.S. 604 (1987). A unanimous Court held that that persons of Arabian ancestry were protected from racial discrimination under Section 1981. The history of the definitions of "race," presented by the Court, is well worth reading because it shows how prior to the 20th century "race" and "ancestry" were synonymous concepts. After outlining the history and usage of the term "race," Justice White and the Court rejected the claim that "a distinctive physiognomy" is essential to qualify for 1981 protection and concluded: "We have little trouble in concluding that Congress intended to protect from discrimination identifiable classes of persons who are subjected to intentional discrimination solely because of their **ancestry or ethnic characteristics.**" William J. Brennan, Jr., in a separate concurrence, added that "Pernicious distinctions among individuals based solely on their **ancestry** are antithetical to the doctrine of equality upon which this nation is founded." (Emphasis supplied).
3. Some of these categories also come from the Race and Hispanic origin questions of the Census. Even though the Ancestry Question captures ethnic responses like Japanese, Korean, Cuban, Mexican and Black or African American, the Census Bureau sanitizes its Ancestry data, so that these responses are only readily available from the Race and Hispanic origin questions.
4. Older analysis of ethnic disimilarity differs from this method because it grouped ancestry responses into larger but far fewer categories such as "Old Stock," "Eastern and Southern European," "Asian," etc. Calculating similarity in 56 dimensional space was simply not possibly with hand calculations employed by previous researchers.

Critical Thinking

1. Were you surprised by the lack of uniform distribution of ethnic groups in America?
2. What is State Similarity Score?
3. Write a narrative that explains the "minimum spanning tree" or the other clustering of closest connections discerned from the Nearest Neighbor Analysis?

Create Central

www.mhhe.com/createcentral

Internet References

American Civil Liberties Union (ACLU)
www.aclu.org

Human Rights Web
www.hrweb.org

Sociosite
www.sociosite.net

U.S. Census Bureau
www.census.gov

Unit 3

UNIT

Prepared by: John A. Kromkowski, *Catholic University of America*

Indigenous Ethnic Groups: The Native Americans

The contemporary issues of Native Americans are clearly a particular case of race and ethnic relations in America. However, treaties, laws and specific relations between various states regulate Native Americans unlike other ethnic groups in the United States. The Native American reality can be viewed in comparative perspective to descendants of all conquered indigenous peoples as they add their weight to the claims for cultural justice, equal protection, and due process throughout the record of human conflict in race and ethic relations. The processes of large-scale political and economic integration are especially problematic for indigenous peoples. Contestation and conquests have marginalized and isolated indigenous small-scale regimes and rural ethnicities. The reclaiming of the history of pre- and post-conquest indigenous cultures is a contemporary effort, in part, informed by the search for meaning and justice rooted in the deepest stirring of human consciousness and its access to symbolization that are embedded in tradition. Such traditions have been articulated in folkloric fashion and have been challenged by acculturation, assimilation and mobility and new patterns of interaction with other ethnic groups and with mainstream America. Traditional relations were challenged during the Civil Rights era. The celebration of the Bicentennial of the American Revolution in 1976 and the re-organization of Native Americans for political action that claimed empowerment over the dominance of the Bureau of Indian Affairs, their victories in the courts and in Congress and their struggle against bureaucracies over payments for mineral royalties that produced the era of renegotiated relationships. Identity politics in 1978 prompted Congress to venture into family law. Congress outlawed the practice of removing Native American children through adoption by non-native-Americans by privileging placement of children within their tribes. In 2013, the Supreme Court decided to hear *Adoptive Couple v, Baby Girl* and ruled on the constitutionality of protection for an unwed father of a child to claim a child adopted outside the tribe.

With new cultural confidence and economic capacity most notably in the gaming industry the descendants of native peoples entered a new epoch, as did the entire country. Native Americans are part of the social texture of American pluralism. While some may argue that the reclamation and revival of tradition and power are unique social and political events a wider view suggests that native populations are but another manifestation of ethnicity and ethnic group articulation of its agenda within the contexts of the American legal and economic order. Popular consciousness of indigenous peoples was heightened by the development of a National Museum on the Mall in Washington DC. The expansion and profitability of Native American gambling casinos, their attendant impact on state and local economies, and the tax exemptions enjoyed by these ventures appear to be headed toward contentions that may spill over into new issues of public order. These issues are restricted to the United States; on the international level, the discussion of human and cultural rights of peoples guaranteed in the United Nations charter and the traditional mode of state sovereignty indicate that a fragile accommodation between indigenous people and the mainstream societies at whose margins they exist may be entering a new phase. Their unequal relationship began with the consolidation of large territorial political and economic regimes. Under scrutiny are personal rights and group rights, pluralistic realms that ensure transnational solidarity, and cultural and religious challenges to those in authority fueled by the passion for power at those intersections between modernity and tradition—the large-scale institutional versus the local and culturally-specific community. Yet life on reservations is harsh, alienating and the movement of the poor into urban areas marks another dimension of injustice articulated both by the social indicators and in the voices of chroniclers and artists that proclaim the problematic struggle of power and meaning and relationships in search of human dignity and solidarity.

Thus questions of race and ethnic relations in these cases extend to claims regarding the rights of sovereign nations and the interests of the U.S. government and its citizens, which also include various Native Americans. These discussions are no longer at the margin of public affairs. The selections in this unit include demographics, historical findings, fictional articulation of cultures in conquest and accounts of life on reservations and the immediate issues of poverty and alienation. On one level the descendants of indigenous peoples are a wide variety of peoples living in various states. On another level these nations and tribes have been grouped into one category and have organized as an interest group that engages in the policy arenas of state and the national government.

Does this complex of particulars and definitions, including group specific protections; beyond the individual rights regimes and tradition transform this instance of ethnicity into an issue of foreign and not domestic policy? Should the claims of ethnic groups in defense of culture, territory, and unique institutions be honored and protected by law and public policy? Why or why not? Is sovereignty real without the power to use force? In fact this is a worldwide phenomenon that can be viewed as part of a wider continuum that includes those populations comprised of thousands of ethnic groups on all continents and islands that have been conquered by the development of the modern state and the creation of large countries and in some situations empires. The process of extending the reach of a regime, which on one level may be described as political military phenomena, is certainly not restricted to modern times. In fact such conquests in the ancient world bear comparison. Most interestingly, because on another level of this phenomena in the ancient world, i.e., the intersections of ethnic groups with overwhelming powers reverberated in the moral, religious and intellectual imagination in ways that continue into our time and have shaped the search for meaning and justice in history and human affairs. The claim that power determines righteousness and that power and ethno-religious superiority are woven into the engines of history and its progress frame many conversations about human affairs that move beyond the horizon of the instruments of successful and efficacious outcomes of various forms of contention.

Ethnicity is built upon the truth and strength of a tradition. Senses of family and community, and an unwillingness to give up, have led to standoffs with many forces within America. From this perspective, this unit details ways in which an ethnic group retrieves its rights and heritage to preserve an ancient culture from amnesia and extinction. Indigenous ethnic communities have encountered a complex array of historical, social, cultural, and economic forces. As a result, in the late twentieth century, the traditions of indigenous ethnic groups have been renegotiated by yet another generation. The North and South American economies and pluralistic cultures, and even Europe near the Arctic Circle as well as of other continents, are at a challenging stage of their quest for self-sufficiency and the preservation of a unique cultural legacy. Current indigenous ethnic leaders challenge past perceptions. Some find interaction easy, but others avoid striking a balance between traditional values and new demands. Native Americans have increasingly interfaced with the American legal system at the state level on issues of land use and gaming, which represent part of this current redefinition. Finally, however, they are challenging themselves to be themselves, and examples of indigenous self-help reveal insights into how personal leadership and service to the community weave the social fabric of civil society.

Article

Prepared by: John A. Kromkowski, *Catholic University of America*

Tribal Philanthropy Thrives

DANIEL GIBSON

Learning Outcomes

After reading this article, you will be able to:

- Describe the philanthropic practices of Native Americans.
- Name the most generous Native American nation and explain why.
- List the types of activities that are supported by Native American philanthropy.

American Indian tribes all have social values that encourage sharing with those in need. Historically, a deer, tapir or walrus brought in by hunters would be split among tribal members or families. Corn, squash and beans from the fields usually went into a common larder. Work was often divided up into group tasks. The emphasis was on survival of all, common goals and a communal spirit. Today those same values are guiding the gifting of millions of dollars each year from tribes benefiting from gaming income to their surrounding non-Indian communities and to non-gaming tribes. Tribes understand what difficult times are all about, and they are stepping up to the plate in a major fashion to aid and assist those less fortunate.

In 2006 alone, tribal governments nationwide gave more than $150 million to charitable causes, according to the National Indian Gaming Association.

Examples abound across the nation. In California, the **Morongo Band of Mission Indians** near Banning has set up a scholarship program open to all California Native students. In recent years, the tribe has also supported programs of the Special Olympics, the Boy Scouts of America, San Gorgonio Memorial Hospital, the Riverside Sheriffs' Association Relief Fund, the local Little League, the American Cancer Society, Big Brothers/Big Sisters, the YMCA, the AIDS Assistance Program, the American Red Cross and the Juvenile Diabetes Association.

In the Southwest, many tribes are generously providing financial assistance to nearby communities and home states. The **Pascua Yaqui Tribe** near Tucson, Arizona donated more than $1.1 million in 2006 and 2007, including $338,000 to the City of Tucson to purchase land for affordable housing, parks and recreation programs; $150,000 for cultural programs and tourism endeavors in the Town of Guadalupe; and $50,000 to the Tucson School District. "The Pascua Yaqui Tribe is committed to investing in the future of our state," notes former tribal chairwoman Herminia Frias.

In fact, when Arizona voters passed Proposition 202 in 2002, which clarified the legal status of Indian gaming in the state, the legislation called for the gaming tribes to donate substantial revenue to the state. Of these funds, 12 percent goes directly to Arizona cities, towns and counties, while the other 88 percent is divided up among a handful of state departments and programs. Of the latter revenue stream, in 2007 alone Arizona tribes provided more than $46 million to the state's Instructional Improvement Fund for charter schools, $23 million to the Trauma & Emergency Services Fund, $6.5 million for the Arizona Office of Tourism, $6.5 million to the Arizona Game & Fish Department's Wildlife Conservation Fund, $8 million to the Arizona Department of Gaming and $1.8 million to the Arizona Office of Problem Gambling.

The **Soboba Band of Luiseño Indians** in southern California has been a good neighbor to its surrounding towns in Riverside County. In June 2003, the tribe gave $400,000 to the City of Hemet Public Library, but that was just one of its many large contributions in the area in recent years. A room at the tribal hall is filled with plaques of appreciation from local youth sports organizations. The tribe has gifted $60,000 in donations to six local football programs, and some 600 other local kids are benefiting from contributions ranging from $10,000 to $20,000 per year to the local parks and recreation program. The Ramona Outdoor Play, a production incorporating local history held annually in Hemet, is now sponsored by the tribe. When the Vietnam Veterans Memorial Moving Wall visited San Jacinto, it was due to a grant from the tribe. Local chamber of commerce events are sponsored by the tribe, which also provides space and staff for the chamber's annual community fair.

"It comes from a lot of years of local people giving us things," explained vice chairwoman Rosemary Morillo in an article in the Riverside *Press-Enterprise* a few years ago. "People would donate oranges, candy and toys for our kids at Christmas. Now we're able to return that gesture." In the same article, tribal administrator Andrew Masiel stated, "We've always had the desire (to contribute to local community events and charitable causes) but not the resources. But now it's different."

The **Forest County Potawatomi** tribe of Wisconsin is actively helping to fund many programs and projects outside of its reservation. Each year in August, the tribe's Community Foundation selects 20 children's charities from Milwaukee, Waukesha, Washington, Racine and Ozaukee counties to receive at least $50,000 each. This August will mark the 15th anniversary of the program, which has provided more than $7 million to date. The funds are derived from the Potawatomi Bingo Casino on Canal Street in Milwaukee, which hosts special Miracle on Canal bingo games, a two-night dinner and auction, and an annual golf event.

The tribe also is active in funding medical programs. Last December, it donated $45,000 to the Medical College of Wisconsin for research and educational programs focused on diabetes treatment and prevention. It was just the most recent gift in a relationship going back several years. "It's a goal of the tribe to be at the forefront when it comes to eliminating this debilitating disease," says Tom Bolter, the executive director of the tribe's Foundation Enterprise Fund. All told, the tribe has given away tens of millions of dollars since its foundation was established in 1999.

The **Confederated Tribes of the Umatilla Indian Reservation** of Oregon established the Wildhorse Foundation in 2001, which is funded by a set percentage of the Wildhorse Resort and Casino's net income. As the resort's business grows, so do the foundation's annual grants. In 2001, grants totaled $294,000; in 2002, $230,000; in 2003, $470,000; in 2004, $503,000; in 2005, $507,000; in 2006, $589,000; and in 2007, $655,000.

Grants range from $500 to $20,000 and are focused on projects and programs in Umatilla, Union, Morrow and Wallowa counties. For instance, in 2007 the tribe gave a $10,000 grant to provide orthodontic and dental treatment to local children through the nonprofit Advantage Smiles for Kids program; $500 for the Cancer Society Relay for Life; $12,000 for the Pendleton Parks Department for new lifeguard chairs; and $10,000 to the Arts Council of Pendleton for public art exhibitions. Other funds were directed to the City of Ukiah and the City of Echo, the Blue Mountain Nordic Club, Eastern Oregon University, Homestead Youth and Family Services, Oregon Historical Society, St. Andrews Mission and Pilot Rock Fire District.

Perhaps the most generous tribe in the nation is the **Shakopee Mdewakanton Sioux Community** of Prior Lake, Minnesota (see Sept./Oct. 2002 issue). Since the tribe opened its first bingo hall in October 1982, it has given away more than $115 million, and in the fiscal year ending last Sept. 30 it hit an annual high mark of $26 million.

"We need to give back—it's the nature of the Dakota people," explains Bill Rudnicki, the tribal administrator for the past 15 years. So far, the tribe has resisted putting a cap on annual donations. "It's gone up every year," says Rudnicki. "The more you help, the more you see the need out there. It's such a good feeling when we get notes from kids, for example, stating that they wouldn't have had textbooks that year if it weren't for our efforts. It really hits home."

The tribe also donates regularly to the American Red Cross, the American Cancer Society, the American Diabetes Association and the American Heart Association, and recently provided $500,000 over a two-year period to the local hospital. It gives more than $200,000 a year at Christmas to some 44 social service organizations in the Twin Cities to buy toys, clothing, food and other gifts. Contributions can be relatively small but play an important role—such as the $1,000 given to the Emily, Minnesota Police Department to acquire and train a German shepherd drug dog. Or they can be huge. On Oct. 19, 2007, the tribe delivered a check for $10.4 million to the University of Minnesota to fund construction of a new stadium, and has committed $2.5 million for university scholarships.

Despite these major gifts that benefit the general Minnesota populace, "The bulk of what we give is actually to other tribes, to specific programs and projects when we hear of unmet needs," Rudnicki notes. Between 1997 and 1998, the tribe created a formal process for annual donations to other tribes. Last year, 19 tribes were on the receiving end of the Shakopees' generosity.

The Red Lake Band of Chippewa of northern Minnesota—scene of a terrible student shooting in March 2005—is one tribal beneficiary. The Red Lake Boys & Girls Club has also been the recipient of $1 million in Shakopee funding. The Red Lake government wanted to restore its once-famous and lucrative walleye fisheries, and with the help of the Shakopees and the state government, they are now undergoing a strong recovery. "I'm really proud of the tribe's being ahead of the times, in terms of funding 'green' initiatives," says Rudnicki.

In January 2008, the Flandreau Santee Sioux Tribe of South Dakota received a $1 million grant to fund construction of an eldercare center. In February, the Spirit Lake Nation of North Dakota was gifted $1 million to build a new courthouse and

Soboba Leader Honored

In April, the chairman of the Soboba Band of Luiseño Indians, Robert Salgado, was recognized for his leadership abilities with the presentation of the Wendell Chino Humanitarian Award from the National Indian Gaming Association. Salgado spent nearly two decades guiding his tribe from obscurity to a high-profile position in southern California's political and economic life.

The tribe has an active program of donating funds to local and regional causes (see main story), but Salgado says perhaps his greatest contribution to his tribe and the region was forging a water-rights pact with the Metropolitan Water District of Southern California and the Eastern Municipal Water District, which came after decades of litigation.

He also oversaw the transformation of his reservation from a pocket of poverty to relative affluence, largely due to revenue derived from the Soboba Casino and the Country Club at Soboba Springs. In 2006, the tribe refurbished The Oaks resort, which included construction of a football stadium for the reservation's Noli Indian High School. A semi-professional football team owned by Salgado also uses the facility, revealing another passion of the chairman. Salgado is still widely remembered in the area for his record-setting role on the local high school football team as a kicker, and later roles as a coach for San Jacinto High School and Mt. San Jacinto College.

undertake other building maintenance and improvement projects. And in March, the Kiowa Tribe of Oklahoma received a $1 million grant to purchase and operate a nearby tourist attraction, Indian City USA.

The tribe is also active in providing loans to tribal governments for economic development and social projects. From 2004 to 2007, $67 million was loaned.

Programs that benefit a wide range of Indian people have also received assistance. For instance, the American Indian College Fund was given $1.8 million over a six-year period. "We've been blessed, and we're grateful for the opportunity to help others," concludes the Shakopee tribal chairman, Stanley Crooks. Details on the tribe's philanthropic program can be found at ccsmdc.org/donations.html.

Critical Thinking

1. Explain the relationship of prosperity to philanthropy.
2. Are philanthropic practices of Native American different from other types of sharing?

Create Central

www.mhhe.com/createcentral

Internet References

American Indian Ritual Object Repatriation Foundation
www.repatriationfoundatfon.org

Native American Home Pages
www.nativeculturalikns.com
www.naha.org

Daniel Gibson has been the editor of *Native Peoples* since February 2001. His most recent book is *Pueblos of the Rio Grande: A Visitor's Guide* (Rio Nuevo Publishers).

Article

Prepared by: John A. Kromkowski, *Catholic University of America*

American Indian and Alaska Native Heritage Month: November 2012

The first American Indian Day was celebrated in May 1916 in New York. Red Fox James, a Blackfeet Indian, rode horseback from state to state, getting endorsements from 24 state governments, to have a day to honor American Indians. In 1990, President George H.W. Bush signed a joint congressional resolution designating November 1990 as "National American Indian Heritage Month." Similar proclamations have been issued every year since 1994. This Facts for Features presents statistics for American Indians and Alaska Natives, as this is one of the six major race categories.

Learning Outcomes

After reading this article, you will be able to:

- List and describe the various social indicators you find about Native Americans.
- Identify the most troubling demographic indicators about Native Americans.

Population

5.1 million

As of the 2011 American Community Survey, the nation's population of American Indians and Alaska Natives, including those of more than one race. They made up 1.6 percent of the total population. Of this total, about half were American Indian and Alaska Native only, and about half were American Indian and Alaska Native in combination with one or more other races.

Source: 2011 American Community Survey http://factfinder2.census.gov/bkmk/table/l.0/en/ACS/ll_1YR/S0201//popgroup~009

8.6 million

The projected population of American Indians and Alaska Natives, including those of more than one race, on July 1, 2050. They would comprise 2 percent of the total population.

Source: Population projections www.census.gov/population/www/projections/summarytables.html

Note: Unless otherwise specified, the statistics in the "Population" section refer to the population who reported a race alone or in combination with one or more other races.

1.1 million

Increase in the nation's American Indian and Alaska Native population between the 2000 Census and 2010 Census. The population of this group increased by 26.7 percent during this period compared with the overall population growth of 9.7 percent.

Source: Census 2000 Brief: Overview of Race and Hispanic Origin http://ww.census.gov/prod/2001pubs/c2kbr01-1.pdf and 2010 Census Brief: Overview of Race and Hispanic Origin www.census.gov/prod/cen2010/briefs/c2010br-02.pdf

689,320

The American Indian and Alaska Native population in California as of the 2011 American Community Survey. California was followed by Oklahoma (502,934) and Arizona (346,380).

Source: 2011 American Community Survey http://factfinder2.census.gov/bkmk/table/1.0/en/ACS/ll_1YR/S0201//popgroup~009

14

Number of states with more than 100,000 American Indian and Alaska Native residents as of the 2011 American Community Survey. These states were California, Oklahoma, Arizona, Texas, New Mexico, Washington, North Carolina, New York, Florida, Michigan, Alaska, Colorado, Oregon and Minnesota.

Source: 2011 American Community Survey http://factfinder2.census.gov/bkmk/table/1.0/en/ACS/ll_1YR/S0201//popgroup~009

19.7%

The proportion of Alaska's population identified as American Indian and Alaska Native as of the 2011 American Community

Survey, the highest rate for this race group of any state. Alaska was followed by Oklahoma (13.3 percent), South Dakota (10.4 percent), and New Mexico (10.4 percent).

Source: 2011 American Community Survey http://factfinder2.census.gov/bkmk/table/l.0/en/ACS/11_lYR/S0201//popgroup~009

31.3

Median age for those who are American Indian and Alaska Native, and no other race. This compares with a median age of 37.3 for the U.S. population as a whole.

Source: 2011 American Community Survey http://factfinder2.census.gov/bkmk/table/l.0/en/ACS/11_lYR/S0201//popgroup~006

Reservations

324

Number of federally recognized American Indian reservations in 2010. All in all, excluding Hawaiian Home Lands, there are 617 American Indian and Alaska Native legal and statistical areas for which the Census Bureau provides statistics.

Source: Census Bureau Geography Division

22%

Percentage of American Indians and Alaska Natives, alone or in combination, who lived in American Indian areas or Alaska Native Village Statistical Areas in 2010. These American Indian areas include federal American Indian reservations and/or off-reservation trust lands, Oklahoma tribal statistical areas, tribal designated statistical areas, state American Indian reservations, and state designated American Indian statistical areas.

Source: 2010 Census Summary File 1

Tribes

566

Number of federally recognized Indian tribes.

Source: Bureau of Indian Affairs www.bia.gov/cs/groups/public/documents/text/idc015898.pdf

100,000+

In the 2010 Census, the tribal groupings with 100,000 or more responses for the American Indian and Alaska Native alone-or-in-any combination population were Cherokee (819,105), Navajo (332,129), Choctaw (195,764), Mexican American Indian (175,494), Chippewa (170,742), Sioux (170,110), Apache (111,810) and Blackfeet (105,304).

Source: 2010 Census Summary File 1, Table PCT3 http://factfinder2.census.gov/bkmk/table/l.0/en/DEC/10_SF1/PCT3

Families

557,425

The number of American Indian and Alaska Native family households in 2011 (households with a householder who was American Indian and Alaska Native alone). Of these, 56.6 percent were married-couple families, including those with children.

Source: 2011 American Community Survey http://factfinder2.census.gov/bkmk/table/l.0/en/ACS/11_1YR/B11001C

29.3 and 27.7

Median age at first marriage for American Indian and Alaska Native men and women age 15 to 54, respectively, in 2011. For the U.S. population as a whole in this age range, the respective numbers were 28.9 and 26.9 years. The differences in the median age at first marriage between American Indian and Alaska Native women and women overall, and between American Indian and Alaska Native men and men overall, were not statistically significant. These statistics include only the American Indian and Alaska Native alone population 15 to 54 years.

Source: 2011 American Community Survey, Table B12007C http://factfinder2.census.gov/bkmk/table/l.0/en/ACS/11_1YR/B12007C

Housing

54%

The percentage of American Indian and Alaska Native alone householders who owned their own home in 2011. This is compared with 65 percent of the overall population.

Source: 2011 American Community Survey http://factfinder2.census.gov/bkmk/table/l.0/en/ACS/11_lYR/S0201//popgroup~006

Languages

27%

Percentage of American Indians and Alaska Natives alone 5 and older who spoke a language other than English at home, compared with 20.8 percent for the nation as a whole.

Source: 2011 American Community Survey http://factfinder2.census.gov/bkmk/table/l.0/en/ACS/ll_lYR/S0201//popgroup~006

68%

Percentage of residents of the Navajo Nation Reservation and Off-Reservation Trust Land, Ariz.-N.M.-Utah, age 5 and older who spoke a language other than English at home.

Source: 2011 American Community Survey, Table S0601 http://factfinder2.census.gov/bkmk/table/l.0/en/ACS/ll_lYR/S0601

http://factfinder2.census.gov/bkmk/table/1.0/en/ACS/11_1YR/S0601/2500000US2430

Education

78.9%

The percentage of American Indians and Alaska Natives alone 25 and older who had at least a high school diploma, GED or alternative credential in 2011. In addition, 13.3 percent obtained a bachelor's degree or higher. In comparison, the overall population had 85.9 with a high school diploma and 28.5 percent with a bachelor's degree or higher.

Source: 2011 American Community Survey
http://factfinder2.census.gov/bkmk/table/1.0/en/ACS/11_1YR/S0201//popgroup~006

42%

Among American Indians and Alaska Natives alone 25 and older who have a bachelor's degree or higher, the percentage whose bachelor's degree is in science and engineering, or science and engineering-related fields in 2011. This compares with 44 percent for all people 25 and older with this level of education.

Source: 2011 American Community Survey
http://factfinder2.census.gov/bkmk/table/1.0/en/ACS/11_1YR/C15010C

65,356

Number of American Indians and Alaska Natives alone 25 and older who had a graduate or professional degree in 2011.

Source: 2011 American Community Survey
http://factfinder2.census.gov/bkmk/table/1.0/en/ACS/11_1YR/B15002C

Businesses

$34.4 billion

Receipts for American Indian- and Alaska Native-owned businesses in 2007, a 28.0 percent increase from 2002. These businesses numbered 236,967, up 17.7 percent from 2002.

45,629

Number of American Indian- and Alaska Native-owned firms in California in 2007, which led the states. Oklahoma and Texas followed. Among the firms in California, 17,634 were in the Los Angeles-Long Beach-Santa Ana metro area, which led all metro areas nationwide.

23,704

Number of American Indian- and Alaska Native-owned firms that had paid employees in 2007. These businesses employed 184,416 people.

30.5%

Percent of American Indian- and Alaska Native-owned firms that operated in construction; and repair, maintenance, personal and laundry services in 2007.

52.9%

Percent of American Indian- and Alaska Native-owned business receipts accounted for by construction, retail trade and wholesale trade in 2007.

4,599

Number of American Indian- and Alaska Native-owned firms with receipts of $1 million or more in 2007.

162

Number of American Indian- and Alaska Native-owned firms with 100 or more employees in 2007. Source for data in this section: Survey of Business Owners-American Indian and Alaska Native Owned Firms: 2007.

www.census.gov/econ/sbo/

Jobs

26.2%

The percentage of civilian-employed American Indian and Alaska Native alone people 16 and older who worked in management, business, science and arts occupations in 2011. In addition, 24.8 percent worked in service occupations and 22.8 percent in sales and office occupations.

Source: 2011 American Community Survey
http://factfinder2.census.gov/bkmk/table/1.0/en/ACS/11_1YR/S0201

Veterans

153,223

The number of American Indian and Alaska Native alone veterans of the U.S. armed forces in 2010.

Source: 2011 American Community Survey
http://factfinder2.census.gov/bkmk/table/1.0/en/ACS/11_1YR/B21001C

Income and Poverty

$35,192

The median income of American Indian and Alaska Native alone households in 2011. This compares with $50,502 for the nation as a whole.

Source: 2011 American Community Survey
http://factfinder2.census.gov/bkmk/table/1.0/en/ACS/11_1YR/S0201//popgroup~006

29.5%

The percent of American Indians and Alaska Natives alone that were in poverty in 2011. For the nation as a whole, the corresponding rate was 15.9 percent.

Source: 2011 American Community Survey
http://factfinder2.census.gov/bkmk/table/l.0/en/ACS/11_1YR/S0201//popgroup~006

Health Insurance

27.6%

The percentage of American Indians and Alaska Natives alone who lacked health insurance coverage in 2011. For the nation as a whole, the corresponding percentage was 15.1 percent.

Source: 2011 American Community Survey
http://factfinder2.census.gov/bkmk/table/l.0/en/ACS/11_1YR/S0201//popgroup~006

Following is a list of observances typically covered by the Census Bureau's *Facts for Features* series:

- African-American History Month (February)
- Super Bowl
- Valentine's Day (Feb. 14)
- Women's History Month (March)
- Irish-American Heritage Month (March)/
- St. Patrick's Day (March 17)
- Asian/Pacific American Heritage Month (May) (November)
- Older Americans Month (May)
- Cinco de Mayo (May 5)
- Mother's Day
- Father's Day
- The Fourth of July (July 4)
- Anniversary of Americans with Disabilities Act (July 26)
- Back to School (August)
- Labor Day
- Grandparents Day
- Hispanic Heritage Month (Sept. 15–Oct. 15)
- Unmarried and Single Americans Week
- Halloween (Oct. 31)
- American Indian/Alaska Native Heritage Month
- Veterans Day (Nov. 11)
- Thanksgiving Day
- The Holiday Season (December)

Critical Thinking

1. What are the causes of population distribution among the various Native Americans and the States?
2. Discuss the various profiles of Native Americans that emerge from the various categories and indicators collected by the Census.

Create Central

www.mhhe.com/createcentral

Internet References

Library of Congress
www.loc.gov

Social Science Information Gateway
http://sosig.esrc.bris.ac.uk

Sociosite
www.sociosite.net

Editor's note—The preceding data were collected from a variety of sources and may be subject to sampling variability and other sources of error.

U.S Census Bureau, 2012.

Article

Prepared by: John A. Kromkowski, *Catholic University of America*

In Montana, An Indian Reservation's Children Feel the Impact of Sequester's Cuts

LYNDSEY LAYTON

Learning Outcomes

After reading this article, you will be able to:

- Identify the causes of poverty on reservations.
- Explain the role, function and importance of schools and education on Native American reservations.

The public schools on the isolated, windswept Fort Peck Indian reservation here are at the frontier of the federal sequester, among the first to struggle with budget cuts sweeping west from Washington.

The superintendent can't hire a reading teacher in an elementary school where more than half the students do not read or write at grade level. Summer school, which feeds children and offers them an alternative to hanging around the reservation's trash-strewn yards, may be trimmed or canceled.

And in a school system where five children recently committed suicide in a single year—and 20 more made the attempt—plans to hire a second guidance counselor at the high school have been scrapped, leaving one person to advise some 200 students.

"The ones who are supposed to help us the most, hurt us the most," said Floyd Azure, the 56-year-old tribal chairman, who views the sequester as another in a long line of promises broken by the federal government. "This is disgraceful."

Few schools in America depend more heavily on the federal government than those on Indian reservations, which have no private landowners to tax. Washington pays about 10 percent of the budget for a typical U.S. public school district; on federal lands, it contributes as much as 60 percent.

While Washington debates the pros and cons of the sequester, the effects are already tangible in Poplar. Even marginal cuts can have a major impact on a reservation struggling with chronic substance abuse, unemployment and other ills, tribal leaders and residents say.

"Five percent isn't a lot when you have a lot," said Florence Garcia, the president of Fort Peck Community College, which is looking to close two community wellness centers because of the sequester. "But when you don't have much, five percent makes a big difference."

The school system—for which federal funding already had been reduced before the sequester—is looking for $1.2 million in additional cuts, partly by not filling jobs that go vacant. The Indian Health Service, the reservation's main source for health care, will also be cut by 8 percent, and Head Start, which serves 240 toddlers, will be cut by 5 percent, officials said.

"Instead of trying to cut, we should be adding," said Kent Hoffman, the vice principal at the high school, who is also filling in as athletic director, another job that will not be filled. "To me, this is insane."

Located in the northeast corner of Montana, north of the Missouri River, Fort Peck is home to two Indian nations, the Sioux and the Assiniboine, which jointly form the Fort Peck tribe. The tribe has roughly 13,000 members, but just half live on the 2-million-acre reservation.

The unemployment rate is more than 50 percent, and problems with alcohol and methamphetamines are widespread, according to tribal leaders. About three of every four children live in poverty. At the high school on any given day, only about half the students show up, said Principal Rayna Neumiller-Hartz.

Stray dogs wander the streets of Poplar, the government seat, which has a few tiny markets, a bar and several gas stations. The streets are littered with the charred remains of buildings because there is no money to clear away debris after a fire.

The struggles of Fort Peck drew national attention three years ago after five middle schoolers committed suicide and 20 others tried to. Tribal leaders declared an emergency, congressional hearings were held and mental health services were beefed up.

"A lot of bad things happen on the rez," said Ashlee Whitman, 15, who went to live with an aunt after her mother committed suicide and dreams of escaping by joining the military. "When people get bored here from watching TV, they smoke weed or get drunk. There's nothing to do here."

Federal dollars are central to keeping Fort Peck's residents afloat.

Isabelle Youngman, who tracks down truant children for the schools, has been helped by aid from Washington all her life. She attended a federally funded Indian boarding school in South Dakota and then Fort Peck Community College before working as a Head Start teacher's aide for 13 years.

With the school system, Youngman holds an $11.95-an-hour job that is partially funded by the federal government. She just bought her own home—a rarity on the reservation—with a mortgage guaranteed through the Agriculture Department's rural housing program. She lives in that two-bedroom, $30,000 house with her great-nephew, who was orphaned and has developmental delays.

Youngman, who is proud to be sober and employed, said the cuts concern her because she knows firsthand how federal dollars can make a difference. "It's scary," she said. "I try not to think about it. I put it in God's hands."

The reservation's three schools, clustered together off the main road, offer a haven of sorts. Some families come before school to shower in the gym because they lack running water at home. Others wash their clothes in the laundry machines at the high school.

The school board bought a movie license so the schools can show first-run films in the evenings or on weekends. "This is the only safe place for many of these kids," said James Rickley, the superintendent.

The federal government contributes about about 30 percent of the $13 million budget for the 830 students attending Poplar's elementary, middle and high schools. The rest comes from the state of Montana.

The sequester is actually a second wave of federal belt-tightening to hit the Poplar school system this year. Poplar had expected to receive 85 percent of the aid that it was qualified to get under a federal funding formula. But Poplar was notified last fall it would receive about 70 percent instead.

That meant a loss of $425,000, plus $800,000 more in sequester cuts through the end of the school year in June, according to school officials. Among other things, school officials won't be able to replace two retiring music teachers or the second high school guidance counselor, who left in February.

Officials are also unable to move ahead with plans for vocational training at the high school, which would allow students to take advantage of the economic boom unfolding 70 miles east at the oil and natural gas fields in North Dakota.

Jobs in the oil fields are plentiful and labor is scarce—employers such as Halliburton are flying in workers from around the country, and the local airwaves are filled with help-wanted ads. But the positions are out of reach for many on the reservation, who frequently lack basic job skills, transportation or the ability to pass a drug test.

The money immediately reduced by the sequester is known as Impact Aid, annual federal payments to schools on Indian reservations, military bases, public housing complexes and other federal properties. In the 2011–2012 school year, the federal government paid about $1.2 billion in Impact Aid to 1,500 districts, according to John Forkenbrock of the National Association of Federally Impacted Schools.

Fort Peck also receives two streams of federal dollars to educate poor children and those with disabilities. That money will be hit by the sequester starting in the fall.

"You guys are getting a triple whammy," Education Secretary Arne Duncan said at a Washington gathering earlier this month with officials from Indian reservations and military bases. "Impact Aid was set up to protect you from the vagaries of the budget. And you're taking the brunt of this."

In Poplar, Rickley thinks he can finish the school year without laying off any of his 152 employees by keeping vacancies open, forgoing purchases, canceling training and relying on everyone to do more.

"We have been very frugal, but we're reeling from this," said Rickley, a 64-year-old Pennsylvania native in his first year as superintendent. "This money is not 'aid.' It's not 'discretionary.' It's what is owed to these people."

Even the little things can matter, officials said. The schools have stopped buying the paper workbooks, printed on flimsy stock, that elementary school students bring home with them.

"These are kids that move from house to house and who don't even know who's picking them up from school," said kindergarten teacher Suzanne Turnbull. "To them, these books are a huge deal."

Critical Thinking

1. Discuss the various causes of the troubling situation described in this article.
2. Discuss the cultural and economic roots of social problems and their relationship to schools and education.

Create Central

www.mhhe.com/createcentral

Internet References

American Indian Ritual Object Repatriation Foundation
www.repatriationfoundatfon.org

Native American Heritage Association
www.naha.org

Native American Home Pages
www.nativeculturalikns.com

Unit 4

UNIT African Americans

Prepared by: John A. Kromkowski, *Catholic University of America*

Ethnic group discrimination and prejudice rooted in brutal and inhumane conquest and slavery that brought Africans to America are a profound and searing legacy. Eighteenth and nineteenth century laws and practices of defining race shaped legal doctrine regarding citizenship and the mentalities of color consciousness, prejudice, and racism in America. Today differentiation by race and ethnicity are aspects of understanding inter-group and intragroup relations, dynamics and definitions. In this respect the process of definition has come a long way since the 1988 New York Times editorial that provides the following account of a group that traces its American ancestry to initial participation as "three-fifths" of a person status in the U.S. Constitution to its later exclusion from the freedoms of this polity altogether by the U.S. Supreme *Courts Dred Scott* decision. The editors of the *Times* wrote (December 22, 1988) "The archaeology is dramatically plain to older adults who in one lifetime, have already heard preferred usage shift from *colored* to *Negro* to *black.* The four lingual layers provided an abbreviated history of naming race and ethnicity in this century" And this process continues: early in 2013, the U.S. Census acknowledged that their polling indicated that the classification "Negro' was offensive and announced that the U. S. Census would no longer used this term in its data collection. Thus another layer of the language of group identity has emerged from popular practice into public policy.

But language and reality intersect to reveal other types of measurable differentiations: income, education, location, occupation, profession, wealth, recent immigration from the Caribbean or an African country, mother tongue, languages, dialects and inter-ethic marriage. The final item is a topic that is rarely broached in mainstream media and ethnic media addresses audiences that are radically different populations interested in other ethnic specific topics:—skin tone, color, hew and hair texture and music and culture aesthetics. Thus the African American community or communities and its various gatekeepers, framers of issues, fashioners of the language of blackness/post-blackness/Afro-centric/cultural-religious markers are essentially more complex and complicated. Discrimination and consciousness of the African American ethnicity and accounts of African American traditions are like all American ethnicities, works in process. This intellectual and cultural ferment suggest that a process model of exploration is most appropriated understanding personal and group identity and the various invocations of tradition and current concerns related to race and ethnic relations. Ethnic groups "share-different" perspectives and experiences about the functions of the self-help community and solidarity, the extended family and on the importance of government as guarantor of civil liberties and civil rights and the political role of the religious ministry. Such dimensions are woven into mentalities and behavior that constitute an ethnic endowment of depth and meaning that is permanent and in flux. These languages of race and ethnic relations are articulated by elected leaders as well as the self-anointed and self-appointed who influenced the direction of social change and ongoing reconfiguring of race and ethnic relations in America.

An article by Lerone Bennett published in *Ebony* more than a decade before the election of president Barack Obama, expressed the thrust of an argument that has defined the discussion within Negro, black, and African American communities. Bennett's argument is that historical moments define a people's identity. A series of pivotal dramatic events inform the identity of African Americans and because of the centrality of this group these moments have shaped the character of group relations as a whole. The key moments include the following epoch making experiences of race and ethnicity: the arrival, the founding of communities and settlements, Nat Turner's War, the multiple moments and venues of emancipation, the Booker T. Washington and W. E. B. Dubois strategic crossroads, migrations, *Brown vs. Board of Education,* the events in Montgomery, Little Rock, and that day in Memphis when time and everything else stopped. Of course, The March on Washington and *Brown v. Topeka* are central to the civil rights era. And the memory and national holiday devoted to Martin Luther King, Jr. are ongoing public memorials. A closer look at a few moments of legal history should be explored to illustrate the role of government in race and ethnic relations.

In *Dred Scott v. Sandford* (1856), the Supreme Court addressed the constitutional status of an African held in bondage that had been moved to a state that prohibited slavery. U.S. Supreme Court Chief Justice Roger B. Taney attempted to resolve the increasingly divisive issue of slavery by declaring that the "Negro African race"—whether free or slave—was "not intended to be included under the word 'citizens' in the Constitution, and can therefore claim none of the rights and privileges that instrument provides for and secures to citizens of the United States. "Contrary to Taney's intentions, however, *Dred Scott* further fractured the country ensuring that only the Civil War would resolve the slavery issue. Even after the Civil War and the inclusion of constitutional amendments that ended slavery and provided for political inclusion of all persons and specifically mandated the loss of representation in the House of Representatives for those states that denied equal protection of the laws to all, exclusionary practices continued. Decisions by the U.S. Supreme Court helped to establish a legal system in which inequality and ethnic discrimination—both political and private—were legally permissible.

In *Plessy v. Ferguson* (1896), the Supreme Court upheld the constitutionality of "Jim Crow" laws that segregated public facilities on the basis of an individual's racial ancestry. The Court reasoned that this "separate but equal" segregation did not violate any rights guaranteed by the U.S. Constitution, nor did it stamp "the colored race with a badge of inferiority." Instead, the Court argued that if "this be so, it is not by reason of anything found in the act but solely because the colored race chooses to put that construction upon it." In contrast, Justice John M. Harlan's vigorous dissent from the Court's *Plessy* opinion contends that "our Constitution is color-blind, and neither knows nor tolerates classes among citizens." The history of the Court's attention to citizenship provides a view of a culturally embedded character of color consciousness and the strict textual dependence of the Justices that interpreted the Constitution.

In *Brown v. Board of Education of Topeka* (1954), the Supreme Court began the ambitious project of dismantling state-supported racial segregation. In *Brown,* a unanimous Court overturned *Plessy v. Ferguson,* arguing that "in the field of public education the doctrine of 'separate but equal' has no place, "because "separate educational facilities are inherently unequal.

The preceding glimpses into the context and content of the African American reality, its struggles, its tradition and community, its achievements, its perceptions of strains and stresses reveal a dense set of dimensions and concerns These pieces of an authentic identity rather than stereotype have replaced earlier dichotomies: "slave/free, black/white, poor/rich", but vestiges are still evident and a variety of group relations based on historic and regional as well as institutional agendas to preserve cultural and racial consciousness have complicated the simple hope for liberty and justice that was shared by many Americans. Many African Americans still face challenges in housing, employment, mobility and education. Growing gaps in education, financial status and class, crime and death rates of young black men paint daunting pictures of past policies and for future.

Article

Prepared by: John A. Kromkowski, *Catholic University of America*

Black (African-American) History Month: February 2013

To commemorate and celebrate the contributions to our nation made by people of African descent, American historian Carter G. Woodson established Black History Week. The first celebration occurred on Feb. 12, 1926. For many years, the second week of February was set aside for this celebration to coincide with the birthdays of abolitionist/editor Frederick Douglass and Abraham Lincoln. In 1976, as part of the nation's bicentennial, the week was expanded into Black History Month. Each year, U.S. presidents proclaim February as National African-American History Month.

Learning Outcomes

After reading this article, you will be able to:

- Explain the origins of Black History Month.
- Identify the most troubling demographic indicators about African Americans.

Population

43.9 million

The number of blacks, either alone or in combination with one or more other races, on July 1, 2011, up 1.6 percent from the census on April 1, 2010.

Source: Population Estimates
www.census.gov/newsroom/releases/archives/population/cb12-90.html

77.4 million

The projected black population of the United States (including those of more than one race) for July 1, 2060. On that date, according to the projection, blacks would constitute 18.4 percent of the nation's total population.

Source: Population projections
www.census.gov/population/projections/data/national/2012/summarytables.html

Note: The reference to the black population in this publication is to single-race blacks ("black alone") except in the first section on "Population." There the reference is to black alone or in combination with other races; in other words, a reference to respondents who said they were one race (black) or more than one race (black plus other races).

3.7 million

The black population in New York, which led all states as of July 1, 2011. Texas had the largest numeric increase since April 1, 2010 (84,000). The District of Columbia had the highest percentage of blacks (52.2 percent), followed by Mississippi (38.0 percent).

Source: Population Estimates
www.census.gov/newsroom/releases/archives/population/cb12-90.html

1.3 million

The black population in Cook, Ill., which had the largest black population of any county in 2011. Fulton, Ga., had the largest numeric increase since 2010 (13,000). Holmes, Miss., was the county with the highest percentage of blacks in the nation (82.9 percent).

Source: Population Estimates
www.census.gov/newsroom/releases/archives/population/cb12-90.html

Serving Our Nation

2.3 million

Number of black military veterans in the United States in 2011.

Source: 2011 American Community Survey
http://factfinder2.census.gov/faces/tableservices/jsf/pages/productview.xhtml?pid=ACS_11_1YR_C21001B&prodType=table.

Education

82.5%

The percentage of blacks 25 and older with a high school diploma or higher in 2011.

Source: 2011 American Community Survey
http://factfinder2.census.gov/bkmk/table/1.0/en/ACS/11_1YR/S0201//popgroup~004.

18.4%
The percentage of blacks 25 and older who had a bachelor's degree or higher in 2011.

Source: 2011 American Community Survey
http://factfinder2.census.gov/bkmk/table/1.0/en/ACS/11_1YR/S0201//popgroup~004

1.6 million
Among blacks 25 and older, the number who had an advanced degree in 2011.

Source: 2011 American Community Survey
http://factfinder2.census.gov/bkmk/table/1.0/en/ACS/11_1YR/S0201//popgroup~004

3.1 million
Number of blacks enrolled in college in 2011, a 74.0 percent increase since 2001.

Source: 2011 Current Population Survey, Table A1
www.census.gov/hhes/school/data/cps/historical/index.html

Voting
11.1 million
The number of blacks who voted in the 2010 congressional election, an increase from 10 percent of the total electorate in 2006 to 12 percent in 2010.

Source: Voting and Registration in the Election of 2010
www.census.gov/newsroom/releases/archives/voting/cb11-164.html

55%
Turnout rate in the 2008 presidential election for the 18- to 24-year-old citizen black population, an 8 percentage point increase from 2004. Blacks had the highest turnout rate in this age group.

Source: Voting and Registration in the Election of 2008
www.census.gov/newsroom/releases/archives/voting/cb09-110.html

65%
Turnout rate among black citizens regardless of age in the 2008 presidential election, up about 5 percentage points from 2004. Looking at voter turnout by race and Hispanic origin, non-Hispanic whites and blacks had the highest turnout levels.

Source: Voting and Registration in the Election of 2008
www.census.gov/newsroom/releases/archives/voting/cb09-110.html

Income, Poverty and Health Insurance
$32,229
The annual median income of black households in 2011, a decline of 2.7 percent from 2010.

Source: U.S. Census Bureau, Income, Poverty and Health Insurance Coverage in the United States: 2011
www.census.gov/prod/2012pubs/p60-243.pdf

27.6%
Poverty rate in 2011 for blacks.

Source: U.S. Census Bureau, Income, Poverty and Health Insurance Coverage in the United States: 2011
www.census.gov/newsroom/releases/archives/income_wealth/cb12-172.html

80.5%
Percentage of blacks that were covered by health insurance during all or part of 2011.

Source: U.S. Census Bureau, Income, Poverty and Health Insurance Coverage in the United States : 2011
www.census.gov/hhes/www/cpstables/032012/health/h01_000.html

Families and Children
61.9%
Among households with a black householder, the percentage that contained a family in 2012. There were 9.7 million black family households.

Source: 2012 Current Population Survey, Families and Living Arrangements, Table F1 and Table HH-2
www.census.gov/hhes/families/data/cps.html

45.2%
Among families with black householders, the percentage that were married couples in 2012.

Source: 2012 Current Population Survey, Families and Living Arrangements, Table F1
www.census.gov/hhes/families/data/cps2012.html

1.2 million
Number of black grandparents who lived with their own grandchildren younger than 18 in 2011. Of this number, 48.5 percent were also responsible for their care.

Source: 2011 American Community Survey
http://factfinder2.census.gov/bkmk/table/1.0/en/ACS/11_1YR/B10051B

Homeownership

43.4%

Nationally, the percentage of households with a householder who was black who lived in owner-occupied homes in 2011.

Source: 2011 American Community Survey
http://factfinder2.census.gov/faces/tableservices/jsf/pages/productview.xhtml?fpt=table

Jobs

28.2%

The percentage of blacks 16 and older who worked in management, business, science and arts occupations.

Source: 2011 American Community Survey
http://factfinder2.census.gov/bkmk/table/1.0/en/ACS/11_1YR/S0201//popgroup~004

Businesses

$135.7 billion

Receipts for black-owned businesses in 2007, up 53.1 percent from 2002. The number of black-owned businesses totaled 1.9 million in 2007, up 60.5 percent.

Source: 2007 Survey of Business Owners
http://factfinder2.census.gov

37.7%

Percentage of black-owned businesses in 2007 in health care and social assistance, repair and maintenance, and personal and laundry services.

Source: 2007 Survey of Business Owners
http://factfinder2.census.gov

10.6%

Percentage of all black-owned firms operating in 2007 in New York, which led all states or state-equivalents. Georgia and Florida followed, at 9.6 percent and 9.4 percent, respectively.

Source: 2007 Survey of Business Owners
http://factfinder2.census.gov

Following is a list of observances typically covered by the Census Bureau's *Facts for Features* series:

- Black History Month (February)
  Labor Day
- Super Bowl
  Grandparents Day
- Valentine's Day (Feb. 14)
  Hispanic Heritage Month (Sept. 15–Oct. 15)
- Women's History Month (March)
  Unmarried and Single Americans Week
- Irish-American Heritage Month (March)/
  Halloween (Oct. 31)
- St. Patrick's Day (March 17)
  American Indian/Alaska Native Heritage Month
- Asian/Pacific American Heritage Month (May)
  (November)
- Older Americans Month (May)
  Veterans Day (Nov. 11)
- Cinco de Mayo (May 5)
  Thanksgiving Day
- Mother's Day
  The Holiday Season (December)
- Hurricane Season Begins (June 1)
- Father's Day
- The Fourth of July (July 4)
- Anniversary of Americans with Disabilities Act (July 26)
- Back to School (August)

Critical Thinking

1. How is Black History Month celebrated in your area?
2. Which of the various demographic indicators are most important?

Create Central

www.mhhe.com/createcentral

Internet References

AIDS and Black New Yorkers
www.villagevoice.comlissues/0024/wright.php

National Association for the Advancement of Colored People (NAACP)
www.naacp.org

National Urban League
www.nul.org

Sociosite
www.sociosite.net

Editor's note—The preceding data were collected from a variety of sources and may be subject to sampling variability and other sources of error.

U.S Census Bureau, 2013.

Article

Prepared by: John A. Kromkowski, *Catholic University of America*

Nationwide Poll of African American Adults

Zogby Analytics

Learning Outcomes

After reading this article, you will be able to:

- Identify the core findings of this opinion poll.
- Identify the most significant issues in this poll.

Methodology

Zogby Analytics was commissioned by Robert L. Johnson to conduct an online survey of 1002 African American adults in the United States. All calls were made from February 14 through February 20, 2013.

Using trusted interactive partner resources, thousands of adults were invited to participate in this interactive survey. Each invitation is password coded and secure so that one respondent can only access the survey one time.

Telephone samples are randomly drawn from lists of adults. Up to three calls are made to reach a sampled phone number, respondents that were not available but qualified to respond were allowed to set appointments to be recalled within the time frame of the field work.

Using information based on census data, voter registration figures, CIA fact books and exit polls, we use complex weighting techniques to best represent the demographics of the population being surveyed. Weighted variables may include age, race, gender, region, party, education, and religion.

Based on a confidence interval of 95%, the margin of error for [1,002] is +/– [3.2%] percentage points. This means that all other things being equal, the identical survey repeated will have results within the margin of error 95 times out of 100.

Subsets of the data have a larger margin of error than the whole data set. As a rule we do not rely on the validity of very small subsets of the data especially sets smaller than 50–75 respondents. At that subset we can make estimations based on the data, but in these cases the data is more qualitative than quantitative.

Additional factors can create error, such as question wording and question order.

Narrative Summary

3–7. *For the following, please indicate your overall view of each–very favorable, somewhat favorable, somewhat unfavorable, very unfavorable–or you are not familiar enough to form an opinion.*

Table 1 Favorable/Unfavorable Ratings

	Overall	Very	Smwht	**Overall**	Very	Smwht		
Barack Obama	**91**	75	16	**6**	3	3	**1**	3
Hillary Clinton	**87**	55	32	**8**	2	6	**1**	4
NAACP	**83**	54	30	**8**	2	6	**4**	5
National Urban League	**69**	37	32	**7**	1	5	**17**	7
Congressional Black Caucus	**68**	33	35	**9**	2	6	**16**	7

Just over nine in ten respondents have a favorable opinion of President Barack Obama, with 6% rating the president unfavorable. Just 1% are not familiar with the president and 3% are not sure how they feel.

Nearly as many respondents (87%) have a favorable opinion of Hillary Clinton, while 8% have an unfavorable opinion of the former Secretary of State. And more than four in five (83%) have a favorable opinion of the NAACP; just 8% are unfavorable.

A majority have an overall favorable opinion of the National Urban League and the Congressional Black Caucus, but 17% and 16% respectively are not familiar with the organizations.

8. *Which of the following speaks for you most often?*

Reverend Al Sharpton, National Action Network	24
Reverend Jesse Jackson, Rainbow PUSH Coalition	11
Congresswoman Maxine Waters (D-CA)	9
Benjamin Jealous, President & CEO, NAACP	8
Assistant Democratic Leader, Congressman James E. Clyburn (D-SC)	5
Marc H. Morial, President & CEO, National Urban League	2
Michael Steele, former Chairman of the Republican National Committee	2
None of the above	40

A plurality (40%) say that none of the people listed speaks for them. The person who most often speaks for respondents is Reverend AI Sharpton (24%). About one in ten say that Reverend Jackson (11%) and Representative Maxine Waters (9%) speaks for them, while 8% say that Ben Jealous of the NAACP most often speaks for them.

One in twenty say that Representative Clyburn speaks for them, while one in fifty each say that Marc MoriaI and Michael Steele most often speaks for them.

9. *Are there any others not mentioned above that you would say speak for you?*

- Barack Obama (81)
- Miscellaneous Democrats (23)
- God/Jesus/Religion (16)
- Myself (14)
- Michelle Obama (11)
- Bill Clinton (9)
- Martin Luther King, Jr. (9)
- Miscellaneous Republican (9)
- Colin Powell (8)
- MSNBC Host/reporter (6)
- Hillary Clinton (4)
- Joe Biden (4)
- Louis Farakhan (3)
- Elijah Cummings (2)
- John Lewis (2)
- Ben Carson (2)
- Eleanor Holmes Norton (2)
- Kwame Mfume (2)
- Sheila Jackson Lee (3)
- Tavis Smiley (3)
- T. D. Jakes (2)
- Oprah (3)
- Entertainer/athlete (3)
- All of the above (3)
- Mentioned in the list (50)
- No one/none (702)

10. *In your opinion, has the election of President Barack Obama helped, hurt, or made no difference in the lives of most African Americans today?*

Helped	72%
Hurt	4
Made no difference	16
Not sure	8

Three in four respondents believe that the election of Barak Obama has helped in the lives of most African Americans, while 16% say the historic election has made no difference. Just 4% think his election has made the lives of African Americans worse and 8% are not sure.

11. *The wealth gap between white Americans and African Americans has increased by $70,000 over the last 20 years. Which of the following do you consider the primary cause?*

Lack of jobs	22%
Lack of access to capital	8
Both	47
Didn't know there was a wealth gap problem	7
Other	10
Not sure	7

Nearly half (47%) of African Americans say that both the lack of jobs and a lack of access to capital are to blame for the wealth gap between whites and African Americans. Twenty-two percent and 8%, respectively,say lack of jobs and lack of access to capital are to blame. Seven percent were not aware of a wealth gap and one in ten say something else is to blame.

12. *Considering your personal finances, would you say you are better off, worse off, or about the same as you were four years ago?*

Better off	30%
Worse off	19
About the same	48
Not sure	3

One in three (30%) respondents consider their personal finances are better off now than they were four years ago and 19% are worse off. Just under half (48%) say their personal finances are about the same and 3% are not sure.

13. *More generally, would you say that African Americans are better off, worse off or about the same as they were four years ago?*

Better off	25%
Worse off	21
About the same	44
Not sure	10

A plurality (44%) say in general that African Americans are about the same as they were four years ago, while respondents are closely divided between better off (25%) and worse off (21%). One in ten are not sure.

14. *Would you say that racial attitudes among non-African Americans toward African Americans are better, worse,*

or about the same since Barack Obama has become President?

Better off	19%
Worse off	25
About the same	48
Not sure	9

Just under half (48%) say that they think that racial attitudes among non-African Americans towards African Americans remains about the same as they were before Obama became President. One in four (25%) believe racial attitudes are worse and 19% think they are better.

15. *African American unemployment has been double that of whites. What do you think is to blame for this?*

Failure of the education system for minorities/African Americans	50
Lack of corporate commitment to hiring minorities/African Americans	48
Lack of good government policies	25
Don't blame anyone or anything	18
Not sure	12

Half (50%) of respondents believe that the unemployment rate of African Americans is double that of whites is because of the failure of the education system, while nearly as many (48%) say the reason for the difference is a lack of corporate commitment to hiring minorities and African Americans. One in four believe the cause is the lack of good government policies and 18% don't blame anyone or anything. Twelve percent are not sure.

16. *As an African American, have you ever been overlooked or felt discounted as a serious contender for employment because of your race?*

Yes	47%
No	39
Not sure	14

Just under half (47%) say they have been overlooked or felt discounted as a serious contender for a job because of their race, while more than one in three (39%) say they have not. Fourteen percent are not sure.

17. *The RLJ Rule is designed to encourage companies to voluntarily establish a best practices policy to identify and interview at least two African Americans at the managerial level and Black businesses for procurement opportunities that are often overlooked because of traditional hiring or procurement practices. The RLJ Rule is adapted from the NFL's Rooney Rule which mandates that teams interview minority candidates when head coaching and general manager positions become available. Overall, would you say that you are very supportive, somewhat supportive, or not supportive of companies voluntarily adopting the RLJ Rule?*

Very supportive	39%
Somewhat supportive	36
Not supportive	6
Not sure	19

Three in four respondents say they are supportive of companies voluntarily adopting the RLJ Rule which identifies and interviews at least two African Americans at the managerial level and Black businesses for procurement opportunities. Just 6% say they do not support adapting the RLJ Rule for business.

18. *If such a rule were in place, do you feel it would help your chances, hurt your chances, or make no difference in your or African Americans chances to be hired or to become a minority supplier?*

Help	47%
Hurt	4
Make no difference	34
Not sure	16

About half (47%) believe that if the RLJ Rule were in place, it would help their chances to be hired to become a minority supplier and one in three (34%) say if the "rule" were in place, it would make no difference. Sixteen percent are not sure and just 4% say it would hurt their chances of being hired or becoming a minority supplier.

19. *If companies did not voluntarily adopt the RLJ Rule, would you want the President to urge Congress to enact legislation to require US companies to interview minorities for jobs and contract opportunities?*

Yes	53%
No	19
Not sure	28

A majority (53%) say that they would the President to urge Congress to enact legislation to require US companies to adopt the RLJ rule so that they would have to interview minorities for jobs and contract opportunities.

20. *In your view, who has been most effective in representing their community's point of view to federal elected and appointed officials?*

African American leadership	15
Lesbian, Gay, Bisexual, Transgendered (LGBT) leadership	13
Religious leaders	9
Hispanic leadership	2
All of the above	39
None of the above	8
Not sure	15

Nearly two in five respondents say that the leadership of all the groups tested have been effective in representing their community's point of view to federal elected and appointed officials. By a narrow margin, respondents say that African American leadership (15%) has been the most effective, followed closely by the LGBT leadership (13%). Just under one in ten say that religious leaders (9%) have been most effective.

Just 2% say Hispanic leadership has been most effective, while 8% say none of the above and 15% are not sure.

21. *Do you believe Hispanics who have come to America illegally should be granted full citizenship. . .?*

Immediately	9%
After 5 years	34
After 10 years	19
Never	16
Other/not sure	21

Thirty-four percent say that Hispanics who have come to America illegally should be granted full citizenship after just 5 years; another 19% say they should be granted citizenship after 10 years. Just under one in ten say they should be allowed to be citizens immediately, while 16% say they should never be allowed to be citizens. One in five are not sure.

22. *Do you believe the US government is doing enough on border security to stem the influx of illegal immigrants?*

Yes	24%
No	48
Not sure	28

About half say that the US government is not doing enough to stem the influx of illegal immigrants, while one in four (24%) say the government is doing enough. Twenty-eight percent are not sure.

23. *Do you believe Hispanic Americans will achieve greater economic growth than African Americans over the next 5 years?*

Yes	51%
No	19
Not sure	30

Just over half believe that the next five years will be better economically for Hispanic Americans that for African Americans, while 30% are not sure.

24. *Do you believe Hispanic Americans will achieve greater economic growth than African Americans over the next 5 years? Why?*

- Hispanics face less racism than African Americans (97)
- Hispanic lifestyle/work ethics (79)
- Hispanics given more opportunity/education is better (77)
- Hispanic population is growing fast/faster (71)
- Hispanics work together as a group/support each other (54)
- Hispanics work for poor wages/bad working conditions (39)
- That's just the way it is (28)
- No response/not sure (528)

25. *The Lesbian Gay, Bisexual, Transgender (LGBT) community asserts they are entitled to certain rights under the law. Do you believe marriage should be restricted to between a man and a woman or do you believe that persons of the same sex should be allowed to marry and receive similar benefits as heterosexual couples?*

Restricted to a man and a woman	42
Same sex couples should be allowed to marry with benefits	40
Same sex couples should be allowed to marry without benefits	4
Not sure	13

26. *Some in the LGBT community claim that rights for LGBT people are the same as rights for African Americans. Do you believe that equal rights for gays are the same as equal rights for African Americans?*

Yes	28%
No	55
Not sure	17

By nearly two to one (55% vs. 28%), respondents say that equal rights for gays are not the same as equal rights for African Americans.

27. *Do you believe ministers who oppose homosexuality, including the rights of gays and lesbians to marry, are. . .?*

Right	34%
Wrong	31
No opinion	35

Despite views on the similarity or difference regarding equal rights for LGBT Americans versus African Americans, respondents are closely divided about whether or not ministers who oppose homosexuality, including the rights of gays and lesbians to marry–about one in three each say the ministers are right to oppose gay marriage (34%), are wrong to oppose gay marriage (31%), and are unsure (35%).

28. *Do you believe the country should ban assault, military-style, high capacity automatic weapons?*

Yes	67%
No	20
Not sure	14

By more than three to one (67% vs. 20%), respondents believe that assault weapons should be banned. Fourteen percent are not sure.

29. *Do you believe the country pays less attention to "Black on Black" crime than it does to gun crimes committed against white Americans?*

Yes	75%
No	14
Not sure	11

The vast majority (75%) of respondents agree that "Black on Black" crime receives less attention than crimes committed against whites in this country.

30. *Are you aware of the plan by the US government along with the private sector, to build a national African American museum in Washington, D. C. on the National Mall?*

Aware	26%
Unaware	66
Not sure	8

Two in three respondents say they are unaware of US government plans to build a national African American museum on the National Mall in Washington, D. C.

31–32 *Overall would you say you are optimistic or pessimistic about each of the following over the next four years.*

White-African American relations	53	23	23
Employment opportunities for African Americans	62	19	20

A majority of African American adults are optimistic about employment opportunities for African Americans (62%) and for white-African American relations (53%) in the next four years.

However, slightly more are pessimistic about relations between whites and African Americans (23%) than are pessimistic about employment opportunities for African Americans (19%)

33. *If the Democratic primary for President were held today, for whom would you vote?*

34. *Who do you think President Obama should endorse to succeed him as the next President of the United States?*

Hillary Clinton	46	39
Joe Biden	19	23
Andrew M. Cuomo	2	1
Julian Castro	1	1
Martin O'Malley	1	1
Deval L. Patrick	1	<1
Someone else	5	4
Cannot/will not vote in primary	6	–
Shouldn't endorse anyone	–	9
***Other (Q34 only)**	–	<1
Not sure	19	21

*Michelle Obama; Allen West; Corey Booker; Christian Socialist candidate

Nearly half (46%) of the respondents say they would support Hillary Clinton for President in the Democratic primary if it were held today and just under two in five (39%) say that President Obama should endorse her to succeed him. About one in five say they will support Vice President Joe Biden if the primary were held today and that President Obama should endorse him.

Two percent or less say they would support any of the other candidates mentioned.

Critical Thinking

1. Discuss the motives for commissioning of this opinion poll.
2. From among the various findings what general lines of opinion seems especially important??

Create Central

www.mhhe.com/createcentral

Internet References

AIDS and Black New Yorkers
www.villagevoice.comlissues/0024/wright.php

Association for the Advancement of Colored People (NAACP)
www.naacp.org

National Urban League
www.nul.org

About Zogby Analytics For three decades, the Zogby companies have produced polls with an unparalleled record of accuracy and reliability. Zogby telephone and interactive surveys have generally been the most accurate in U.S. Presidential elections since 1996.

Zogby Analytics is composed entirely of senior level executives from Zogby International. Zogby Analytics, along with renowned pollster John Zogby, have continued in the tradition of conducting telephone and interactive surveys, while keeping an eye on the future by incorporating social media tracking and analysis into our work.

Zogby Analytics conducts a wide variety of surveys internationally and nationally in industries, including banking, IT, medical devices, government agencies, colleges and universities, non-profits, automotive, insurance and NGOs.

Article

Prepared by: John A. Kromkowski, *Catholic University of America*

What Black Parents Tell their Sons

Trayvon Martin's Killing Confirms Worst Fears

DAHLEEN GLANTON

Learning Outcomes

After reading this article, you will be able to:

- Describe Trayvon Martin.
- Explain why this event became more than a personal, family, and locally sad and painful event?

When their son was about to enter his teens, Paul and Jeanne Miller, of Flossmoor, decided it was time to have the talk.

Because you are an African-American male, they told him, some people will make judgments about you and view you with suspicion based solely on your race.

Recently, as Jeremy, 16, was preparing to get his driver's license, his father told him what to do if he were ever stopped by police: Keep your hands visible on the steering wheel at all times.

And when he asked to take part in Assassins, a popular suburban game in which teens stalk each other with airsoft guns, his parents' answer was an unequivocal no, lest someone mistake the toy that fires plastic pellets for a real weapon.

The story of 17-year-old Trayvon Martin's death in Sanford, Fla., a suburb of Orlando, has struck a particularly sensitive chord with African-American parents such as the Millers, many of whom said they live with a nagging fear that their teenage boys could be harassed or attacked.

"We live in a fairly affluent interracial neighborhood with fantastic people who don't see color, but I know there are people out there who do," said Paul Miller. "I constantly tell him, 'Don't forget you're black.' I don't want him to run into that guy who does see color one day when he's walking down the street."

Martin was shot to death last month by a man on a neighborhood watch patrol who confronted the African-American teenager because he thought he looked suspicious in the gated community. Martin, who was unarmed, was walking back to his father's house after going to the store for a can of tea and candy.

George Zimmerman claimed he acted in self-defense when he shot Martin and was not charged in the shooting, prompting protests across the country, including two Friday in Chicago and one scheduled for noon Saturday at Daley Plaza.

The case once again placed a spotlight on race in America and forced discussions about the negative perceptions some people have regarding African-American men. The recurring theme at many of the rallies has been that Martin could have been the son of any African-American.

On Friday, President Barack Obama weighed in, saying, "If I had a son, he'd look like Trayvon."

"When I think about this boy, I think about my own kids," Obama said. "And I think every parent in America should be able to understand why it is absolutely imperative that we investigate every aspect of this, and that everybody pulls together—federal, state and local—to figure out exactly how this tragedy happened."

With the election of Obama four years ago, some people mistakenly believe America is now a post-racial country, according to Cathy Cohen, a political science professor at the University of Chicago. But many young black men remain targets of racism that still exists, she said.

"The reality is that many Americans . . . perceive young black men to be 'suspicious' individuals who will rob them, confront them and carry a firearm to threaten their safety, independent of whether it is true or not," said Cohen.

"Young black men go through the world being harassed, watched and stereotyped. They live with that every day, and far too many of us have ignored their reality," she said.

Marguerite Alston, of Chicago Heights, said she rarely allows her 16-year-old son, Michael, to walk home from school, but when he does, she insists that he goes with a group.

"At least there is another set of eyes if there's a problem," she said. "Someone can go and get help."

Sometimes, however, she worries when her son asks to go to a mall with a group of African-American boys, fearing that they could be accused of making trouble even if they are not.

"I know they are good kids, but it's like a red flag goes up in people's mind when they see a group of black boys," said Alston. "The first thing they think about is what they see on the news or what they've heard about. And just that quickly, something could go wrong."

Michael said he is familiar with the suspicious look to which his mother is referring.

"Sometimes when you are in certain areas that don't have a lot of black young men around, people might watch you a little more, and it can be uncomfortable," he said. "It makes me feel like I don't belong there. Not necessarily scared, but it makes me feel out of place."

Alston and her husband, Jeff, started talking to their son when he was a preteen. Growing up, Alston's five brothers had the same conversations with their mother, who stressed the importance of telling Alston's son how to avoid racially charged confrontations, Alston said.

African-American men long have claimed that they are unfairly harassed by police while driving, particularly in predominantly white neighborhoods. It has become so common that it is referred to as "driving while black."

There are tools their children can use to lessen the chances that a routine police stop could escalate into violence, they said, but there is no way to prepare them for situations such as the one that left Martin, who was wearing a hoodie and talking on a cellphone, dead.

"I have a group of kids who get stopped just walking down the street. Their pants are not even hanging off their behind. They don't have on any hoodies. They're just going through everyday life," said Cecil Reddit, who mentors teenage boys and facilitates a fathers support group for Family Focus Lawndale.

The challenge for many parents is how to prepare the boys without frightening them or making them feel their parents are being overly protective. It is also important, they said, not to make them feel as though they are less important than anyone else.

"I get very angry about this because, as Americans, we are all men," said Reddit. "We should be able to live the same way everyone else is doing and not be targeted for these types of things, but it is reality."

Jocilyn Floyd, a single mother raising a 7-year-old son in the West Chesterfield neighborhood on the South Side, said she already has begun teaching him to understand what it means to be African-American, though he is fair-skinned with green eyes and sandy brown hair.

"He is just black enough but not white enough," said Floyd, adding that her son's father is half Italian. "I'm trying to get him to understand that he can't follow along with everybody. He can't get into trouble like some kids and that you have to be careful that you're not pegged the kid with bad behavior."

To keep him grounded, she said, she has enrolled him in a private Afrocentric school, which she hopes will give him more self-esteem. But she acknowledges that how people perceive him is out of her hands.

"My concern for my son would be that, by perception or ignorance, that he could easily be a victim of an incident just like Trayvon if he's in the wrong place at the wrong time," said Floyd. "There is no way to prepare him for walking down the street while being black. When he gets older, I can guarantee you there will be a part of me that will be terrified and praying every day."

Critical Thinking

1. Discuss the media presentation of the killing of Trayvon Martin.
2. Discuss the experiences of fearfulness and suspicion of others.

Create Central

www.mhhe.com/createcentral

Internet References

National Association for the Advancement of Colored People (NAACP)
www.naacp.org

Sociosite
www.sociosite.net

The National Urban League
www.nul.org

Article Prepared by: John A. Kromkowski, *Catholic University of America*

Poverty Rates for Selected Detailed Race and Hispanic Groups by State and Place: 2007–2011

SUZANNE MACARTNEY, ALEMAYEHU BISHAW, AND KAYLA FONTENOT

Learning Outcomes

After reading this article, you will be able to:

- Identify the five concentrations of poverty.
- Determine whether the measurement of poverty reveals race and ethnic or place-specific causes and/or correlations.

Introduction

Poverty rates are important indicators of community well-being and are used by government agencies and organizations to allocate need-based resources. The American Community Survey (ACS) 5-year data allow for the analysis of poverty rates by race arid Hispanic origin for many levels of geography.

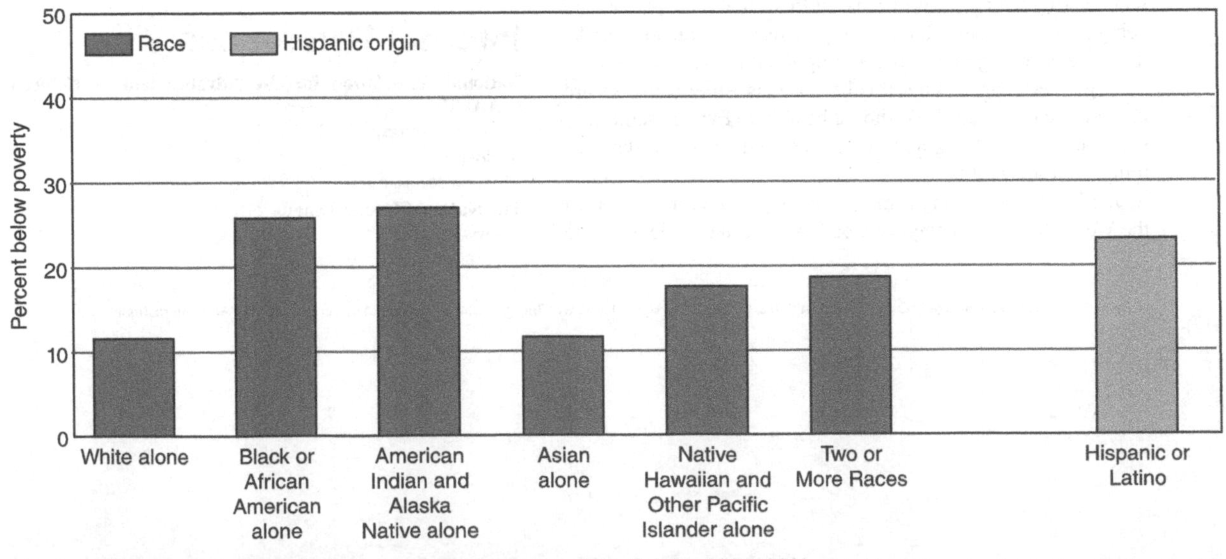

Figure 1 U.S. Poverty Rates by Race and Hispanic or Latino Origin: 2007–2011 (For information on confidentiality protection, sampling error, nonsampling error, and definitions, see *www.census.gov/acs/www/*)

Note: Persons who report only one race among the six defined categories are referred to as the race-alone population, while persons who report more than one race category are referred to as the Two or More Races population. This figure shows data using the race-alone approach. Use of the single-race population does not imply that it is the preferred method of presenting or analyzing data. The Census Bureau uses a variety of approaches. Because Hispanics may be of any race, data in this figure for Hispanics overlap with data for race groups.

Source: U.S. Census Bureau, 2007–2011 American Community Survey.

In this report, poverty rates are summarized by race and Hispanic origin for the United States, each state, and the District of Columbia.

Poverty rates are also presented for selected retailed race and origin groups in the cities and towns with the largest populations of these groups. For the nation and selected places, poverty rates are summarized for detailed Asian groups with populations of 750,000 or more, detailed Native Hawaiian and Other Pacific Islander groups with populations of 25,000 or more, and detailed Hispanic groups with populations of 1 million or more.

Highlights

- According to the 2007–2011 ACS, 42.7 million people or 14.3 percent of the U.S. population had income below the poverty level.
- By race, the highest national poverty rates were for American Indians and Alaska Natives (27.0 percent) and Blacks or African Americans (25.8 percent).
- Native Hawaiians and Other Pacific Islanders had a national poverty rate of 17.6 percent.
- For the Asian population, poverty rates were higher for Vietnamese (14.7 percent) and Koreans (15.0 percent), and lower for Filipinos (5.8 percent).[1]
- Among Hispanics, national poverty rates ranged from a low of 16.2 percent for Cubans to a high of 26.3 percent for Dominicans.
- Nine states had poverty rates of about 30 percent or more for American Indians and Alaska Natives (Arizona, Maine, Minnesota, Montana, Nebraska, New Mexico, North Dakota, South Dakota, and Utah).
- For Asians, nine states had poverty rates of about 10 percent or less (Connecticut, Delaware, Hawaii, Maryland, Nevada, New Hampshire, New Jersey, Virginia, and South Carolina).
- The 2007–2011 national poverty rate for Whites was 11.6 percent, and most states (43) as well as the District of Columbia had poverty rates lower than 14.0 percent for this group.

Understanding Race and Hispanic Origin Concepts

Individuals who responded to the question on race by indicating only one race are referred to as the race-alone population or the group who reported only one race category. The text and figures of this report show estimates for the race-alone population. Six categories make up this population: White alone, Black or African American alone, American Indian and Alaska Native alone, Asian alone, Native Hawaiian and Other Pacific Islander alone, and Some Other Race alone. Individuals who chose more than one of the six race categories are referred to as the Two or More Races population. All respondents who indicated more than one race can be collapsed into the Two or More Races category which, combined with the six race-alone categories, yields seven mutually exclusive and exhaustive categories. Thus, the six race-alone categories and the Two or More Races category sum to the total population.

Hispanics may be of any race. For each race group, data in this report include people who reported they were of Hispanic origin and people who reported they were not Hispanic. Because Hispanics may be of any race, data in this report for Hispanics overlap with data for race groups. For more information on the concepts of race and Hispanic origin, see Humes, K., N. Jones, and R. Ramirez, "Overview of Race and Hispanic Origin: 2010," U.S. Census Bureau, 2010 Census Briefs, 2011, available at www.census.gov/prod/cen2010/briefs/c2010br-02.pdf.

See Census Briefs and Reports, 2010 Census, at www.census.gov/2010census/ discussed in this for more information on the race and origin groups report.

The estimates contained in this report are based on the 2007-2011 ACS. The ACS is conducted every month with income data collected for the 12 months preceding the interview. The 5-year estimates are period estimates. They represent the characteristics of the population and housing over the specific data collection period.

National

During the 2007 to 2011 period, 42.7 million people or 14.3 percent of the U.S. population had income below the poverty level (Table 1). National poverty rates differed widely across race groups and by Hispanic or Latino origin.[2]

Two groups had poverty rates more than 10 percentage points higher than the U.S. rate for the total population: American Indian and Alaska Native (27.0 percent) and Black or African American (25.8 percent). Rates were above the overall national average for Native Hawaiians and Other Pacific Islanders (17.6 percent) while poverty rates for Whites (11.6 percent) and Asians (11.7 percent) were lower than the overall rate (14.3 percent).[3] The Hispanic population had a poverty rate of 23.2 percent, about 9 percentage points higher than the overall U.S. rate (Figure 1).

For a particular race group, poverty rates may differ by detailed race or origin. Some detailed race or origin groups are listed on the ACS questionnaire such as Filipino, Native Hawaiian, or Puerto Rican.

Categories not listed may be handwritten and the responses tabulated within major race groups. Poverty differed across detailed Asian groups. Poverty rates also differed by detailed Native Hawaiian and Other Pacific Islander groups.

An estimated 17.6 percent of the Native Hawaiian and Other Pacific Islander population had income below the poverty level over the 2007 to 2011 period (Figure 2). Within this group, poverty rates ranged from a low of 6.4 percent for Fijians to a high of about 18.0 percent for Samoans and Tongans.[4] The largest detailed group, Native Hawaiian, had a poverty rate of 14.4 percent, a rate not statistically different from the U.S. average for the total population. For Guamanians or Chamorros, poverty was estimated at 11.6 percent, a rate lower than the U.S. average for the total population.

Figure 3 shows that for the Asian population, poverty was estimated at 8.2 percent for both Asian Indians and Japanese. Higher rates were found for Vietnamese (14.7 percent) and Koreans (15.0 percent),[5] and lower rates were found for Filipinos (5.8 percent).

Many Hispanic groups had poverty rates higher than the overall U.S. rate for the 2007 to 2011 period (Figure 4). Salvadorans and Cubans had poverty rates of 18.9 percent and 16.2 percent, respectively. For Mexicans and Guatemalans, the rates were about 25.0 percent. Similar rates were found for Puerto Ricans (25.6 percent) and Dominicans (26.3 percent).

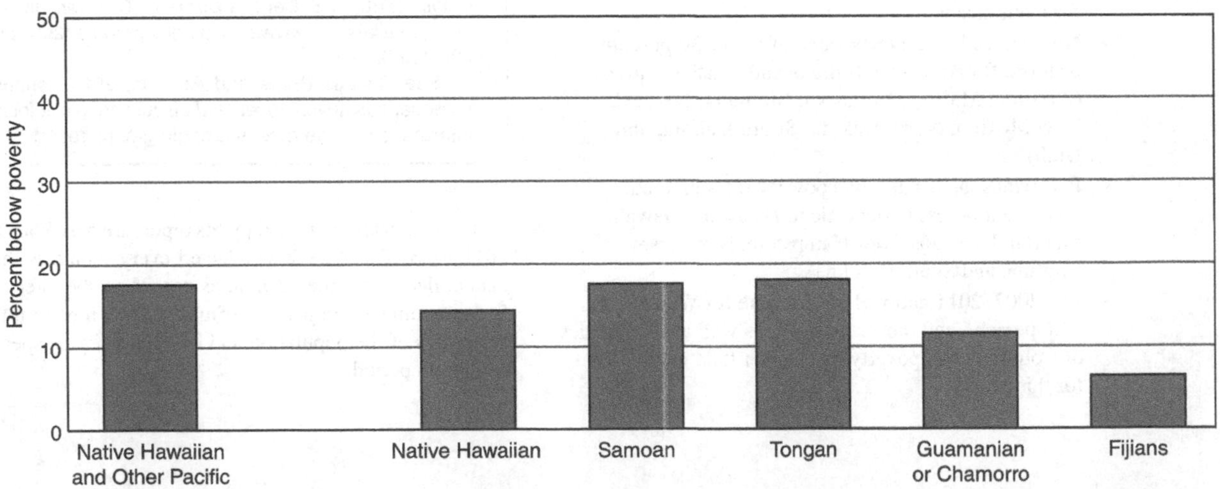

Figure 2. U.S. Poverty Rates for the Native Hawaiian and Other Pacific Islander Alone Population and Selected Detailed Groups: 2007–2011 (For information on confidentiality protection, sampling error, nonsampling error, and definitions, see www.census.gov/acs/www/)

Note: Persons who report only one race among the six defined categories are referred to as the race-alone population, while persons who report more than one race category are referred to as the Two or More Races population. This figure shows data using the race-alone approach. Use of the single-race population does not imply that it is the preferred method of presenting or analyzing data. The Census Bureau uses a variety of approaches.

Source: U.S. Census Bureau, 2007–2011 American Community Survey.

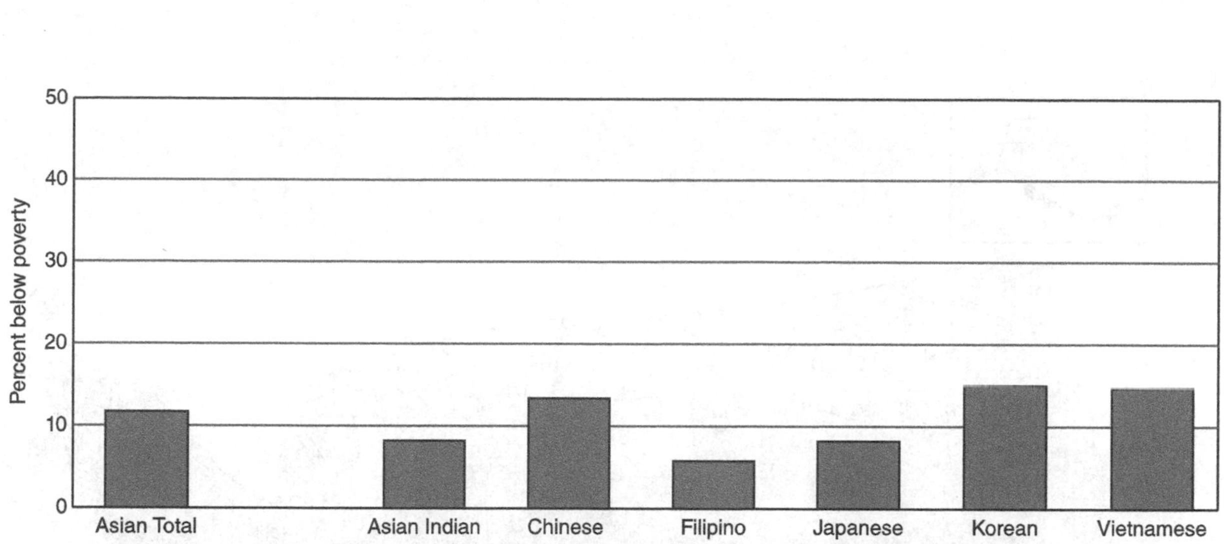

Figure 3. U.S. Poverty Rates for the Asian Alone Population and Selected Detailed Groups: 2007–2011 (For information on confidentiality protection, sampling error, nonsampling error, and definitions, see www.census.gov/acs/www/)

Note: Persons who report only one race among the six defined categories are referred to as the race-alone population, while persons who report more than one race category are referred to as the Two or More Races population. This figure shows data using the race-alone approach. Use of the single-race population does not imply that it is the preferred method of presenting or analyzing data. The Census Bureau uses a variety of approaches.

Source: U.S. Census Bureau, 2007–2011 American Community Survey.

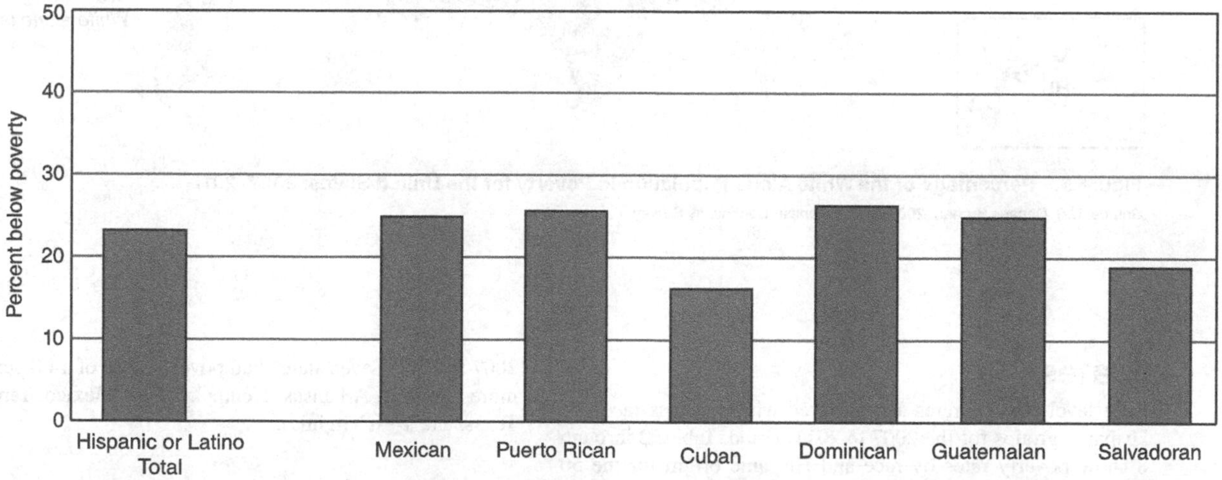

Figure 4. U.S. Poverty Rates for the Hispanic Population and Selected Detailed Groups: 2007–2011 (For information on confidentiality protection, sampling error, nonsampling error, and definitions, see www.census.gov/acs/www/)

Note: Hispanics may be of any race. For more information, see Ennis, S., M. Rios-Vargas, and N. Albert, "The Hispanic Population: 2010," U.S. Census Bureau, *2010 Census Briefs*, C2010BR-04, 2011, available at www.census.gov/prod/cen2010/briefs/c2010br-04.pdf.

Source: U.S. Census Bureau, 2007–2011 American Community Survey.

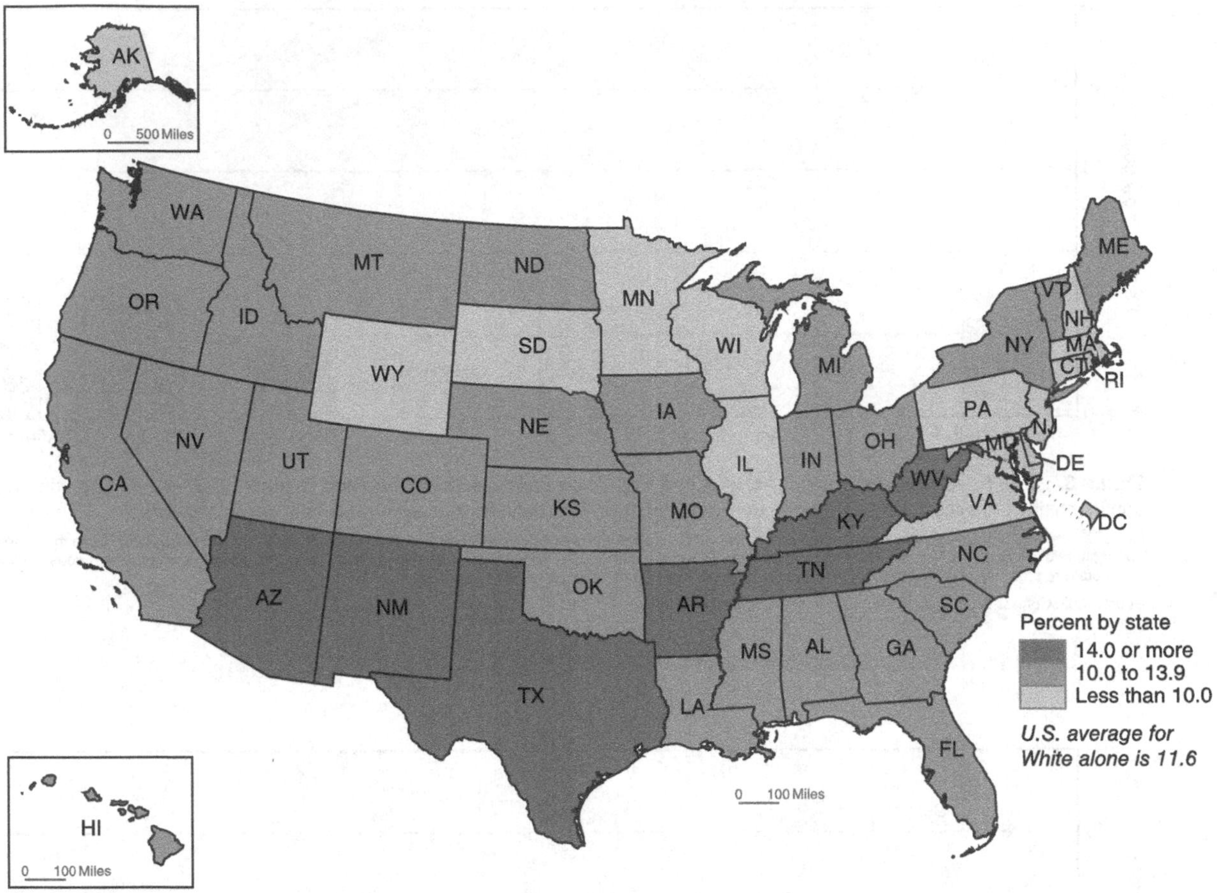

Figure 5. Percentage of the White Alone Population in Poverty for the United States: 2007–2011

Source: U.S. Census Bureau, 2007–2011 American Community Survey.

States

State-level poverty rates also differed widely across race and Hispanic groups for the 2007 to 2011 period. Tables 2 through 8 show poverty rates by race and Hispanic origin for the 50 states and the District of Columbia. Figures 5 through 9 show the variation in poverty levels across the United States for selected race and Hispanic groups.

White

Figure 5 shows the distribution of poverty for the White population. Forty-three states and the District of Columbia had poverty rates for the White population lower than 14.0 percent for 2007 to 2011. Seven states had poverty rates of 14.0 percent or more (Arizona, Arkansas, Kentucky, New Mexico, Tennessee, Texas, and West Virginia).[6]

Black

Figure 6 shows that during the 2007 to 2011 period for the Black population, 43 states and the District of Columbia had poverty rates of 20.0 percent or higher. Iowa, Maine, Mississippi, and Wisconsin had rates above 35.0 percent. Six states had poverty rates for Blacks that were about 20.0 percent or less (Alaska, Delaware, Hawaii, Maryland, New Jersey, and Virginia).

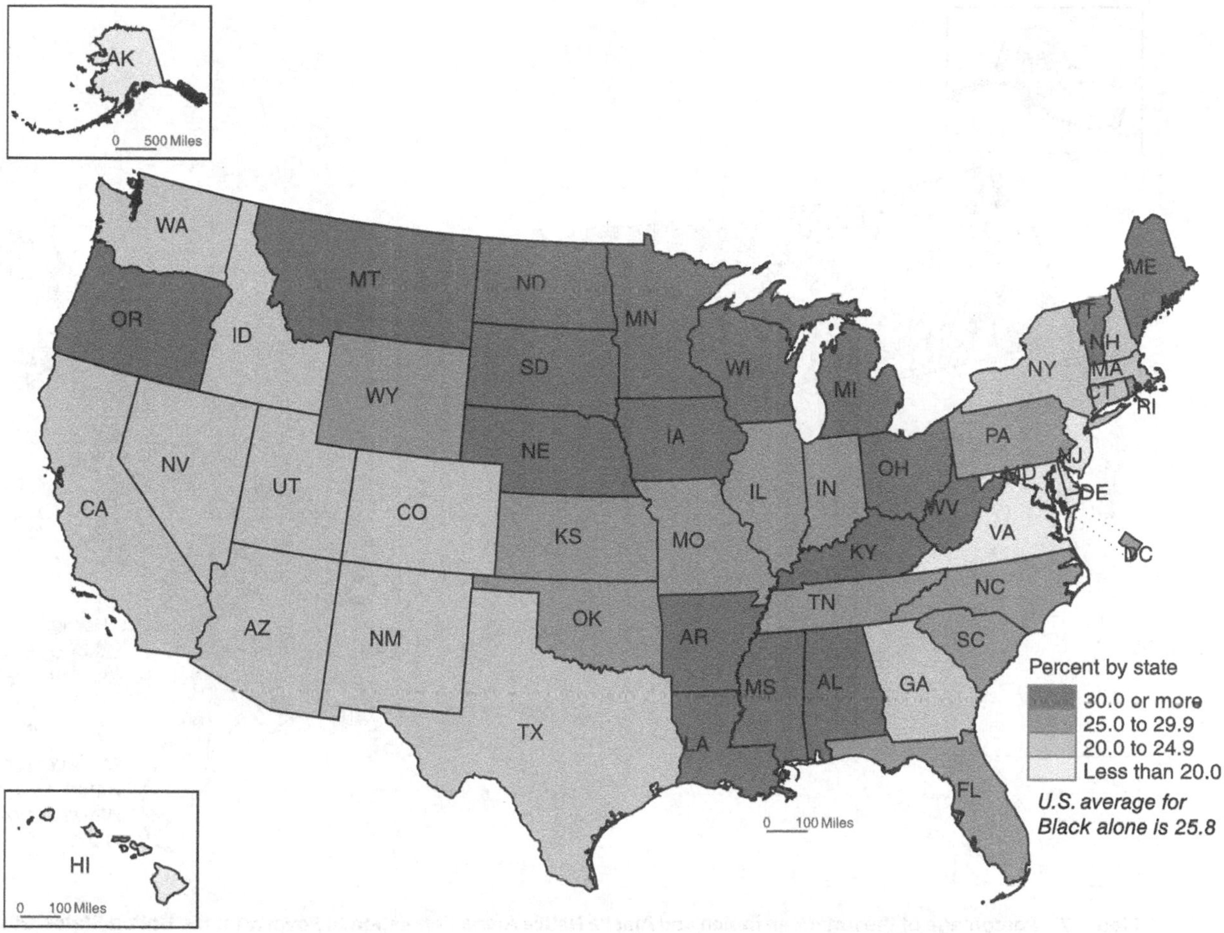

Figure 6. Percentage of the Black Alone Population in Poverty for the United States: 2007–2011
Source: U.S. Census Bureau, 2007–2011 American Community Survey.

American Indian and Alaska Native

Table 2 shows poverty rates for the American Indian and Alaska Native alone population. For American Indians and Alaska Natives, the poverty rates in Maryland (13.9 percent), New Hampshire (15.8 percent), and Virginia (13.8 percent) were among the lowest of any states.[7] By comparison, South Dakota (48.3 percent) had the highest poverty rate for this group. North Dakota was next at 41.6 percent.[8] Seven other states had poverty rates of about 30.0 percent or more (Arizona, Maine, Minnesota, Montana, Nebraska, New Mexico, and Utah) (Figure 7). Table 3 shows poverty rates for persons identified as American Indian and Alaska Native alone or in combination with one or more other races.[9]

Native Hawaiian and Other Pacific Islander

The 2007-20 ACS poverty rates for the Native Hawaiian and Other Pacific Islander alone population are shown in Table 4. Connecticut (7.0 percent), Illinois (8.6 percent), and New Hampshire (6.6 percent) were among the states with the lowest poverty rates for this group.[10] Poverty rates for Arkansas (41 .8 percent), Nebraska (50.8 percent), and Oklahoma (37.0 percent) were among the highest rates.[11] Table 5 shows poverty rates for persons identified as Native Hawaiian and Other Pacific Islander alone or in combination with one or more other races.

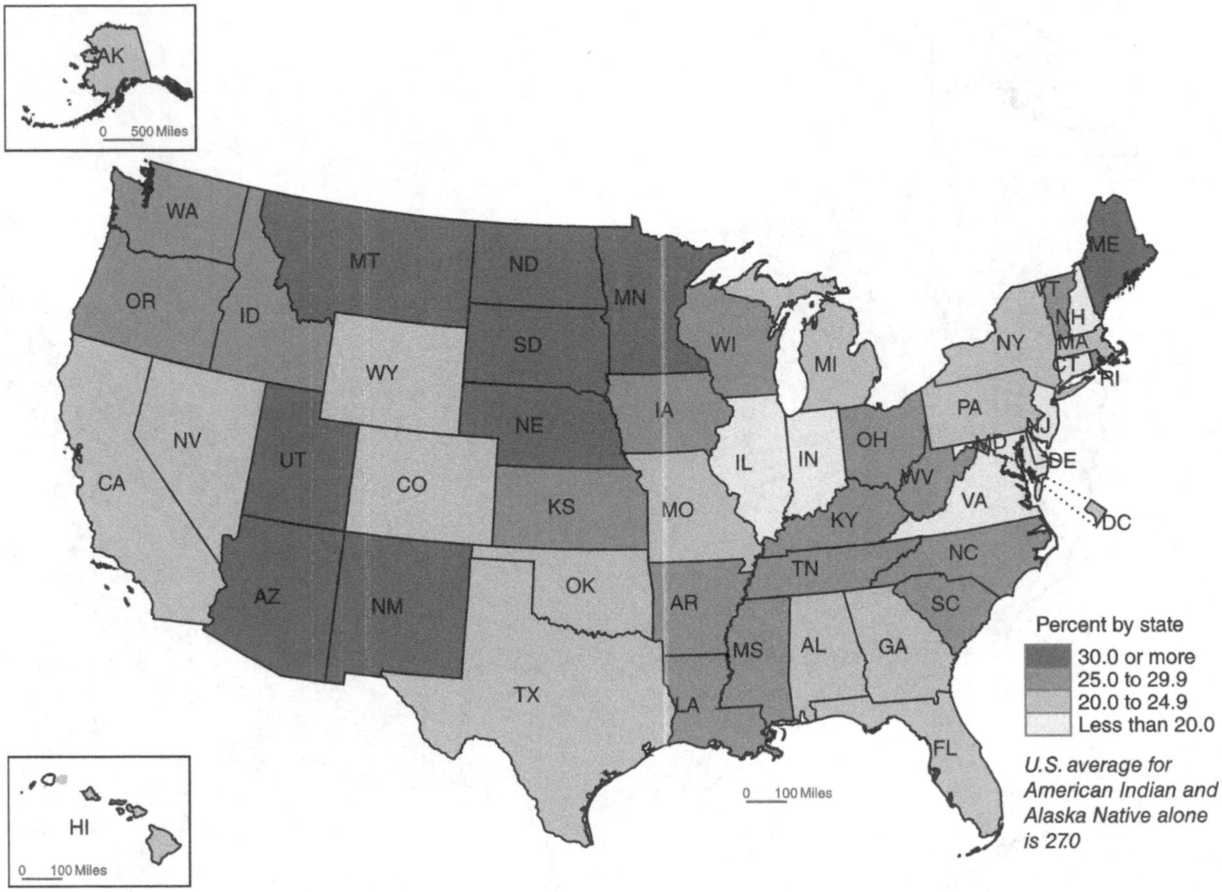

Figure 7 Percentage of the American Indian and Alaska Native Alone Population in Poverty for the United States: 2007–2011
Source: U.S. Census Bureau, 2007–2011 American Community Survey.

Asian

Table 6 shows that for the Asian alone population, Delaware (7.9 percent), Hawaii (6.4 percent), and New Jersey (6.8 percent) had some of the lowest state poverty rates for the 2007 to 2011 periodY Figure 8 shows six other states with poverty rates of about 10.0 percent or less for Asians (Connecticut, Maryland, New Hampshire, Nevada, South Carolina, and Virginia). By comparison, Idaho (19.7 percent), Indiana (19.2 percent), and North Dakota (22.3 percent) had some of the highest poverty rates.[13] Table 7 shows poverty rates for persons identified as Asian alone or in combination with one or more other races.

Hispanic or Latino

For the Hispanic or Latino population, Alaska (10.3 percent) had the lowest level of poverty during the 2007 to 2011 period while Kentucky (31.5 percent), Pennsylvania (31.6 percent), and

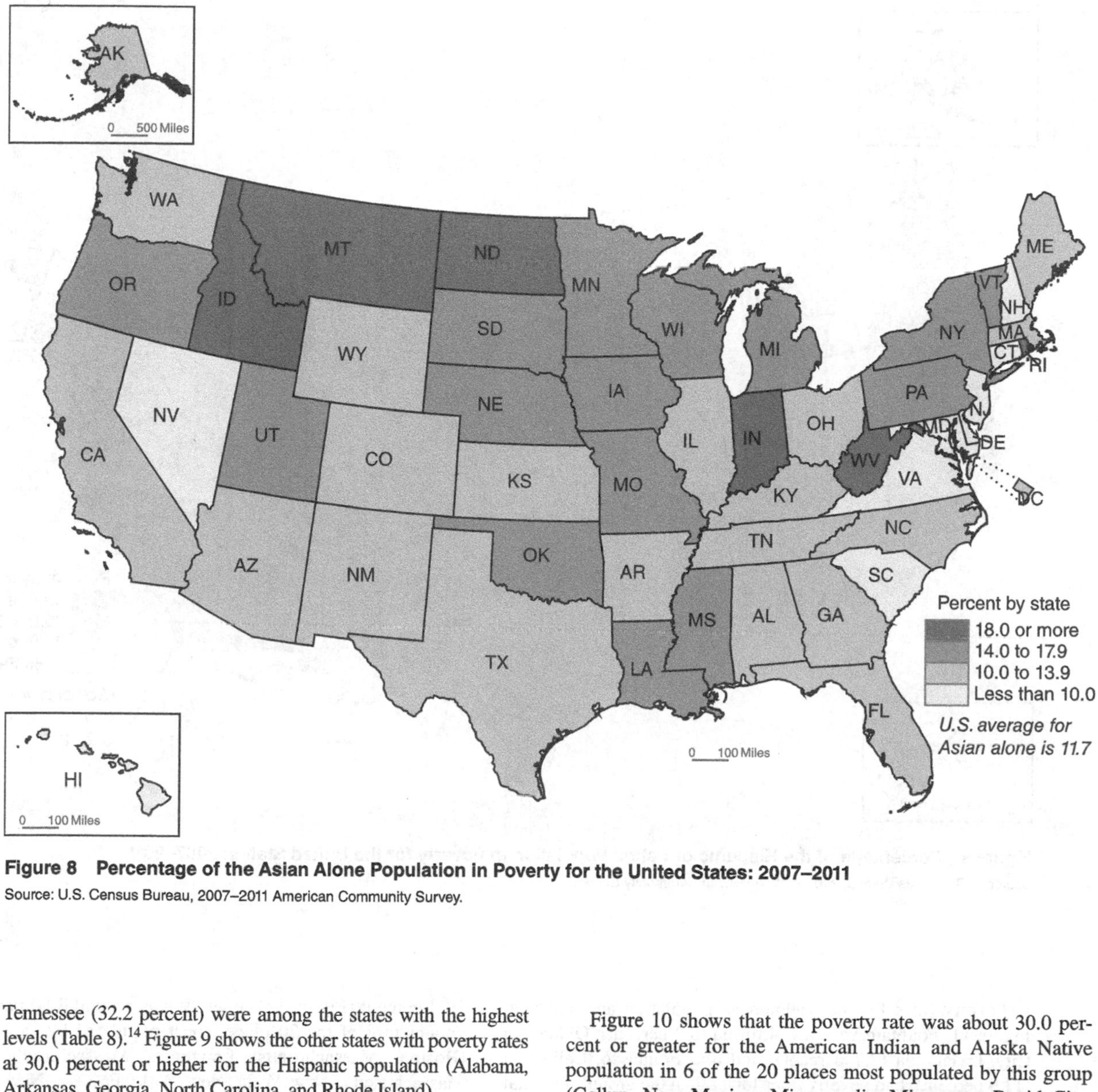

Figure 8 Percentage of the Asian Alone Population in Poverty for the United States: 2007–2011

Source: U.S. Census Bureau, 2007–2011 American Community Survey.

Tennessee (32.2 percent) were among the states with the highest levels (Table 8).[14] Figure 9 shows the other states with poverty rates at 30.0 percent or higher for the Hispanic population (Alabama, Arkansas, Georgia, North Carolina, and Rhode Island).

Cities

Poverty rates for selected detailed race and Hispanic groups by city or place are shown in Figures 10, 11, and 12.

Figure 10 shows that the poverty rate was about 30.0 percent or greater for the American Indian and Alaska Native population in 6 of the 20 places most populated by this group (Gallup, New Mexico; Minneapolis, Minnesota; Rapid City, South Dakota; Shiprock, New Mexico; Tucson, Arizona; and Zuni Pueblo, New Mexico). The poverty rate in Rapid City, South Dakota (50.9 percent) for American Indians and Alaska Natives was around three times the rate in Anchorage, Alaska (16.6 percent).

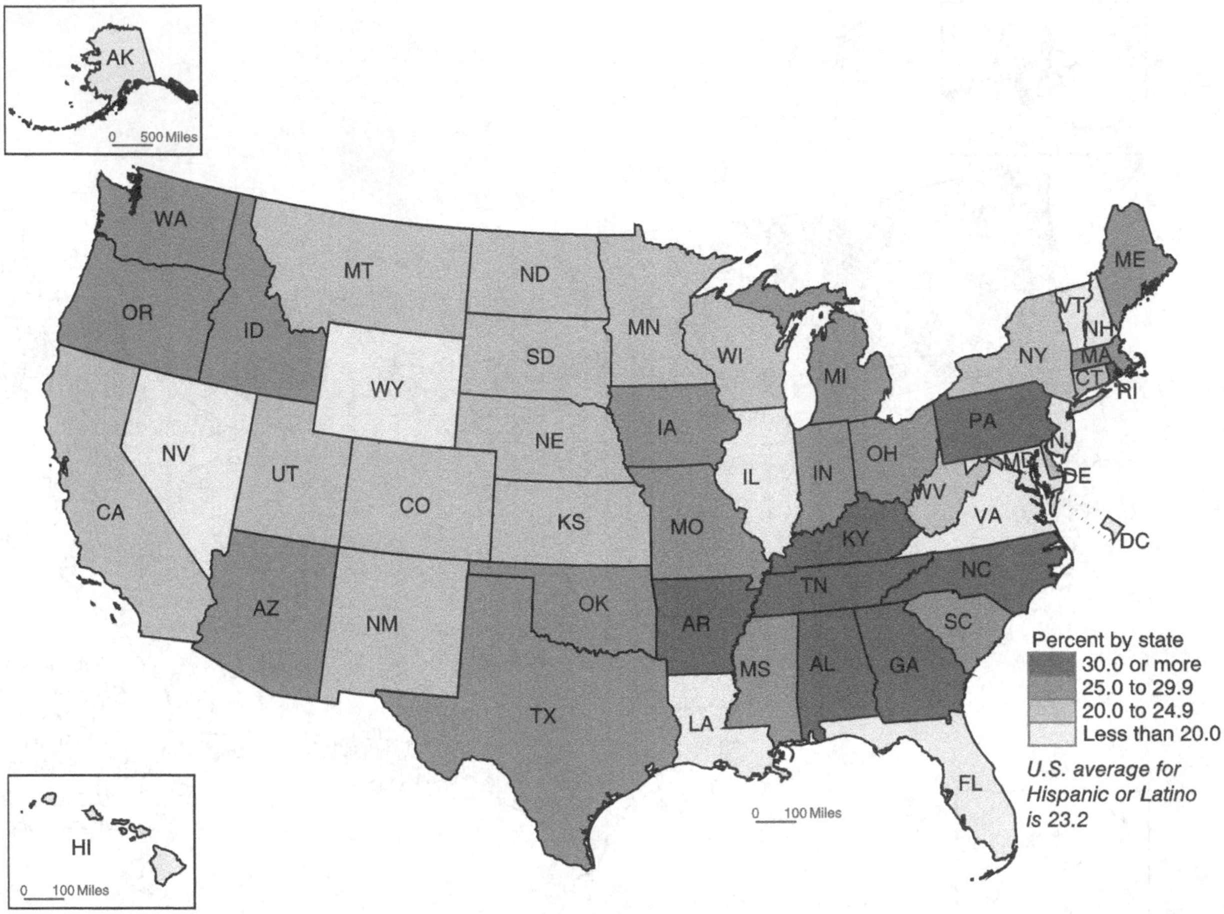

Figure 9 Percentage of the Hispanic or Latino Population in Poverty for the United States: 2007–2011
Source: U.S. Census Bureau, 2007–2011 American Community Survey.

Poverty rates for the Vietnamese population are shown in Figure 11. Fountain Valley, California (8.2 percent); Oklahoma City, Oklahoma (7.7 percent); and San Francisco, California (11.9 percent), had poverty rates lower than the group's national rate (14.7 percent). By comparison, the poverty rate for Vietnamese in Boston, Massachusetts (35.8 percent), was around three times the U.S. rate for this group.

In cities or places with large populations of Dominicans, poverty rates for this group ranged from 43.2 percent to 10.0 percent (Figure 12). Poverty was around 30.0 percent or greater in 8 of the 20 places most populated by Dominicans (Boston, Massachusetts; Lawrence, Massachusetts; Lynn, Massachusetts; New York, New York; Passaic, New Jersey; Philadelphia, Pennsylvania; Providence, Rhode Island; and Reading, Pennsylvania).

(For additional poverty rates by city or place for selected detailed race and Hispanic groups, please see the appendix tables.)

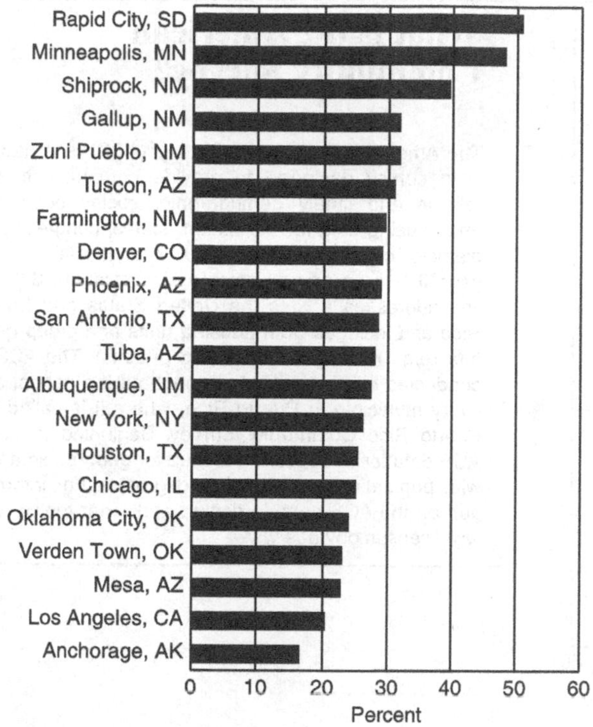

Figure 10. Poverty Rates for the American Indian and Alaska Native (AIAN) Alone Population in 20 U.S. Cities Most Populated by AIAN Alone: 2007–2011 (For information on confidentiality protection, sampling error, nonsampling error, and definitions, see www.census.gov/acs/www/)

Source: U.S. Census Bureau, 2007–2011 American Community Survey.

How Poverty Is Measured

Poverty status is determined by comparing annual income to a set of dollar values called poverty thresholds that vary by family size, number of children, and the age of the householder. If a family's before-tax money income is less than the dollar value of their threshold, then that family and every individual in it are considered to be in poverty. For people not living in families, poverty status is determined by comparing the individual's income to his or her poverty threshold.

The poverty thresholds are updated annually to allow for changes in the cost of living using the Consumer Price Index (CPI-U). They do not vary geographically.

The ACS is a continuous survey and people respond throughout the year. Since income is reported for the previous 12 months, the appropriate poverty threshold for each family is determined by multiplying the base-year poverty threshold (1982) by the average of monthly CPI-U values for the 12 months preceding the survey month.

For more information see "ACS Poverty Definition" and "How Poverty is Calculated in the ACS" at www/census.gov/hhes/www/poverty/methods/definitions.html.

Figure 11. Poverty Rates for the Vietnamese Alone Population in the 20 U.S. Cities Most Populated by Vietnamese Alone: 2007–2011 (For information on confidentiality protection, sampling error, nonsampling error, and definitions, see www.census.gov/acs/www/)

Note: To illustrate the data available in the appendix tables of this report, selected groups with comparatively higher rates of poverty and geographic dispersion are highlighted in these figures.

Persons who report only one race among the six defined categories are referred to as the race-alone population, while persons who report more than one race category are referred to as the Two or More Races population. This figure shows data using the race-alone approach. Use of the single-race population does not imply that it is the preferred method of presenting or analyzing data. The Census Bureau uses a variety of approaches.

Source: U.S. Census Bureau, 2007–2011 American Community Survey.

What Is the American Community Survey?

The American Community Survey (ACS) is a nationwide survey designed to provide communities with reliable and timely demographic, social, economic, and housing data for the nation, states, congressional districts, counties, places, and other localities every year. It has an annual sample size of about 3.3 million addresses across the United States and Puerto Rico and includes both housing units and group quarters (e.g., nursing facilities and prisons). The ACS is conducted in every county throughout the nation, and every municipio in Puerto Rico, where it is called the Puerto Rico Community Survey. Beginning in 2006, ACS data for 2005 were released for geographic areas with populations of 65,000 and greater. For information on the ACS sample design and other topics, visit www.census.gov/acs/www.

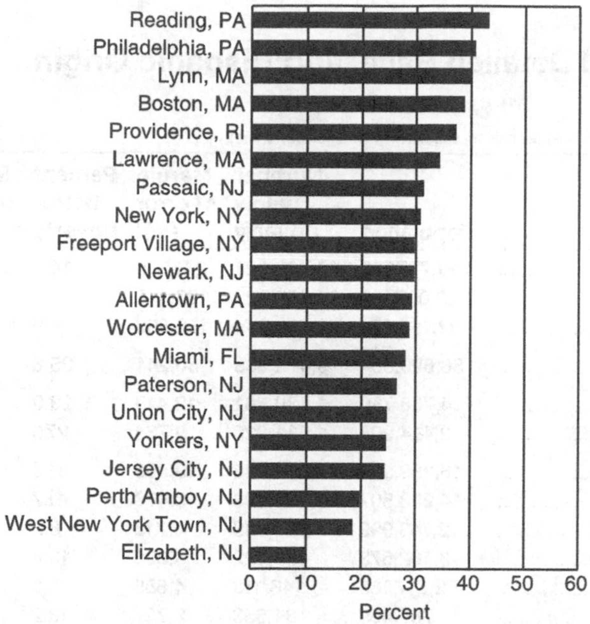

Figure 12. Poverty Rates for the Dominican Population in the 20 U.S. Cities Most Populated by Dominicans: 2007–2011 (For information on confidentiality protection, sampling error, nonsampling error, and definitions, see www.census.gov/acs/www/)

Note: To illustrate the data available in the appendix tables of this report, selected groups with comparatively higher rates of poverty and geographic dispersion are highlighted in these figures.

Source: U.S. Census Bureau, 2007–2011 American Community Survey.

Source and Accuracy

The data presented in this report are based on the ACS sample interviewed between 2007 and 2011. The estimates based on this sample approximate the actual values and represent the entire household and group quarters population. Sampling error is the difference between an estimate based on a sample and the corresponding value that would be obtained if the estimate were based on the entire population (as from a census). Measures of the sampling errors are provided in the form of margins of error for all estimates included in this report. All comparative statements in this report have undergone statistical testing, and comparisons are significant at the 90 percent level unless otherwise noted. In addition to sampling error, nonsampling error may be introduced during any of the operations used to collect and process survey data such as editing, reviewing, or keying data from questionnaires. For more information on sampling and estimation methods, confidentiality protection, and sampling and nonsampling errors, please see the 2011 ACS Accuracy of the Data document located at www.census.gov/acs/www/Downloads/data_documentation/Accuracy/ACS_Accuracy_of_Data_2011.pdf.

Table 1
U.S. Poverty Rates by Race, Selected Detailed Race, and Hispanic Origin Groups: 2007–2011[1,2]

(For information on confidentiality protection, sampling error, nonsampling error, and definitions, see www.census.gov/acs/www/)

Race and Hispanic or Latino origin	Population	Number below poverty	Margin of error (±)[3]	Percent below poverty	Margin of error (±)[3]
Total	**298,787,989**	**42,739,924**	**277,336**	**14.3**	**0.1**
White alone	222,007,105	25,659,922	193,148	11.6	0.1
White alone, non-Hispanic	192,160,374	18,959,814	152,602	9.9	0.1
Black or African American alone	36,699,584	9,472,583	50,241	25.8	0.1
American Indian and Alaska Native alone or in combination	4,738,750	1,130,661	12,413	23.9	0.3
American Indian and Alaska Native alone	2,414,908	651,226	9,734	27.0	0.4
Asian alone or in combination	16,389,524	1,899,448	19,805	11.6	0.1
Asian alone	14,223,507	1,663,303	19,470	11.7	0.1
Asian Indian	2,743,999	224,343	7,718	8.2	0.3
Chinese	3,162,573	424,322	7,305	13.4	0.2
Filipino	2,517,885	146,113	4,685	5.8	0.2
Japanese	782,469	64,553	2,727	8.2	0.3
Korean	1,378,830	206,241	5,340	15.0	0.3
Vietnamese	1,554,143	228,381	6,674	14.7	0.4
Native Hawaiian and Other Pacific Islander alone or in combination	992,614	156,717	5,039	15.8	0.5
Native Hawaiian and Other Pacific Islander alone	485,892	85,346	3,634	17.6	0.7
Native Hawaiian	151,905	21,937	1,485	14.4	1.0
Samoan	99,860	17,606	1,616	17.6	1.6
Tongan	39,893	7,221	1,421	18.1	3.0
Guamanian or Chamorro	70,669	8,197	1,007	11.6	1.4
Fijians	27,158	1,738	488	6.4	1.8
Other Pacific Islander[4]	96,407	28,647	2,643	29.7	2.3
Some Other Race alone	15,393,344	3,792,156	47,496	24.6	0.2
Two or More Races	7,563,658	1,415,388	13,717	18.7	0.2
Hispanic origin	48,190,992	11,197,648	77,014	23.2	0.2
Mexican	31,157,323	7,744,050	65,971	24.9	0.2
Guatemalan	1,054,350	262,575	7,506	24.9	0.6
Salvadoran	1,708,491	323,317	8,870	18.9	0.5
Cuban	1,727,550	279,011	5,969	16.2	0.4
Dominican	1,387,724	364,523	6,591	26.3	0.5
Puerto Rican	4,466,054	1,142,216	13,907	25.6	0.3

[1]Poverty status is determined for individuals in housing units and noninstitutional group quarters. The poverty universe excludes children under age 15 who are not related to the householder, people living in institutional group quarters, and people living in college dormitories or military barracks.

[2]The Census Bureau does not advocate the use of the alone population over the alone-or-in-combination population or vice versa. The use of the alone population in sections of this brief does not imply that it is the preferred method of presenting or analyzing data. Data on race from the American Community Survey can be presented and discussed in a variety of ways. Hispanics and Latinos may be of any race. For more information see the 2010 Census Brief, Overview of Race and Hispanic Origin, at www.census.gov/prod/cen2010/briefs/c2010br-02.pdf.

[3]Data are based on a sample and are subject to sampling variability. A margin of error is a measure of an estimate's variability. The larger the margin of error in relation to the size of the estimate, the less reliable the estimate. This number when added to or subtracted from the estimate forms the 90 percent confidence interval.

[4]Includes Other Micronesian (25,000), Other Pacific Islander not specified (17,000), Marshallese (17,000), Other Native Hawaiian (8,000), Other Pacific Islander (7,000), Palauan (6,000), Other Polynesian (5,000), Chuukese (2,000), Pohnpeian (1,000), Tahitian (1,000), and other detailed groups.

Source: U.S. Census Bureau, 2007–2011 American Community Survey.

Table 2
Poverty Rates for the American Indian and Alaska Native Alone Population by State: 2007–2011[1]

(For information on confidentiality protection, sampling error, nonsampling error, and definitions, see www.census.gov/acs/www/)

State	American Indian and Alaska Native alone[2]				
	Population	Number below poverty	Margin of error (±)[3]	Percent below poverty	Margin of error (±)[3]
United States	**2,414,908**	**651,226**	**9,734**	**27.0**	**0.4**
Alabama	25,905	5,746	1,049	22.2	3.4
Alaska	94,670	19,896	918	21.0	0.9
Arizona	272,710	95,654	3,469	35.1	1.3
Arkansas	16,962	4,242	551	25.0	2.7
California	277,564	60,743	3,014	21.9	1.0
Colorado	45,497	10,775	1,219	23.7	2.4
Connecticut	7,578	1,504	386	19.8	4.3
Delaware	3,076	588	260	19.1	7.6
District of Columbia	1,711	370	155	21.6	8.8
Florida	56,251	13,118	1,264	23.3	2.0
Georgia	23,011	5,410	823	23.5	3.3
Hawaii	2,807	585	210	20.8	7.0
Idaho	18,627	4,947	681	26.6	3.1
Illinois	24,269	4,448	495	18.3	2.1
Indiana	14,173	2,519	349	17.8	2.2
Iowa	9,122	2,351	357	25.8	3.1
Kansas	22,097	5,606	728	25.4	2.8
Kentucky	8,489	2,147	418	25.3	4.3
Louisiana	27,618	7,263	1,013	26.3	3.2
Maine	6,814	2,257	294	33.1	4.1
Maryland	15,985	2,222	475	13.9	2.5
Massachusetts	11,665	2,789	560	23.9	3.9
Michigan	52,770	13,128	1,017	24.9	1.8
Minnesota	54,191	20,795	1,174	38.4	1.9
Mississippi	13,488	3,437	750	25.5	5.5
Missouri	21,535	4,804	580	22.3	2.4
Montana	59,102	21,469	1,497	36.3	2.4
Nebraska	15,074	5,738	665	38.1	3.9
Nevada	28,633	5,883	657	20.5	2.0
New Hampshire	2,530	399	154	15.8	5.7
New Jersey	19,998	3,365	742	16.8	3.1
New Mexico	183,672	57,585	2,904	31.4	1.5
New York	65,396	15,955	1,531	24.4	2.1
North Carolina	106,000	29,526	2,031	27.9	1.8
North Dakota	34,151	14,195	896	41.6	2.5
Ohio	20,331	5,679	605	27.9	2.7
Oklahoma	251,022	55,559	2,064	22.1	0.8
Oregon	55,341	15,874	1,664	28.7	2.5
Pennsylvania	17,196	3,996	489	23.2	2.7
Rhode Island	4,396	1,307	482	29.7	9.2
South Carolina	14,394	3,737	571	26.0	3.5
South Dakota	65,779	31,792	1,563	48.3	2.3
Tennessee	14,836	4,264	814	28.7	4.4
Texas	120,664	24,476	1,678	20.3	1.2
Utah	29,570	9,366	995	31.7	3.0
Vermont	1,722	435	153	25.3	8.0
Virginia	24,342	3,370	608	13.8	2.0
Washington	90,775	23,342	1,654	25.7	1.6
West Virginia	2,749	756	214	27.5	6.7
Wisconsin	46,330	13,071	956	28.2	1.9
Wyoming	12,320	2,743	595	22.3	4.6

[1] Poverty status is determined for individuals in housing units and noninstitutional group quarters. The poverty universe excludes children under age 15 who are not related to the householder, people living in institutional group quarters, and people living in college dormitories or military barracks.

[2] Persons who report only one race among the six defined categories are referred to as the race-alone population, while persons who report more than one race category are referred to as the Two or More Races population. This table shows data using the race-alone approach. Use of the single-race population does not imply that it is the preferred method of presenting or analyzing data. The Census Bureau uses a variety of approaches.

[3] Data are based on a sample and are subject to sampling variability. A margin of error is a measure of an estimate's variability. The larger the margin of error in relation to the size of the estimate, the less reliable the estimate. This number when added to or subtracted from the estimate forms the 90 percent confidence interval.

Source: U.S. Census Bureau, 2007–2011 American Community Survey.

Table 3
Poverty Rates for the American Indian and Alaska Native Alone or in Combination Population by State: 2007–2011[1]

(For information on confidentiality protection, sampling error, nonsampling error, and definitions, see www.census.gov/acs/www/)

	American Indian and Alaska Native alone or in combination[2]				
State	Population	Number below poverty	Margin of error (±)[3]	Percent below poverty	Margin of error (±)[3]
United States	**4,738,750**	**1,130,661**	**12,413**	**23.9**	**0.3**
Alabama	56,295	12,919	1,310	22.9	2.2
Alaska	131,007	24,959	1,090	19.1	0.8
Arizona	323,816	107,026	3,906	33.1	1.1
Arkansas	45,783	11,447	903	25.0	1.9
California	630,094	122,663	4,458	19.5	0.6
Colorado	98,741	21,175	1,479	21.4	1.4
Connecticut	27,868	3,989	691	14.3	2.4
Delaware	8,276	1,366	414	16.5	4.7
District of Columbia	4,587	977	248	21.3	5.2
Florida	142,232	29,727	2,017	20.9	1.3
Georgia	65,927	12,979	1,457	19.7	2.0
Hawaii	31,673	5,987	1,051	18.9	2.9
Idaho	34,867	9,136	838	26.2	2.3
Illinois	74,187	13,959	1,072	18.8	1.4
Indiana	52,897	10,526	742	19.9	1.3
Iowa	26,040	8,022	806	30.8	2.5
Kansas	58,099	13,650	988	23.5	1.5
Kentucky	29,163	8,488	951	29.1	2.7
Louisiana	52,740	13,021	1,345	24.7	2.3
Maine	18,940	5,659	467	29.9	2.4
Maryland	51,675	7,503	1,334	14.5	2.4
Massachusetts	40,200	8,413	873	20.9	2.0
Michigan	133,069	32,588	1,739	24.5	1.1
Minnesota	93,419	30,553	1,423	32.7	1.5
Mississippi	26,625	6,233	968	23.4	3.3
Missouri	76,974	17,971	1,499	23.3	1.6
Montana	73,585	25,096	1,512	34.1	2.0
Nebraska	30,471	10,528	1,105	34.6	3.0
Nevada	49,984	9,812	902	19.6	1.6
New Hampshire	9,565	1,270	270	13.3	2.7
New Jersey	57,876	8,615	1,235	14.9	1.9
New Mexico	208,247	63,107	3,157	30.3	1.4
New York	154,839	34,498	2,040	22.3	1.1
North Carolina	169,155	45,587	2,210	26.9	1.2
North Dakota	39,848	15,384	876	38.6	2.2
Ohio	87,119	24,136	1,604	27.7	1.6
Oklahoma	466,618	101,415	3,284	21.7	0.7
Oregon	111,593	29,403	1,966	26.3	1.4
Pennsylvania	67,249	15,209	1,183	22.6	1.7
Rhode Island	11,718	2,985	602	25.5	5.0
South Carolina	36,831	8,586	807	23.3	1.9
South Dakota	76,671	34,623	1,498	45.2	2.0
Tennessee	54,978	13,496	1,226	24.5	2.0
Texas	272,544	49,386	2,358	18.1	0.8
Utah	44,921	12,106	1,169	26.9	2.4
Vermont	7,029	1,301	212	18.5	3.0
Virginia	69,782	9,834	1,017	14.1	1.3
Washington	184,571	42,025	1,882	22.8	1.0
West Virginia	18,379	5,390	619	29.3	2.8
Wisconsin	79,938	21,746	1,129	27.2	1.3
Wyoming	20,045	4,187	695	20.9	3.5

[1]Poverty status is determined for individuals in housing units and noninstitutional group quarters. The poverty universe excludes children under age 15 who are not related to the householder, people living in institutional group quarters, and people living in college dormitories or military barracks.

[2]Persons who report only one race among the six defined categories are referred to as the race-alone population, while persons who report more than one race category are referred to as the Two or More Races population. This table shows data using the race-alone-or-in-combination approach. The race alone-or-in-combination population is the total number of people who reported a particular race, whether or not they reported any other races. Use of this approach does not imply that it is the preferred method of presenting or analyzing data. The Census Bureau uses a variety of approaches.

[3]Data are based on a sample and are subject to sampling variability. A margin of error is a measure of an estimate's variability. The larger the margin of error in relation to the size of the estimate, the less reliable the estimate. This number when added to or subtracted from the estimate forms the 90 percent confidence interval.

Source: U.S. Census Bureau, 2007–2011 American Community Survey.

Table 4
Poverty Rates for the Native Hawaiian and Other Pacific Islander Alone Population by State: 2007–2011[1]

(For information on confidentiality protection, sampling error, nonsampling error, and definitions, see www.census.gov/acs/www/)

	Native Hawaiian and Other Pacific Islander alone[2]				
State	Population	Number below poverty	Margin of error (±)[3]	Percent below poverty	Margin of error (±)[3]
United States	**485,892**	**85,346**	**3,634**	**17.6**	**0.7**
Alabama	1,210	230	116	19.0	8.2
Alaska	6,677	1,183	490	17.7	7.4
Arizona	10,827	2,041	625	18.9	5.6
Arkansas	4,960	2,071	539	41.8	10.8
California	138,273	18,221	1,831	13.2	1.3
Colorado	5,492	893	444	16.3	8.0
Connecticut	1,268	89	105	7.0	7.8
Delaware	(NA)	(NA)	(NA)	(NA)	(NA)
District of Columbia	(NA)	(NA)	(NA)	(NA)	(NA)
Florida	10,619	1,604	457	15.1	4.1
Georgia	4,294	1,120	334	26.1	7.6
Hawaii	126,799	24,213	1,993	19.1	1.5
Idaho	2,413	352	181	14.6	7.5
Illinois	3,090	265	138	8.6	4.4
Indiana	1,197	299	169	25.0	11.9
Iowa	986	357	196	36.2	14.1
Kansas	1,550	190	101	12.3	5.7
Kentucky	2,274	490	319	21.5	11.9
Louisiana	1,644	421	324	25.6	16.0
Maine	296	81	66	27.4	18.0
Maryland	2,417	265	143	11.0	5.1
Massachusetts	1,471	305	189	20.7	12.0
Michigan	2,461	586	270	23.8	9.1
Minnesota	2,088	379	154	18.2	7.3
Mississippi	557	90	67	16.2	14.2
Missouri	5,491	941	395	17.1	7.0
Montana	571	119	92	20.8	11.8
Nebraska	1,121	569	195	50.8	14.5
Nevada	16,112	2,924	819	18.1	4.9
New Hampshire	288	19	16	6.6	7.5
New Jersey	1,959	261	168	13.3	8.3
New Mexico	1,105	247	153	22.4	12.5
New York	6,347	1,160	390	18.3	6.6
North Carolina	4,429	445	211	10.0	4.5
North Dakota	340	59	50	17.4	14.0
Ohio	2,035	303	148	14.9	6.9
Oklahoma	4,151	1,536	472	37.0	10.1
Oregon	13,111	4,119	767	31.4	5.0
Pennsylvania	2,513	609	214	24.2	6.8
Rhode Island	436	163	117	37.4	27.0
South Carolina	1,802	332	226	18.4	11.4
South Dakota	(NA)	(NA)	(NA)	(NA)	(NA)
Tennessee	3,054	395	246	12.9	7.8
Texas	19,121	3,195	677	16.7	3.4
Utah	24,705	4,767	1,061	19.3	4.3
Vermont	(NA)	(NA)	(NA)	(NA)	(NA)
Virginia	4,981	619	229	12.4	4.1
Washington	36,379	6,568	1,050	18.1	2.8
West Virginia	(NA)	(NA)	(NA)	(NA)	(NA)
Wisconsin	1,435	216	97	15.1	6.7
Wyoming	158	26	30	16.5	17.3

(NA) Not available. Data cannot be displayed because the number of sample cases is too small.

[1]Poverty status is determined for individuals in housing units and noninstitutional group quarters. The poverty universe excludes children under age 15 who are not related to the householder, people living in institutional group quarters, and people living in college dormitories or military barracks.

[2]Persons who report only one race among the six defined categories are referred to as the race-alone population, while persons who report more than one race category are referred to as the Two or More Races population. This table shows data using the race-alone approach. Use of the single-race population does not imply that it is the preferred method of presenting or analyzing data. The Census Bureau uses a variety of approaches.

[3]Data are based on a sample and are subject to sampling variability. A margin of error is a measure of an estimate's variability. The larger the margin of error in relation to the size of the estimate, the less reliable the estimate. This number when added to or subtracted from the estimate forms the 90 percent confidence interval.

Source: U.S. Census Bureau, 2007–2011 American Community Survey.

Table 5
Poverty Rates for the Native Hawaiian and Other Pacific Islander Alone or in Combination Population by State: 2007–2011[1]

(For information on confidentiality protection, sampling error, nonsampling error, and definitions, see www.census.gov/acs/www/)

	Native Hawaiian and Other Pacific Islander alone or in combination[2]				
State	Population	Number below poverty	Margin of error (±)[3]	Percent below poverty	Margin of error (±)[3]
United States	**992,614**	**156,717**	**5,039**	**15.8**	**0.5**
Alabama	2,746	538	184	19.6	5.6
Alaska	9,797	1,793	581	18.3	5.5
Arizona	20,234	3,107	675	15.4	3.2
Arkansas	6,041	2,312	551	38.3	9.2
California	240,453	29,709	2,156	12.4	0.9
Colorado	12,003	1,670	496	13.9	3.9
Connecticut	2,767	279	185	10.1	6.1
Delaware	1,005	53	55	5.3	5.4
District of Columbia	(NA)	(NA)	(NA)	(NA)	(NA)
Florida	23,077	3,419	733	14.8	3.1
Georgia	8,508	2,038	509	24.0	5.6
Hawaii	331,970	52,044	2,977	15.7	0.9
Idaho	4,845	966	357	19.9	6.9
Illinois	8,523	782	306	9.2	3.5
Indiana	3,368	668	270	19.8	7.2
Iowa	2,525	623	254	24.7	9.1
Kansas	3,102	435	182	14.0	5.8
Kentucky	3,536	865	312	24.5	7.5
Louisiana	2,994	806	367	26.9	9.8
Maine	786	119	91	15.1	10.2
Maryland	5,738	737	286	12.8	4.1
Massachusetts	4,491	828	266	18.4	5.8
Michigan	6,657	1,379	361	20.7	4.7
Minnesota	5,342	931	275	17.4	5.0
Mississippi	1,110	217	128	19.5	9.6
Missouri	8,800	1,357	447	15.4	5.0
Montana	1,602	373	186	23.3	10.0
Nebraska	1,874	713	216	38.0	10.7
Nevada	30,228	4,700	952	15.5	3.3
New Hampshire	939	78	73	8.3	8.3
New Jersey	6,531	1,151	416	17.6	5.8
New Mexico	2,508	472	223	18.8	8.3
New York	13,842	2,307	546	16.7	4.0
North Carolina	10,071	1,951	514	19.4	4.1
North Dakota	826	112	78	13.6	8.6
Ohio	6,551	1,185	355	18.1	5.0
Oklahoma	7,793	2,402	583	30.8	7.3
Oregon	23,492	6,227	967	26.5	3.8
Pennsylvania	6,713	1,357	365	20.2	4.9
Rhode Island	1,116	339	176	30.4	16.4
South Carolina	3,764	860	534	22.8	11.3
South Dakota	(NA)	(NA)	(NA)	(NA)	(NA)
Tennessee	5,538	800	307	14.4	5.6
Texas	33,684	5,665	755	16.8	2.2
Utah	33,825	6,390	1,197	18.9	3.5
Vermont	(NA)	(NA)	(NA)	(NA)	(NA)
Virginia	12,080	1,412	405	11.7	3.0
Washington	62,461	9,642	1,193	15.4	1.9
West Virginia	936	183	122	19.6	12.1
Wisconsin	3,730	558	181	15.0	4.6
Wyoming	539	66	67	12.2	12.0

(NA) Not available. Data cannot be displayed because the number of sample cases is too small.

[1]Poverty status is determined for individuals in housing units and noninstitutional group quarters. The poverty universe excludes children under age 15 who are not related to the householder, people living in institutional group quarters, and people living in college dormitories or military barracks.

[2]Persons who report only one race among the six defined categories are referred to as the race-alone population, while persons who report more than one race category are referred to as the Two or More Races population. This table shows data using the race-alone-or-in-combination approach. The race alone-or-in-combination population is the total number of people who reported a particular race, whether or not they reported any other races. Use of this approach does not imply that it is the preferred method of presenting or analyzing data. The Census Bureau uses a variety of approaches.

[3]Data are based on a sample and are subject to sampling variability. A margin of error is a measure of an estimate's variability. The larger the margin of error in relation to the size of the estimate, the less reliable the estimate. This number when added to or subtracted from the estimate forms the 90 percent confidence interval.

Source: U.S. Census Bureau, 2007–2011 American Community Survey.

Table 6
Poverty Rates for the Asian Alone Population by State: 2007–2011[1]

(For information on confidentiality protection, sampling error, nonsampling error, and definitions, see www.census.gov/acs/www/)

State	Asian alone[2]				
	Population	Number below poverty	Margin of error (±)[3]	Percent below poverty	Margin of error (±)[3]
United States	**14,223,507**	**1,663,303**	**19,470**	**11.7**	**0.1**
Alabama	51,579	6,752	913	13.1	1.8
Alaska	35,533	3,606	820	10.1	2.3
Arizona	169,293	21,147	1,895	12.5	1.1
Arkansas	34,273	4,316	715	12.6	2.0
California	4,758,104	521,442	9,163	11.0	0.2
Colorado	131,648	13,680	1,268	10.4	0.9
Connecticut	128,737	10,020	1,245	7.8	0.9
Delaware	28,433	2,238	536	7.9	1.9
District of Columbia	19,143	2,671	436	14.0	2.2
Florida	449,557	53,911	3,097	12.0	0.7
Georgia	301,347	34,804	2,569	11.5	0.8
Hawaii	515,593	33,153	1,727	6.4	0.3
Idaho	18,300	3,607	742	19.7	3.9
Illinois	571,519	60,800	3,011	10.6	0.5
Indiana	94,842	18,172	1,374	19.2	1.4
Iowa	50,461	7,126	778	14.1	1.5
Kansas	65,265	9,076	1,154	13.9	1.7
Kentucky	46,559	6,087	879	13.1	1.8
Louisiana	68,009	10,949	1,077	16.1	1.6
Maine	13,154	1,621	404	12.3	3.1
Maryland	307,872	22,761	1,774	7.4	0.6
Massachusetts	330,917	45,624	2,456	13.8	0.7
Michigan	237,499	33,233	2,052	14.0	0.8
Minnesota	203,691	34,965	2,229	17.2	1.1
Mississippi	24,891	4,379	847	17.6	3.3
Missouri	89,889	13,455	1,123	15.0	1.2
Montana	5,731	1,085	294	18.9	4.9
Nebraska	29,669	4,222	676	14.2	2.2
Nevada	189,126	15,835	1,612	8.4	0.8
New Hampshire	26,703	2,514	567	9.4	2.1
New Jersey	705,933	48,140	2,948	6.8	0.4
New Mexico	26,739	3,391	670	12.7	2.5
New York	1,383,969	229,552	5,208	16.6	0.4
North Carolina	197,435	25,447	1,870	12.9	0.9
North Dakota	6,247	1,394	246	22.3	3.9
Ohio	185,506	22,400	1,552	12.1	0.8
Oklahoma	61,837	8,972	897	14.5	1.4
Oregon	136,765	20,259	1,473	14.8	1.1
Pennsylvania	329,095	48,723	2,410	14.8	0.7
Rhode Island	29,347	5,563	1,010	19.0	3.4
South Carolina	54,679	4,798	660	8.8	1.2
South Dakota	7,307	1,048	369	14.3	5.0
Tennessee	88,464	10,202	1,072	11.5	1.2
Texas	928,236	109,895	3,840	11.8	0.4
Utah	53,973	9,508	1,181	17.6	2.1
Vermont	6,989	1,267	358	18.1	4.9
Virginia	422,299	34,165	2,354	8.1	0.5
Washington	463,863	51,854	2,641	11.2	0.6
West Virginia	11,159	1,932	369	17.3	3.3
Wisconsin	122,474	21,082	1,549	17.2	1.3
Wyoming	3,854	460	158	11.9	4.0

[1]Poverty status is determined for individuals in housing units and noninstitutional group quarters. The poverty universe excludes children under age 15 who are not related to the householder, people living in institutional group quarters, and people living in college dormitories or military barracks.

[2]Persons who report only one race among the six defined categories are referred to as the race-alone population, while persons who report more than one race category are referred to as the Two or More Races population. This table shows data using the race-alone approach. Use of the single-race population does not imply that it is the preferred method of presenting or analyzing data. The Census Bureau uses a variety of approaches.

[3]Data are based on a sample and are subject to sampling variability. A margin of error is a measure of an estimate's variability. The larger the margin of error in relation to the size of the estimate, the less reliable the estimate. This number when added to or subtracted from the estimate forms the 90 percent confidence interval.

Source: U.S. Census Bureau, 2007–2011 American Community Survey.

Table 7
overty Rates for the Asian Alone or in Combination Population by State: 2007–2011[1]

(For information on confidentiality protection, sampling error, nonsampling error, and definitions, see www.census.gov/acs/www/)

State	Asian alone or in combination[2]				
	Population	Number below poverty	Margin of error (±)[3]	Percent below poverty	Margin of error (±)[3]
United States	**16,389,524**	**1,899,448**	**19,805**	**11.6**	**0.1**
Alabama	62,319	8,281	964	13.3	1.5
Alaska	46,317	4,663	949	10.1	2.0
Arizona	214,481	26,481	2,100	12.3	1.0
Arkansas	40,761	5,567	920	13.7	2.1
California	5,321,945	575,061	9,712	10.8	0.2
Colorado	174,187	18,548	1,612	10.6	0.9
Connecticut	144,994	11,309	1,297	7.8	0.9
Delaware	32,567	2,564	559	7.9	1.7
District of Columbia	23,182	3,107	447	13.4	1.8
Florida	544,305	63,704	3,332	11.7	0.6
Georgia	339,803	39,355	2,744	11.6	0.8
Hawaii	757,432	59,509	2,805	7.9	0.4
Idaho	27,498	5,515	810	20.1	2.8
Illinois	635,049	67,473	3,267	10.6	0.5
Indiana	114,356	21,148	1,526	18.5	1.3
Iowa	59,364	8,684	840	14.6	1.4
Kansas	77,992	10,823	1,211	13.9	1.5
Kentucky	56,810	7,822	1,036	13.8	1.8
Louisiana	78,678	12,539	1,184	15.9	1.5
Maine	16,947	2,107	456	12.4	2.7
Maryland	351,143	25,454	1,920	7.2	0.5
Massachusetts	365,383	49,109	2,572	13.4	0.7
Michigan	276,666	39,319	2,199	14.2	0.8
Minnesota	232,548	37,814	2,284	16.3	1.0
Mississippi	28,942	5,089	842	17.6	2.9
Missouri	113,583	17,500	1,286	15.4	1.1
Montana	10,019	1,815	360	18.1	3.3
Nebraska	37,761	5,547	749	14.7	2.0
Nevada	229,015	19,955	1,699	8.7	0.7
New Hampshire	32,248	3,064	616	9.5	1.9
New Jersey	759,407	52,013	3,067	6.8	0.4
New Mexico	35,700	4,492	772	12.6	2.1
New York	1,495,346	243,108	5,515	16.3	0.4
North Carolina	232,911	29,980	1,943	12.9	0.8
North Dakota	8,273	1,866	351	22.6	4.1
Ohio	222,707	27,624	1,601	12.4	0.7
Oklahoma	78,957	11,955	1,052	15.1	1.3
Oregon	176,765	24,985	1,677	14.1	0.9
Pennsylvania	370,657	53,682	2,479	14.5	0.7
Rhode Island	33,252	6,029	1,031	18.1	3.1
South Carolina	68,383	6,754	949	9.9	1.4
South Dakota	9,091	1,454	425	16.0	4.6
Tennessee	105,470	12,677	1,101	12.0	1.1
Texas	1,041,268	121,643	4,084	11.7	0.4
Utah	73,059	12,162	1,118	16.6	1.5
Vermont	9,189	1,635	400	17.8	4.2
Virginia	489,098	38,829	2,541	7.9	0.5
Washington	571,426	62,376	2,970	10.9	0.5
West Virginia	14,376	2,686	421	18.7	2.8
Wisconsin	142,298	23,876	1,673	16.8	1.2
Wyoming	5,596	696	220	12.4	3.9

[1]Poverty status is determined for individuals in housing units and noninstitutional group quarters. The poverty universe excludes children under age 15 who are not related to the householder, people living in institutional group quarters, and people living in college dormitories or military barracks.

[2]Persons who report only one race among the six defined categories are referred to as the race-alone population, while persons who report more than one race category are referred to as the Two or More Races population. This table shows data using the race-alone-or-in-combination approach. The race alone-or-in-combination population is the total number of people who reported a particular race, whether or not they reported any other races. Use of this approach does not imply that it is the preferred method of presenting or analyzing data. The Census Bureau uses a variety of approaches.

[3]Data are based on a sample and are subject to sampling variability. A margin of error is a measure of an estimate's variability. The larger the margin of error in relation to the size of the estimate, the less reliable the estimate. This number when added to or subtracted from the estimate forms the 90 percent confidence interval.

Source: U.S. Census Bureau, 2007–2011 American Community Survey.

Table 8
Poverty Rates for the Hispanic or Latino Population by State: 2007–2011[1]

(For information on confidentiality protection, sampling error, nonsampling error, and definitions, see www.census.gov/acs/www/)

State	Hispanic or Latino[2]				
	Population	Number below poverty	Margin of error (±)[3]	Percent below poverty	Margin of error (±)[3]
United States	**48,190,992**	**11,197,648**	**77,014**	**23.2**	**0.2**
Alabama	170,351	53,203	3,032	31.2	1.8
Alaska	37,976	3,925	614	10.3	1.6
Arizona	1,817,790	469,009	10,185	25.8	0.6
Arkansas	174,123	53,978	2,833	31.0	1.6
California	13,503,094	2,803,788	25,767	20.8	0.2
Colorado	985,873	240,274	6,643	24.4	0.7
Connecticut	449,691	110,895	3,844	24.7	0.9
Delaware	68,418	15,645	1,859	22.9	2.7
District of Columbia	51,852	7,268	958	14.0	1.9
Florida	4,057,788	790,397	13,282	19.5	0.3
Georgia	804,180	240,966	7,118	30.0	0.9
Hawaii	114,599	17,869	1,541	15.6	1.3
Idaho	164,689	45,994	2,208	27.9	1.3
Illinois	1,959,070	376,023	8,442	19.2	0.4
Indiana	367,774	100,729	3,823	27.4	1.0
Iowa	139,236	35,990	1,962	25.8	1.4
Kansas	280,455	68,985	3,426	24.6	1.2
Kentucky	119,640	37,685	2,232	31.5	1.9
Louisiana	177,171	35,182	2,196	19.9	1.2
Maine	16,612	4,774	560	28.7	3.4
Maryland	442,416	56,112	3,267	12.7	0.7
Massachusetts	587,872	175,533	5,106	29.9	0.9
Michigan	420,184	117,043	3,324	27.9	0.8
Minnesota	237,023	58,356	2,601	24.6	1.1
Mississippi	70,914	19,714	1,615	27.8	2.2
Missouri	199,949	50,199	2,563	25.1	1.3
Montana	26,996	6,708	750	24.8	2.7
Nebraska	154,497	37,563	2,104	24.3	1.4
Nevada	689,331	136,444	4,921	19.8	0.7
New Hampshire	34,822	6,051	868	17.4	2.5
New Jersey	1,487,862	268,776	6,940	18.1	0.5
New Mexico	915,122	220,754	5,430	24.1	0.6
New York	3,282,749	818,211	10,517	24.9	0.3
North Carolina	747,738	235,175	6,769	31.5	0.9
North Dakota	12,443	2,703	392	21.7	3.1
Ohio	333,626	95,465	3,969	28.6	1.2
Oklahoma	308,731	87,596	3,285	28.4	1.1
Oregon	427,756	113,281	4,504	26.5	1.1
Pennsylvania	662,044	209,169	5,812	31.6	0.9
Rhode Island	123,727	37,085	2,020	30.0	1.6
South Carolina	214,207	63,858	3,236	29.8	1.5
South Dakota	20,286	4,632	653	22.8	3.2
Tennessee	270,686	87,068	3,610	32.2	1.3
Texas	9,035,286	2,340,708	23,191	25.9	0.3
Utah	336,479	75,690	3,562	22.5	1.1
Vermont	8,886	1,618	269	18.2	3.0
Virginia	588,949	87,109	3,904	14.8	0.7
Washington	710,202	185,613	5,723	26.1	0.8
West Virginia	19,725	4,399	633	22.3	3.2
Wisconsin	314,991	75,040	3,197	23.8	1.0
Wyoming	45,111	7,396	901	16.4	2.0

[1]Poverty status is determined for individuals in housing units and noninstitutional group quarters. The poverty universe excludes children under age 15 who are not related to the householder, people living in institutional group quarters, and people living in college dormitories or military barracks.

[2]Because Hispanics may be any race, data in this report for Hispanics overlap with data for race groups. Data users should exercise caution when interpreting aggregate results for race groups or for the Hispanic population because these populations consist of many distinct groups that differ in socioeconomic characteristics, culture, and recency of immigration. For more information see the 2010 Census Brief, Overview of Race and Hispanic Origin, at www.census.gov/prod/cen2010/briefs/c2010br-02.pdf.

[3]Data are based on a sample and are subject to sampling variability. A margin of error is a measure of an estimate's variability. The larger the margin of error in relation to the size of the estimate, the less reliable the estimate. This number when added to or subtracted from the estimate forms the 90 percent confidence interval.

Source: U.S. Census Bureau, 2007-2011 American Community Survey.

Notes

1. Poverty rates for Vietnamese and Koreans were not statistically different from one another.
2. Definitions of the race and Hispanic-origin groups used in this brief are available in the 2010 ACS Subject Definitions Guide available at www.census.gov/acs/www/data_documentation/documentation_main/.

   Individuals who responded to the question on race by indicating only one race are referred to as the race-alone population (e.g., "White alone," "Black alone," etc.). As a matter of policy, the U.S. Census Bureau does not advocate the use of the alone population over the alone-or-in-combination population or vice versa. The text and figures of this report focus on the race-alone population. This approach does not imply that it is a preferred method of presenting or analyzing data. The tables in this report show data using both approaches.

   Because Hispanics may be of any race, data for Hispanics overlap with data for race groups. Therefore, data users should exercise caution when comparing aggregate results for race population groups and the Hispanic population.
3. Poverty rates for Whites and Asians were not statistically different from one another.
4. Poverty rates for Samoans (17.6 percent) and Tongans (18.1 percent) were not statistically different from one another.
5. Poverty rates for Vietnamese and Koreans were not statistically different from one another.
6. Poverty rates for the White population in Arizona and Tennessee were not statistically different from one another. The poverty rate for the White population in Idaho was not statistically different from Tennessee.
7. Poverty rates for American Indian and Alaska Native (AIAN) in Maryland, New Hampshire, and Virginia were not statistically different from one another.
8. The poverty rate for AIAN in North Dakota was not statistically different from the rate for AIAN in Nebraska.
9. The maximum number of people who reported a particular race is reflected in the race alone-or-in-combination population. The race alone-or-in-combination population is the total number of people who reported a particular race, whether or not they reported any other races.
10. Poverty rates for the White population in Arizona and Tennessee were not statistically different from one another. The poverty rate for the White population in Idaho was not statistically different from Tennessee.
11. Poverty rates for Asians in Idaho, Indiana, and North Dakota were not statistically different from one another.
12. Poverty rates for Hispanics in Kentucky, Pennsylvania, and Tennessee were not statistically different from one another.
13. Poverty rates for Native Hawaiian and Other Pacific Islander (NHPI) in Connecticut, Illinois, and New Hampshire were not statisti- cally different from one another.
14. Poverty rates for NHPI in Arkansas, Nebraska, and Oklahoma were not statistically different from one another.

Critical Thinking

1. Evaluate the causes and remedies for poverty.
2. Discuss the opportunities and obstacles of entering the workforce.

Create Central

www.mhhe.com/createcentral

Internet References

National Association for the Advancement of Colored People (NAACP)
www.naacp.org

Sociosite
www.sociosite.net

The National Urban League
www.nul.org

U.S Census Bureau, 2013.

Unit 5

UNIT

Prepared by: John A. Kromkowski, *Catholic University of America*

Hispanic/Latino/a Americans

Hispanic/Latino Americans are a composite of ethnicities. The clustering of these ethnicities and nationalities and the experiences of groups that are recent immigrants or refugees and populations that were coercively incorporated into the United States as well as their relationship to the Spanish language, seem to be sufficient evidence of the commonalities that constitute the shared expression of this complex of memory and contemporary politics. Yet the use of "Hispanic" and "Latino" that differentiates them from Anglo-American foundations, and their social expression as they search for a cultural and political terrain, are but the surface of the process of intergroup dynamics in the United States. A wider horizon into which this topic can be placed can be gained by recalling that the term *Hispanic* emerged from an act of political will and cultural entrepreneurship. This substantive and consequential emergence of community leadership and coalition building during the urban ferment of the 1960s is most relevant to understanding race and ethnic relations. The achievement of initiating the process which transcended the names of ethnic groups such Puerto Rican, Mexican American, and Cuban American and the construction and implementation of this new paradigm by the US Census that began with the work of The National Council of LaRaza (NCLR) and Congressman Robert Garcia, University of Notre Dame Professor Julian Samora, Henry Santiestevan, and Herman Gallegos and scores of others yielded The Hispanic Question of 1970 as an addition to the US Census. In 1980 a coalition of other ethnic leaders associated with National Center for Urban Ethnic Affairs (NCUEA) and the Racial Ethnic Council of the Bicentennial of the American Revolution (BERC) and thousands of others convinced Congress and the US Bureau of the Census that "If You're Not Counted You Don't Count." The 1980 US Census Long Form added the fullest range of ethnicities by including the Ancestry Question that initiated a new era ethnic measures to the process of identity research, politics and public policy. In 2000 the U.S. Census broke new ground when it began to collect multiple race and ethnic identities. Such data collection policy shifts have implications for the restructuring of our understanding of pluralism. By formatting demographic data in ways that legitimate and institutionalize the relevance of pluralism at the personal level, the question of group participation and exclusion based on a simplistic vision of dichotomous differentiation and values has been made more complex and fittingly more indicative of the persistence and diversity of ethnic identity in modern societies. Moreover, the clustering of groups in and the particularities of places rivet our attention on the importance of local knowledge and to characteristics of enclave cultures and regional variety.

The overall and interrelated character and mobility of ethnic groups and the particularity of locations are both relevant for the serious consideration of the Hispanic/Latino presence in The United States. The following examples frame the importance of a place specific approach to understanding the ethnicity in general and in this case variations found in the Hispanic presence.

- The Hispanic presence in New York, Connecticut and Cleveland could focus on Puerto Ricans.
- The Hispanic presence in New York could focus on relations among newer Hispanics, such as Mexicans and Dominicans and long-time residents of New York, the Puerto Ricans.
- The Hispanic presence in Miami could not ignore Cubans.
- The Hispanic presence in Texas, Arizona, California and New Mexico could focus on border cities.
- The Hispanic presence in New Mexico and Arizona could address the differences in state political cultures that seem to drive fundamentally different approaches to governance and ethnic relations.
- The Hispanic presence in Hazelton, Pennsylvania and Arizona and Alabama could address other very recent uses of city ordinances and state laws that terrorized and removed populations.
- The Hispanic presence in the executive suites of major corporations could be assessed as measures of economic mobility from the margin to the mainstream.
- The Hispanic presence in prisons and gangs and criminal action could be assessed.
- The Hispanic presence in arts, music, film and literature could be tracked and translations of classics of various ethnic/national traditions as well as new literature from the experiences of immigrant and ethnic communities could be reviewed.
- The Hispanic presence in the restaurant industry could be compared to the Italian American presence.
- The Hispanic presence in professional baseball could be assessed as a mobility strategy.
- The Hispanic presence in the faculties of higher education and in other professions and various private sector segments of the economy can be measured and indices of dissimilarity can be tabulated.

- The Hispanic presence in immigrants from Caribbean and Central American countries could be contrasted with immigrants from Mexico and South American countries.
- The Hispanic presence in Caribbean and Central American countries immigrants and their social and economic mobility can be measured against immigrants from Caribbean countries that were part of French, Dutch, British empires.
- The Hispanic presence and the immigration experiences could be compared to immigrant experiences of recent African American immigrants whose experiences and traditional memories do include the trauma and struggle to overcome slavery, peonage, *dejure* segregation and large scale incarceration and generations of encounters with economic and governmental sectors of America.
- The Hispanic presence in immigrants from Caribbean, Central American, South American countries and Mexico could be compared to the grandchildren of immigrants from these and other countries.
- The Hispanic presence in Congress, the presidential cabinet and as ambassadors, in policy development and leadership positions in congressional staffs, in federal agencies, and in national advocacy and research organizations and in major public affairs journals, media and communication organizations could be analyzed.
- The Hispanic presence in military services could be compared to the African-Americans and Polish American presence in the armed forces and compared without attention to race and ethnicity, but to economic class and age cohorts.
- The Hispanic presence that emerges from content analysis of local radio, television and advertising and its impact on self-images identity and community build, and an inventory of ownership and origins of positive and negative programming. The Hispanic presence can be measured in the institutional capacity of the organizations and associations, religious congregations and the level of funding, fields of action, adequacy of remediation, and self-sufficiency.
- The Hispanic presence as measured by a full social, economic and housing demography and comparative indicia for each ethnic group and each location.
- The Hispanic presence located in Virginia, Maryland, and the Federal District as well as dis-aggregation by counties cities, towns, and neighborhoods.

What does Hispanic/Latino really mean? Am I Hispanic because I am a fluent Spanish speaking person and an immigrant from Romania and Brazil? If not, then, what does Hispanic/Latino really mean? For what purposes are such meanings and questions of meaning, belonging or participating in a Hispanic aspect of being? Posing such questions and other less cosmic and exotic enquiries about various dimensions of ethnic identity and ethnic issues provocatively shifts perspectives toward the fact of immigration and group participation of immigrants and their children and grandchildren in the United States. American mentalities vary from region to region and what may be clear in many eastern and midwestern states are contentious concerns in many western and southwestern states and sources of confusion, bafflement and anger in some southern states.

Article

Prepared by: John A. Kromkowski, *Catholic University of America*

Profile America: Facts for Features, Cinco de Mayo

Cinco de Mayo celebrates the legendary Battle of Puebla on May 5, 1862, in which a Mexican force of 4,500 men faced 6,000 well-trained French soldiers. The battle lasted four hours and ended in a victory for the Mexican army under Gen. Ignacio Zaragoza. Along with Mexican Independence Day on Sept. 16, Cinco de Mayo has become a time to celebrate Mexican heritage and culture.

Learning Outcomes

After reading this article, you will be able to:

- Identify the most troubling demographic indicators about Hispanic/Latino/a Americans.
- Explain if this report is hopeful or pessimistic about the future for Hispanic/Latino/a Americans.
- Explain whether this report is hopeful or pessimistic about immigration?

Mexican Population

31.8 million

The number of U.S. residents of Mexican origin, according to the 2010 Census. These residents accounted for about three-quarters (63 percent) of the 50.5 million Hispanics and increased 54 percent, growing from 20.6 million in 2000 to 31.8 million in 2010.

Source: The Hispanic Population: 2010
http://www.census.gov/prod/cen2010/briefs/c2010br-04.pdf

25.5

Median age of people in the United States of Mexican origin. The total Hispanic population had a median age of 27.2 and for the total population it was 37.2.

Source: 2010 American Community Survey 1-Year Estimates
http://factfinder2.census.gov table S0201

Geographic Distribution

61%

Percentage of the Mexican-origin population in the United States that resided in California (11.4 million) and Texas (8.0 million) in 2010.

Source: The Hispanic Population: 2010
www.census.gov/prod/cen2010/briefs/c2010br-04.pdf

40

Number of states in which the Mexican-origin population represented the largest Hispanic group, according to the 2010 Census. More than half these states were in the South and West regions of the country, two in the Northeast region, and in all 12 states in the Midwest region.

Source: The Hispanic Population: 2010
www.census.gov/prod/cen2010/briefs/c2010br-04.pdf

Military

685,000

Number of U.S. military veterans of Mexican origin.

Source: 2010 American Community Survey
http://factfinder2.census.gov

Education

1.5 million

Number of people of Mexican descent 25 and older with a bachelor's degree or higher. This included about 404,000 who had a graduate or professional degree.

Source: 2010 American Community Survey
http://factfinder2.census.gov table S0201

Families

34.0%

Percentage of married-couple families, with own children younger than 18, among households with a householder of Mexican origin. For all households, the corresponding percentage was 20 percent.

Source: 2010 American Community Survey
http://factfinder2.census.gov table S0201

4.2 people

Average size of families with a householder of Mexican origin in 2010. The average size of all families was 3.2 people.

Source: 2010 American Community Survey
http://factfinder2.census.gov table S0201

Jobs

67.8%

Percentage 16 and older of Mexican origin in the labor force. The percentage was 64 percent for the population as a whole.

Source: 2010 American Community Survey
http://factfinder2.census.gov table S0201

16.2%

Percentage of civilians employed 16 years and older of Mexican origin who worked in management, business, science and arts occupations. In addition, 27 percent worked in service occupations; 21 percent in sales and office occupations; 18 percent in natural resources, construction and maintenance occupations; and 18 percent in production, transportation and material moving occupations.

Source: 2010 American Community Survey
http://factfinder2.census.gov table S0201

Income and Wealth

$39,264

Median family income in 2010 for households with a householder of Mexican origin. For the population as a whole, the corresponding amount was $60,609.

Source: 2010 American Community Survey
http://factfinder2.census.gov table S0201

26.6%

Poverty rate in 2010 for all people of Mexican heritage. For the population as a whole, the corresponding rate was 15.3 percent.

Source: 2010 American Community Survey
http://factfinder2.census.gov table S0201

24.2%

Poverty rate in 2010 for all families of Mexican heritage. For all families, the corresponding family poverty rate was 11.3 percent.

Source: 2010 American Community Survey
http://factfinder2.census.gov table S0201

Ownership

49.2%

Percentage of householders of Mexican origin in occupied housing units who owned the home in which they lived. This compared with 65.4 percent for the population as a whole.

Source: 2010 American Community Survey
http://factfinder2.census.gov table S0201

Foreign-Born

11.7 million

Number of Mexican-born U.S. residents in 2010, representing 29 percent of the foreign-born population.

Source: 2010 American Community Survey
http://factfinder2.census.gov

Language Spoken at Home

75.3%

Percentage of Mexican-origin people who spoke a language other than English at home; among these people, 36 percent spoke English less than "very well." Among the population as a whole, the corresponding figures were 21 percent and 9 percent, respectively.

Source: 2010 American Community Survey
http://factfinder2.census.gov

Trade with Mexico

$460.6 billion

The value of total goods traded between the United States and Mexico in 2011, Mexico was our nation's third-leading trading partner, after Canada and China. The leading U.S. export commodity to Mexico in 2011 was unleaded gasoline ($11.6 billion); the leading U.S. import commodity from Mexico in 2011 was crude petroleum ($29.9 billion).

Source: Foreign Trade Statistics
www.census.gov/foreign-trade/statistics/highlights/top/top1112yr.html and https://www.usatradeonline.goy/

Businesses

1.0 million

Number of firms owned by people of Mexican origin in 2007. They accounted for 45.8 percent of all Hispanic-owned firms. Mexicans led all Hispanic subgroups.

Source: Hispanic-Owned Firms: 2007
www.census.gov/econ/sbo/get07sof.html?11

$154.9 billion

Sales and receipts for firms owned by people of Mexican origin in 2007, 44.2 percent of all Hispanic-owned firm receipts.

Source: Hispanic-Owned Firms: 2007
www.census.econ/sbo/get07sof.html?11

47.8%

Percentage increase in the number of businesses owned by people of Mexican origin between 2002 and 2007.

Source: Hispanic-Owned Firms: 2007
http://www.census.gov/newsroom/releases/archives/business_ownership/cb10-145.html

70.5%

Percent of all Mexican-owned U.S. businesses in either California or Texas in 2007. California had the most Mexican-owned U.S. firms (36.1 percent), followed by Texas (34.4 percent) and Arizona (4.1 percent).

Source: Hispanic-Owned Firms: 2007
http://www.census.gov/econ/sbo/get07sof.html?11

16.5%

Ratio of Mexican-owned firms to all firms in Texas, which led all states. New Mexico was next (15.1 percent), followed by California (10.9 percent), Arizona (8.6 percent) and Nevada (4.9 percent).

Source: Hispanic-Owned Firms: 2007
http://www.census.gov/econ/sbo/get07sof.html?11

32.3%

Percentage of Mexican-owned U.S. firms in the construction and repair, maintenance, personal and laundry services sectors. Mexican-owned firms accounted for 5.1 percent of all U.S. businesses in these sectors.

Source: Hispanic-Owned Firms: 2007
http://www.census.gov/econ/sbo/get07sof.html?11

Mexican Food

$100.4 million

Product shipment value of tamales and other Mexican food specialties (not frozen or canned) produced in the United States in 2002.

Source: 2002 Economic Census
http://www.census.gov/econ/census02/guide/INDRPT31.HTM

$48.9 million

Product shipment value of frozen enchiladas produced in the United States in 2002. Frozen tortilla shipments were valued even higher at $156 million.

Source: 2002 Economic Census
http://www.census.gov/econ/census02/guide/INDRPT31.HTM

374

Number of U.S. tortilla manufacturing establishments in 2008. The establishments that produce this unleavened flat bread employed 16,311 people. Tortillas, the principal food of the Aztecs, are known as the "bread of Mexico." One in three of these establishments was in Texas.

Source: County Business Patterns: 2008
http://www.census.gov/econ/cbp/

Following is a list of observances typically covered by the Census Bureau's Facts for Features series:

- Black History Month (February)
- Super Bowl
- Valentine's Day (Feb. 14)
- Women's History Month (March)
- Irish-American Heritage Month (March)/
- St. Patrick's Day (March 17)
- Asian/Pacific American Heritage Month (May)
- Older Americans Month (May)
- Cinco de Mayo (May 5)
- Mother's Day
- Hurricane Season Begins (June 1)
- Father's Day
- The Fourth of July (July 4)
- Anniversary of Americans with Disabilities Act (July 26)
- Back to School (August)
- Labor Day
- Grandparents Day
- Hispanic Heritage Month (Sept. 15-Oct. 15)
- Unmarried and Single Americans Week
- Halloween (Oct. 31)
- American Indian/Alaska Native Heritage Month (November)
- Veterans Day (Nov. 11)
- Thanksgiving Day
- The Holiday Season (December)

Critical Thinking

1. What do demographic indicators reveal about an ethnic group?
2. Is there evidence for improving outcomes?

Create Central

www.mhhe.com/createcentral

Internet References

Hispanic Access Foundation
www.haf.org

Latino American Network Information Center (LANIC)
http:llanic.utexas.edu

League of United Latino Citizens
www.lulac.org

National Association of Latin American Elected Officials
www.naleo.org
National Catholic Bishops Conference
www.USCCB.org
National Council of La Raza (NCLR)
www.nclrorg
Social Science Information Gateway
http://sosig.esrc.bris.ac.uk
Sociosite
www.sociosite.net

Editor's note—The preceding data were collected from a variety of sources and may be subject to sampling variability and other sources of error. Facts for Features are customarily released about two months before an observance in order to accommodate magazine production timelines. Questions or comments should be directed to the Census Bureau's Public Information Office: telephone: 301-763-3030; fax: 301-763-3762; or e-mail: pio@census.gov.

U.S Census Bureau, 2012.

Article

Prepared by: John A. Kromkowski, *Catholic University of America*

The Foreign Born from Latin America and the Caribbean: 2010

Learning Outcomes

After reading this article, you will be able to:

- Identify the most troubling demographic indicators about the foreign-born population from Central America.
- Explain whether this report is hopeful or pessimistic about the future for Hispanic/Latino/a Americans?
- List the countries from which Hispanic/Latino/a immigrants are coming to the United States.

Introduction

During the last 50 years, the number of foreign born from Latin America and the Caribbean has increased rapidly, from less than 1 million in 1960 to 21.2 million in 2010.[1] Currently, the foreign born from Latin America represent over half of the total foreign-born population. This brief will discuss the size, place of birth, citizenship status, and geographic distribution of the foreign born from Latin America in the United States. It presents data on the foreign born from Latin America at the national and state levels based on the 2010 American Community Survey (ACS).

Defining Nativity Status: Who Is Foreign Born?

Nativity status refers to whether a person is native or foreign born. The native-born population includes anyone who was a U.S. citizen at birth. Respondents who were born in the United States, Puerto Rico, a U.S. Island Area (U.S. Virgin Islands, Guam, American Samoa, or the Commonwealth of the Northern Mariana Islands), or abroad of a U.S. citizen parent or parents, are defined as native born. The foreign-born population includes anyone who was not a U.S. citizen at birth, including those who have become U.S. citizens through naturalization.

In 2010, 309.3 million people lived in the United States, including 40.0 million foreign born (13 percent of the total population). In 2000, 31.1 million of the 281.4 million U.S. residents were foreign—born—11 percent of the total population.[2] Over the decade, the foreign-born population increased by 8.8 million.

Over half (53 percent) of all foreign-born U.S. residents in 2010 were from Latin America (Table 1). Another 28 percent were from Asia. The next largest world region-of-birth group, the foreign born from Europe, represented 12 percent of all foreign born—less than half the size of the foreign born from Asia. About 4 percent of the foreign born were born in Africa and 3 percent were from other regions, including Oceania and Northern America. The single largest country-of-birth group was from Mexico (29 percent of all foreign born).

Findings

In 2000, 16.1 million foreign born from Latin America lived in the United States. Over the last 10 years, the foreign-born population from Latin America increased by 5.1 million, reaching 21.2 million in 2010.

The majority of the foreign born from Latin America were from Central America (70 percent), followed by the Caribbean (18 percent), and South America (13 percent) (Table 2). Mexico accounted for more than half (55 percent) of the foreign born from Latin America. El Salvador and Cuba each represented more than 5 percent. Among the foreign born from the Caribbean, those born in Cuba (30 percent) and the Dominican Republic (24 percent) represented the largest proportion of all foreign born. Over three-fourths of all foreign born from Central America were born in Mexico (79 percent). Colombia represented the largest share of the foreign born from South America (23 percent).

Although the foreign born from Latin America were found across the country, most were concentrated in only a few states. In 2010, 26 percent (or 5.5 million) of the foreign born from Latin America lived in California, 14 percent (or 3.0 million) in Texas, 13 percent (or 2.8 million) in Florida, and 10 percent (or 2.2 million) in New York (Figure 1). When combined, these four states accounted for 63 percent (or 13.4 million) of the total Latin American foreign born.

Table 1 Foreign-Born Population by Region of Birth: 2010

Region of birth	Number		Percent	
	Estimate	Margin of error (±)[1]	Estimate	Margin of error (±)[1]
Total	39,956	115	100.0	(X)
Africa	1,607	33	4.0	0.1
Asia	11,284	47	28.2	0.1
Europe	4,817	44	12.1	0.1
Latin America and the Caribbean	21,224	90	53.1	0.1
Caribbean	3,731	42	9.3	0.1
Central America	14,764	90	36.9	0.2
Mexico	11,711	83	29.3	0.2
Other Central America[2]	3,053	46	7.6	0.1
South America	2,730	42	6.8	0.1
Other regions[3]	1,024	19	2.6	—

(Numbers in thousands. Data based on sample. For information on confidentiality protection, sampling error, nonsampling error, and definitions, see *www.census.gov/acs/www*)
— Represents or rounds to zero.
(X) Not applicable.
[1]Data are based on a sample and are subject to sampling variability. A margin of error is a measure of an estimate's variability. The larger the margin of error is in relation to the size of the estimate, the less reliable the estimate. This number when added lo and subtracted from the estimate forms the 90 percent confidence interval.
[2]Other Central America includes Belize, Costa Rica, El Salvador, Guatemala, Honduras, Nicaragua, and Panama.
[3]Other regions includes Oceania and Northern America.
Source: U.S. Census Bureau, 2010 American Community Survey.

In 19 states, the foreign-born population from Latin America composed over half of the state's foreign-born population (Figure 2). In the South and West, the foreign-born population from Latin America represented 65 percent or more of the total foreign-born population in Arizona, Arkansas, Florida, New Mexico, and Texas. In Florida and New Mexico, approximately 75 percent of the foreign-born population were born in Latin America. In just nine states, the foreign-born population from Latin America represented less than 25 percent of the foreign-born population. In Maine and North Dakota, they were approximately 10 percent. In Hawaii, they were less than 10 percent.

In over three-fourths of all states and the District of Columbia, the foreign-born populations from Central America represented more than half of the Latin American foreign born (Table 3). The foreign born from Mexico represented about 9 out of 10 foreign born from Latin America in New Mexico, Arizona, and Idaho. The foreign born from the Caribbean represented about one-third of the Latin American foreign born in seven states. Two of these states—Florida (55 percent) and New York (49 percent)—each have Latin American foreign-born populations of 2 million or more.

In 2010, 32 percent of the foreign-born population from Latin America were naturalized citizens (Table 4). The foreign-born population from Central America had the lowest percent

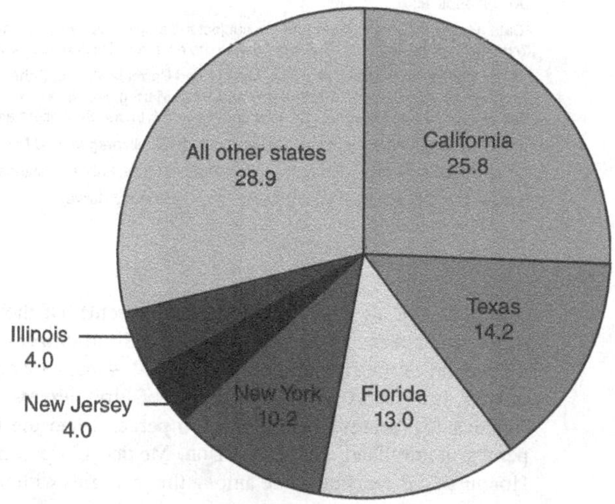

Figure 1. Distribution of the Latin American and Caribbean Foreign Born by State: 2010 (Percent distribution. Data based on sample. For information on confidentiality protection, sampling error, nonsampling error, and definitions, see *www.census.gov/acs/www*)
Source: U.S. Census Bureau, 2010 American Community Survey.

Table 2 Foreign-Born Population From Latin America and the Caribbean by Country of Birth: 2010

Region and country of birth	Number		Percent of total		Percent of region	
	Estimate	Margin of error (±)[1]	Estimate	Margin of error (±)[1]	Estimate	Margin of error (±)[1]
Total	21,224	90	100.0	(X)	(X)	(X)
Caribbean	3,731	42	17.6	0.2	100.0	(X)
Cuba	1,105	27	5.2	0.1	29.6	0.6
Dominican Republic	879	24	4.1	0.1	23.6	0.6
Haiti	587	21	2.8	0.1	15.7	0.6
Jamaica	660	20	3.1	0.1	17.7	0.5
Other Caribbean[2]	500	17	2.4	0.1	13.4	0.4
Central America	14,764	90	69.6	0.2	100.0	(X)
Mexico	11,711	83	55.2	0.3	79.3	0.3
El Salvador	1,214	34	5.7	0.2	8.2	0.2
Guatemala	831	29	3.9	0.1	5.6	0.2
Honduras	523	24	2.5	0.1	3.5	0.2
Other Central America[3]	485	17	2.3	0.1	3.3	0.1
South America	2,730	42	12.9	0.2	100.0	(X)
Brazil	340	15	1.6	0.1	12.4	0.5
Colombia	637	19	3.0	0.1	23.3	0.6
Ecuador	443	20	2.1	0.1	16.2	0.6
Peru	429	18	2.0	0.1	15.7	0.6
Other South America[4]	882	23	4.2	0.1	32.3	0.7

(Numbers in thousands. Data based on sample. For information on confidentiality protection, sampling error, nonsampling error, and definitions, see *www.census.gov/acs/www*)

(X) Not applicable.

[1]Data are based on a sample and are subject to sampling variability. A margin of error is a measure of an estimate's variability. The larger the margin of error is in relation to the size of the estimate, the less reliable the estimate. This number when added to and subtracted from the estimate forms the 90 percent confidence interval.

[2]Other Caribbean includes Anguilla, Antigua and Barbuda, Aruba, Bahamas, Barbados, British Virgin Islands, Cayman Islands, Dominica, Grenada, the former country of Guadeloupe (including St. Barthélemy and Saint-Martin), Martinique, Montserrat, the former country of the Netherlands Antilles (including Bonaire, Curaçao, Saba, Sint Eustatius, and Sint Maarten), St. Kitts and Nevis, St. Lucia, St. Vincent and the Grenadines, Trinidad and Tobago, and Turks and Caicos Islands.

[3]Other Central America includes Belize, Costa Rica, Nicaragua, and Panama.

[4]Other South America includes Argentina, Bolivia, Chile, Falkland Islands, French Guiana, Guyana, Paraguay, Suriname, Uruguay, and Venezuela.

Source: U.S. Census Bureau, 2010 American Community Survey.

naturalized of all regions of birth (24 percent). Of those born in the Caribbean, 54 percent were naturalized citizens. About 44 percent of the foreign born from South America were naturalized citizens. Among the country-of-birth groups shown, Jamaica (61 percent) and Cuba (56 percent) had the highest percent naturalized. By comparison, Mexico (23 percent) and Honduras (21 percent) were among the countries with the lowest percent naturalized.

Source and Accuracy

Data presented in this report are based on people and households that responded to the ACS in 2010. The resulting estimates are representative of the entire population. All comparisons presented in this report have taken sampling error into account and are significant at the 90 percent confidence level unless otherwise noted. Due to rounding, some details may not sum to totals. For information on sampling and estimation methods, confidentiality protection, and sampling and nonsampling errors, please see the "2010 ACS Accuracy of the Data" document located at www.census.gov/acs/www/Downloads/data_documentation/Accuracy/ACS_Accuracy_of_Data_2010.pdf.

What is the American Community Survey?

The American Community Survey (ACS) is a nationwide survey designed to provide communities with reliable and timely demographic, social, economic, and housing data for the nation, states, congressional districts, counties, places, and other localities every year. It has an annual sample size of about 3 million addresses across the United States and Puerto

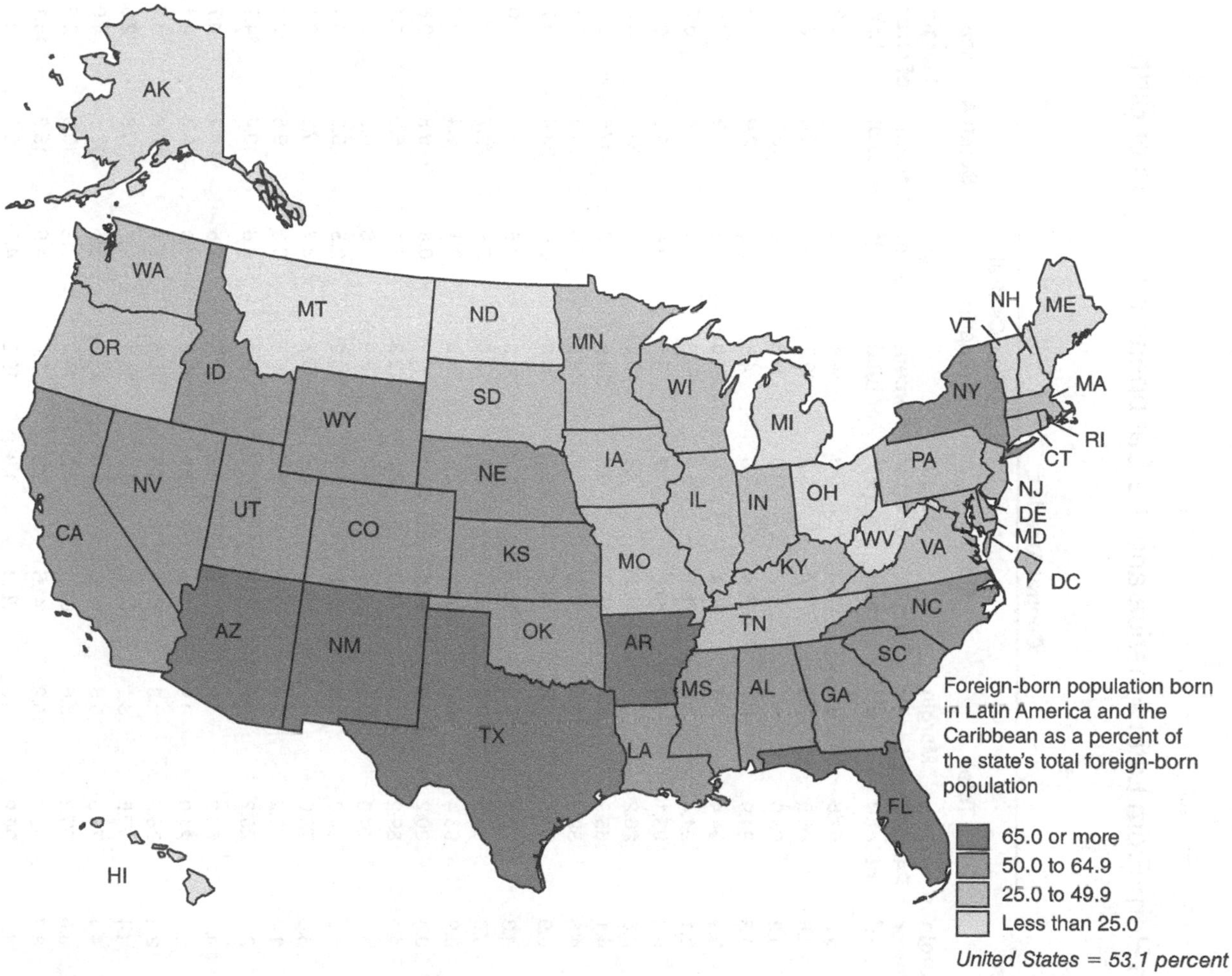

Figure 2. Foreign Born From Latin American and the Caribbean by State: 2010 (Data based on sample. For information on confidentiality protection, sampling error, nonsampling error, and definitions, see *www.census.gov/acs/www*)

Source: U.S. Census Bureau, 2010 American Community Survey.

Rico and includes both housing units and group quarters (e.g., nursing facilities and prisons). The ACS is conducted in every county throughout the nation, and every municipio in Puerto Rico, where it is called the Puerto Rico Community Survey. Beginning in 2006, ACS data for 2005 were released for geographic areas with populations 65,000 and greater. For information on the ACS sample design and other topics, visit www.census.gov/acs/www.

Table 3 Percent Distribution of the Foreign Born From Latin America and the Caribbean by Region of Birth and State: 2010

Area	Latin America		Caribbean		Central America						South America	
					Total		Mexico		Other Central America[1]			
	Number	Margin of error (±)[2]	Percent of total	Margin of error (±)[2]	Percent of total	Margin of error (±)[2]	Percent of total	Margin of error (±)[2]	Percent of total	Margin of error (±)[2]	Percent of total	Margin of error (±)[2]
United States	21,224	90	17.6	0.2	69.6	0.2	55.2	0.3	14.4	0.2	12.9	0.2
Alabama	98	5	5.4	1.6	86.8	2.6	70.0	3.8	16.7	3.5	7.8	2.1
Alaska	9	2	16.4	9.3	68.0	9.0	56.2	11.5	11.8	8.2	15.6	6.2
Arizona	572	13	2.2	0.5	94.9	0.7	90.4	1.0	4.5	0.9	2.9	0.5
Arkansas	88	5	1.7	0.9	94.4	1.6	73.4	3.6	21.0	3.6	3.9	1.5
California	5,477	43	1.3	0.1	94.4	0.2	78.8	0.5	15.6	0.4	4.4	0.2
Colorado	275	11	2.4	0.6	93.1	1.0	84.5	1.7	8.6	1.4	4.5	0.9
Connecticut	205	11	36.3	2.6	26.2	3.0	10.2	1.9	16.0	2.7	37.5	3.2
Delaware	34	3	16.5	4.1	65.9	6.3	49.7	7.9	16.2	5.6	17.6	5.4
District of Columbia	36	3	20.8	4.8	59.8	6.7	10.8	5.1	49.0	7.5	19.4	5.1
Florida	2,752	30	55.1	0.9	21.5	0.8	9.6	0.5	11.9	0.6	23.4	0.7
Georgia	515	12	16.4	1.3	72.5	1.5	56.3	2.0	16.2	1.6	11.1	1.0
Hawaii	13	3	14.7	7.9	55.6	9.0	41.0	9.1	14.6	5.8	29.7	7.9
Idaho	54	4	1.2	0.9	93.4	2.0	88.2	3.1	5.2	3.1	5.4	1.8
Illinois	842	16	3.0	0.4	90.2	0.9	84.1	1.1	6.1	0.8	6.8	0.8
Indiana	143	6	4.9	1.1	89.2	1.8	76.9	2.6	12.3	2.1	5.9	1.4
Iowa	60	4	2.1	1.2	91.0	2.6	75.0	4.4	16.0	3.8	6.9	2.5
Kansas	106	6	1.0	0.5	94.0	1.5	83.8	2.5	10.2	2.5	5.0	1.4
Kentucky	60	4	16.3	3.3	76.0	3.9	60.7	4.8	15.3	3.7	7.8	2.1
Louisiana	93	5	11.3	2.4	79.2	2.8	32.6	3.5	46.6	3.6	9.5	2.4
Maine	4	1	34.5	12.6	25.2	14.0	11.8	10.9	13.4	8.8	40.4	14.2
Maryland	312	9	16.9	1.6	63.0	1.9	11.3	1.5	51.7	2.5	20.1	1.7
Massachusetts	356	13	42.6	2.1	24.0	1.9	4.4	0.9	19.6	1.9	33.4	2.1
Michigan	118	7	11.9	2.2	78.3	2.9	67.7	3.5	10.6	2.1	9.8	1.7
Minnesota	104	5	4.7	1.4	77.5	3.1	63.4	3.7	14.1	2.7	17.8	2.8
Mississippi	32	3	8.9	4.4	78.5	5.5	64.3	6.5	14.3	5.1	12.5	4.9
Missouri	72	6	11.9	3.0	77.2	3.6	62.5	4.2	14.7	3.2	10.9	2.5
Montana	2	1	6.7	6.7	45.0	16.2	41.5	17.3	3.6	4.5	48.3	16.1
Nebraska	61	4	1.9	1.1	94.2	1.8	75.0	4.8	19.3	4.7	3.9	1.6
Nevada	291	8	6.7	1.0	88.4	1.4	75.1	1.8	13.3	1.7	5.0	0.9

(continued)

Area	Latin America		Caribbean		Central America						South America	
					Total		Mexico		Other Central America[1]			
	Number	Margin of error (±)[2]	Percent of total	Margin of error (±)[2]	Percent of total	Margin of error (±)[2]	Percent of total	Margin of error (±)[2]	Percent of total	Margin of error (±)[2]	Percent of total	Margin of error (±)[2]
New Hampshire	14	3	31.4	9.9	35.2	11.0	20.8	11.0	14.4	6.0	33.5	10.8
New Jersey	852	15	32.4	1.5	30.9	1.3	15.2	1.1	15.6	1.1	36.8	1.5
New Mexico	163	9	2.2	0.7	95.1	1.4	91.4	1.6	3.7	1.3	2.7	1.0
New York	2,155	28	49.3	0.9	23.9	0.9	11.7	0.8	12.1	0.7	26.8	0.8
North Carolina	414	11	7.1	1.2	83.2	1.5	63.5	2.3	19.7	1.8	9.7	1.1
North Dakota	1	1	25.4	17.6	63.7	13.4	50.7	18.5	13.0	13.9	10.9	8.9
Ohio	101	6	13.7	3.6	70.3	4.3	53.8	4.8	16.5	3.0	16.0	3.1
Oklahoma	121	6	1.6	0.9	93.4	1.7	83.3	2.8	10.1	2.4	5.0	1.5
Oregon	175	8	2.2	0.8	94.0	1.1	86.2	2.0	7.9	2.0	3.7	0.8
Pennsylvania	221	11	39.6	2.8	38.2	2.7	26.7	2.3	11.5	1.7	22.2	2.3
Rhode Island	60	4	45.4	5.3	36.1	4.9	6.9	2.5	29.2	4.8	18.5	4.7
South Carolina	120	6	7.6	1.8	81.6	2.8	57.8	4.0	23.8	3.8	10.7	2.1
South Dakota	6	1	1.5	1.9	87.0	6.2	64.1	15.4	22.9	14.8	11.5	6.0
Tennessee	143	7	5.3	1.4	87.4	2.4	63.3	4.7	24.1	3.8	7.3	1.7
Texas	3,013	35	2.0	0.2	94.0	0.3	82.5	0.5	11.5	0.5	4.0	0.3
Utah	139	6	1.6	0.9	82.5	2.4	73.8	2.7	8.8	1.7	15.9	2.3
Vermont	3	1	18.0	11.9	40.1	20.5	33.7	22.0	6.5	5.7	41.9	15.7
Virginia	338	9	8.5	1.1	63.7	2.1	19.1	2.3	44.6	2.6	27.8	2.1
Washington	277	8	2.0	0.5	91.5	1.1	84.2	1.6	7.4	1.1	6.4	1.0
West Virginia	5	1	21.5	9.7	57.7	11.7	22.9	8.9	34.8	13.0	20.8	10.0
Wisconsin	110	6	3.7	1.0	88.1	2.3	80.3	2.5	7.7	1.8	8.2	2.0
Wyoming	9	2	—	—	84.4	9.5	75.1	10.3	9.3	6.7	15.6	9.5

(Numbers in thousands. Data based on sample. For information on confidentiality protection, sampling error, nonsampling error, and definitions, see *www.census.gov/acs/www*)

— Represents or rounds to zero.

[1]Other Central America includes Belize, Costa Rica, El Salvador, Guatemala, Honduras, Nicaragua, and Panama.

[2]Data are based on a sample and are subject to sampling variability. A margin of error is a measure of an estimate's variability. The larger the margin of error is in relation to the size of the estimate, the less reliable the estimate. This number when added to and subtracted from the estimate forms the 90 percent confidence interval.

Source: U.S. Census Bureau, 2010 American Community Survey.

Table 4 Percent of the Foreign Born From Latin America and the Caribbean Who Are Naturalized U.S. Citizens by Place of Birth: 2010

Region and country of birth	Percent	
	Estimate	Margin of error (±)[1]
Total	32.1	0.3
Caribbean	54.1	0.6
Cuba	55.7	1.2
Dominican Republic	47.7	1.4
Haiti	50.0	1.6
Jamaica	61.2	1.5
Other Caribbean[2]	57.7	1.6
Central America	24.3	0.3
Mexico	22.9	0.3
El Salvador	27.9	1.0
Guatemala	24.1	1.3
Honduras	21.1	1.4
Other Central America[3]	52.1	1.5
South America	44.4	0.6
Brazil	28.2	1.7
Colombia	48.2	1.3
Ecuador	40.7	1.8
Peru	43.2	1.7
Other South America[4]	50.3	1.1

(Data based on sample. For information on confidentiality protection, sampling error, nonsampling error, and definitions, see *www.census.gov/acs/www*)

[1]Data are based on a sample and are subject to sampling variability. A margin of error is a measure of an estimate's variability. The larger the margin of error is in relation to the size of the estimate, the less reliable the estimate. This number when added to and subtracted from the estimate forms the 90 percent confidence interval.

[2]Other Caribbean includes Anguilla, Antigua and Barbuda, Aruba, Bahamas, Barbados, British Virgin Islands, Cayman Islands, Dominica, Grenada, the former country of Guadeloupe (including St. Barthélemy and Saint-Martin), Martinique, Montserrat, the former country of the Netherlands Antilles (including Bonaire, Curaçao, Saba, Sint Eustatius, and Sint Maarten), St. Kitts and Nevis, St. Lucia, St. Vincent and the Grenadines, Trinidad and Tobago, and Turks and Caicos Islands.

[3]Other Central America includes Belize, Costa Rica, Nicaragua, and Panama.

[4]Other South America includes Argentina, Bolivia, Chile, Falkland Islands, French Guiana, Guyana, Paraguay, Suriname, Uruguay, and Venezuela.

Source: U.S. Census Bureau, 2010 American Community Survey.

Notes

1. The term *Latin America and the Caribbean* includes countries in Central and South America and the Caribbean. *Central America* includes Belize, Costa Rica, El Salvador, Guatemala, Honduras, Mexico, Nicaragua, and Panama. *South America* includes Argentina, Bolivia, Brazil, Chile, Colombia, Ecuador, Falkland Islands, French Guiana, Guyana, Paraguay, Peru, Suriname, Uruguay, and Venezuela. *Caribbean* includes Anguilla, Antigua and Barbuda, Aruba, Bahamas, Barbados, British Virgin Islands, Cayman Islands, Cuba, Dominica, Dominican Republic, Grenada, the former country of Guadeloupe (including St. Barthélemy and Saint-Martin), Haiti, Jamaica, Martinique, Montserrat, the former country of the Netherlands Antilles (including Bonaire, Curaçao, Saba, Sint Eustatius, and-Sint Maarten), St. Kitts and Nevis, St. Lucia, St. Vincent and the Grenadines, Trinidad and Tobago, and Turks and Caicos Islands. Note that people born in Puerto Rico and the U.S. Virgin Islands are native born to the United States and are not included in the list of countries in the Caribbean. Throughout the remainder of this report, the term *Latin America* refers to all of these areas.
2. Gibson, Campbell and Kay Jung, 2006. "Historical Census Statistics on the Foreign-Born Population in the United States: 1850 to 2000." U.S. Census Bureau: Population Division Working Paper, Number 81 available on the Census Bureau's Web site at www.census.gov/population/www/techpap.html.

Critical Thinking

1. Explain troubling and hopeful evidence in this report.
2. Do the concentrations of populations from countries of origin have positive and negative consequences?

Create Central

www.mhhe.com/createcentral

Internet References

Hispanic Access Foundation
www.haf.org

Latino American Network Information Center (LANIC)
http:Illanic.utexas.edu
League of United Latino Citizens
www.lulac.org
National Association of Latin American Elected Officials
www.naleo.org
National Catholic Bishops Conference
www.USCCB.org
National Council of La Raza (NCLR)
www.nclrorg
Social Science Information Gateway
http://sosig.esrc.bris.ac.uk
Sociosite
www.sociosite.net
The International Center for Migration, Ethnicity, and Citizenship
www.newschool.edu/icmec

U.S Census Bureau, 2010.

Article

Prepared by: John A. Kromkowski, *Catholic University of America*

Latino Agricultural Workers and their Young Families: Advancing Theoretical and Empirically Based Conceptualizations

SANDRA BARRUECO, PHD AND ROBERT O'BRIEN, PHD

Learning Outcomes

After reading this article, you will be able to:

- Describe the developmental Contests of Children within Agricultural Worker Families.
- Describe the elements of the Cultural Experiences Model.

The widely—circulated image of a frightened preschooler clinging to her mother during the heart of the recent immigration raids has led to increased awareness of the agricultural worker community in the United States. Developing a deeper understanding of the plight and strengths of this largely Mexican immigrant community has also become a priority for early childhood intervention programs, which are increasingly available in rural areas (Barnett, Epstein, Friedman, Sansanelli, & Hustedt, 2009; Barnett & Yarosz, 2007). As both researchers and service providers prepare to engage more with agricultural worker families, a thorough description and multidisciplinary review of findings from the fields of psychology, health, education, and services is needed. This paper synthesizes and discusses these findings within a comprehensive, theoretical framework, with the goal of further understanding the key characteristics that should be considered when collaborating with this community[1]. Research and practice implications are presented at the end of this paper to further dialogue along these multiple avenues. Indeed, aspects of this work have been presented to the government to assist in the creation of a nationally representative study of Migrant and Seasonal Head Start (MSHS), a federally—funded comprehensive early childhood intervention program tailored to young agricultural worker families (O'Brien, Barrueco, López, & D'Elio).

Theoretical Framework and Developmental Pathway

The lives of agricultural worker families are comprised of a complex constellation of physical, psychological, sociological, political, and even meteorological facets. The role of each facet, and their interaction among one another, may be conceptualized from the perspective of the theoretical gestalt and more detailed conceptual pathway presented in Figures 1 and 2. These models are adapted from the cultural conceptualizations of human development by Bronfenbrenner (1979) and Super & Harkness (1999), as well as frameworks utilized in other studies of young children (e.g., ACF, 2006; NCES, 2002; West et al., 2007).

The contextual model presented in Figure 1 focuses on children, which reflects both the concentration of early interventions services on agricultural children's developmental and school readiness outcomes, as well as the central role that children (and dedication to one's children) play in the lives of Latino agricultural worker families (e.g., Gloria & Segura-Herrera, 2004; Parra-Cardona, Bulock, Imig, Villarruel, & Gold, 2006). A particularly apt feature of this model is the placement of MSHS, directly affecting children's development while concurrently influencing family and home experiences through its services to parents, families, and the community. The broader institutional contexts influence each of the layers within the model: formal State and Federal policies—as well as more informal community contexts—impact the families, children, and early childhood programs, such as MSHS. These larger institutional influences can strongly affect families and programs simultaneously; an example is the current focus on the status and role of immigrants in the United States. Touching upon all of these is the larger context of values, beliefs, and practices from both the

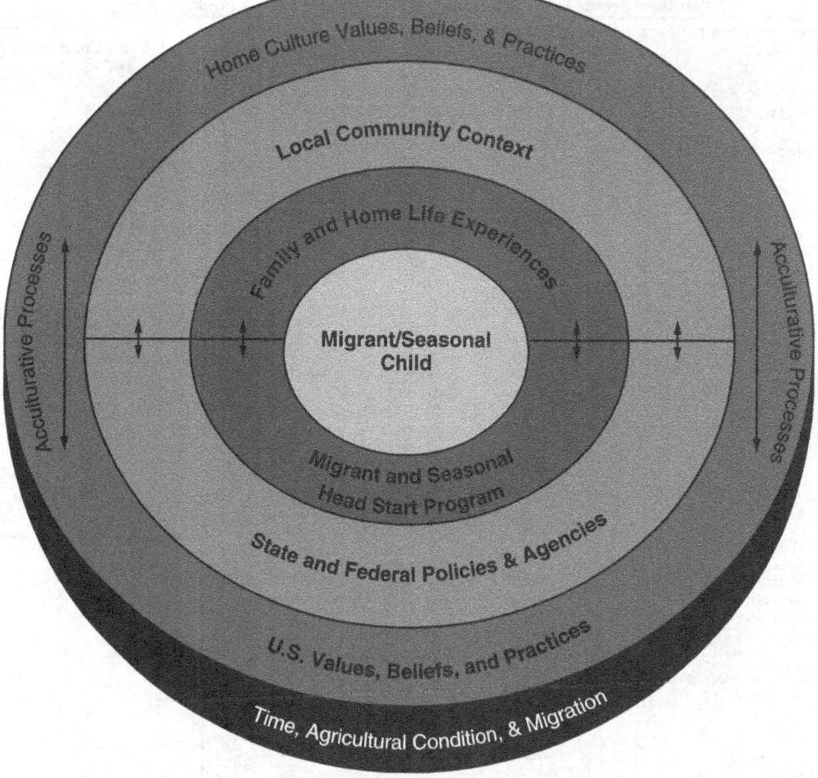

Figure 1 Developmental Contexts of Children within Agricultural Worker Families Participating in MSHS.

United States and the home country of the agricultural worker family, such as cultural variations in parents' approaches to child rearing. Finally, an overarching force in the systems of this child contextual model are the less predictable impacts of time and weather that play a central role in the daily functioning of families and programs for agricultural workers. In all, family practices, program participation, communities, policies, culture, time, weather, and even children's own individual characteristics come together to influence development in a dynamic, interrelated fashion.

The conceptual pathway presented in Figure 2 provides a more detailed analysis of the familial, programmatic, and sociocultural influences implicated in the development of young children of agricultural worker families. Providing a strong influence on this pathway was Super and Harkness' (1999) developmental niche, which identifies three concurrent and culturally-relevant facts to the familial experience.[2] Due to space considerations, this paper focuses primarily on elucidating these family influences, along with the community, cultural, and meterological factors at play in the development of young children within agricultural worker families. Individuals interested in reading more about classroom-based practices and other intervention approaches for this community are referred to O'Brien, Barrueco, López, & D'Elio.

Understanding Agricultural Workers and their Young Children

Regions of Origin, Language and Education

Significant percentages of agricultural workers originate from Mexico (94%, with 2% from Central America and 1% from other countries). Given the strong Latin American presence among agricultural workers, it may not be surprising that the overwhelming majority of agricultural workers participating in MSHS primarily speak Spanish (86%; ACF, 2007). However, Mexico is also comprised of communities with indigenous heritages and languages, particularly in the southern region. In recent decades, the proportion of agricultural workers from Veracruz, Guerrero, Oaxaca, Mòrelos, Chiapas, and Puebla doubled from 9% in 1993–1994 to 19% in 2001–2002

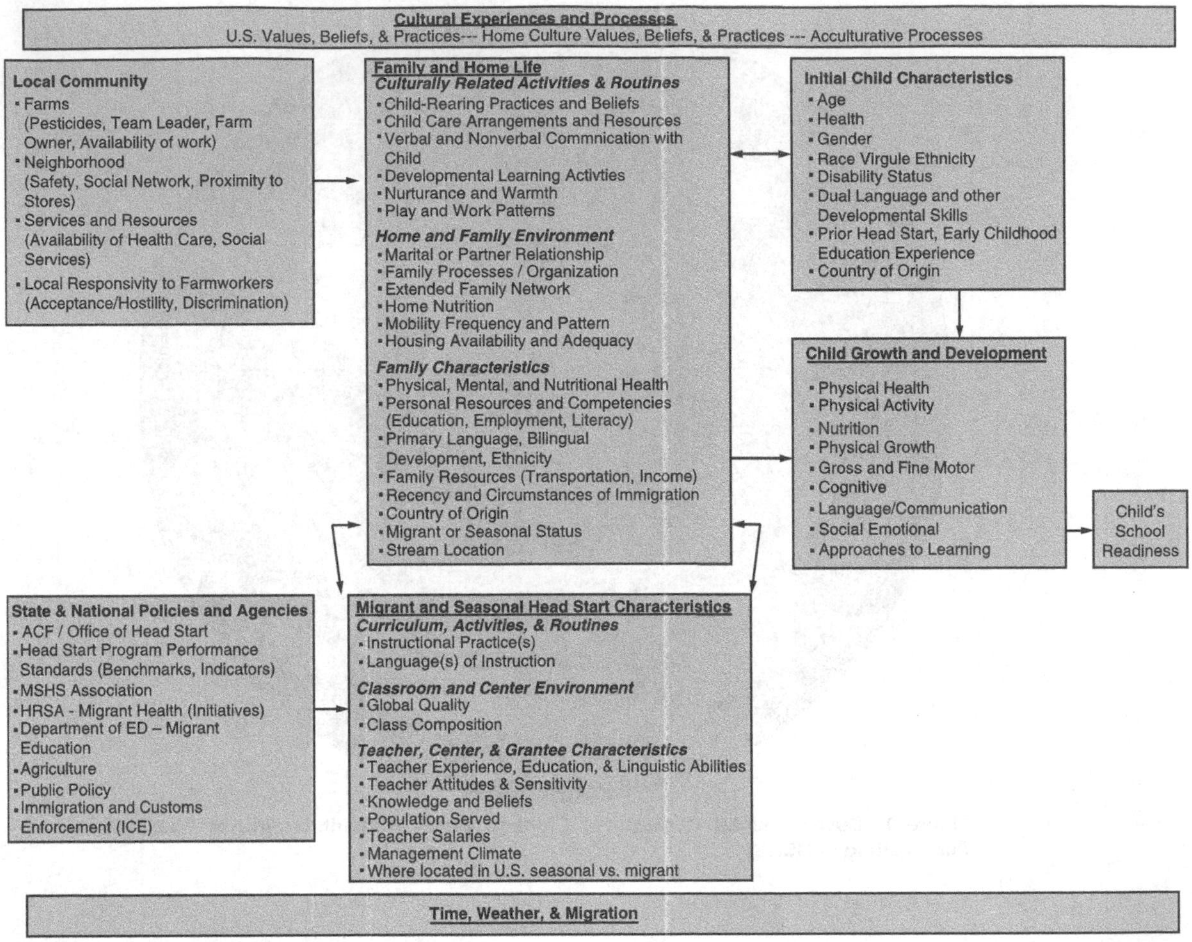

Figure 2 Contextual Pathway

(U.S. Department of Labor, 2005). A greater diversity of non-Spanish languages are spoken in these areas, including 2 types of Huasteco, 5 types of Mazateco, 14 types of Nahuatl (Aztec), 9 types of Otomi, and 4 types of Popoluca, among many others (Gordon, 2005). Creole, Mixteco, and Kanjobal are specifically among the most prevalent non-Spanish/non-English languages within the general agricultural community (U.S. Department of Labor, 2005). Given such changes, attention needs to be placed on the particular region that Mexican agricultural workers may be emigrating from *and* the languages they speak.

Yet, regardless of the specific language or languages spoken by farm worker families, literacy rates appear to be limited. 85% of migrant agricultural workers are estimated to struggle to gain information from printed materials in any language (U.S. Department of Labor, 2000). Average educational levels among farm worker parents participating in the MSHS program fall in the 7th to 8th grade range, reflecting Mexican educational policies where citizens pay for their own schooling after the 6th grade (ACF, 1999a). Such limited years of formal education and literacy skills certainly influence the development of their young children; importantly, the provision of quality early childhood interventions also can play a vital role in language and literacy facility (e.g., Ezell, Gonzales, and Randolph, 2000).

Mobility within the United States

There has been a tradition in migrant agricultural research, and perhaps within the migrant community itself, to discuss the patterns of North-South annual migrations in terms of three overarching paths: the West Coast, Midwest and East Coast 'streams' (Figure 3) (MSHS TAC-12/National Collaboration Office/AED, 2007). However, the simplicity of this organization currently appears to be a matter of convenience and not accuracy, as family migratory patterns now cross from one stream to another. In addition, families may or may not follow the same pattern from year to year, making the job of anticipating movement and enrollment even more difficult for local programs serving this community. Two national studies (ACF, 1999a; 1999b) explored the reasons why migrant agricultural workers choose one migrational stream over another, while occasionally engaging in interstream migration. These studies

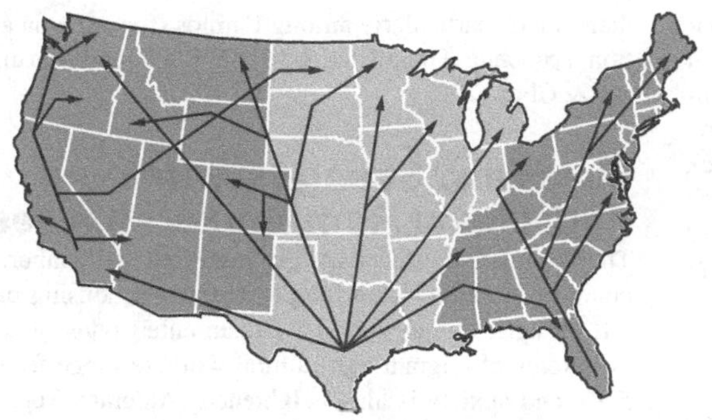

Figure 3 Current Diversity of Agricultural Workers' Migratory Patterns, Overlapping the Traditional 'Streams': Western, Midwestern, and East Coast (MSHS TAC-12/National Collaboration Office/AED, 2007)

identified agricultural and cultural factors, as well as practical factors (i.e., availability of subsidized health care, child care, legal, and MSHS services), as influences on the choice of migration patterns. Meteorological occurrences may play a particularly strong role in any given year. Shifting weather patterns influence the timing of crop development (e.g., planting, maintenance, and harvesting), while hurricanes, fires and other catastrophes decimate crops (and farm worker's livelihoods) in entire regions.

Concomitant with 'stream' participation, migrant families served by MSHS programs typically engage in four *types* of migration. In the first type, families travel to one or two locations during the annual harvest period and return to their "home-base" after the harvest.[3] In the second type, families travel from farm to farm for an extended period of time, sometimes covering more than one annual harvest, before returning home. For some families, this means moving to various areas of the country before returning to an area that they consider more of a "home base." In a third type of migration, families continually move without returning to a consistent home base. Finally, other families move within a relatively small area, traveling from farm to farm, such as nut and grape farmers in the Central Valley in California. Many of these families with a narrower migration zone reside permanently in one area while one member of the family, usually the father (or an adult male), travels relatively short distances for agricultural work (Klayman & Hubbell-McKey, 2000).

Farming and Living Conditions

The circumstances and poverty of agricultural workers often necessitates that both parents work, and some families may not have extended family to assist them due to immigration and continued mobility. Thus, agricultural children may be brought to the fields and other workplaces from infancy, experiencing unhealthy and dangerous conditions including high heat and toxin exposures (e.g., Frank, McKnight, Kirkhorn, & Gunderson, 2004; Koch, 1988). Once in the field, there can be a tendency for children to assist their parents with the field work as soon as they are able (e.g., Bey, 2003). Since both parents in agricultural farm worker families often work long hours and most days of the week, such strenuous and unhealthy activities have serious implications for children's development. Over past decades, the presence of children in the fields greatly decreased as federal agencies worked to target this problem through regulatory approaches as well as the provision of MSHS itself (ACF, 1999).

While the direct exposure of migrant children to negative farming conditions may have attenuated, some researchers remain concerned about indirect effects of living in an agricultural community. For example, pesticides deposited near homes on farms can seep into homes through the water supply, plumbing, house tiles, and other methods (McCauley, Beltran, Phillips, Lasarev, & Sticker, 2001). Parents may carry the pesticides home on clothing and shoes, which can adversely affect young children. Rohlman et al. (2005) identified slower response speed and higher latency rates on fine motor tasks among preschoolers living in agricultural areas, which is consistent with the effects of organophosphate pesticides. In addition, the housing conditions of young migrant children and their families are often poor, leading to exposure to high levels of heat, pest infestation, lead, and plumbing difficulties (e.g., Slesinger, 1992).

Health and Mental Health

As may be expected, poorer health among agricultural farmworkers and their children have been evidenced. Illness, fatigue, and pain are experienced by many agricultural workers from working long hours in difficult conditions. Further, specific health difficulties include poor nutrition, eye and skin damage from exposure to the sun, musculoskeletal problems, pesticide poisoning, and parasitic infections (e.g., Bechtel, 1998; CDC, 2006; Kandel, 1998; Thompson, 2003). Given that few agricultural positions allow for paid sick leave or worker's compensation, many parents may not attend to health issues in order to keep working. For example, only 42% of agricultural parents participating in MSHS report receiving medical or dental care and 51% report receiving prental care (ACF, 2004). Lack of insurance and paucity of rural medical services are major obstacles. Further, few resources can be brought to bear on physical health maintenance (e.g., regular check-ups, proper nutrition, disease prevention, stress reduction), given that their family household incomes fall in the median range of $12,500 to $14,999, which is well below poverty level (ACF, 2004). As such, agricultural workers may have high morbidity and mortality, with life expectancies that are much shorter than typical U.S. life expectancies (e.g., Kloosterman, Skiffington, Sanchez, & Kiron, 2003; Slesinger, 1992).

Unfortunately, higher mortality rates are also evidenced among migrant children (Slesinger, Christenson, & Cautley, 1986). Although recent relevant data is sparse, studies across the last three decades consistently identify deficits in nutrition, timely immunizations, infection control, and dental health (Koch, 1988; Weathers, Minkovitz, Ocampo, & Diener-West, 2003). For example, nearly a third of migrant children had a Vitamin A deficiency, as well as deficiencies in Vitamin C, Calcium, and Riboflavin; these deficiencies in turn can contribute to infection rates (Chase et al., 1971; Thomas, 1996). While no single cause of these health issues is determinable, it appears that the combination of a higher likelihood of pesticide exposure, along with inadequate nutrition, poor access to medical treatment, poor housing conditions, and extreme poverty contribute to the poorer health of children of agricultural workers. Further, a "lack of an independent means of transportation, lack of knowledge of where to go for needed care, and very high caretaker pressure to work contribute[d] to unmet medical need among migrant children" (Weathers, Minkovitz, O'Campo, & Diener-West, 2004, p. 281). Fortunately, comprehensive early childhood programs aim to address this need, with positive effects evidenced in improved growth rates among Mexican-American migrant children (Dewey, Chavez, Gauthier, Jones, & Ramirez., 1993).

Local Community

Agricultural workers and their families do not exist in isolation. As reflected in Figure 1, they are embedded within, and influenced by the communities in which they live. For example, contributing factors to their health are the availability and proximity of medical care (both traditional and non-traditional), pharmacies, and other health and human resources in the large expanses of rural land where they live. Further, agricultural workers' general well-being and mental health are influenced by the attitudes and behaviors of the local community towards them, including the farm owners and team leaders themselves (Hovey & Magaña, 2000; Hovey, Magaña, & Booker, 2001; Hovey & Magaña, 2002a; 2002b). Even discrimination evidenced at the broader community context is a salient feature in the lives of agricultural workers (Dalla & Christensen, 2005; Parra-Cardona et al., 2006; Ruiz, 2002; Wirth & Dollar, 2004). Finally, the children themselves are not immune from negative community experiences. In an exploratory study by Martin, Gordon, & Kupersmidt (1995), 52% of children from agricultural worker families had experienced some form of violence, either as witnesses (46%) or as victims (19%). Such violence exposure exceeds national estimates and approximates those of poverty-stricken, high-crime urban areas (Richters & Martinez, 1993).

Cultural Experiences and Processes

Surrounding many of the aforementioned influences are cultural experiences and processes. The acculturative process is not necessarily a simple linear process; the immigrant family does not always move from being more "ethnic" to more "American" (Chun, Organista, & Marín, 2003). Rather, bi-dimensional models (such as those conceptualized by Berry [1980; 1997] and others) have stronger empirical support.[4] These models of the acculturative process posit that there are two separate influences: 1) the values, beliefs, practices, and language(s) of the home country, and 2) the values, beliefs, practices, and language(s) of the United States. As such, individuals may become *bicultural* by retaining strong ethnic practices and beliefs as they develop American ones. Alternative outcomes may be *assimilation* (low ethnic, high American), *unacculturation* (high ethnic, low American), or *marginalization* (low ethnic, low American). Notably, bicultural individuals exhibit more positive outcomes in health and mental health than others, particularly among Latinos (for more on acculturation, see Chun, Organista, & Marín, 2003, and Marín, Organista, & Chun, 2005).

Stress and Strengths within Agricultural Farm Worker Families

The cumulative effects of acculturation, hard labor, medical conditions, and unstable employment and housing can take a toll on agricultural workers. Documented rates of depressive symptoms of migrant agricultural workers range from 20% to 57%, and anxiety is also heightened (Alderate, Vega, Kolody, & Aguilar-Gaxiola, 1999; Hovey & Magaña, 2000; Hovey, Magaña, & Booker, 2001; Hovey & Magaña, 2002a; 2002b). The recent increase in immigration raids and suspicion of all immigrants (whether legal or not) have led to documented strain among both parents and children in agricultural communities (e.g., Capps, Casteñeda, Chaudry, & Santos, 2007).

Yet, in the face of such challenges, the agricultural worker community possesses multiple sources of strength. For example, a qualitative study by Parra-Cardona and colleagues (2006) found that being family-focused was a strong contributor to parents' report of their resiliency. Children are a "source of inspiration when facing adversity and extreme hardship" (372). Like many Latino immigrant parents, agricultural workers are wholeheartedly dedicated to their children's educational success and linguistic proficiency in English and Spanish (e.g., Gloria & Segura-Herrera, 2004). Further, pride in "*trabajando duro*" (working hard) and a belief that such work improves their children's lives contribute to making meaning of adversity and supporting stronger life satisfaction (Parra-Cardona et al., 2006; Walsh, 2003). Finally, maintaining strong relationships with family and friends can improve farm worker's resiliency and even relate to their children's own socioemotional functioning, as independently rated by MSHS teachers (De Leon, Siantz, & Smith, 1993).

Research and Practice Recommendations

The agricultural worker community plays a critical role in the health and development of all Americans; it is through their arduous labor that a bountiful array of fruits and vegetables is made available each year. Further, agricultural workers contribute to a $100 billion agricultural industry for rather meager wages (U.S. Environmental Protection Agency, 2009). While agricultural workers are grateful for and invested in their livelihood, it comes with significant risks to themselves and their young children. Given these considerations, the following recommendations are provided.

Research

- There is scarce information on the development of young children in agricultural worker families, particularly within the areas of language, numeracy and socioemotional functioning. Much of the health and safety information (an area that should not be overlooked) is also becoming outdated. Given the greater investments in early childhood programs by states and others, this dearth creates a barrier to creating, validating, and providing appropriate and effective interventions for this population.

- Greater proportions of farm workers are of indigenous heritage yet relatively little is understood about individuals stemming from these southern Mexican communities. For example, what are their approaches to child-rearing, community engagement, and verbal and non-verbal communication styles? Even the most basic information is limited, such as the percentage of children and parents who are bilingual (Spanish/English; indigenous language/English) or even trilingual (indigenous language/Spanish/English). Such information would improve the development of appropriate early childhood interventions, including staffing, trainings, and materials.

Practice

- Innovative methods in providing interventions and services for agricultural worker families are required. One approach is to match the flexibility of the workers' schedules and mobility by providing services at the times and locations they need them. Some MSHS programs open and close centers as farm workers move through an area, while others provide teachers and staff that follow them through the migratory patterns. Such approaches may be fruitful within the health, mental health, and educational arenas. Recent technological advances could also provide another avenue for service or intervention provision. Pay-as-you-go cellular phones and computers at public libraries and schools could provide mechanisms for maintaining connections with service providers and teachers while families are migrating to the most distant rural areas.
- Finally, the process of gaining *la confianza* (trust) of the agricultural community can not be overlooked. Given the past and present experiences of this population, *confianza* can be slow to develop. It often entails frequent and respectful interactions, though this process can be quickened if introductions are made by trusted individuals within or outside the community. Regardless of approach, it is necessary to understand that *confianza* is built on at least three levels: the broader agricultural worker community, the family, and the individual. Addressing and discussing all three in both everyday discussions and when planning intervention and research efforts demonstrates cultural competency and lays the foundation for successful engagement. Therefore, the aspiring practitioner, researcher, or teacher must approach and acknowledge all three in order to successfully understand, collaborate with, and contribute to this important community in the American tapestry.

Notes

1. Occasionally, relatively dated studies are included in this chapter when no better information could be found and the findings contributed to a greater understanding of agricultural children and families.
2. These components are called "Customs of Child Care and Child Rearing," "Physical and Social Settings of Daily Life," and "Psychology of the Caretakers," respectively, in Super and Harkness (1997) original writings. Titles are adapted to better reflect the terminology of the early childhood field.
3. The term "home base" is often used to describe the families' identification of an area to which they almost always return; these are often located in warmer locations for winter housing, although this is not always the case.
4. Research in the past decade has even begun to support a multidimensional process capturing more nuanced patterns and variations in underlying cultural processes, such as the separation of linguistic and cultural practices (e.g., Berry, 2003; Sue, 2003).

References

Alderete, E., Vega, W.A., Kolody, B., & Aguilar-Gaxiola, S. (1999). Depressive symptomatology: Prevalence and psychosocial risk factors among Mexican migrant farmworkers in California. *Journal of Community Psychology, 27,* 457–471.

Administration on Children and Families (1999a). *A Descriptive Study of Children and Families Served by Head Start Migrant Programs.* Washington, D.C.: U.S. Department of Health and Human Services.

Administration on Children and Families (1999b). *Descriptive study of migrant and seasonal farmworker families.* Washington, D.C.: U.S. Department of Health and Human Services.

Administration for Children and Families (ACF), (2004). Executive Summary: Migrant and Seasonal Head Start Research Design Development Project 2002–2004. Washington, DC: U.S. Department of Health and Humand Services.

Administration for Children and Families (ACF), (2006). Head Start Family and Child Experiences Survey (FACES), 2006 Cohort: Supporting Statement for Request for OMB Approval of Data Collection Instruments. Washington, DC: U.S. Department of Health and Human Services.

Administration for Children and Families (ACF), (2007). Head Start Program Fact Sheet: Fiscal Year 2007. Washington, DC: U.S. Department of Health and Human Services.

Barnett, W.S., Epstein, D.J., Friedman,, A.H., Sansanelli, R.A., & Hustedt,, J.T. (2009). *The State of Preschool 2009: State Preschool Yearbook.* Rutgers, NJ: The National Institute for Early Education Research.

Barnett, W.S., & Yarosz, D.J. (2007). *Who Goes to Preschool and Why Does it Matter?* Rutgers, NJ: The National Institute for Early Education Research.

Berry, J. W. (1980). Acculturation as a variety of adaptation. In A. M. Padilla (Ed.), *Acculturation: Theory, models and some new findings* (pp. 9–25). Boulder, CO: Westview.

Berry, J. W. (1997). Immigration, acculturation, and adaptation. *Applied Psychology: An International Review, 46* (1), 5–34.

Bechtel, G.A. (1998). Parasitic infections among migrant farm families. *Journal of Community Health Nursing, 15,* 1–7.

Bey, M. (2003). The Mexican child: From work with the family to paid employment. *Childhood: A Global Journal of Child Research, 10,* 287–299.

Bronfenbrenner, U. (1979). *The Ecology of Human Development: Experiments by Nature and Design.* Cambridge: MA: Harvard University Press.

Capps, R., Casteñeda, R.M., Chaudry, A. & Santos, R. (2007). *Paying the Price: The Impact of Immigration Raids on America's Children.* Washington, DC: Urban Institute.

Centers for Disease Control and Prevention. (2006). Worker illness related to ground application of pesticide-Kern County, California, 2005. *Morbidity and Mortality Weekly Report, 55,* 486–488.

Chase, H. P., Kumar, V., Dodds, J. M., Sauberlich, H.E., Hunter, R.M., Burton, R.S., & Spalding, V. (1971). Nutritional status of preschool Mexican American migrant farm children. *American Journal of Diseases of Children, 122,* 316–324.

Chun, K.M., Organista, P.B. & Marin, G. (2003). *Acculturation: Advances in theory, measurement, and applied research.* Washington, DC: American Psychological Association.

Dalla, R. L., & Christensen, A. (2005). Latino immigrants describe residence in rural Midwestern meatpacking communities: A longitudinal assessment of social and economic change. *Hispanic Journal of Behavioral Sciences,* 27, 23–42.

De Leon Siantz, M. L. & Smith, M. S. (1993). Parental factors correlated with developmental outcome in the Migrant Head Start child. *Early Childhood Research Quarterly, 9,* 481–504.

Dewey, K. G., Chavez, M. N., Gauthier, C. L., Jones, L. B., & Ramirez, R. E. (1983). Anthropometry of Mexican-American migrant children in northern California. *American Journal of Clinical Nutrition, 37,* 828–833.

Ezell, H. K., Gonzales, M. D., & Randolph, E. (2000). Emergent literacy skills of migrant Mexican-American preschoolers. *Communication Disorders Quarterly, 21,* 147–153.

Frank, A.L., McKnight, R., Kirkhorn, S.R. & Gunderson, P. (2004). Issues of agricultural safety and health. *Annual Review of Public Health, 25,* 225–245.

Gloria, A. M., & Segura-Herrera, T. A. (2004). !!!Somos! Latinas and Latinos in the United States. In D. R. Atkinson (Ed.), *Counseling American Minorities* (6th ed., pp. 279–299). Boston: McGraw Hill.

Gordon, R. G. (Ed.). (2005). *Ethnologue: Languages of the World* (15th ed.). Dallas, TX: SIL International.

Hovey, J.D., & Magana, C.G. (2000). Acculturative stress, anxiety, and depression among Mexican farmworkers in the Midwest United States. *Journal of Immigrant Health, 2,* 119–131.

Hovey, J.D., & Magana, C.G. (2002). Exploring the mental health of Mexican migrant farm workers in the Midwest: Psychosocial predictors of psychological distress and suggestions for prevention and treatment. *The Journal of Psychology, 136,* 493–513.

Hovey, J.D., & Magana, C.G. (2002a). Cognitive, affective, and physiological expressions of anxiety symptomatology among Mexican migrant farmworkers: Predictors and generational differences. *Community Mental Health Journal, 38,* 223–237.

Hovey, J.D., & Magana, C.G. (2002b). Psychosocial predictors of anxiety among immigrant Mexican migrant farmworkers: Implications for prevention and treatment. *Cultural Diversity & Ethnic Minority Psychology, 8,* 274–289.

Kandel, W. (2008). *Profile of Hired Farmworkers: A 2008 Update* (Economic Research Report 60). Washington, DC: United States Department of Agriculture.

Klayman, D. & McKey, R.H. (2000). *Descriptive Study of Migrant and Seasonal Farmworker Families.* Department of Health and Human Services: Washington, DC.

Kloosterman, Skiffington, Sanchez, & Kiron, (2003). *Migrant and Seasonal Head Start and Child Care Partnerships: A Report from the Field.* Education Development Center: Newton, MA.

Koch, D. (1988). Migrant day care and the health status of migrant preschoolers: A review of the literature. *Journal of Community Health Nursing, 5,* 221–233.

Marín, G., Organista, P.B., & Chun, K. M. (2005). Accultural research: Current issues and findings. In G. Bernal, J.E., Trimble, A.K., Burlew, & F. T. Leong. (2003). *Handbook of Racial and Ethnic Minority Psychology* (pp. 208–219). Thousand Oaks, CA: Sage Publications.

Martin, S.L., Gordon, T.E., & Kupersmidt, J.B. (1995). Survey of exposure to violence among the children of migrant and seasonal farm workers. *Public Health Reports. 110,* 268–276.

MSHS TAC-12/National Collaboration Office/AED (2007). *Migrant and Seasonal Head Start center locator directory.* Washington, DC: Migrant and Seasonal Head Start Collaboration Office.

McCauley, L.A., Beltran, M., Phillips, J., Lasarev, M., & Sticker, D. (2001). The Oregon Migrant Farmworker Community: An Evolving Model for Participatory Research. *Environmental Health Perspective, 109,* 449–455.

National Center for Education Statistics (2002). *Early Childhood Longitudinal Study, Birth Cohort, 9-month data collection: 2001–02.* Washington, DC: U.S. Department of Education.

National Center for Farmworker Health (NCFH). (2003). Overview of America's farmworkers: Farmworker health. Retrieved from www.ncfh.org/aaf_03.php

O'Brien, R., Barrueco, S., López, M.L., & D'Elio, M.A. (in press). *Design of the National Migrant and Seasonal Head Start Survey.* Washington, DC: Department of Health and Human Services.

Parra-Cardona, J., Bulock, L.A., Imig, D.R., Villarruel, F.A., & Gold, S.J. (2006). "Trabajando duro todos los días": Learning from the life experiences of Mexican-origin migrant families. *Family Relations, 55,* 361–375.

Richters, J.E. & Martinez, P. (1993). The NIMH Community Violence Project: I. Children as victims and witnesses to violence. *Psychiatry, 56,* 7–21.

Rohlman, D. S., Arcury, T. A., Quandt S. A., Lasarev, M., Rothlein, J., Travers, R., Alys Tamulinas, A., Scherer, J., Early, J., Marín, A., Phillips, J., & McCauley, L. (2005). Neurobehavioral performance in preschool children from agricultural and non-agricultural communities in Oregon and North Carolina. *Neuro Toxicology, 26,* 589–598.

Ruiz, P. (2002). Hispanic access to health/mental health services. *Psychiatric Quarterly, 73,* 85–91.

Slesinger, D.P., Christenson, B.A. & Cautley, E. (1986). Health and mortality of migrant farm children, *Social Science & Medicine, 23,* 65–74.

Slesinger, D P. (1992). Health status and needs of migrant farm workers in the United States: a literature review. *Journal of Rural Health, 8,* 227–234.

Super, C.M., & Harkess, S. (1997). The cultural structuring of child development. In J. Berry, P.R & T. S. Dasen, (Eds.), *Handbook of cross-cultural psychology: Basic processes and human development* (2nd ed., vol. 2, pp. 1–39). Boston, MA: Allyn & Bacon.

Super, C. M., & Harkness, S. (1999). The environment as culture in developmental research. In S. L. Friedman & T. D. Wachs (Eds.), *Measuring environment across the life span: Emerging methods and concepts* (pp. 279–326). Washington, DC: American Psychological Association.

Thomas, E.C. (1996). *Bitter Sugar: Migrant Farmworker Nutrition and Access to Service in Minnesota.* St. Paul, MN: The Urban Coalition.

Thompson, B., Coronado, G.D., Grossman, J.E., Puschel, K., Solomon, C.C., Islas, I., Curl, C.L., Shirai, J.H., Kissel, J.C., & Fenske, R.A. (2003). Pesticide take-home pathway among children of agricultural workers: Study design, methods, and baseline findings. *Journal of Occupational and Environmental Medicine, 45,* 42–53.

U.S. Department of Labor. (2000). Findings from the National Agricultural Workers Survey (NAWS) 1997–1998: A demographic and employment profile of United States farmworkers (Research Report No. 9). Washington, DC: U.S. Department of Labor.

U.S. Department of Labor (2005). Findings from the National Agricultural Workers Survey (NAWS) 2001–2002: A Demographic and Employment Profile of United States Farm Workers (Research Report No. 9). Washington, DC: U.S. Department of Labor.

U.S. Environmental Protection Agency (2009). *Major Crops Grown in the United States.* Retrieved from www.epa.gov/agriculture/ag101/cropmajor.html

Walsh, F. (2003). Family resilience: A framework for clinical practice. *Family Process, 42,* 1–18.

Weathers A, Minkovitz C, O'Campo P, Diener-West M. (2003). Health services use by children of migratory agricultural workers: exploring the role of need for care. *Pediatrics, 111,* 956–963.

Weathers, A., Minkovitz, C., O'Campo, P., & Diener-West, M. (2004). Access to care for children of migratory agricultural workers: Factors associated with unmet need for medical care. *Pediatrics, 113,* 276–282.

West, J. Tarullo, L., Aikens, N., Sparchman, S., Ross, C., & Carlson, B.L. (2007). *FACES 2006: Study Design.* Washington, DC: U.S. Department of Health and Human Services.

Wirth, J. B., & Dollar, S. C. (2004). Concerns of Hispanics and service providers in southwest Missouri. *Great Plains Research, 14,* 253–270.

Acknowledgments—Funding was provided in part by the U.S. Department of Health and Human Services (DHHS), HHSP23320045009XI. The contents do not necessarily represent the positions or policies of the DHHS, and endorsement by the Federal government should not be assumed. Our heart-felt gratitude goes to Wendy DeCourcey, Ph.D. who provided invaluable feedback. We also thank Michael López, Ph.D., Mary Ann D'Elio, and many other colleagues for their suggestions.

Critical Thinking

1. What five aspects of this report are most revealing of the condition of agricultural workers?
2. Can a 'family support' policy for agricultural workers be improved by the states or the national government?
3. Are the private sector and our overall pattern of food production and consumption as well as international commerce dependent of legal and illegal workers? What does this mean for America?

Create Central

www.mhhe.com/createcentral

Internet References

Hispanic Access Foundation
www.haf.org

Latino American Network Information Center (LANIC)
http:Illanic.utexas.edu

League of United Latino Citizens
www.lulac.org

National Association of Latin American Elected Officials
www.naleo.org

National Catholic Bishops Conference
www.USCCB.org

National Council of La Raza (NCLR)
www.nclrorg

The International Center for Migration, Ethnicity, and Citizenship
www.newschool.edu/icmec

Unit 6

UNIT

Prepared by: John A. Kromkowski, *Catholic University of America*

Asian Americans

The Asian American ethnic groups provide unique and varied perspectives on the adjustment of immigrants and their reception in various regimes and cultures. Asian Americans are engaged in the ongoing issue of cultural formation, the recovery of tradition, and the incorporation of new ethnicities from Asian into mainstream cultural entertainment. The political and economic forces that frame relationships at the personal and cultural levels pose dilemmas and attendant choices that define current situations and the artifices used to heighten or diminish Asian ethnicities in America. The variety of religious traditions that Asian immigrants bring to America is another dimension of cultural and moral importance. In what respect are non-Judeo-Christian/Islamic faith traditions issues of consequence? The aftermath of conflict and resulting analysis have riveted attention on the ethnic factor. The details of familial and cultural development within these Asian American communities compose worlds of meaning that are rich sources of material from which both insights and troubling questions of personal and group identity emerge. Pivotal periods of conflict in the drama of the American experience provide an occasion for learning as much about us as about one of the newest clusters of ethnicities: the Asian Americans.

Asian Americans are engaged in the ongoing issue of cultural formation, the recovery of tradition and the incorporation of new ethnicities from Asia into mainstream cultural entertainment. The political and economic forces that frame relationships at personal and cultural levels pose dilemmas and attendant choices that define current situations and the artifices used to heighten or diminish Asian ethnicities in America. The intrinsic complexity of immigration as a social issue is one reason for the lack of comprehensive and long-range planning evidenced by U.S. immigration laws. The extreme diversity in our immigration sources clearly adds to the complexity of this issue. Throughout this nation's history, immigration has been both praised and reviled. Immigrant success stories are mingled with fear that the foreigner will take jobs and that our infrastructure will be strained. The late 1900s is a turning point in U.S. immigration history, not only because it signals the beginning of direct federal controls but also because it reflects new immigrant sources, whose ability to assimilate will be questioned. The first general immigration law was enacted in 1882. Generally, it established a 50-cent head tax per immigrant and gave the treasury secretary jurisdiction over immigration matters. The 1882 act also excluded convicts, paupers, and mentally defective aliens. Earlier that year Congress had passed the Chinese Exclusion Act, which based ineligibility for admission to the United States on national origin. The act also prohibited foreign-born Chinese from becoming citizens and placed a 10-year ban on the admission of Chinese workers. In 1890 there were 107,488 Chinese aliens on the American mainland; because of the Exclusion Act, that number had dwindled to 61,639 by 1920. Thousands of Chinese aliens had come to the West Coast as contract laborers to build the railroads in the mid-1850s. By 1880 there were 189,000 Chinese in the United States. Their sheer numbers coupled with the fact that most were unskilled and worked for low wages generated hostility and adverse public opinion. Calls for restrictive measures grew until Congress responded with the 1882 act. However, the issue did not disappear after the act's passage. In the next several decades, Congress would take further restrictive measures against the Chinese. In 1884 in fact, Congress amended the Chinese Exclusion Act. The section dealing with Chinese workers was extended to cover all Chinese, regardless of whether they were Chinese subjects. The immigrant head tax increased to $1.00 in 1884. Thousands of Japanese immigrants arrived in the late 1800s. Initially, Hawaiian sugar plantations were their destination, where they worked as contract labor. Canadians and Mexicans also streamed across our land border in this period to work in factories and fields. Congress amended the 1882 Chinese Exclusion Act again in 1892, as it was about to expire. The 1892 act extended the exclusion provisions for an additional 10 years and required all Chinese workers to obtain a residence certificate within 1 year. In 1893 Congress passed an act that reinforced prior immigration laws. It also required ship owners to collect information about incoming aliens to help identify those who were excludable. Boards of inquiry were established in 1893 to deal with immigration problems, including deportation. Calls for more regulation and restriction of immigrants continued through the turn of the century. Various members of Congress proposed a literacy test again and again as an immigration control to exclude aliens who were unable to read inane language. Legislation to accomplish this was vetoed by presidents Cleveland, Taft, and Wilson. In 1917 a literacy test for incoming aliens was enacted over President Wilson's veto. Between 1901 and 1920, 14,531,197 immigrants entered the United States. In 1901 an immigrant anarchist assassinated President McKinley. Theodore Roosevelt, who succeeded McKinley, told Congress that U.S. policy should be to systematically exclude and deport anarchists. Two years later, Congress responded by adding anarchists to the growing list of excludable aliens in the first federal law making political ideas and beliefs grounds for deportation. The 1903 immigration act also barred epileptics, insane persons, and professional beggars from entry. In addition, it raised the head tax to $2.00 and re-codified the contract labor law. Congress passed a subsequent statute in 1907, which raised the head tax to $4.00 and earmarked these revenues for use in defraying the costs of enforcing U.S. immigration laws. The 1907 act also created a commission to study immigration, which came to be known as the Dillingham Commission after the senator who chaired it. The commission submitted 42-volume report in 1911. It concluded that the immigrants who started coming to the United States in the late 1800s adversely affected the American labor movement. The growth of the Asian American population since the immigration reform of 1965, the emergence of China as international financial powers and the image of Asian American intellectual and financial success have heightened interest in this cluster of ethnic groups.

Article

Prepared by: John A. Kromkowski, *Catholic University of America*

The Foreign Born from Asia: 2011

THOMAS GRYN AND CHRISTINE GAMBINO

Learning Outcomes

After reading this article, you will be able to:

- Identify Asian counties that are losing population because of immigration.
- Develop a profile of new immigrants from Asia.

Introduction

During the last 50 years, the number of foreign born from Asia increased rapidly in the United States, from about 0.5 million in 1960 to 11.6 million in 2011.[1,2,3] In 2011, the foreign born from Asia represented over one-fourth of the total foreign-born population in the nation. This brief discusses the size, place of birth, citizenship status, educational attainment, and geographic distribution of the foreign born from Asia in the United States. Data on the foreign-born population from Asia are presented at the national and state levels based on the 2011 American Community Survey (ACS).

Defining Nativity Status; Who Is Foreign Born?

Nativity status refers to whether a person is native or foreign born. The native-born population includes anyone who was a U.S. citizen at birth. Respondents who were born in the United States, Puerto Rico, a U.S. island Area (U.S. Virgin Islands, Guam, American Samoa, or the Commonwealth of the Northern Mariana Islands), or abroad of a U.S. citizen parent or parents, are defined as native born. The foreign-born population includes anyone who was not a U.S. citizen at birth, including those who have become U.S. citizens through naturalization.

Findings

In 2011, there were 311.6 million people in the United States, including 40.4 million foreign born (13 percent of the total population). Over half (53 percent) of all foreign born were born in Latin America and the Caribbean (Table 1). Additionally, over one-fourth (29 percent) were born in Asia. The next largest world region-of-birth group, the foreign born from Europe, represented 12 percent of ail foreign born—less than half the size of the foreign born from Asia. About 4 percent of the foreign born were born in Africa and 3 percent in other regions, including Oceania and Northern America.

The foreign-born population from Asia increased from 8.2 million in 2000 to 11.6 million in 2011. Of the 11.6 million foreign born from Asia, 34 percent were from South Eastern Asia, 32 percent from Eastern Asia, 26 percent from South Central Asia, and 8 percent from Western Asia. There were five countries of birth with over 1 million people living in the United States: China, India, Korea, the Philippines, and Vietnam (Table 2). China accounted for 19 percent of the foreign born from Asia, while India and the Philippines each represented about 16 percent, Vietnam about 11 percent, and Korea 9 percent.

Four states had more than half a million foreign born from Asia: California (3.7 million), New York (1.2 million), Texas (778,000), and New Jersey (593,000) (Table 3). When combined, these four states represented over half (54 percent) of all foreign born from Asia. California alone represented almost one-third of the total foreign born from Asia.

Among states with foreign-born populations from Asia over 10,000, the proportions of foreign born from subregions of Asia differed widely. Half or more of the foreign born from Asia in Hawaii (66 percent), Nevada (61 percent), Louisiana (54 percent), and Minnesota (54 percent) were from South Eastern Asia (Table 3). The foreign born from South Central Asia represented 45 percent of the foreign born from

Table 1 Foreign-Born Population by Region of Birth: 2011

Region of birth	Number		Percent	
	Estimate	Margin of error (±)[1]	Estimate	Margin of error (±)[1]
Total	**40,378**	**125**	**100.0**	**(X)**
Africa	1,664	30	4.1	0.1
Asia[2]	11,562	47	28.6	0.1
Eastern Asia	3,640	34	9.0	0.1
South Central Asia	3,010	35	7.5	0.1
South Eastern Asia	3,939	41	9.8	0.1
Western Asia	932	30	2.3	0.1
Europe	4,890	50	12.1	0.1
Latin America and the Caribbean	21,245	99	52.6	0.2
Other regions[3]	1,016	20	2.5	–

(Numbers in thousands. Data based on sample. For information on confidentiality protection, sampling error, nonsampling error, and definitions, see *www.census.gov/acs/www*)

–Rounds to zero.

(X) Not applicable.

[1] Data are based on a sample and are subject to sampling variability. A margin of error is a measure of an estimate's variability. The larger the margin of error is in relation to the size of the estimate, the less reliable the estimate. When added to and subtracted from the estimate, the margin of error forms the 90 percent confidence interval.

[2] Includes an estimated 41,000 persons whose region of birth was classified as "Asia not elsewhere classified" and are not included in the four Asian subregions.

[3] "Other regions" includes Northern America, Oceania, and those born at sea.

Source: U.S. Census Bureau, 2011 American Community Survey.

Table 2 Foreign-Born Population From Asia by Country of Birth: 2011

Country of birth	Number		Percent	
	Estimate	Margin of error (±)[1]	Estimate	Margin of error (±)[1]
Total	**11,562**	**47**	**100.0**	**(X)**
Bangladesh	184	13	1.6	0.1
China[2]	2,231	28	19.3	0.2
India	1,857	31	16.1	0.3
Iran	362	15	3.1	0.1
Japan	318	12	2.8	0.1
Korea[3]	1,083	23	9.4	0.2
Pakistan	304	14	2.6	0.1
Philippines	1,814	35	15.7	0.3
Thailand	240	13	2.1	0.1
Vietnam	1,259	26	10.9	0.2
All other countries in Asia	1,910	34	16.5	0.3

(Numbers in thousands. Data based on sample. For information on confidentiality protection, sampling error, nonsampling error, and definitions, see *www.census.gov/acs/www*)

(X) Not applicable.

[1] Data are based on a sample and are subject to sampling variability. A margin of error is a measure of an estimate's variability. The larger the margin of error is in relation to the size of the estimate, the less reliable the estimate. When added to and subtracted from the estimate, the margin of error forms the 90 percent confidence interval.

[2] China includes respondents who reported their country of birth as China, Hong Kong, Macau, Paracel Islands, or Taiwan.

[3] Korea includes respondents who reported their country of birth as Korea, South Korea, or North Korea.

Source: U.S. Census Bureau, 2011 American Community Survey.

Table 3 Percentage Distribution of the Foreign-Born Population From Asia by Region of Birth and State: 2011

Area	Total[1]		Eastern Asia		South Central Asia		South Eastern Asia		Western Asia	
	Number	Margin of error (±)[2]	Percent	Margin of error (±)[2]	Percent	Margin of error (±)[2]	Percent	Margin of error (±)[2]	Percent	Margin of error (±)[2]
United States	**11,562**	**47**	**31.5**	**0.3**	**26.0**	**0.3**	**34.1**	**0.3**	**8.1**	**0.2**
Alabama	43	2	33.5	3.6	24.3	4.4	37.3	5.3	4.8	1.9
Alaska	27	2	27.5	5.9	4.0	1.9	66.5	6.2	1.9	2.0
Arizona	155	7	27.2	3.3	23.5	2.9	35.7	3.2	13.2	2.7
Arkansas	27	2	26.0	7.2	22.6	7.1	43.3	8.2	7.5	3.8
California	3,735	26	32.1	0.6	18.7	0.5	42.1	0.5	6.9	0.3
Colorado	107	5	35.3	3.2	21.6	3.0	35.3	3.5	7.7	2.2
Connecticut	112	4	27.3	2.9	42.1	4.0	22.3	3.7	7.5	2.0
Delaware	23	1	34.8	7.1	44.8	7.5	16.9	4.9	2.9	2.0
District of Columbia	16	2	36.4	7.4	22.4	6.1	25.8	7.5	15.3	4.7
Florida	370	13	20.6	1.6	27.0	2.2	38.7	2.2	13.3	2.2
Georgia	252	10	33.6	3.0	31.9	3.1	28.7	2.9	5.7	1.5
Hawaii	193	10	32.9	2.3	0.6	0.4	66.2	2.3	0.2	0.1
Idaho	19	2	40.7	11.1	35.1	11.9	20.6	7.7	2.7	2.3
Illinois	494	9	27.1	1.6	35.8	1.7	25.4	1.7	10.2	1.3
Indiana	90	5	36.4	3.4	30.9	3.2	24.2	2.9	7.7	2.8
Iowa	45	3	30.3	4.8	30.6	6.2	34.1	6.0	4.7	2.1
Kansas	60	4	23.9	3.6	24.7	4.4	40.6	4.4	10.2	4.7
Kentucky	46	3	31.7	5.2	31.9	6.1	26.6	5.1	8.8	3.5
Louisiana	56	3	19.4	3.6	18.4	3.7	53.6	4.7	8.2	3.1
Maine	11	1	29.2	7.6	17.0	8.2	44.0	8.5	9.9	6.1
Maryland	263	7	35.9	2.2	33.6	2.4	25.7	2.1	4.7	0.8
Massachusetts	288	7	38.2	2.2	23.5	1.9	27.3	1.9	10.7	1.4
Michigan	278	9	22.0	1.4	25.7	1.9	16.5	1.7	34.9	2.2
Minnesota	139	5	23.5	2.6	20.5	2.2	53.3	3.0	2.5	0.8
Mississippi	20	2	25.3	8.2	20.3	6.0	45.9	8.4	6.7	4.5
Missouri	88	4	29.7	3.0	32.7	3.7	26.8	3.2	10.3	2.7
Montana	(B)	(B)	(B)	(B)	(B)	(B)	(B)	(B)	(B)	(B)
Nebraska	31	3	22.4	4.3	20.2	6.6	48.6	6.2	8.8	4.1
Nevada	147	7	22.1	3.1	10.5	2.5	60.7	3.9	6.6	1.8
New Hampshire	26	2	25.9	5.5	38.5	6.5	26.5	7.7	9.1	4.1
New Jersey	593	8	29.4	1.4	43.0	1.6	20.1	1.2	7.1	0.6
New Mexico	21	2	34.0	6.9	28.1	7.0	33.4	7.6	4.4	2.6
New York	1,176	16	46.1	1.1	31.3	1.0	13.3	0.8	8.9	0.7
North Carolina	160	7	26.5	3.1	35.6	3.3	30.7	3.1	5.7	1.4
North Dakota	(B)	(B)	(B)	(B)	(B)	(B)	(B)	(B)	(B)	(B)
Ohio	175	7	32.2	2.8	33.1	2.6	20.5	2.6	12.5	1.8
Oklahoma	53	2	23.1	3.1	20.2	4.0	48.9	5.0	7.7	2.5
Oregon	111	5	38.9	3.8	17.9	2.6	36.2	3.6	6.4	2.7
Pennsylvania	283	6	32.2	1.7	32.0	2.0	28.6	2.0	6.5	1.0
Rhode Island	25	2	27.3	7.1	24.2	6.9	38.3	6.9	10.3	3.9
South Carolina	49	3	34.7	5.0	24.3	6.0	34.3	5.9	6.5	3.2
South Dakota	(B)	(B)	(B)	(B)	(B)	(B)	(B)	(B)	(B)	(B)
Tennessee	83	5	23.9	3.3	34.5	4.7	29.6	3.8	12.0	2.6
Texas	778	14	21.8	1.3	33.8	1.5	38.0	1.7	6.2	0.8
Utah	40	3	33.8	5.1	21.1	5.7	38.9	5.1	6.1	2.5
Vermont	(B)	(B)	(B)	(B)	(B)	(B)	(B)	(B)	(B)	(B)
Virginia	366	8	27.6	2.4	35.6	2.4	30.6	2.3	6.0	1.0
Washington	362	9	34.3	2.2	16.5	1.7	44.9	2.2	4.2	0.8
West Virginia	(B)	(B)	(B)	(B)	(B)	(B)	(B)	(B)	(B)	(B)
Wisconsin	87	4	24.4	3.1	26.0	3.7	43.1	4.0	6.3	2.1
Wyoming	(B)	(B)	(B)	(B)	(B)	(B)	(B)	(B)	(B)	(B)

(Numbers in thousands. Data based on sample. For information on confidentiality protection, sampling error, nonsampling error, and definitions, see *www.census.gov/acs/www*)

(B) Population born in Asia was less than 10,000.

[1] Includes an estimated 41,000 persons whose region of birth was classified as "Asia not elsewhere classified" and are not included in the four Asian subregions.

[2] Data are based on a sample and are subject to sampling variability. A margin of error is a measure of an estimate's variability. The larger the margin of error is in relation to the size of the estimate, the less reliable the estimate. When added to and subtracted from the estimate, the margin of error forms the 90 percent confidence interval.

Source: U.S. Census Bureau, 2011 American Community Survey.

Asia in Delaware, 43 percent in New Jersey, and 42 percent in Connecticut.[4] In Michigan, 35 percent of Asian foreign born were from Western Asia. The foreign born from Eastern Asia accounted for 46 percent of the Asian foreign born in New York.

When considering the geographic distribution of the five largest country-of-birth groups from Asia, the largest proportion of each of these groups resided in California, ranging between 21 percent of the foreign born from India to 45 percent of the foreign born from the Philippines (Table 4). For two

Table 4 Foreign-Born Population From Asia by State, for Five Largest Countries of Birth: 2011

Country of birth and state[1]	Number		Percent of total		Percent of country	
	Estimate	Margin of error (±)[2]	Estimate	Margin of error (±)[2]	Estimate	Margin of error (±)[2]
Total	**11,562**	**47**	**100.0**	**(X)**	**100.0**	**(X)**
China[3]	2,231	28	19.3	0.2	100.0	(X)
California	761	18	6.6	0.2	34.1	0.7
New York	410	11	3.5	0.1	18.4	0.5
Texas	108	8	0.9	0.1	4.8	0.3
New Jersey	92	7	0.8	0.1	4.1	0.3
Massachusetts	82	5	0.7	–	3.7	0.2
India	1,857	31	16.1	0.3	100.0	(X)
California	381	18	3.3	0.2	20.5	0.9
New Jersey	210	10	1.8	0.1	11.3	0.5
Texas	162	9	1.4	0.1	8.7	0.5
New York	145	9	1.3	0.1	7.8	0.5
Illinois	127	8	1.1	0.1	6.9	0.4
Philippines	1,814	35	15.7	0.3	100.0	(X)
California	812	18	7.0	0.2	44.8	0.8
Hawaii	112	9	1.0	0.1	6.2	0.5
New Jersey	87	7	0.7	0.1	4.8	0.4
Texas	86	9	0.7	0.1	4.8	0.5
Illinois	85	8	0.7	0.1	4.7	0.4
Vietnam	1,259	26	10.9	0.2	100.0	(X)
California	485	16	4.2	0.1	38.5	1.0
Texas	153	11	1.3	0.1	12.1	0.9
Washington	58	7	0.5	0.1	4.6	0.5
Florida	51	6	0.4	0.1	4.0	0.5
Virginia	43	5	0.4	–	3.4	0.4
Korea[4]	1,083	23	9.4	0.2	100.0	(X)
California	334	13	2.9	0.1	30.9	0.9
New York	103	8	0.9	0.1	9.5	0.7
New Jersey	71	6	0.6	0.1	6.5	0.6
Virginia	58	7	0.5	0.1	5.4	0.7
Illinois	50	6	0.4	–	4.7	0.5

(Numbers in thousands. Data based on sample. For information on confidentiality protection, sampling error, nonsampling error, and definitions, see *www.census.gov/acs/www*)

– Represents or rounds to zero.

(X) Not applicable.

[1] Countries of birth are shown for those countries with over 1 million foreign born living in the United States.

[2] Data are based on a sample and are subject to sampling variability. A margin of error is a measure of an estimate's variability. The larger the margin of error is in relation to the size of the estimate, the less reliable the estimate. When added to and subtracted from the estimate, the margin of error forms the 90 percent confidence interval.

[3] China includes respondents who reported their country of birth as China, Hong Kong, Macau, Paracel Islands, or Taiwan.

[4] Korea includes respondents who reported their country of birth as Korea, South Korea, or North Korea.

Source: U.S. Census Bureau, 2011 American Community Survey.

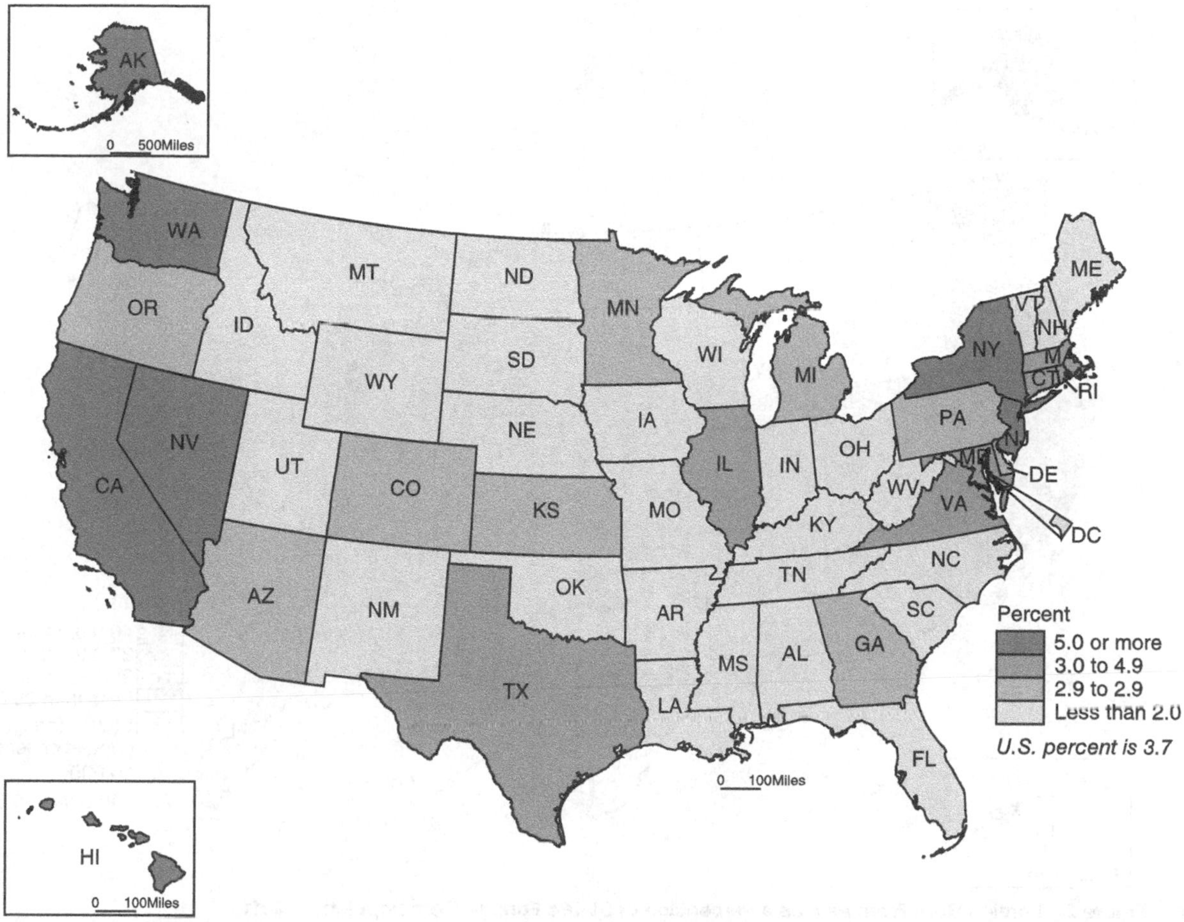

Figure 1 Foreign Born From Asia as a Percentage of Total State Population: 2011
Source: U.S. Census Bureau, 2011 American Community Survey.

country of birth groups—China (18 percent) and Korea (10 percent)—New York was the second-largest state proportion. For Vietnam, the second-largest was Texas (12 percent), for India it was New Jersey (11 percent), and for the Philippines it was Hawaii (6 percent).

States with the highest percentage of their total population consisting of foreign born from Asia included Hawaii (14 percent), California (10 percent), New Jersey (7 percent), New York (6 percent), Washington (5 percent), and Nevada (5 percent) (Figure 1). Among states with at least 50,000 foreign born, Hawaii (79 percent), Alaska (52 percent), and Michigan (46 percent) had the highest percentage of Asian born in their foreign-born populations (Figure 2).

When compared with the foreign born from all other regions, the foreign born from Asia were more likely to have graduated from high school and to have a bachelor's degree or higher. In 2011, 83 percent of the foreign born from Asia aged 25 and older were high school graduates or higher, while 48 percent had received a bachelor's degree or higher (Table 5).

What Is the American Community Survey?

The American Community Survey (ACS) is a nationwide survey designed to provide communities with reliable and timely demographic, social, economic, and housing data for the nation, states, congressional districts, counties, places, and other localities every year. It has an annual sample size of about 3.3 million addresses across the United States and Puerto Rico and includes both housing units and group quarters (e.g., nursing facilities and prisons). The ACS is conducted in every county throughout the nation, and every municipio in Puerto Rico, where it is called the Puerto Rico Community Survey. Beginning in 2006, ACS data for 2005 were released for geographic areas with populations of 65,000 and greater. For information on the ACS sample design and other topics, visit www.census.gov/acs/www.

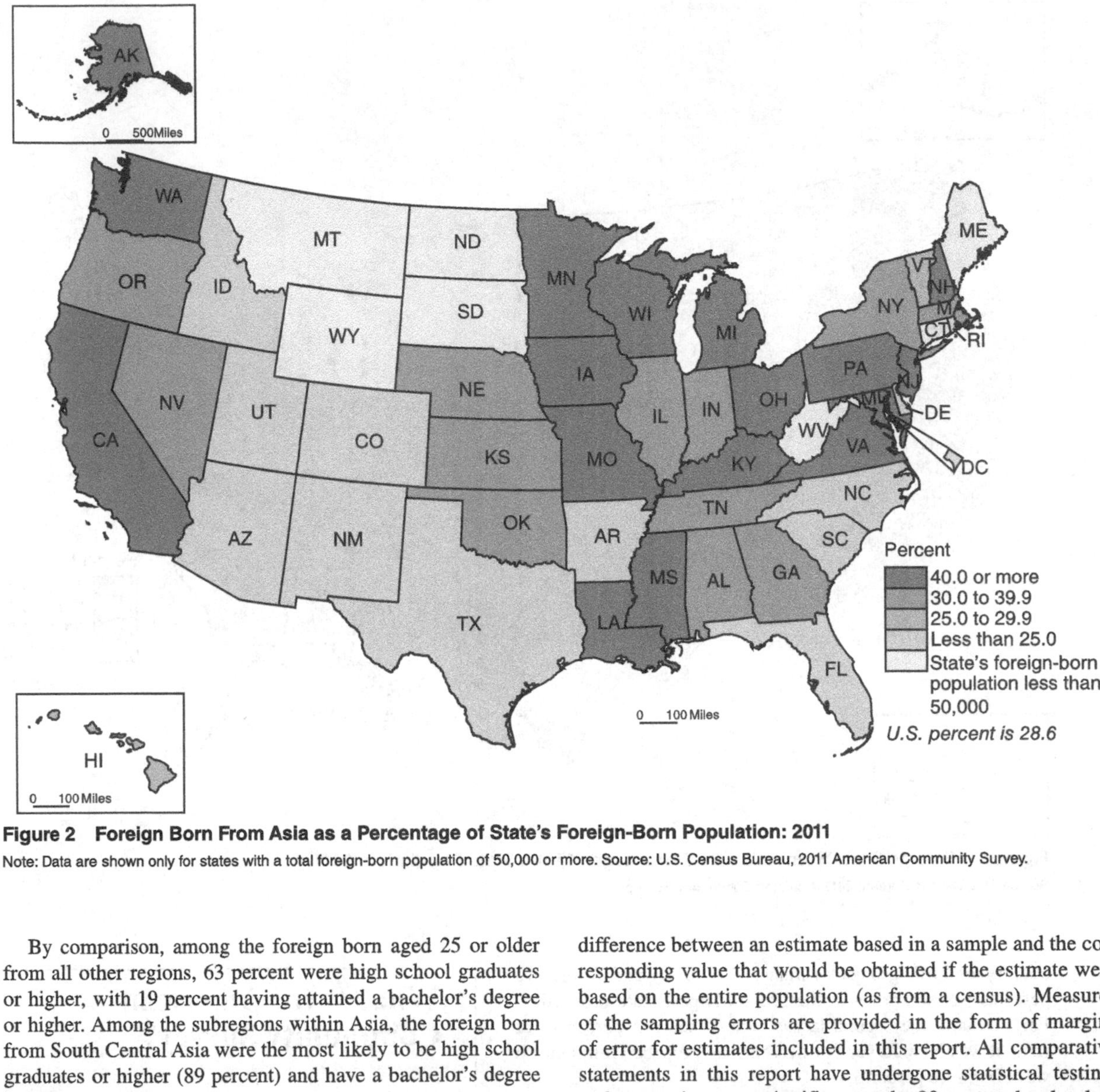

Figure 2 Foreign Born From Asia as a Percentage of State's Foreign-Born Population: 2011

Note: Data are shown only for states with a total foreign-born population of 50,000 or more. Source: U.S. Census Bureau, 2011 American Community Survey.

By comparison, among the foreign born aged 25 or older from all other regions, 63 percent were high school graduates or higher, with 19 percent having attained a bachelor's degree or higher. Among the subregions within Asia, the foreign born from South Central Asia were the most likely to be high school graduates or higher (89 percent) and have a bachelor's degree or higher (65 percent).

The foreign born from Asia were also more likely than the foreign born from all other world regions to be naturalized citizens (Figure 3). Fifty-eight percent of the foreign born from Asia were naturalized citizens, compared with 40 percent of the foreign born from all other world regions. Among regions within Asia, the foreign born from South Eastern Asia were the most likely to be naturalized citizens (66 percent).

Source and Accuracy

The data presented in this report are based on the ACS sample interviewed in 2011. The estimates based on this sample approximate the actual values and represent the entire household and group quarters population. Sampling error is the difference between an estimate based in a sample and the corresponding value that would be obtained if the estimate were based on the entire population (as from a census). Measures of the sampling errors are provided in the form of margins of error for estimates included in this report. All comparative statements in this report have undergone statistical testing, and comparisons are significant at the 90 percent level unless otherwise noted. In addition to sampling error, nonsampling error may be introduced during any of the operations used to collect and process survey data such as editing, reviewing, or keying data from questionnaires. For more information on sampling and estimation methods, confidentiality protection, and sampling and nonsampling errors, please see the 2011 ACS Accuracy of the Data document located at www.census.gov/acs/www/Downloads/data_documentation/Accuracy/ACS_Accuracy_of_Data_2011.pdf.

Notes

1. This report refers to the foreign-born population born in Asia, not those who report their race as Asian.

Table 5 Foreign-Born Population Aged 25 and Older by Region of Birth and Educational Attainment: 2011

Educational attainment	Total	Asia: Total[1]	Asia: Eastern Asia	Asia: South Central Asia	Asia: South Eastern Asia	Asia: Western Asia	All other regions[2]
Number							
Total	**34,383**	**9,908**	**3,057**	**2,579**	**3.474**	**764**	**24,475**
Less than 9th grade	6,889	984	307	145	446	82	5,905
9th to 12th grade, no diploma	3,926	659	187	130	284	56	3,266
High school graduate (includes equivalency)	7,734	1,632	532	291	644	157	6,102
Some college, no degree	4,544	1,211	308	217	576	105	3,333
Associate's degree	1,907	630	189	111	274	54	1,277
Bachelor's degree	5,498	2,748	795	801	972	172	2,750
Graduate or professional degree	3,887	2,044	738	884	278	139	1,842
Percent high school graduate or higher	68.5	83.4	83.8	89.3	79.0	82.1	62.5
Percent bachelor's degree or higher	27.3	48.4	50.2	65.3	36.0	40.7	18.8
Margin of Error (±)[3]							
Total	**98**	**40**	**31**	**28**	**36**	**24**	**90**
Less than 9th grade	50	17	11	9	11	5	49
9th to 12th grade, no diploma	39	15	8	8	9	5	35
High school graduate (includes equivalency)	58	24	15	13	14	10	50
Some college, no degree	41	21	10	9	16	7	35
Associate's degree	24	15	8	6	12	5	20
Bachelor's degree	47	32	15	17	18	9	34
Graduate or professional degree	37	26	16	19	10	8	28
Percent high school graduate or higher	0.2	0.2	0.4	0.5	0.4	0.8	0.2
Percent bachelor's degree or higher	0.2	0.3	0.6	0.6	0.5	1.2	0.2

(Numbers in thousands. Data based on sample. For information on confidentiality protection, sampling error, nonsampling error, and definitions, see *www.census.gov/acs/www*)

[1] Includes an estimated 41,000 persons whose region of birth was classified as "Asia not elsewhere classified" and are not included in the four Asian subregions.

[2] "All other regions" includes all non-Asian countries, including those in Africa, Europe, Latin America, North America, and Oceania.

[3] Data are based on a sample and are subject to sampling variability. A margin of error is a measure of an estimate's variability. The larger the margin of error is in relation to the size of the estimate, the less reliable the estimate. When added to and subtracted from the estimate, the margin of error forms the 90 percent confidence interval.

Source: U.S. Census Bureau, 2011 American Community Survey.

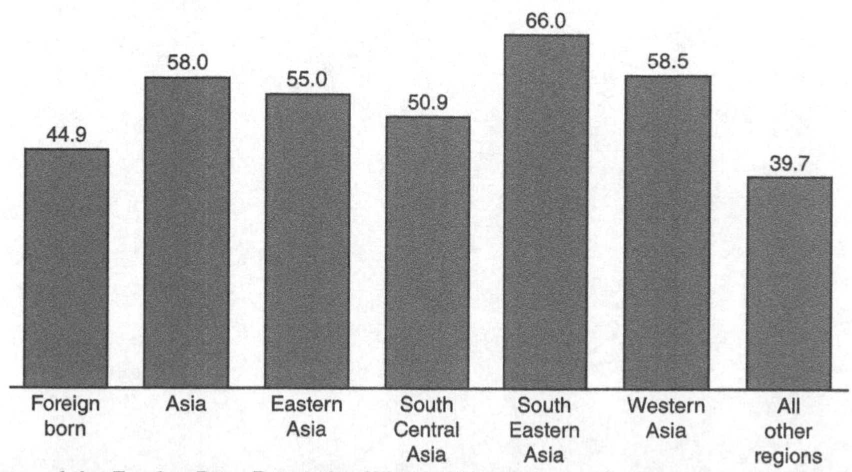

Figure 3 Percentage of the Foreign-Born Population Who Are Naturalized U.S. Citizens by Region of Birth: 2011 (Data based on sample. For information on confidentiality protection, sampling error, nonsampling error, and definitions, see www.census.gov/acs/www/)

Source: U.S. Census Bureau, 2011 American Community Survey.

2. The term Asia includes countries in Eastern, South Central, South Eastern, and Western Asia. Eastern Asia includes China (including China, Hong Kong, Taiwan, Macau, and the Paracel islands), Japan, Korea (including South Korea and North Korea), and Mongolia. South Central Asia includes Afghanistan, Bangladesh, Bhutan, India, Iran, Kazakhstan, Kyrgyzstan, Maldives, Nepal, Pakistan, Sri Lanka, Tajikistan, Turkmenistan, and Uzbekistan. South Eastern Asia includes Brunei, Burma, Cambodia, Indonesia, Laos, Malaysia, Philippines, Singapore, Thailand, Timor-Leste, and Vietnam. Western Asia includes; Armenia, Azerbaijan, Bahrain, Cyprus, Georgia, Iraq, Israel, Jordan, Kuwaiti Lebanon, Oman, Qatar, Saiidt Arabia, Syria, Turkey, United Arab Emirates, and Yemen. Throughout the remainder of this report, the term Asia refers to all of these areas and also any responses classified as "Asia not elsewhere classified."
3. Gibson, Campbell and Kay Jung, 2006, "Historical Census Statistics on the Foreign-Born Population in the United States: 1850 to 2000," U.S. Census Bureau, Population Division Working Paper, Number 81, available on the Census Bureau's Web site at www.census.gov/population/www/techpap.html.
4. The percentages of foreign born from Asia who were from South Central Asia in Delaware, New Jersey, and Connecticut were not statistically different.

Critical Thinking

1. What are the root causes of migration?
2. Are Asian immigrants the model minority population?

Create Central

www.mhhe.com/createcentral

Internet References

Asian American for Equality
www.aafe.org

Asian American Studies Center
www.aasc.ucla.eduldefault.asp

Asian-Nation
www asian-nation.orglindex_shtml

Social Science Information Gateway
http://sosig.esrc.bris.ac.uk

Sociosite
www.sociosite.net

U.S Census Bureau, 2012.

Article

Prepared by: John A. Kromkowski, *Catholic University of America*

Profile America: Facts for Features, Asian/Pacific American Heritage Month: May 2013

In 1978, a joint congressional resolution established Asian/Pacific American Heritage Week. The first 10 days of May were chosen to coincide with two important milestones in Asian/Pacific American history: the arrival in the United States of the first Japanese immigrants (May 7, 1843) and contributions of Chinese workers to the building of the transcontinental railroad, completed May 10, 1869. In 1992, Congress expanded the observance to a monthlong celebration. Per a 1997 Office of Management and Budget directive, the Asian or Pacific Islander racial category was separated into two categories: one being Asian and the other Native Hawaiian and Other Pacific Islander. Thus, this Facts for Features contains a section for each.

Learning Outcomes

After reading this article, you will be able to:

- Know when Congress established Asian/Pacific American Heritage Week.
- Identify the most troubling demographic indicators about Asian/Pacific Americans.

Asians

18.2 million

The estimated number of U.S. residents in 2011 who were Asian, either alone or in combination with one or more additional races.

Source: 2011 Population Estimates Table 3 www.census.gov/popest/data/index.html. For additional information, see www.census.gov/popest/data/national/asrh/2011/index.html.

5.8 million

The Asian alone or in combination population in California in 2011. The state had the largest Asian population, followed by New York (1.7 million). The Asian alone-or-in-combination population represented 57 percent of the total population in Hawaii.

Source: 2011 Population Estimates Table 5 www.census.gov/popest/data/index.html. For additional information, see www.census.gov/popest/data/state/asrh/2011/index.html.

46%

Percentage growth of the Asian alone or in combination population between the 2000 and 2010 censuses, which was more than any other major race group.

Source: U.S. Census Bureau, 2010 Census Redistricting Data (Public Law 94–171) Summary File, Custom Table 3, www.census.gov/2010census/news/xls/cbllcn123_us_2010redistr.xls. For additional details, see Hoeffel, E., S. Rastogi, M. Kim, and H. Shahid. 2011. *The Asian Population: 2010,* U.S. Census Bureau, 2010 Census Briefs, C2010BR-11, available at www.census.gov/prod/cen2010/briefs/c2010br-ll.pdf.

4 million

Number of Asians of Chinese, except Taiwanese, descent in the U.S. in 2011. The Chinese (except Taiwanese) population was the largest Asian group, followed by Filipinos (3.4 million), Asian Indians (3.2 million), Vietnamese (1.9 million), Koreans (1.7 million) and Japanese (1.3 million). These estimates represent the number of people who reported a specific detailed Asian group alone, as well as people who reported that detailed Asian group in combination with one or more other detailed Asian groups or another race(s).

Source: U.S. Census Bureau, 2011 American Community Survey, Table B02018 http://factfinder2.census.gov/bkmk/table/1.0/en/ACS/11_1YR/B02018

Income, Poverty and Health Insurance

$67,885

Median household income for the Asian alone population in 2011.

Source: U.S. Census Bureau, 2011 American Community Survey, Table S0201, http://factfinder2.census.gov/bkmk/table/1.0/en/ACS/11_1YR/S020l//popgroup~031 Median household income differed greatly by Asian group. For Asian Indians, for example, the median income in 2011 was $92,418; for Bangladeshi, it was $45,185. (These figures represent the Asian alone population.)

Source: U.S. Census Bureau, 2011 American Community Survey, Table S0201,
http://factfinder2.census.gov/bkmk/table/1.0/en/ACS/11_1YR/S0201//popgroup~013 and
http://factfinder2.census.gov/bkmk/table/1.0/en/ACS/11_1YR/S0201//popgroup~014

12.8%

The poverty rate for the Asian alone population in 2011.

Source: U.S. Census Bureau, 2011 American Community Survey, Table S1701
http://factfinder2.census.gov/faces/tableservices/jsf/pages/productview.xhtml?pid=ACS_11_1YR_S1701

15.4

Percentage of single-race Asians without health insurance coverage in 2011.

Source: U.S. Census Bureau, 2011 American Community Survey, Table S0201
http://factfinder2.census.gov/bkmk/table/1.0/en/ACS/11_1YR/S0201/popgroup~012

Education

50%

The percentage of the Asian alone population 25 and older who had a bachelor's degree or higher level of education. This compared with 28.5 percent for all Americans 25 and older.

Source: U.S. Census Bureau, 2011 American Community Survey, Table S0201,
http://factfinder2.census.gov/bkmk/table/1.0/en/ACS/11_1YR/S0201//popgroup~012 and
http://factfinder2.census.gov/bkmk/table/1.0/en/ACS/11_1YR/S0201

85.1%

The percentage of the Asian alone population 25 and older who had at least a high school diploma. This is not statistically different from the percentage for the total population or the percentage of Native Hawaiian or Other Pacific Islander alone, 86 and 85 percent, respectively.

Source: U.S. Census Bureau, 2011 American Community Survey, Table S0201,
http://factfinder2.census.gov/bkmk/table/l.0/en/ACS/11_1YR/S0201

20.7%

The percentage of the Asian alone population 25 and older who had a graduate (e.g., master's) or professional degree. This compared with 10.6 percent for all Americans 25 and older.

Source: U.S. Census Bureau, 2011 American Community Survey, Table S0201,
http://factfinder2.census.gov/bkmk/table/1.0/en/ACS/11_1YR/S0201 and
http://factfinder2.census.gov/bkmk/table/1.0/en/ACS/11_1YR/S020l//popgroup~031

Voting

589,000

The additional number of the Asian alone population who voted in the 2008 presidential election than in the 2004 election. All in all, 48 percent of Asians turned out to vote in 2008—up 4 percentage points from 2004. A total of 3.4 million Asians voted.

Source: U.S. Census Bureau, Voting and Registration in the Election of November 2008,
www.census.gov/newsroom/releases/archives/voting/cb09-110.html

Businesses

Source for the statements referenced in this section, unless otherwise indicated: U.S. Census Bureau, 2007 Survey of Business Owners via American FactFinder,

http://factfinder2.census.gov/bkmk/table/1.0/en/SBO/2007/00CSA01/0100000US/naics~00

1.5 million

Number of businesses owned by Asians in 2007, an increase of 40.4 percent from 2002.

$506.0 billion

Total receipts of businesses owned by Asians in 2007, up 54.9 percent from 2002.

44.7%

Percentage of Asian-owned businesses that operated in repair and maintenance, personal and laundry services; professional, scientific and technical services; and retail trade in 2007.

47.2%

Percentage of businesses in Hawaii owned by people of Asian descent. It was 14.9 percent in California and 10.1 percent in New York.

508,969

California had the most Asian-owned firms at 508,969 (32.8 percent of all such firms), followed by New York with 196,825 (12.7 percent) and Texas with 114,297 (7.4 percent).

Serving Our Nation

264,695

The number of the Asian alone population military veterans in 2011. About one in three veterans was 65 and older.

Source: U.S. Census Bureau, 2011 American Community Survey, Table B21001D, http://factfinder2.census.gov/bkmk/table/1.0/en/ACS/11_1YR/B21001D

Jobs

48.5%

The proportion of civilian employed single-race Asians 16 and older who worked in management, business, science and arts occupations, such as financial managers, engineers, teachers and registered nurses in 2011. Additionally, 17.4 percent worked in service occupations, 21.1 percent in sales and office occupations, 9.6 percent in production, transportation and material moving occupations and 3.3 percent in natural resources, construction and maintenance occupations.

Source: U.S. Census Bureau, 2011 American Community Survey, Table S0201,
http://factfinder2.census.gov/bkmk/table/1.0/en/ACS/11_1YR/S0201//popgroup~012

Internet Use

80%

Percentage of Asians in 2009 living in a household with Internet use—the highest rate among race and ethnic groups.

Source: U.S. Census Bureau, Reported Internet Usage for Households, by selected Householder Characteristics; Current Population Survey: 2009
www.census.gov/population/www/socdemo/computer/2009.html

Age Distribution

33.5

Median age of the Asian alone or in combination population in 2011. The corresponding figure was 37.3 years for the population as a whole.

Source: U.S. Census Bureau, 2011 American Community Survey, Tables S0201,
http://factfinder2.census.gov/bkmk/table/1.0/en/ACS/11_1YR/S0201//popgroup~031 and
http://factfinder2.census.gov/bkmk/table/1.0/en/ACS/11_1YR/S0201

25.6%

Percent of the Asian alone or in combination population that was under age 18 in 2011, while 9.0 percent was 65 or older.

Source: U.S. Census Bureau, 2011 American Community Survey, Table S0201
http://factfinder2.census.gov/bkmk/table/1.0/en/ACS/11_1YR/S0201//popgroup~031

Native Hawaiians and Other Pacific Islanders

1.4 million

The estimated number of U.S. residents in 2011 who were Native Hawaiian or Other Pacific Islander, either alone or in combination with one or more additional races.

Source: 2011 Population Estimates Table 3
www.census.gov/popest/data/index.html. For additional information, see
www.census.gov/popest/data/national/asrh/2011/index.html.

359,000

Hawaii had the largest population of Native Hawaiians and Other Pacific Islanders among the alone or in combination population with 359,000, followed by California (329,000) in 2011. Hawaii had the largest proportion of Native Hawaiians and Other Pacific Islanders (26 percent).

Source: 2011 Population Estimates Table 4
www.census.gov/popest/data/index.html. For additional information, see
www.census.gov/popest/data/state/asrh/2011/index.html.

40%

Percentage growth of the Native Hawaiian and Other Pacific Islander alone or in combination population between the 2000 and 2010 censuses.

Source: U.S. Census Bureau, 2010 Census Redistricting Data (Public Law 94–171) Summary File, Custom Table 3, www.census.gov/2010census/news/xls/cb11cn123_us_2010redistr.xls. For additional details, see Hixson, L., B. Hepler, and M. Kim. 2011. *The Native Hawaiian and Other Pacific Islander Population: 2010,* U.S. Census Bureau, 2010 Census Briefs, C2010BR-12, available at
www.census.gov/prod/cen2010/briefs/c2010br-12.pdf.

518,000

Number of Native Hawaiians in the U.S. in 2011. The Native Hawaiian population was the largest detailed Native Hawaiian and Other Pacific Islanders (NHPI) group, followed by Samoan (174,000) and Guamanian or Chamorro (108,000). These estimates represent the number of people who reported a specific detailed NHPI group alone, as well as people who reported that detailed NHPI group in combination with one or more other detailed NHPI groups or another race(s).

Source: U.S. Census. Bureau, 2011 American Community Survey, Table B02019
http://factfinder2.census.gov/bkmk/table/1.0/en/ACS/11_1YR/B02019

Income, Poverty and Health Insurance

$49,378

The median income of households headed by the Native Hawaiians and Other Pacific Islanders alone in 2011.

Source: U.S. Census Bureau, 2011 American Community Survey, Table S0201

http://factfinder2.census.gov/bkmk/table/1.0/en/ACS/11_1YR/S0201//popgroup~050

21.5%

The poverty rate in 2011 Native Hawaiians and Other Pacific Islanders alone population.

Source: U.S. Census Bureau, 2011 American Community Survey, Table S0201,
http://factfinder2.census.gov/bkmk/table/1.0/en/ACS/11_1YR/S0201//popgroup~050

18.5%

The percentage without health insurance in 2011 for single-race Native Hawaiians and Other Pacific Islanders.

Source: U.S. Census Bureau, 2011 American Community Survey, Table S0201,
http://factfinder2.census.gov/bkmk/table/1.0/en/ACS/11_1YR/S0201//popgroup~050

Education

14.5%

The percentage of the Native Hawaiians and Other Pacific Islanders alone 25 and older who had a bachelor's degree or higher in 2011. This compared with 28.5 percent for the total population.

Source: U.S. Census Bureau, 2011 American Community Survey, Tables S020I
http://factfinder2.census.gov/bkmk/table/1.0/en/ACS/11_1YR/S0201//popgroup~050 and
http://factfinder2.census.gov/bkmk/table/1.0/en/ACS/11_1YR/S0201

85.1%

The percentage of the Native Hawaiians and Other Pacific Islanders alone 25 and older who had at least a high school diploma in 2011. This compared with 85.9 percent of the total population.

Source: U.S. Census Bureau, 2011 American Community Survey Tables S0201
http://factfinder2.census.gov/bkmk/table/1.0/en/ACS/11_1YR/S020l//popgroup~050 and
http://factfinder2.census.gov/bkmk/table/1.0/en/ACS/11_1YR/S0201

4.3%

The percentage of the Native Hawaiians and Other Pacific Islanders alone 25 and older who had obtained a graduate or professional degree in 2011. This compared with 10.6 percent for the total population this age.

Source: U.S. Census Bureau, 2011 American Community Survey, Tables S0201
http://factfinder2.census.gov/bkmk/table/1.0/en/ACS/11_1YR/S0201//popgroup~050 and
http://factfinder2.census.gov/bkmk/table/1.0/en/ACS/11_1YR/S0201

Businesses

Source for the statements referenced in this section, unless otherwise indicated: U.S. Census Bureau, 2007 Survey of Business Owners via American FactFinder
http://factfinder2.census.gov/bkmk/table/1.0/en/SBO/2007/00CSA01/0100000US/naics~00

37,687

The number of Native Hawaiian and Other Pacific Islander-owned businesses in 2007, up 30.2 percent from 2002.

$6.3 billion

Total receipts of these businesses in 2007, up 47.7 percent from 2002.

44.5%

The percent of all Native Hawaiian and Other Pacific Islander-owned business revenue that construction and retail trade accounted for in 2007.

9.5%

The percent of businesses in Hawaii owned by Native Hawaiian and Other Pacific Islanders in 2007, highest among all states.

Serving Our Nation

27,469

The number of the Native Hawaiian and Other Pacific Islander alone military veterans. About one in five veterans was 65 years and older.

Source: U.S. Census Bureau, 2011 American Community Survey, B21001E,
http://factfinder2.census.gov/bkmk/table/1.0/en/ACS/10_1YR/B21001E

Jobs

24%

The proportion of civilian employed the Native Hawaiians and Other Pacific Islanders alone 16 and older who worked in management, business, science and arts occupations, such as financial managers, engineers, teachers and registered nurses in 2011. The percents for management, business, science and arts occupations, sales and office occupations and service occupations are not statistically different from one another. Additionally, 25.7 percent worked in service occupations, while 26.6 percent worked in sales and office occupations, 15.2 percent in production, transportation and material moving occupations and 8.6 percent in natural resources, construction and maintenance occupation.

Source: U.S. Census Bureau, 2011 American Community Survey, Table S0201,

http://factfinder2.census.gov/bkmk/table/1.0/en/ACS/11_1YR/S0201//popgroup~050

Age Distribution

27.1

The median age of the Native Hawaiian and Other Pacific Islander population alone or in combination in 2011. The median age was 37.3 for the population as a whole.

Source: U.S. Census Bureau, 2011 American Community Survey, http://factfinder2.census.gov/bkmk/table/1.0/en/ACS/11_1YR/S0201//popgroup~060 and http://factfinder2.census.gov/bkmk/table/l.0/en/ACS/11_1YR/S0201

33.5%

Percentage of the Native Hawaiian and Other Pacific Islander alone or in combination population that was under age 18 in 2011, while 5.5 percent was 65 or older.

Source: U.S. Census Bureau, 2011 American Community Survey, Table S0201, http://factfinder2.census.gov/bkmk/table/1.0/en/ACS/11_1YR/S0201//popgroup~060

Following is a list of observances typically covered by the Census Bureau's *Facts for Features* series:

- Black History Month (February)
- Super Bowl
- Valentine's Day (Feb. 14)
- Women's History Month (March)
- Irish-American Heritage Month (March)/
- St. Patrick's Day (March 17)
- Asian/Pacific American Heritage Month (May)
- Older Americans Month (May)
- Cinco de Mayo (May 5)
- Mother's Day
- Hurricane Season Begins (June 1)
- Father's Day
- The Fourth of July (July 4)
- Anniversary of Americans with Disabilities Act (July 26)
- Back to School (August)
- Labor Day
- Grandparents Day
- Hispanic Heritage Month (Sept. 15–Oct. 15)
- Halloween (Oct. 31)
- American Indian/Alaska Native Heritage Month (November)
- Veterans Day (Nov. 11)
- Thanksgiving Day
- The Holiday Season (December)

Critical Thinking

1. Are Asian immigrants acculturating and assimilating or are these concepts irrelevant in a globalized world?
2. Discuss the positive and troubling consequences related to highly skilled immigrants.

Create Central

www.mhhe.com/createcentral

Internet References

Asian American for Equality
www.aafe.org

Asian American Studies Center
www.aasc.ucla.eduldefault.asp

Asian-Nation
www.asian-nation.orglindex_shtml

Social Science Information Gateway
http://sosig.esrc.bris.ac.uk

Sociosite
www.sociosite.net

Editor's note—As a matter of policy, the Census Bureau does not advocate the use of the *alone* population over the *alone-or-in-combination* population or vice versa. The use of the *alone* population in sections of this report does not imply that it is a preferred method of presenting or analyzing data. The same is true for sections of this report that focus on the *alone-or-in-combination* population. Data on race can be presented and discussed in a variety of ways.

The preceding data were collected from a variety of sources and may be subject to sampling variability and other sources of error.

U.S Census Bureau, 2013.

Article

Prepared by: John A. Kromkowski, *Catholic University of America*

Filipino Americans: An Introduction to Their (Mostly) Recent Historiography

ROLAND L. GUYOTTE

Learning Outcomes

After reading this article, you will be able to:

- Understand whether or not written history always involves the selection of relevant events.
- Understand the concept and purpose of a "usable past"?

Filipino Americans are unique in several ways. *First,* they hail from the United States' most populous overseas colony, over which American mainlanders ruled from 1899 to 1946. Filipinos have thus been more likely to have at least some English than many other immigrants. Second, during most of the era of Asiatic exclusion Filipinos as colonial "nationals" could travel freely back and forth from the United States to the islands, making them inherently transnational, though most could not become citizens and faced racial and legal exclusions such as west coast anti-miscegenation laws and many states' restriction oflicensed professional work to U. S. citizens. Third, although the 1934 legislation authorizing the independence of the Philippines basically closed the door to Filipinos until the Immigration Reform Act of 1965, Filipinos subsequently rushed to enter the United States, were naturalized at higher rates than almost all other groups, and actively pursued a form of strategic citizenship for extended kin networks, based on family reunification provisions of recent legislation. According to the Census Bureau's American Community Survey, by 2008, as many as 2.9 million Americans could claim some Filipino ancestry. A generational distinction among Filipino Americans reflects a contrast between those who migrated to—and stayed in—the United States before 1935 and those who came after 1965. While a few Filipinos migrated to Louisiana before the twentieth century, the earliest substantial Filipino . . . immigration, far . . . more male than female, came when young, single men sought work, study, adventure or a combination of these. They intended their stay to be temporary, but some became "unintentional immigrants." More than half of the approximately 100,000 Filipinos in the United States in 1940 lived in Hawaii, where sugar planters had recruited about 120,000 of their countrymen as contract labor between 1909 and 1934. The vast majority of the 45,000 Filipinos on the mainland lived on the west coast, often traveling seasonally to the fields and canneries of California, Oregon, Washington, and Alaska, though some also combined study with work. Many of the farm workers remained single, although some married Mexican or Alaska native women. "Little Manilas" emerged before World War IT in Seattle, Los Angeles, and Stockton, CA, among other places, as Filipinos either drifted in from the countryside between planting and harvesting, or found personal service or restaurant work. Smaller groups of Filipinos lived in Midwestern and east coast cities, often after having attempted or completed schooling inthe United States. A substantial portion of the 2000 or so Filipinos settling in Chicago before 1940 found niche employment as postal clerks or as attendants on Pullman Company railroad dining and club cars. The small communities of Filipino immigrants in Washington, DC or Virginia included Filipino veterans of the U.S. Navy, who under certain conditions could gain citizenship.

These "old-timers" have long had their chroniclers, and recent scholarship has deepened and altered the original portraiture. The semi-memoir of Carlos Bulosan (1912–1956) *America is in the Heart* (1946) has for decades been a primary source for information about the harsh conditions faced by California Filipino farm labor, and is useful for teaching purposes, but it should be supplemented by Linda España-Maram's outstanding *Creating Masculinity in Los Angeles's Little Manila: Working Class Filipinos and Popular Culture, 1920s–1950s* (2006), which details their leisure as well as their work lives—at boxing matches, taxi-dance halls, and gambling dens. España-Maram emphasizes the role of the automobile as a means for maintaining "mobile community" ties among young transients. Robert Vallangca, *Pinoy: The First Wave, 1898–1941* (1977) has interviews of early Filipino migrants not always in sync with Bulosan's account, while Rick Baldoz's ambitious *The Third Asiatic Invasion: Empire and Migration in Filipino America, 1898–1946* (2011), adds new detail to west coast anti-Filipino violence and immigrant resistance to it. A fine memoir edited by Craig Scharlin and Lilian Villanueva, *Philip Vera Cruz: A Personal History of Filipino Immigrants and the Farmworkers Movement* (2000) traces his career from the 1920s to the 1970s. Dorothy Fugita-Rony, *American Workers, Colonial Power: Philippine Seattle and the Transpacific West, 1919–1941* (2003), and Chris Friday, *Organizing Asian American Labor: The Pacific Coast Canned Salmon Industry, 1870–1942* (1994), provide important information respectively about Filipino labor contractors and the labor unions that sometimes battled them in the prewar era. Melinda Tria Kerkvliet, *Unbending Cane: Pablo Manlapit, a Filipino Labor Leader in Hawaii* (2003) personalizes the early Hawaiian Filipino experience. Barbara Posadas's pioneering articles, sometimes co-authored with this writer, contrast the west coast agricultural and service workers with those Midwestern students, a substantial number of whom married women of European descent and did not return to the Philippines. And two recent works on broader. topics have fine chapters which place Filipinos in context with other immigrant groups: Elliott R. Barkan, *From All Points: America's Immigrant West, 1870s–1952* (2007), and Mae M. Ngai, *Impossible Subjects: Illegal Aliens and the Making of Modern America* (2004), which recounts the failed attempt by U.S. federal authorities to "repatriate" Filipinos to the Islands in the late 1930s. Among older volumes, Bruno Lasker's monumental survey, *Filipino Immigration: To Continental United States and Hawaii* (1931) is still useful, and Fred W. Cordova's *Filipinos: Forgotten Asian Americans: A Pictorial Essay/1763-circa-1963* (1983) remains unsurpassed for visual material in the years it covers.

The "old-timers'" offspring, usually born between the 1920s and the 1940s, and those war brides, Exchange Visitor Act nurses, or other Filipinos who managed to enter the U. S. between 1935 and 1965, sometimes refer to themselves as the "bridge" generation, and have done much to collect and preserve interviews, photographs, and other documentary material about their parents' and their own cohorts. Caridad Conception Vallangca carried on her late husband's work in *The Second Wave: Pinoy and Pinay, 1945–1960* (1987), which has particularly good interviews with military brides and female professionals. Joseph A. Galura and Emily Lawsin, *Filipino Women in Detroit, 1945–1955* (2002) provides Midwestern detail. Several "bridge" Filipinos have written their own stories. In *Growing Up Brown: Memoirs of a Filipino American* (2006), Peter Jamero, a social services executive, recounts the political activism of his Seattle contemporaries. Other notable memoirs include Evangeline Canonizado Buell's *Twenty-Five Chickens and a Pig for a Bride: Growing Up in a Filipino Immigrant Family* (2006), and Patricia Justiniani McReynolds, *Almost Americans: A Quest for Dignity* (1997), which recounts the travails of her Filipino immigrant father and Norwegian immigrant mother in southem California.

"Bridge" and post-1965 immigrants more likely kept up ties with the Philippines than those "old-timers" who stayed in the United States, though some of the latter traveled back and forth over several decades, sent remittances, or corresponded frequently long before historians took note. Two outstanding recent scholarly works emphasize the transnational character of intellectuals and nurses, respectively. In *Five Faces of Exile: The Nation and Filipino Exiles* (2005), Augusto Fauni Espiritu traces the varied careers of five figures, including American-educated Carlos Romulo, later Philippine foreign minister and president of the United Nations General Assembly, and Bulosan, who achieved American literary prominence in the 1940s but died a decade later in obscurity without ever returning "home." Catherine Ceniza Choy's *Empire of Care: Nursing and Migration in Filipino American History* (2003) ranges widely to delineate American-designed nursing education in the Philippines, the migration of nurses, and their fate in the United States. By 1960, the "old-timers," the "bridge" generation and their offspring totaled about 175,000 of Philippine descent, but their numbers paled by comparison with post-1965 immigrants, 55 percent of whom were still Philippine-born in 2008.

The post-1965 immigrants came mainly because of a surplus of educated workers in the Philippines in such professions as health, science, and engineering, and because of the continuing poverty, corruption, and instability in their class-riven nation. Educated before arriving in the United States, they had likely married and begun families in the Philippines, and because of the Islands' post-independence shift to Tagalog as the national language they resembled other recent immigrants more than their predecessors by speaking a language other than English at home. They settled in substantial enclaves, not only in Hawaii, California, and the Pacific Northwest, but also in New York, New Jersey, Illinois, and elsewhere in the Midwest. Many sought doggedly to combine economic success—often achieved through a household's paychecks and lower-waged employment for which they were overqualified—with retention of "Philippine values," especially in the raising of their children, a difficult task under any circumstances, but complicated in the post-1965 era by exposure to American popular culture *and* the ease of contact with the homeland.

Not surprisingly, historians have not written as much about post-1965 Filipino Americans as have social scientists. The major exception, albeit in a relatively brief survey because of the format of the "New Americans Series" in which it appeared, is Barbara M. Posadas, *The Filipino Americans* (1999), which draws upon the author's familiarity with the Filipinos' American past to place the newcomers in a historical context. Works by social scientists include Maria P. P. Root (ed.), *Filipino Americans: Transformation and Identity* (1997), containing almost two dozen articles, among them Theodore S. Gonzalves, "The Day the Dancers Stayed: On Filipino Cultural Nights," an ethnography of a contemporary college tradition that rallies local Filipino American communities throughout the United States. Rick Bonus, *Locating Filipino Americans: Ethnicity and the Cultural Politics of Space* (2000), adds material on shopping centers, community newspapers, and beauty pageants. The particular hazards of growing up female in Filipino America are treated in Yen Le Espiritu, *Home Bound: Filipino American Lives across Cultures, Communities, and Countries* (2003), focused on San Diego, and Diane L. Wolf, "There's No Place Like 'Home': Emotional Transnationalism and the Struggles of Second-Generation Filipinos," in Peggy Levitt and Mary C. Waters (eds.), *The Changing Face of Home: The Transnational Lives of the Second Generation* (2002). An engaging, highly teachable memoir, is Pati Navalta Poblete, *The Oracles: My Filipino Grandparents in America* (2006). Rhacel Salazar Parreñas treats Filipina women's international labor migration comparatively in her study of Los Angeles and Rome, *Servants of Globalization: Women, Migration and Domestic Work* (2001). In *Global Divas: Filipino Gay Men in the Diaspora* (2003), Martin F. Manalansan IV profiles a distinctive subculture in contemporary New York City.

Finally, a substantial portion of Filipino American fiction has depicted conflicts among generations or Filipinos' difficulties in America. A sampling of the possibilities are Bienvenido Santos's poignant stories about "old-timers" in *The Scent of Apples: A Collection of Stories* (1979), Peter Bacho's tales of fathers and sons in *Dark Blue Suit, and Other Stories* (1997), and Jessica Tarahata Hagedorn's fast-paced account of San Francisco and New York Filipino punk rock cultures in *The Gangster of Love* (1997). Significantly, several Filipino American writers have published novels set in either country: Hagedorn's acclaimed *Dogeaters* (1991), Bacho's *Cebu* (1991) and R. Zamora Linmark's *Leche* (2011), are all centered in the Philippines.

Critical Thinking

1. Has the history of U.S. relations to the Philippine Islands been part of your American history course?
2. Discuss the concept and uses of memory and history in the creation of an ethnic tradition.

Create Central

www.mhhe.com/createcentral

Internet References

Asian American for Equality
www.aafe.org

Asian American Studies Center
www.aasc.ucla.eduldefault.asp

Asian-Nation
www asian-nation.orglindex_shtml

Center for Research in Ethnic Relations
www.warwickac.ukllaclsoc/CRER_RC

Yale University Guide to American Ethnic Studies.
www.fibrary.yale.edulrsc/ethniclintemethtml

Roland L. Guyotte is Professor of History and All-University Morse Alumni Distinguished Teaching Professor at the University of Minnesota, Morris.

Unit 7

UNIT

Prepared by: John A. Kromkowski, *Catholic University of America*

Euro/Mediterranean Ethnic Americans

The American experience from 1870 to 1924 addressed the influence of these groups and in so doing shifted American consciousness of itself. Even 100 years later, America's public mind continues to identify and divide its history as an immigrant-receiving country into two periods: The Old Immigration, meaning Northern Europeans, and the New Immigration, meaning Others—the Mediterranean and eastern European as well as Asian and Hispanic populations. One marker of this division can be found in the ***Report of the Dillingham Commission (1910)***, a congressional and presidential blue ribbon panel that warned America that the eastern European and Mediterranean character was less capable of Americanization than the Nordics and Teutonic who had peopled America.

The considerable fluidity of the immigrant experiences, as well as the complex processes of cultural identity and political use of cultural symbols, such as race and ethnicity, the search for more analytical rigor in this field is far from complete. Some guide to discernable and measurable features of ethnic phenomena and characteristics that are attributes of ethnicity was developed in a fine collection of materials on this topic, ***The Harvard Encyclopedia of American Ethnic Groups,*** which lists the following markers of ethnic groups: common geographic origin, migratory status, language/dialect, religious faith(s), ties that transcend kinship, neighborhood, and community boundaries, shared traditions values, and symbols, literature, folklore, music, food preferences, settlement and employment patterns, special interests in regard to politics in the homeland and in the United States, institutions that specifically serve and maintain the group, and internal sense of distinctiveness and an external perception of distinctiveness. With the addition of a demographic database developed by the US Census a much more rigorous set of analytics can be applied to anthropological and humanistic approaches to ethnic groups.

The U.S Census reveals the ongoing process of peopling America and the remarkably "lumpy" distribution of geographic patterns in various states and regions. The persistence of ethnic identification and the arrival of new immigrants are measured in these data and can now be accessed and systematically analyzed. The specific dynamics of group isolation and integration point to the complexity generated by public policy, most importantly the designations available for racial and ethnic identity offered for the first time in the 2000 U.S. Census. The plentitude of resources and the social imagination of community leaders as well as specific characteristics of race and ethnic populations—their size, scale, and scope—and the range of governmental policies determine race and ethnic relations. As a guide for your own study, the U.S. Commission on Civil Rights has noted the following issues for both recent arrivals and Americans by birth:

- Employment: The areas of occupation selected by or imposed upon various ethnic populations trace ethnic group mobility strategies and ethnic succession in the workplace, especially in manufacturing, hospitals, restaurants, and maintenance and custodial positions. Some ethnic populations appear to have greater numbers of highly educated persons in professional or semi-professional positions.
- Institutional and societal barriers: The job preferences and discrimination against the ethnic enclaves and persons install communities that are isolated from mainstream English-speaking society suggest the value of second-language competencies. Mutual accommodation is required to minimize the effect of inadequate language skills and training and difficulties in obtaining licenses, memberships, and certification.
- Exploitation of workers: The most common form is the payment of wages below minimum standards. Alien workers have been stereotyped as a drain on public services. Such scapegoating is insupportable.
- Taking jobs from Americans: Fact or fiction?: The stunning fact is that immigrants are a source of increased productivity and a significant, if not utterly necessary, addition to the workforce as well as to the consumer power that drives the American economy.

The U.S. Census in 1980 and 1990 began the systematic collection of ethnic data. Census data on ethnicity is derived from self-identification. This method captures the respondent's sense of personal and group identity. Prior to 1980 the paucity of quantified information on ethnic variety was a profound impediment to the analysis of the ethnic composition of America and to the electoral participation of ethnic voters and ethnic organizations. Appreciating the variety of ethnicities that constitute the American population begins with dispelling the conventional categories and counts. Personal reflections on the relevance of ethnicity to one's self-concept and the search for clearer expressions of group identity are included in this unit. Readers may be interested in exploring the concept of social distance and group affinity in relation to information provided in these articles and as tools for testing and discovering patterns of race and ethnic interest in various issues. In addition to those mentioned, recent concerns of ethnic groups include language preservation, fair hearings for homeland interests, enclave neighborhoods, inclusion in ethnic studies, and their articulation of historical American expressions of fairness, justice, and equity, as well as the collection of accurate data from all ethnic groups in America. These values are thoroughly patterned into their worldview and they propriated the expansive promise of the American icon: the Statue of Liberty.

Moynihan and Glazer in *Beyond the Melting Pot* (1964), the report of the Kerner Commission, and findings of the National Center for Urban Ethnic Affairs confirmed that ethnicity was a salient factor. The descendants of Mediterranean and eastern European immigrants, even into the fourth generation, were just barely moving toward the middle class, absent in the professions, and rarely admitted to prestigious universities or colleges. More specifically, Italian and Polish people, like blacks and Hispanics/Latinos, were found to be excluded from the executive suites and boardrooms of America's largest corporations, publicly regulated utilities, and philanthropies.

Ethnicity is often associated with immigrants and with importation of culture, language, stories, and foods from foreign shores. Appalachian, Western, and other regional ethnicities are evidence of multigenerational ethnic cultural development within the American reality. The persistent, ongoing process of cultural formation and personal identity are expressed locally in unique and intriguing folkways, dialects, languages, myths, festivals, food displays, and other enduring monuments and visible signs of the past and of the public dimension of cultural consciousness that constitutes ethnicity. The emergence of interest in retracing the pathways of these immigrant groups and assessing their participation in intergroup relations in America are topics of many scholarly disciplines.

Article Prepared by: John A. Kromkowski, *Catholic University of America*

Neither Natural Allies nor Irreconcilable Foes

Alliance Building Efforts between African Americans and Immigrants

ANDREW GRANT-THOMAS, YUSUF SARFATI, AND CHERYL STAATS

Learning Outcomes

After reading this article, you will be able to:

- Understand the reasons for friction between African Americans and immigrants.
- Identify strategies that can alleviate misunderstanding or develop convergent issues.

African American – immigrant relations have been under increased scrutiny by a range of stakeholders, including researchers, community organizers, policy makers, and philanthropic leaders. From gang violence to political representation, from labor concerns to negative stereotypes, black Americans and immigrants face a variety of challenges. In some communities, in certain arenas, each group regards the other as a rival. A pervasive media storyline that underscores instances of conflict while all but ignoring signs of cooperation only exacerbates the difficulties. Nevertheless, opportunities to unite are present, and some community organizers are working actively, and successfully, to form strong alliances between the groups. In this article, we briefly outline some of the key challenges, opportunities, and strategies that define these alliances.

Numerous barriers confront those who try to forge constructive relationships between African American and immigrant communities. Structural challenges include the socioeconomic marginalization that marks many African American and immigrant communities and often leads members of each group to live in close proximity to each other, sometimes provoking tensions over the allocation of limited resources. Whether at the federal, state, or local government level, or at the community level, most immigrants receive little help with integrating socially, economically, or politically into their new communities. Conversely, the members of receiving communities typically receive little help anticipating or accommodating the community changes that often accompany the new arrivals, creating fertile ground for inter-group friction. These strains are compounded by the unfavorable perceptions that African Americans and immigrants too often harbor about each other, the existence of an anti-immigrant wedge movement, and the prevalence of a conflict narrative in the mainstream media that encourages a zero-sum mentality among both groups.

These and other significant challenges notwithstanding, opportunities to unite and to achieve important relationship-building and policy successes exist. A great many African Americans and immigrants share the need for education reform in low-opportunity neighborhoods, for better workplace safety measures and wage reforms, for an end to racial profiling practices, and so on. Many progressives regard the two communities as core constituents within any viable, broad-based movement for expanded social justice in the United States. Current alliance-building efforts may yet prove to be the seedbed for such a movement.

From our conversations with dozens of organizers representing a wide range of social justice organizations and alliances, we identified a set of approaches based on alternative logics around which African American-immigrant alliances are formed: *intercultural relationship-building, issue-based organizing,* and *workplace-based organizing.* These three do not exhaust the range of alliance-building efforts in the field; nor are they mutually exclusive.

Community organizers who espouse an intercultural relationship-building approach aspire to build strong multicultural communities. For them, establishing healthy relationships among people of color is an important value in itself. Insofar as relationship-building reshapes identities and interests, it is also seen as a prerequisite for effective issue campaigns. These organizers suggest that interpersonal trust between the communities needs to be established first, and can be done only by addressing commonly held misconceptions through the deliberate re-education of each community. Without the trust born of solid relationships, racial and xenophobic tensions invariably emerge, and partnership development becomes episodic at best.

Re-education measures can range from preparing simple cultural exchange events to engaging in specialized curriculums and trainings.

While acknowledging the importance of relationship building, issue-based organizers argue that the best way to build solidarity across lines of race, ethnicity, and nativity is through appeals to shared "bread and butter" interests. Trust develops most surely as a byproduct of common struggle, preferably one that yields tangible successes. In contrast, these organizers claim that inter-group relationship challenges, as such, provide uncertain motivation for partnerships, especially among poor and working-class people likely to have more pressing concerns. "Issue-first" alliances are typically formed between organizations, rather than within particular organizations.

Finally, in some sectors of the economy, especially in low-paying jobs, African Americans and immigrants work side by side, making workplaces the frontlines of negotiations and *de facto* solidarity between the groups. These sectors include construction work, the hotel industry, restaurants, and the meat-packing industry. Some workplaces are home to initiatives that operate in the absence of formal coalitions. Unlike initiatives shaped by the first two approaches, these initiatives mobilize constituents not around their identities as "African Americans," "immigrants," or people of color, but around their common identity as workers. In other words, the goal of the organization is not to support immigrant or African American issues, as such, but to promote worker issues. The goal is presented in a color-blind manner, and the organizers try to emphasize the salience of associational rather than communal identities.

No matter which strategy or combination of strategies community organizers use, ongoing efforts and existing opportunities for further collaboration offer grounds for hope about the future of African American – immigrant alliance building work.

Creating alliances that endure and prosper is a challenging task, but the potential benefits make such efforts worthwhile. Cooperation between African Americans and immigrants in the United States is crucially important for creating an inclusive pluralistic democracy in which people of different races and cultures thrive by recognizing both their differences and similarities and working for common goals.

Critical Thinking

1. What are the reasons for friction between African Americans and immigrants?
2. What can be done to alleviate misunderstandings between African Americans and recent immigrants?
3. Do the long-term attitudes of African Americans and immigrants really extend beyond two generations?
4. What institutional, regional and structural factors have pitted groups into competitive relations?

Create Central

www.mhhe.com/createcentral

Internet References

American Indian Ritual Object Repatriation Foundation
www.repatriationfoundatfon.org

Center for Research in Ethnic Relations
www.warwickac.ukllaclsoc/CRER_RC

The International Center for Migration, Ethnicity, and Citizenship
www.newschool.edu/icmec

Yale University Guide to American Ethnic Studies
www.fibrary. yale. edulrsc/ethniclintemet.html

Article

Prepared by: John A. Kromkowski, *Catholic University of America*

Irish-American Heritage Month (March) and St. Patrick's Day (March 17): 2013

Originally a religious holiday to honor St. Patrick, who introduced Christianity to Ireland in the fifth century, St. Patrick's Day has evolved into a celebration for all things Irish. The world's first St. Patrick's Day parade occurred on March 17, 1762, in New York City, featuring Irish soldiers serving in the English military. This parade became an annual event, with President Truman attending in 1948. Congress proclaimed March as Irish-American Heritage Month in 1995, and the president issues a proclamation commemorating the occasion each year.

Learning Outcomes

After reading this article, you will be able to:

- Identify the most troubling demographic indicators about Irish Americans.
- Discuss the origins of the celebrations related to Irish Americans?

Population Distribution

34.5 million

Number of U.S. residents who claimed Irish ancestry in 2011. This number was more than seven times the population of Ireland itself (4.68 million). Irish was the nation's second most frequently reported ancestry, trailing only German.

Source: 2011 American Community Survey http://factfinder2.census.gov/bkmk/table/1.0/en/ACS/11_1YR/S0201//popgroup~541 Ireland Central Statistics Office http://www.cso.ie/en/media/csoie/releasespublications/documents/latestheadlinefigures/popmig_2012.pdf

150,990

Number of Irish-born naturalized U.S. residents in 2011.

Source: 2011 American Community Survey http://factfinder2.census.gov/bkmk/table/1.0/en/ACS/11_1YR/S0201//popgroup~541

39.3 years old

Median age of U.S. residents who claim Irish ancestry is higher than the U.S. residents median age as a whole (37.3 years).

Source: 2011 American Community Survey http://factfinder2.census.gov/bkmk/table/1.0/en/ACS/11_1YR/S0201//popgroup~541

12.9%

Percent of New York state residents who were of Irish ancestry in 2011. This compares with a rate of 11.1 percent for the nation as a whole.

Source: 2011 American Community Survey http://factfinder2.census.gov/bkmk/table/1.0/en/ACS/11_1YR/DP02/0400000US36 http://factfinder2.census.gov/bkmk/table/1.0/en/ACS/11_1YR/DP02/0100000US

Irish-Americans Today

33.3%

Percentage of people of Irish ancestry, 25 or older, who had a bachelor's degree or higher. In addition, 92.9 percent of Irish-Americans in this age group had at least a high school diploma. For the nation as a whole, the corresponding rates were 28.5 percent and 85.9 percent, respectively.

Source: 2011 American Community Survey http://factfinder2.census.gov/bkmk/table/1.0/en/ACS/11_1YR/S0201//popgroup~541 http://factfinder2.census.gov/bkmk/table/1.0/en/ACS/11_1YR/DP02/0100000US

$57,319

Median income for households headed by an Irish-American, higher than the $50,502 for all households. In addition, 7.3

percent of families of Irish ancestry were in poverty, lower than the rate of 11.7 percent for all Americans families.

Source: 2011 American Community Survey
http://factfinder2.census.gov/bkmk/table/1.0/en/ACS/11_1YR/S0201//popgroup~541
http://factfinder2.census.gov/bkmk/table/1.0/en/ACS/11_1YR/DP03/0100000US

41%

Percentage of employed civilian Irish-Americans 16 or older who worked in management, professional and related occupations. Additionally, 25.9 percent worked in sales and office occupations; 16.0 percent in service occupations; 9.3 percent in production, transportation and material moving occupations; and 7.8 percent in construction, extraction, maintenance and repair occupations.

Source: 2011 American Community Survey
http://factfinder2.census.gov/bkmk/table/1.0/en/ACS/11_1YR/S0201//popgroup~541

69.3%

Percentage of householders of Irish ancestry who owned the home in which they live, with the remainder renting. For the nation as a whole, the homeownership rate was 64.6 percent.

Source: 2011 American Community Survey
http://factfinder2.census.gov/bkmk/table/1.0/en/ACS/11_1YR/S0201//popgroup~541
http://factfinder2.census.gov/bkmk/table/1.0/en/ACS/11_1YR/DP04/0100000US

Places to Spend the Day

7

Number of places in the United States named Shamrock, the floral emblem of Ireland. Mount Gay-Shamrock, W.Va., and Shamrock, Texas, were the most populous, with 1,585 and 1,929 residents, respectively. Shamrock Lakes, Ind., had 228 residents and Shamrock, Okla., 101. Three Shamrock Townships in Minnesota, Nebraska and Missouri had populations of 1,273, 301 and 40, respectively.

Source: 2010 Demographic Profile
http://factfinder2.census.gov/faces/tableservices/jsf/pages/productview.xhtml?pid=ACS_11_5Y R_DP05&prodType=table

13

Number of places in the United States that share the name of Ireland's capital, Dublin. The most populous of these places is Dublin, Calif., with a population of 43,572.
Source: 2011 American Community Survey

If you're still not into the spirit of St. Paddy's Day, then you might consider paying a visit to Emerald Isle, N.C., with 3,702 residents.
Source: 2010 Demographic Profile
http://factfinder2.census.gov/faces/tableservices/jsf/pages/productview.xhtml?pid=ACS_11_5YR_DP02&prodType=table

Other appropriate places in which to spend the day: the township of Irishtown, Ill., several places or townships named Clover (in South Carolina, Illinois, Minnesota, Pennsylvania and Wisconsin) and the township of Cloverleaf, Minn.

Irish Imports and Celebrations!

In the month of St. Patrick's Day, the value of U.S. imports of beer made from malt increased, going from $288,073,597 in February 2012 to $374,076,005 in March 2012; in April of that same year the value of beer imports went back down to $334,769,134.

Source: U.S. Census Bureau: Foreign Trade Division USA Trade ® Online U.S. Import and Export Merchandise trade
https://www.usatradeonline.gov/
http://www.census.gov/foreign-trade/

The pattern was the same for nonalcoholic beer. The value of its U.S. imports increased, going from $1,114,450 in February 2012 to $1,234,910 in March 2012; in April of that same year the value of nonalcoholic beer imports went back down to $1,173,111.

Source: U.S. Census Bureau: Foreign Trade Division USA Trade ® Online U.S. Import and Export Merchandise trade
https://www.usatradeonline.gov/

$39.4 billion

The total value of imports from Ireland in 2011 to the U.S.

Source: Foreign Trade Division
http://www.census.gov/foreign-trade/statistics/product/enduse/imports/c4190.html

$532.1 million

The total value of alcoholic beverages except wine and related products imported from Ireland in 2011 to the United States. The total amount of wine and related products imported from Ireland in 2011 to the U.S. was $6.0 million.

Source: Foreign Trade Division
https://www.usatradeonline.gov/

$2.8 billion and $28.6 million

Value of beef and cabbage imported to the U.S. in 2011. Corned beef and cabbage is a traditional St. Patrick's Day dish.

Source: Foreign Trade Division
https://www.usatradeonline.gov/

Following is a list of observances typically covered by the Census Bureau's *Facts for Features* series:

- African-American History Month (February)
- Super Bowl
- Valentine's Day (Feb. 14)
- Women's History Month (March)

- Irish-American Heritage Month (March)/ St. Patrick's Day (March 17)
- Earth Day (April 22)
- Asian/Pacific American Heritage Month (May)
- Older Americans Month (May)
- Cinco de Mayo (May 5)
- Mother's Day
- Hurricane Season Begins (June 1)
- Father's Day
- The Fourth of July (July 4)
- Anniversary of Americans With Disabilities Act (July 26)
- Back to School (August)
- Labor Day
- Grandparents Day
- Hispanic Heritage Month (Sept. 15–Oct. 15)
- Unmarried and Single Americans Week
- Halloween (Oct. 31)
- American Indian/Alaska Native Heritage Month (November)
- Veterans Day (Nov. 11)
- Thanksgiving Day
- The Holiday Season (December)

Critical Thinking

1. Do large and apparently mainstream ethnic populations understand group relations in fundamentally different ways than minority groups?
2. Is it still "true" that everyone is Irish on Saint Patrick's Day, March 17th, or is that common statement disappearing from the popular culture?

Create Central

www.mhhe.com/createcentral

Internet References

The American Irish Historical Society
www.aihs.org

The Ancient Order of Hibernians
www.aoh.org

National Catholic Bishops Conference
www.USCCB.org

Editor's note—The preceding data were collected from a variety of sources and may be subject to sampling variability and other sources of error. Facts for Features are customarily released about two months before an observance in order to accommodate magazine production timelines. Questions or comments should be directed to the Census Bureau's Public Information Office: telephone: 301-763-3030; fax: 301-763-3762; or e-mail: PIO@census.gov.

U.S. Census Bureau, 2013.

Article

Prepared by: John A. Kromkowski, *Catholic University of America*

Arab Voices: Listening and Moving Beyond Myths

JAMES ZOGBY

Learning Outcomes

After reading this article, you will be able to:

- Identify and dispel the myths about Arab Americans.
- Find the origins of images about ethnic groups.

After decades spent trying to better explain the Arab World to other Americans, all too often I have found myself running up against the same mythologies and half-truths that, year after year, stubbornly maintain an alarming ability to shape thinking about the region.

One of the reasons I wrote *Arab Voices: What They Are Saying to Us and Why It Matters* was to challenge these myths head on. Unlike so many other books or articles that have been written about this region, *Arab Voices* is neither a retelling (or an interpretation) of history, nor is it a collection of personal anecdotes. These approaches can be useful, and there are excellent examples that have made real contributions to our understanding. But they are also susceptible to bias or to what I call "bad science" – as in the case of writers with a penchant for elevating an observation or a conversation into a generalized conclusion (the musings of Tom Friedman come to mind).

My starting point is hard data, derived from more than a decade of polling Zogby International has conducted across the Middle East. Where I use personal anecdotes, it is to "put flesh on the bones" of the numbers in order to help tell the stories of those Arabs whose realities we must understand.

I love polling (and not merely because my brother John is the business). Polling opens a window and lets in voices we seldom hear. When we ask 4,000 Arabs from Morocco to the United Arab Emirates to tell us their attitudes toward the United States, to identify their most important political concerns, their attitudes toward women in the workplace, or what programs they watch on television – and when we organize their responses by country, and then by age or gender or class, and then listen to what they are saying – we are able pierce through the fog of myth and learn.

And learning is important, because for too long our understanding of this region and its peoples have been clouded by distorted stereotypes and myths. They have dominated our thinking and, in some cases, have shaped our policies. I look at each of these myths in "Arab Voices" and then contrast the assumptions and misperceptions behind them with polling data that reveal what Arabs really think.

The five myths I examine are:

1. Are Arabs all the same and can they, therefore, be reduced to a "type" (as in "all Arabs are this or that")? Reading the broad generalizations and crude caricatures of Arabs found in Raphael Patai's *Arab Mind* (used as a training manual by the U.S. military in Iraq) or Tom Friedman's *Mid East Rules to Live By* might lead one to think so. But our polling reveals a very different view. What we find when we survey public opinion is a rich and varied landscape across the Arab World that defies stereotype. Not only are there diverse sub-cultures and unique histories that give texture to life, making Egyptians different than Saudis or Lebanese. There are also generational differences. For example, younger Arabs (who are 60% of the population of this region) are caught up with globalization and change. They share different concerns and aspire to different goals than their parents. They are more open to gender equality and are less tied to tradition.
2. Are Arabs so diverse that they do not constitute a world at all? That's what "The Economist" would have us believe. In a special 2009 issue of this magazine, the editors described the region as "a big amorphous thing and arguably not a thing at all." Once again, our polling reveals quite the opposite. Across the region, Arabs do identify as "Arabs" and they describe themselves as tied to one another by a common language (and the common history that implies) and shared political concerns, with majorities of all generations and in all countries demonstrating a strong attachment to Palestine and the fate of the Iraqi people.

3. Are Arabs all angry, hating us, "our values" and "our way of life"? In a recent poll, we found this view to be shared by a plurality of Americans. But our work in the Arab World finds quite the opposite to be true. Arabs like the American people, and they not only respect our education and our advances in science and technology, they also like our values of "freedom and democracy." What they don't like are our policies toward them, which lead them to believe that we don't like them. As one Arab businessman said to me, "we feel like jilted lovers."
4. Are Arabs are driven by religious fanaticism? Arabs are, like many in the West, "people of faith," with their values shaped by their religious traditions. But mosque attendance rates across the Middle East are about the same as church attendance rates here in the U.S. And when we ask Arabs what programs they prefer to watch on TV, the list is as varied as those favored by American viewers. In Egypt, Morocco and Saudi Arabia (the largest countries covered in our polls) the top rated programs are movies and soap operas. Religious programs are near the bottom of the list. And when we ask Arabs to list their most important concerns, not surprisingly, the top two are the quality of their work and their families.

   So in contrast to the mythic notion that "Arabs go to bed at night hating America, wake up hating Israel, and spend their days either watching news or listening to preachers who fuel that anger," the reality is that "Arabs go to bed each night thinking about their jobs, wake up each morning thinking about their kids, and spend each day thinking about how to improve the quality of their lives."
5. Lastly there is the myth that Arabs reject reform and will not change, unless the West pushes them. This has been a fundamental tenet of the neo-conservatives. Derived from the writings of Bernard Lewis, this myth provided one of the rationales for the Iraq war – the idea being that we would destroy the "old regime" giving birth to "the new Middle East."

What our polling shows, however, is that Arabs do want reform, but the reform they want is theirs, not ours. Their top domestic priorities are: better jobs, improved health care and expanded educational opportunities (sound familiar?). Our findings further demonstrate that most Arabs do not want us meddling in their internal affairs, but they would welcome our assistance in helping their societies build capacity to provide services and improve the quality of their lives.

When we look at the Arab World more closely and listen to Arabs more carefully, we learn that this region and its people are not as they have been imagined by Hollywood or projected by political ideologues with an axe to grind. They can not be reduced to the mythic stereotypes that have so warped our understanding and contributed to distorting our policies. With this realization will come the ability to engage productively with the people of this region which has become so critical to our national interests.

Critical Thinking

1. Have your views about Arab Americans changed over the years?
2. Do you see Arabs as a diverse group?

Create Central

www.mhhe.com/createcentral

Internet References

Arab American Institute
www.aai.org

National Association of Arab Americans
www.naaa.org

Article

Prepared by: John A. Kromkowski, *Catholic University of America*

Arab Americans: The Zogby Culture Polls 2000–2004

Learning Outcomes

After reading this article, you will be able to:

- Know what is most important for the Arab-American population.
- See the role that heritage plays among Arab-Americans.

As the first table in our study would suggest, Arab Americans did not demonstrate any significant increase or decrease in their ethnic pride during the period from 2000 to 2003. Indeed, in response to the question, "On a scale of 1 to 5, with 1 being not at all and 5 being extremely, how proud are you of your ethnic heritage?" 85.5% of those polled reported being 'proud' of their ethnic background in our recent study (that is to say, a response· of 4 or 5 with regards to the question), a marginal decrease of 4.5% when compared with 2000.

Table 1 Ethnic Pride

	2000	2003
Proud	90.0	85.5
Average Pride	7.0	10.1
Not Proud	3.0	3.8

If we break down ethnic pride into several categories we see that no significant mutations have taken place over the past five years. Regardless of their level of education, income, sex or age, Arab Americans all demonstrate a substantial amount of pride in their ethnicity. And while the numbers in 2003 correspond with the slight decrease in pride overall, it should be noted that ethnic pride remains well over 80% for each sub-group. As in 2000, high school graduates with no college education have slightly more ethnic pride than those with college degrees. Arabs who earn around $75,000 in yearly income also tend to exhibit more ethnic pride than their counterparts in the $25–50,000 income bracket, while females have a slight edge over males. One interesting trend is the ever-widening gap between the ethnic pride of Arabs aged 18 to 34 and those aged 55 to 69. The ethnic pride of younger generation Arabs increased from 91.0% to 95.3% between 2000 and 2003, while that of the older generation decreased from 91.0% to 85.9%.

Table 2 Ethnic Pride in 2000

All	High School	$25–50,000	Male	18–34
	92.5	89.5	89.0	91.0
90.0	**College**	**$75,000**	**Female**	**55–69**
	88.5	90.0	90.5	91.0

Table 3 Ethnic Pride in 2003

All	High School	$25–50,000	Male	18–34
	91.8	82.2	83.6	95.3
85.5	**College**	**$75,000**	**Female**	**55–69**
	87.4	87.0	87.4	85.9

As is the case with regards to ethnic pride, Arab Americans continue to demonstrate a tremendous recognition for the importance of their ethnic heritage. When asked, "how important is your ethnic heritage in defining you as a person?" 55.6% of those polled in 2003 claimed that their heritage was very important to them (an increase of 4.1% from 2000). An additional 29.9% acknowledged their heritage to be at least somewhat important, comparable to the figure of 35.0% in 2000. Perhaps most striking of all, only 14.0% of the respondents in 2003 place no importance on ethnic heritage— nearly identical to the 13.0% figure of 2000.

Table 4 Importance of Heritage

	2000	2003
Very	51.5	55.6
Somewhat	35.0	29.9
Not important	13.0	14.0

When we observe the importance of ethnic heritage as it pertains to various different groups, several figures stand out. Amongst 18 to 34 year-olds, for example, the percentage of those who claimed their heritage to be very important increased from 52.0 to 73.3 from 2000 to 2003. Over the same period the importance of ethnic heritage actually decreased from 59.0% to 51.3% in the 55-to-69 age bracket. This reality mirrors the trend we remarked upon in tables 2 and 3 regarding ethnic pride, suggesting that younger Arab Americans are increasingly cognizant of their ethnic background while the older generation grows more and more disinterested. We also note the increase in the percentage of college graduates and males who consider their ethnic heritage to be very important, while the numbers for high school graduates and individuals whose annual income is $75,000 and above decreased over the same period.

Table 5 Importance of Heritage in 2000

All	High School	$25–50,000	Male	18–34
	73.0	54.0	42.5	52.0
51.5	**College**	**$75,000**	**Female**	**55–69**
	38.5	48.5	61.0	59.0

Table 6 Importance of Heritage in 2003

All	High School	$25–50,000	Male	18–34
	65.1	57.1	50.0	73.3
55.6	**College**	**$75,000**	**Female**	**55–69**
	53.9	54.8	61.2	51.3

Arab Americans maintain relatively strong ties to their land of heritage, although not quite to the extent that they did in 2000. According to our latest poll, only 39.7% of respondents have strong emotional ties to their country of heritage, compared to 55.5% in the year 2000. This reality suggests that Arab Americans are becoming less and less attached to their country and region of origin as time goes by. Nonetheless, the percentage of individuals who claim to have no emotional ties to their land of heritage remains very low (21.5% in 2003).

Table 7 Emotional Ties to Land of Heritage

	2000	2003
Strong	55.5	39.7
Moderate	24.0	38.7
None	20.0	21.5

Critical Thinking

1. In your opinion, do other cultures share the same pride in their heritage as Arab Americans?
2. Do you believe many Arab Americans will continue to drift away from their roots, as has been the case with other cultures that have assimilated into American life?

Create Central

www.mhhe.com/createcentral

Internet References

Arab American Institute
www.aai.org

National Association of Arab Americans
www.naaa.org

Article

Prepared by: John A. Kromkowski, *Catholic University of America*

Blood in the Marketplace: The Business of Family in the *Godfather* Narratives

THOMAS J. FERRARO

Learning Outcomes

After reading this article, you will be able to:

- Discuss whether movies shape our self images and images of others.
- Discuss the general question of imagination, art and values.

Giorgio introduces me to his friend Piero Paco, hero of the Italo-American breach into American literature. He looks like a massive gangster but turns out to be a plain, nice guy with a lot of folksy stories and no complexes. He doesn't feel guilty about blacks, doesn't care about elevating Italo-American prestige. He's no missionary for wops. No gripes about the Establishment. He just decided in the best American way to write a book that would make half a million bucks because he was tired of being ignored.

> *"You don't think struggling Italo-Americans should stick together and give each other a push up from the bottom of the pile where they've always been?" I ask him. But he's no struggling half-breed anymore. He's made his pile; he's all-American now.*
>
> *"I'm not going to push that crap," he says engagingly.*
>
> *—Helen Barolini, Umbertina (1979)*

I

What, after all, could be more American than the success stories of penniless immigrant boys clawing their way to wealth and respectability by private enterprise? What legitimate American business tycoon ever objected to being called "ruthless," to being credited (like the good boxer) with the "killer instinct" . . . ?

> *What is more, The Godfather could be seen to represent not only some of the continuing principles of the American way of life, but the ancestral ideals it had somehow inexplicably lost on the way. In Don Corleone's world bosses were respected and loved by their subordinates as surrogate fathers. Men were men and women were glad of it. Morality rules unchallenged, and crime, for the most part, was kept off the streets. Families stuck together under patriarchal control. Children obeyed—fathers, and virtuous wives were not afraid of losing their status to mistresses.... No wonder New York magazine exclaimed (according to the paperback edition's blurb): "You'll find it hard to stop dreaming about it."*
>
> *—E.J. Hobsbawm, "Robin Hoodo"*

In his 1969 blockbuster, *The Godfather,* Mario Puzo presented an image of the Mafia that has become commonplace in American popular culture. Since Puzo, it has been taken for granted that the Mafia operates as a consortium of illegitimate businesses, structured along family lines, with a familial patriarch or "godfather" as the chief executive officer of each syndicate.[1] Puzo's version of the Mafia fuses into one icon the realms of family and economy, of southern Italian ethnicity and big-time American capitalism, of *blood* and the *marketplace.* "Blood" refers to the violence of organized crime. "Blood" also refers to the familial clan, and its extension through the fictive system of the *compare,* or "co-god parenthood." In *The Godfather,* the representation of the Mafia fuses ethnic tribalism with the all-American pursuit of wealth and power. Since its publication, we have regarded this business of family in *The Godfather* as a figment of Puzo's opportunistic imagination, which it remains in part. But the business of family in Puzo's Mafia is also a provocative revision of accepted notions of what ethnicity is and how it works—the new ethnic sociology in popular literary form.

During the late seventies and early eighties, there was a short outburst of scholarly interest in *The Godfather* and its myriad offspring. A consensus about the meaning of the saga's popularity emerges from the books and essays of Fredric Jameson, Eric Hobsbawm, John Cawelti, and John Sutherland. The portrayal of the Corleone family collective allows Americans, in the post-Vietnam era, to fantasize about the glory days of "closely knit traditional authority." The portrayal of the power and destructive greed of the Mafia chieftains permits Americans to vent their rage at "the managerial elite who hold the reins of corporate power and use it for their own benefit."[2] The family and business thematics are, in each instance, disengaged from one another. As Jameson puts it: on the one hand, the ethnic family imagery satisfies "a Utopian longing" for collectivity; on the other hand, "the substitution of crime for big business" is the narrative's "ideological function."[3] In standard treatments like these, Puzo's narrative is regarded as a brilliant (or brilliantly lucky) instance of satisfying two disparate appetites with a single symbol. This perspective, formulated in the late seventies, seems to have settled the issue of the novel's popularity.

I want to reopen that issue. We need to return to *The Godfather* because we have too easily dismissed its representation of the Mafia as a two-part fantasy. Of course, *The Godfather* is not reliable as a roman à clef or as a historical novel: Puzo's details are fuzzy, mixed-up, and much exaggerated.[4] "There was things he stretched," as Huck would put it, and everyone knows it. But critics have been too ready to accept his major sociological premise—family and business working in tandem—as pure mythology. The importance of *The Godfather* lies not in a double mythology, I would argue, but in its taking of the fusion of kinship and capitalist enterprise *seriously.* Its cultural significance lies not in the simultaneous appeals of "family" and "business" imagery but rather in the appeal of an actual structural simultaneity: *the business of family.* By failing to pause long enough to consider its surface narrative, critics have underestimated not only the strategies of the novel but the insights and intuitions of its huge audience as well.

Readers have underestimated the business of family because little in traditional theories of the family, ethnicity, and advanced capitalism has prepared them to recognize it. In both scholarly and popular treatments, ethnic culture and extended kinship are interpreted as barriers to the successful negotiation of the mobility ladder, particularly its upper ranks. Southern Italian immigrants and their descendants have long been thought to exemplify the principle that the more clannish an ethnic group, the slower its assimilation and economic advancement.[5] Herbert Guns's *Urban Villagers,* Virginia Yans-McLaughlin's *Family and Community,* Thomas Kessner's *The Golden Door,* and Thomas Sowell's *Ethnic America* essentially update the social-work perspectives of writers such as Phyllis H. Williams and Leonard Covello.[6] In 1944, Covello wrote,

> *Any social consciousness of Italo-Americans within "Little Italies" appertains primarily to sharing and adhering to the family tradition as the main motif of their philosophy of life. . . . The retention of this cultural "basis" is essentially the source of their retarded adjustment.*[7]

This long-standing tradition of identifying the Italian family structure as a dysfunctional survival runs aground on the Mafia.

Historians and sociologists attest to the difficulty of interpreting the Mafia in terms of a linear model of assimilation and upward mobility. All commentators recognize that the Mafia was not simply transported here; that it grew up from the multiethnic immigrant streets, rather than being passed on from father to son; and that Prohibition was the major factor in shaping its growth. In *A Family Business,* the sociologist Francis A. J. Ianni concedes these points, only to stress the family structure of the syndicates and the origin of this familialism in southern Italy:

> *[The Lupullo crime organization] feels like a kinship-structured group; familialism founded it and is still its stock in trade. One senses immediately not only the strength of the bond, but the inability of members to see any morality or social order larger than their own.*

Ianni's research tempts him into abandoning the tradition of placing ethnic phenomena on a linear continuum running from Old World marginality to New World centrality.[8] His research supports and his analysis anticipates (if it does not quite articulate) the cutting edge of ethnic theory. It is time for the criticism of ethnic literature generally, and of *The Godfather* in particular, to take advantage of such theory.

Scholars in a number of fields are working to change the way we think about ethnicity, ethnic groups, and ethnic culture. In identifying the social bases of ethnicity, theorists are shifting emphasis from intergenerational transmission to arenas of conflict in complex societies. They argue that we need to examine ethnic cultures not as Old World survivals (whatever their roots) but as strategies to deal with the unequal distribution of wealth, power, and status. In this light, ethnic groups are seen to include not only socially marginal peoples but any groups who use symbols of common descent and tradition to create or maintain power. From a historian's perspective, European family structures and traditions do not necessarily dissolve in the face of capitalism but rather, as they have always done, evolve to meet its changing needs.[9] Herbert Guns has spoken of "cost-free" ethnicity among the middle classes, but ethnicity is often *profitable* as well.[10]

In his work, the anthropologist Abner Cohen conceives of ethnic groups as "interest groups," in which ethnic symbols function in lieu of more formal structures such as the law. By the symbolic apparatus of ethnicity, he means the emphasis on common history and tradition, endogamy and social boundary maintenance, religion and ritual, and everyday encoded behavior, including "accent, manner of speech, etiquette, style of joking, play," and so forth: the rhetoric and codes of "blood."[11] As Cohen explains, the symbolic apparatus of "ethnicity" incites genuine loyalty and emotion, whose power and idiosyncrasy should not be underestimated. But the apparatus also serves utilitarian purposes within society at large, including the economic marketplace. In many of our most familiar examples, the function of ethnic ritual is primarily defensive, organizing a group on the margins of society: but the uses of ethnicity can be quite aggressive as well. The Italian-American Mafia is a case in point. As Ianni and others have demonstrated, it is the ethos of ethnic solidarity that puts the *organization* into Italian-American organized crime.

In her discussion of *The Godfather,* Rose Basile Green comes the closest of any critic, I think, to unpacking in Cohen's fashion what she herself calls the "socioeconomic ethnic image" of the Corleone crime syndicate. Unlike almost everyone else, Green takes seriously Puzo's portrayal of the syndicates not as a historical novel about actual gangsters but as a treatise (however romanticized) "dealing with the contemporary strategy of gaining and securing power." Yet her analysis splits into typical parallel paths: crime as a means for social mobility versus the family as a locus of traditional southern Italian responsibility. Although Green identifies "a subtle line between personal interest and structural power," she too fails to make the strongest connection between the private family life ascribed to Don Corleone and the illegitimate enterprise he heads. When Green says that *The Godfather* explores "the contemporary strategy of gaining and securing power," she means by "strategy" the tactics of bribery, intimidation, the brokerage of votes, intergang warfare, and so forth, with which Don Corleone conducts business outside the confines of his own organization. But the most noteworthy device for gaining and securing power in Puzo's depiction is internal to the Corleone syndicate. The device is not a gun or payola but, quite simply and obviously, that mystified entity the "southern Italian family."[12]

II

"Tell the old man I learned it all from him and that I'm glad I had this chance to pay him back for all he did for me. He was a good father."

—Michael Corleone

As narrator in *The Godfather,* Puzo adopts the familiar role of cultural interpreter, mediating between outside readers and an ethnic secret society. Puzo's agenda, implicit yet universally understood, is to explain why Sicilian-Americans have made such good criminals. The answer, generally speaking, is their cult of family honor. The Corleones believe with a kind of feudal fervor, in patriarchy, patronage, and protection. *The Godfather* is saturated with the imagery of paternity, family, and intimate friendship; with the rhetoric of respect, loyalty, and the code of silence; with references to Sicilian blood and the machismo attributed to it; with the social events—weddings, christenings, funerals, meals, and so forth—that embody the culture of family honor. Always the business of crime is interlaced with the responsibilities of family. In the film, for instance, Clemenza frets over a request from his wife even as he presides over the execution of Paulie Gatto: "Don't forget the cannolis!" Don Vito himself is a true believer. He believes in the mutual obligation of kinfolk. He seeks to expand his wealth and power to protect his dependents and to make his protection available to more and more people. He recruits from within his family to keep the business "all in the family" for the family's sake. "It was at this time that the Don got the idea that he ran his world far better than his enemies ran the greater world which continually obstructed his path."[13] At the same time, "not his best friends would have called Don Corleone a saint from heaven"; there is always "some self-interest" in his generosity (*G,* 215). For everyone recognizes the wisdom of family honor—Corleone's honor—given the special exigencies of operating in a big way in an outlawed underground economy.

In his analysis of the ethnic group as an interest group, Abner Cohen stresses the growth potential wherever there is a sector of an economy that has not been organized formally:

> *Even in the advanced liberal industrial societies there are some structural conditions under which an interest group cannot organize itself on formal lines. Its formal organization may be opposed by the state or by other groups within the state, or may be incompatible with some important principles in the society; or the interests it represents may be newly developed and not yet articulated in terms of a formal organization and accommodated with the formal structure of the society. Under these conditions the group will articulate its organization on informal lines making use of the kinship, friendship, ritual, ceremonial and other symbolic activities that are implicit in what is known as a style of life.*[14]

The ethnic ethos means sticking together, respecting the authority of the group rather than that of outsiders, defending the group's turf, and abiding by tradition. The reasoning comes full circle, for tradition is equated with group solidarity. The family is the core element of the group and its most powerful symbol. Under the appropriate conditions the ethos of "ethnicity" is by no means anachronistic in the advanced stages of capitalism, no matter how rooted such values might be to the past of particular groups. Wherever ethnicity can facilitate enterprise, capitalism as a system can be said to be one of ethnicity's primary motors, not its antithesis. Focusing on the old moneyed elite of London, Cohen has argued that ethnicity functions among the privileged as well as the impoverished and among "core" castes as well as racial and national minorities. In another case study, the historian Peter Dobkin Hall implicates family and tradition in the mercantilism of Massachusetts elites, 1700–1900.[15] As both Cohen and Hall contend, a precondition for capitalized ethnicity is a legal vacuum. Here I wish to add a corollary based on the history of the Mafia: the desire to engage in enterprise, not simply in a vacuum (where there is no law or formal arrangements) but in an economic zone outside the law and *against* formal arrangements, makes some form of family and ethnic organization a necessity.

The seemingly "feudal" ethos of family honor, deeply internalized, cements individuals together in American crime, structuring syndicates and giving them their aggrandizing momentum. Loyalty and devotion to group honor are the values around which individuals are motivated, recruited, judged, and policed in the Mafia. These values are especially good in binding criminals together and in making criminals out of those otherwise not drawn to the outlaw life. They came into the forefront in America when Prohibition created an enormous unorganized sector of the national economy, legally proscribed, but promoted by immense appetites and the willingness of the actual legal structure to play along, especially "for a price." They are also especially needed to hold together the large-scale enterprises, not structured or protected by law, that prohibition creates but that survive after it: rackets devoted to gambling, loan-sharking, prostitution, various forms of extortion, and eventually drugs. In legitimate business, a prized executive who sells himself and perhaps a secret or two to another company is regarded as an unexpected operating loss. A *capo-regime* who becomes a stool pigeon can bring the whole system down. The ideology of tradition and of group solidarity, principally of the family, is ideal for rationalizing crime syndicates, in both senses of the term "rationlize": ideal for organizing them because it is ideal for justifying their existence and their hold over their members.

Scholars report that actual mafiosi crime syndicates are family based. In *A Family Business,* Ianni analyzes the structure of a major American Mafia clan—the "Lupullo" family—abstracting four general rules of organization:

> *the merging of social and business functions into one kin-centered enterprise, the assignment of leadership positions on the basis of kinship; the correlation between closeness of kin relationship and the hierarchy of position; and the requirement of close consanguineal or affinal relationship for inclusion in the core group....*[16]

Ianni produces several diagram to illustrate his thesis: a genealogical table of actual and fictive (godparent-godchild) relations; a flowchart of the subdivisions and their operations within the crime syndicate; and a third table, which combines the preceding two.[17] The third table diagrams what Ianni calls the "power alliances" (relations of respect and deference) between leaders within the Lupullo crime hierarchy. The pattern of authority within the syndicate mimics the pattern within the patriarchal clan.

In *The Godfather,* Mario Puzo provides a narrative equivalent of the Lupullo's power chart. During the wedding scene, Puzo introduces the Corleones in terms of their dual roles as family members and company executives. Vito Corleone is president and chief executive officer, as well as father or godfather to everyone within the organization. Genco Abbandando, *"consigliori"* (right-hand man), has been his best friend during his American childhood, his honorary brother, the son of the man who took him in and gave him his first job. But Genco is dying, and it is suspected that Tom Hagen, Vito Corleone's "adopted" son, will be taking over as counselor. Vito's eldest, Sonny, operates one of the principal three divisions or *regimes* of the family. The other two division leaders *(capo-regimes),* Tessio and Clemenza, are *compari* of Vito, godparents to each other's children. Fredo, the second son, serves his father as bodyguard and executive secretary. Michael, the youngest son, is the black sheep of the family and has nothing to do with its business. By tradition, the women are "civilians." But Connie's groom, Carlo Rizzi (an old boyhood chum of Sonny), expects, through this marriage, to rise quickly in the syndicate.

The network of nuclear family, extended kin by blood or marriage, and honorary kinship is not simply a structural convenience. The ideology of family operates neither as false consciousness in the vulgar sense nor as rhetoric that is entirely and self-consciously hypocritical. The rhetoric of solidarity works to organize the Corleone syndicate *because* of its hold over the imaginations and passions of leaders and those in the common ranks alike. As Cohen explains it, ethnic symbols function in lieu of formal structures precisely because of their trans-utilitarian, emotional appeal. This "dual" nature of symbolization is illustrated especially well in Puzo's depiction of Tom Hagen's admission into the Corleone syndicate.

Sonny Corleone had brought Tom Hagen, an orphaned waif of German-Irish extraction, into the Corleone household, where he was alllowed to remain. "In all this the Don acted not as a father but rather as a guardian." Only after Hagen goes to work for Don Corleone is he treated as a fourth son:

> *After he passed the bar exam, Hagen married to start his own family. The bride was a young Italian girl from New Jersey, rare at that time for being a college graduate. After the wedding, which was of course held in the home of Don Corleone, the Don offered to support Hagen in any undertaking he desired, to send him law clients, furnish his office, start him in real estate.*
>
> *Tom Hagen had bowed his head and said to the Don, "I would like to work for you."*
>
> *The Don was surprised, yet pleased. "You know who I am?" he asked.*
>
> *Hagen nodded. . . . "I would work for you like your sons," Hagen said, meaning with complete loyalty, with complete acceptance of the Don's parental divinity. The Don, with that understanding which was even then building the legend of his greatness, showed the young man the first mark of fatherly affection since he had come into his household. He took Hagen into his arms for a quick embrace and afterward treated him more like a true son, though he would sometimes say, "Tom, never forget your parents," as if he were reminding himself as well as Hagen. (G, 51–52)*

In the scene above, Hagen moves into the Don's inner circle. It is a *dual* movement, enacted simultaneously, into the inner realm of Don Vito's familial affections and into the ranks of his crime organization. Tom touches the Don's heart by volunteering, despite his origins, to submit himself to the Don's will and risk his life and freedom in the company. By the same token, the Don rewards Hagen's voluntary show of respect with a symbolic "adoption" that signifies the bond of loyalty upon which their futures as gangsters will depend. The symbol of paternity here works emotionally and pragmatically at the same time. Indeed, the father-son bonding is all the more powerful because of its economic component, while its utility depends, in the absence of biological paternity, quite precisely upon the psychological density of the tie.[18]

So far I have been juxtaposing the sociology of ethnic and familial interest groups with various elements of *The Godfather,* treating the latter as if it were merely an illustration of the former—as if *The Godfather* were a kind of sociological tract or social-work guide to the Mafia. Of course, *The Godfather* is not exposition, but a novel; not sociology, but story. Yet the populist, fictional composition of *The Godfather* does not mean it is any less effective than the scholarship of Cohen or Ianni as a medium for implicating the ethnic family in capitalism. Puzo uses the resources of fiction—imagery and rhetoric, characterization, and, most of all, narrative—to make a case for the interpenetration of family and business. In the instance of Tom Hagen's admission to the Corleone family, Puzo rigs a set of circumstances and unfolds an event in such a fashion that the strands of father-son emotion and corporate personnel management are not phenomenologically separable. Hagen's recruitment/initiation functions as a microcosm for the interpenetration of family and business in the narrative as a whole. Through melodrama, Puzo undermines the still common assumption that family and business operate as separate spheres. Puzo combines family and business within the same narrative site. He also subverts the reader's desire, in keeping with a purified notion of the family and a vilified notion of the economy, to subordinate one phenomenon to the other, as cause and effect, in any given instance. In *The Godfather* the syndicate never, or almost never, uses family imagery *merely* to structure itself in lieu of better alternatives, thereby "corrupting" the forms and values of an otherwise sacrosanct ethnic tribe. On the other hand, the family never engages in business *simply* to support itself, dirtying its hands to keep head and heart clean. Always the two phenomena are causally intermingled. By the deviousness of situation and event, Puzo contextualizes the ethnic family within the capitalist economy while excavating the contribution of ethnic culture and the rhetoric of ethnicity to illegitimate enterprise.

To a greater extent perhaps than we have become used to in analyzing modernist, high-brow literature, the story line is crucial to *The Godfather.* Even the critics most hostile to Puzo admit that his great gift is storytelling, including the creation of memorable characters, but especially the creation and maintenance of suspense—of beginnings that captivate, middles the keep you going, and endings that satisfy. In *The Godfather,* Puzo narrates two plots that lock together into a single, resounding conclusion.[19] When the novel opens, a breakdown in filial obedience exposes the Corleone syndicate to "a hostile take-over bid" from the Barzini-Tattaglia group. At the same time, business matters threaten the lives of Corleone family members and precipitate dissent among them. This double crisis is the hook that captures our attention: a business in trouble, a family in trouble. We cheer for a solution to both crises—nothing less will satisfy—and Puzo contrives brilliantly to give it to us. Both crises, potentially disastrous, are solved when Don Vito's youngest son, Michael, ascends to his father's place and successfully squelches the Barzini-Tattaglia threat. It is a stunning Illustration of the structural logic of family business in narrative terms. The return of the prodigal son alleviates the problem of managerial succession while the resurrection of the syndicate's power base restores the primacy of family values and commitments. Puzo's story is "dual" in the sense that the ethnic symbols of the Mafia are dual and that Tom Hagen's adoption as a Corleone is dual. So tightly constructed is Puzo's plot around the theme of duality that the novel's denouement seems inevitable. To save the business, you must regroup the family; to save the family, you must regroup the business.

In *The Godfather,* Puzo uses Connie Corleone's wedding to illustrate the overlapping structures of family and business in the American Mafia of the 1940s. In the *Godfather* film (the lens of which constantly obscures our view of the novel), Coppola plays with a contrast between the beneficent private life of the Corleones (the sunlit wedding feast) and their business escapades (inside the darkened house, inside their hearts of darkness).[20] Yet, Coppola's moral allegory reifies a distinction between the private and the corporate, home and work, explicitly undermined by the novel. In Puzo's design, business associates *are* the proper wedding guests, because one's family and friends are one's proper coworkers and retainers. The specter of communal solidarity, embodied in the wedding, marks a plateau of harmonious unity from which the Corleones are about to fall. As Puzo introduces the members of the Corleone family at Connie's wedding and their environment, he not only unpacks the functional interdependence of family and business. He explicates and foreshadows a disturbance in family-business equilibrium, reciprocally engendered, mutually threatening, that is the medium for the *Godfather* narrative. As Puzo imagines it, the incipient threat to the Corleone empire is analytically inseparable from the breakdown in the familial solidarity of the syndicate—including Genco's death, the Don's creeping senility, Sonny's disobedience, the disloyalty of Carlo and Tessio, Hagen' intransigent foreignness, Michael's rebellion. At the same time, tensions in the family arise directly out of the involvement in the business of crime.

At the opening of the novel, Don Corleone is nearing retirement, which has him justifiably worried about the leadership of the syndicate. In standard corporate management, such a problem can be handled either by promotion of the best available personnel from within company ranks or by recruitment from outside the company (intercorporate "raiding"). But for the Corleones, of course, the problem of the company executive is strictly a family matter, and that makes it a problem indeed. The right-hand man, Genco Abbandando, dies on the day of the wedding, leaving Don Corleone no choice but to promote Tom Hagen, an adopted son whose German-Irish descent precludes consideration for the top post of don. Both Clemenza and Tessio, the two *capo-regimes,* are nearing retirement themselves; moreover, they are not quite family enough. Of the don's own sons, neither Sonny nor Fredo seems finally to have the mettle to be don, while Michael, once favored to head the family, is now an outcast:

> *[Sonny] did not have his father's humility but instead a quick, hot temper that led him into errors of judgment. Though he was a great help in his father's business, there were many who doubted that he would become the heir to it.... The second son, Fredrico ... did not have that personal magnetism, that animal force, so necessary for a leader of men, and he too was not expected to inherit the family business.... The third son, Michael, did not stand with his father and his two brothers but sat at a table in the most secluded corner of the garden. (G, 17)*

The leadership vacuum, familially engendered, is the weak link that tempts the Barzini-Tattaglia consortium (fronted by Sollozzo, the drug dealer) to take over the Corleone rackets. Weaknesses in the character of family members and in their relations with one another expose the Corleone family to, quite literally, a hostile takeover bid.

Concomitantly, and inseparably, business tensions have precipitated disputes within the intimate family circle. Michael has fallen out with his family because he objects to the way its members make a living, committing himself instead to the defense of his country and the "straight arrow" mobility of a Dartmouth education. Connie's oldfashioned Sicilian wedding seems to symbolize the unity of the Corleone generations. Yet the garden celebration actually screens dissent between Connie and her father, traceable to Corleone involvement in the rackets. "Connie had consented to a 'guinea' wedding to please her father because she had so displeasured him in her choice of a husband" (G, 20). The persistence of the Corleone syndicate means that one of the qualifications for a Corleone son-in-law is potential for criminal leadership. Don Corleone objects to Carlo Rizzi as his daughter's husband not because he doubts Carlo's qualities as a mate but because he questions Carlo's ability and trustworthiness as a gangster. For his own part, Carlo marries Connie not only out of love but also because he hopes to rise in the Corleone syndicate. When Don Corleone violates the principle of familial promotion, providing Carlo with a living but not an executive role, Carlo seeks revenge on his father-in-law and the family. Carlo sets up the assassination of Sonny, bringing the syndicate to the brink of disaster. By Puzo's design, as demonstrated in this instance, any analysis of family-business disrepair comes full circle: we trace family problems to business questions, only to find the intrusion of business into family life returning to haunt the business.

Carlo's betrayal, like that of Paulie Gatto and ultimately of Tessio himself, illustrates the point of vulnerability in a family business within a competitive market. The principles of maximizing profits and employing insiders are not always compatible. Syndicate leaders are tempted, for the sake of performance, to slight certain inept family members. Syndicate members are tempted, for personal gain, to betray their organizations. As long as a doctrine of familial loyalty is obeyed to the letter, neither temptation wins the day. But when family principles break down, the company is in danger.

The leadership vacuum in the Corleone syndicate Is filled by the reestablishment of order in the Corleone patriarchy, when Michael returns to his family, his descent culture, and his filial "destiny." In *The Godfather,* the crisis of managerial succession is a crisis, as Cawelti notes, of "family succession" which can be solved only *familially.*[21] Puzo resolves the dual crisis by having Michael grow a familial conscience and an ethnic consciousness, mandating his ascent to his father's position as patriarch. At the novel's opening, Michael is a family *pariah—scomunicato,* excommunicated.[22] Before the war, Michael was the chosen heir to his father's regime, but later he refuses to have anything to do with the business and barely anything to do with the members of his family. He courts an "Adams" for a wife. Puzo's narrative counteracts the seeming decline of the Corleone syndicate by charting Michael's rebirth as a Corleone family member and a businessman of crime.

Michael's return as a once prodigal son is enacted in a steplike progression that mirrors the rhythms of religious initiation—baptism, confirmation, the sacrament of marriage or the priesthood. Killing Sollozzo and the police captain, Michael commits himself to his father's honor and a life of crime, *simultaneously.* In Sicily, he is symbolically rebaptized a Sicilian, learning the history of the Italian Mafia, converting to the old traditions, even taking a local wife (subsequently killed). Back in America, he is apprenticed to his father. When Don Corleone dies, Michael takes over the business and the family, becoming godfather to Connie's firstborn and "Don Michael" to his business associates. During the actual christening of his godson (as Coppola depicts it), Michael's henchmen execute a series of murders that restore the internal solidarity of the Corleone syndicate and enlarge its boundaries and standing. When he acts his father's part, even Michael's face begins to resemble Don Vito's in his prime. Puzo's drama of monarchical, Oedipal succession reverses the familiar convention of second-generation "orphanhood" with which the novel begins.[23]

Any analytic attempt to separate what Michael does out of an emotional recommitment to his father or his ethnic past from what Michael accomplishes out of a pragmatic enlistment in his father's company is doomed to echo in the wilderness. Readers even vaguely familiar with the *Godfather* narrative know that the brutal simultaneous killings at the end of the novel reestablish and indeed improve the Corleones' standing in the American Mafia. But it is less well recognized, and the film underplays, how the ending reintegrates the Corleone household. Critics argue that Puzo deploys family imagery to win sympathy for Michael's otherwise morally egregious plans. Critics misconstrue the strategies of the novel, however, when they subordinate the familial pleadings of the narrative to its capitalist melodrama, as if the reintegration of the family were merely an ideological cover for the reincorporation of the syndicate. The two structures are interrelated; neither can rightly be subordinated to the other.

Standing godfather to his nephew, Michael accepts family leadership and embodies family unity, literalizing his newly won title as patriarch of an extended family, crowned "Don" Michael Corleone. Michael tightens the family circle around him. Hagen returns from Nevada. Traitors to family honor—Gatto, Rizzi, Tessio—are weeded out. Michael's success in restoring the Corleone empire is as much the act of a truly obedient son as his godfatherhood is a basis for taking over the syndicate, for the crime organization becomes a structure on which the Corleones are reunited. Coppola's film version leaves us with a trace of dissent in the air, ending with Kay's recognition of Michael's ruthless criminality. In the novel, Puzo restores the equanimity of husband and wife and, by symbolic extension, of the Corleone family at large. Tom Hagen explains to Kay why it was necessary, from the standpoint of their ethos, for Michael to order the executions of Carlo Rizzi, Tessio, and the others. Kay acquiesces to Hagen's explanation and Michael's desire that she come home. She undergoes a rite of cultural self-transformation, to make herself into the kind of Italian-American woman the criminal environment expects. Whereas the film ends with Kay's anguish, the novel ends with Kay's conversion to Catholicism. Every morning she goes to mass with her mother-in-law, there to say in the final words of the novel, "the necessary prayers for the soul of Michael Corleone" (*G* 446). The peace of the Corleones is thereby restored. Michael does not mend matters with Kay simply to make the company perform better, any more than he restores the power of the syndicate simply to win his wife back and reintegrate his family; as Puzo has rigged the plot, the two go hand in hand.

III

> *The single aspect of The Godfather that seems to have made the deepest impact on the American public is Puzo's use of the central symbol of "the family." This symbol's influence has virtually changed overnight the American public's favorite term for a criminal organization.*
>
> —*John Cawelti*

For its depiction of an ethnic subculture that functions as an interest group, *The Godfather* would warrant attention from scholars—even if, like *The Fortunate Pilgrim,* the novel had disappeared into obscurity upon publication. But the novel has had a major impact on popular culture. The figure of "the godfather" outstrips all but the most ubiquitous cultural symbols, falling somewhere between Huckleberry Finn and Superman, perhaps better known than Uncle Sam himself.[24] The novel has possibly been the best-seller of all time. By 1971, when the first film was released, there were over one million hardcover copies in circulation—multiple copies in every library in every town in America—with at least ten million more paperbacks.[25] Historically, the reading of the novel framed the film—not, as in academic criticism, the other way around. The novel still sells, another five or ten million to date, in a $1.95 paperback series of "classic bestsellers." The most immediate spin-offs were the two films; versions of those films rearranged for television; and the video format, which frequently offers both films on a single cassette. By 1975, 260 more books on the Mafia theme had been released, principally of the hard-boiled variety.[26] In 1984, Puzo himself tried again with *The Sicilian,* his fictional account of Salvatore Giuliano. Ethnicity in crime has figured in several major films, including *The Cotton Club* (coscripted by Coppola, Puzo, and William Kennedy), *The Gang Who Couldn't Shoot Straight, Mean Streets, Broadway Danny Rose, Heart of the Dragon, Scarface,* and *Once upon a Time in America.* The popularity of the family "dynasty" sagas, especially in their many ethnic varieties, can be traced in part to Puzo's model. More telling still has been the ceaseless production of *Godfather* clones, emphasizing the fusion of family and crime. Practically a genre of their own, they include (auto)biographical works like Gay Talese's *Honor Thy Father,* Joseph Bonanno's *Man of Honor,* and Antoinette Giancana's *Mafia Princess;* novels like Vincent Patrick's *Family Business* and Richard Condon's *Prizzi's Honor;* academic studies like Francis A. J. Ianni's *A Family Business;* and films and teleplays, including "Our Family Honor," ABC's ill-fated attempt to combine Italian-American gangsters with Irish-American cops.

What are we to make of the lasting fascination with *The Godfather?* Since its appearance, scholars have recognized *The Godfather* as an artifact of what is called, perhaps misleadingly, the "new ethnicity." The timing of the novel and its immediate offspring, from the book's publication in 1969 to the television series in the late seventies, corresponds to the rise of a celebratory attitude toward ethnic identity. This celebration encompassed not only groups by and large still marginal—blacks, Indians, newcomers from Asia and the Hispanic Americas—but also the descendants of European immigrants, including the Italians who were increasingly well established in the middle classes. Necessarily, the connections drawn between the increased salience of ethnicity and *The Godfather's* popularity have been premised on the prevailing interpretation of *The Godfather* as a two-part fantasy, in which family sanctuary and successful corporate enterprise are polar opposites. My reading of *The Godfather,* emphasizing the complicity of family and business, calls for a reexamination of the novel's role in the new ethnic self-consciousness. Both the popularity of *The Godfather* and the celebration of ethnicity are complex phenomena, reflecting a myriad of attitudes toward race, class, and gender as well as toward ehnicity—attitudes often in conflict with one another. By claiming that *The Godfather* articulates the business of family, I do not wish to mute these other voices. My ambition is to point the way toward evaluating the voice of family business within the larger cacophony of debate.

Scholars like Jameson and Cawelti, working within the frame of traditional *Godfather* interpretation, seek to locate in the novel an anticapitalist energy—not an overt critique so much as an impulse, the energy of a potential critique partially veiled and misdirected. Both critics argue that Puzo portrays the Mafia as the center of a capitalist conspiracy and, simultaneously and irreconcilably, as a refuge from the conspiracy of capitalism. Because Puzo's Mafia functions as "the mirror-image of big-business," its brutality provides a focus for anticapitalist anxiety and an outlet for anticapitalist anger.[27] Similarly, the juxtaposed, equally powerful image of the family reflects, in Jameson's terms, a "Utopian longing" for escape from the prison house of capitalism. "The 'family' is a fantasy of tribal belongingness," echoes Cawelti, "that protects and supports the individual as opposed to the coldness and indifference of the modern business or government bureaucracy."[28]

In the standard view, *The Godfather's* putative double fantasy reflects the misdirected energies of the new ethnicity; the new ethnicity arises from frustration with capitalism yet mutes its resistance in clamor about the decline of the family and traditional values.[29] My analysis of *The Godfather* suggests we might hesitate, however, before accepting the majority opinion, that the family in the novel embodies a refuge from capitalism. We need especially to question whether a case for the subsersive nature of *The Godfather* can rest on the myth of the Italian-American family as a precapitalist collectivity, when Puzo mounts all his forces to undermine this false dichotomy. The representation of the southern Italian family in *The*

Godfather is not the kind of saccharine portrayal of innocent harmony—the haven in a heartless world—that scholars take as the benchmark of ethnic nostalgia. In *The Godfather,* capitalism is shown to accommodate, absorb, and indeed accentuate the structures of family and ethnicity. Americans respond to *The Godfather* because it presents the ethnic family not as a sacrosanct European institution, reproduced on the margins of America, but as a central American structure of power, successful *and* bloodied.

The desire of scholars to identify ethnic pietism as a locus of anticapitalist energy has blinded them to an alliance between the new ethnicity and procapitalist celebration of the family. This alliance is an insufficiently recognized strain in recent popular culture. At least until World War II, and perhaps into the 1970s, the dominant attitude toward the ethnic family in the United States assumed its incompatibility with capitalism, whether ethnicity was favored or not. The rabid Americanizers of the early decades attempted to strip immigrant workers of their familial and cultural loyalties. Among immigrants themselves, many feared that the price of upward mobility might be family solidarity, even as most in their midst deployed the family as a basis for group enterprise and mutual financial support. And intellectuals who were skeptical of capitalism, whether partly or wholly, based one strand of their critique on the damage that capitalism supposedly inflicted upon traditional family cultures. These family doomsayers tend less and less to be nativist Americanizers and guardians of ethnic tradition, but the nostalgia among scholars remains loud and clear. While the myth of the natural ethnic family still holds sway among intellectuals, the general public has come increasingly to accept and indeed welcome the idea of compatibility between ethnicity and capitalism. To accent the Italian example, for instance, public figures ranging from Lee Iacocca to Geraldine Ferraro and Mario Cuomo emphasize the contribution of family values to their own success stories, occasionally stretching our imaginations.[30] Similar rhetoric appears in the reemergence of the critique of the black family, in the widespread lauding of Asian- and Caribbean-American merchants and their schoolchildren, and in the general appeal for a new American work ethic. In this light, *The Godfather* feeds upon a strain of American rhetoric and expectation that has reached full salience only in the last decade.

Perhaps no artifact of American culture, popular or serious, has made the case for the business of family with quite the force of *The Godfather.* At no time in United States history has ethnicity enjoyed the vogue that it first achieved in the years of *The Godfather's* greatest popularity and, in large measure, now maintains. The congruence is no coincidence. *The Godfather* does indeed participate in the new ethnicity by celebrating the ethnic family. But the Mafia achieves its romantic luster not because Puzo portrays the Italian-American family as a separate sphere, lying outside of capitalism, but because the Italian-American family emerges as a potent structure within it. The ethnic family in *The Godfather* feeds off a market sensibility rather than undermining it.[31] The Corleones can provide protection from the market only because they have mastered it. Indeed, the height of romance is reached in *The Godfather* with Puzo's choice of the Mafia as a model for family enterprise, for illegal family enterprises are capable of growing and expanding to an extent that the structure and regulation of legitimate capitalism will ultimately not support.

If *The Godfather* does indeed harbor anticapitalist energies, as a thorough reading of the novel might suggest, then perhaps scholars have been looking for that energy in the wrong places. Jameson concludes,

> *When indeed we reflect on an organized conspiracy against the public, one which reaches into every corner of our daily lives and our political structures to exercise a wanton and genocidal violence at the behest of distant decision–makers and in the name of an abstract conception of profit—surely it is not about the Mafia, but rather about American business itself that we are thinking, American capitalism in its most systematized and computerized, dehumanized, "multi-national" and corporate form.*[32]

Jameson and the others may be correct in insisting that fascination with *The Godfather* is motivated, at a deeper level, by anticapitalist anxiety. But the real scare occasioned by *The Godfather,* however much suppressed, is about capitalism not in its "most systematized and computerized, dehumanized" form, but rather in its more "intimate" varieties—ethnic, familial, personal. My reading of *The Godfather* suggests that if we wish to press charges against capitalism, we press charges against family and ethnicity, too. One strand of rhetoric in twentieth-century America, familiar to us from Howells's *Hazard of New Fortunes* and sources pervasive in our culture, suggests that Americans can go home to escape the specter of capitalism. Professionals often complain about taking work home with them, mentally if not literally. How much more frightening, then, is the alternative represented by Puzo: when some Americans go home to papa, they end up confronting the boss. Critics have been quick to interpret the brutality of the Mafia as a symbol for the violence to the invididual inherent in capitalism, and to assume that the family represents an escape from that violence. Yet the melodrama of *The Godfather* implicates the family not only in the success of the Corleone empire but in its cycle of self-destructive violence as well. Michael reintegrates the family business only *after* burying a brother, murdering a brother-in-law, alienating a sister, and betraying the trust of his wife. For Americans who experience family and economy as interwoven pressures (if not actual combined enterprises), the Mafia genre may allow a focusing of resentments, even if, inevitably, a Mafia analogy overstates them. For the cost of employing blood in the marketplace is finding the company at home.

My speculations notwithstanding, there is no direct way to study popular opinion and pinpoint the popular interpretation of *The Godfather.* Indeed, it would be a mistake to assume there is any single interpretation (any more than there is a single "mind of the masses"). The great strength of popular literature may be its ability to entertain different, even contrary readings. But we can at least consider how other American artists catering to mass audiences have read the message of Puzo's novel. Two of the novel's best offspring—the film *Godfather II* (1974) and *Prizzi's Honor* (1982) by Richard Condon—illuminate the novel's reception. Although Puzo receives credit for the *Godfather II* screenplay, along with Coppola, the film offers a perspective on the Corleones very different from either that of the novel or that of its reasonable facsimile, the first film. Pauline Kael actually throws almost all the credit for *Godfather ll* to Coppola: "This second film . . . doesn't appear to derive from the book as much as from what Coppola learned while he was making the first."[33] For our purposes, however, it is not essential to distribute praise or blame, but simply to note that the film differs significantly enough from the original narrative to constitute a "rereading" of it (even if it is, in part, Puzo's own). Whereas the original *Godfather* narrative winds the fates of the Corleone family and the Corleone business together, Coppola's *Godfather II* separates the two strands. In *Prizzi's Honor,* on the other hand, Richard Condon uses all the devices in Puzo's novel, plus some of his own, to bond family and business tighter than ever. *Prizzi's Honor* surgically extracts Puzo's theme from underneath his excesses and Coppola's sermonizing and exposes it to a scintillating parody. The greatest testament to *The Godfather* has been paid not by critics or scholars but by Condon and John Huston, who directed the 1985 film version from Condon's own screenplay. Together, *Godfather II* and *Prizzi's Honor* can be construed as leading voices in a debate about the meaning of Puzo's novel and the future of the genre in which all three works participate.

Notes

1. It is not unreasonabale to assume that Puzo derived his emphasis on the familial aspect of the Mafia from the reports of Joseph Valachi, whose Senate hearings were in 1963 and whose book came out in 1967. In *The Italians,* itself a nonfiction leading seller of 1964, Luigi Barzini summarized how Valachi's testimony reshaped common American ideas about organized crime:

   > *The convicted American gangster, Joseph Valachi . . . explained the facts of life of the Sicilian village, probably as old as Mediterranean civilization, the principles guiding Homeric kings and heroes in their decisions, to a Senate committee and an awestruck twentieth-century television audience. He patiently pointed out that an isolated man was a dead duck in the American underworld; that he had to belong to a family, his own, or one which accepted him; that families were gathered in alliances, and the alliances in a loose federation called Cosa Nostra, governed by an unwritten code.*

   Luigi Barzini, *The Italians* (New York: Bantam, 1965), 284. Puzo may have derived his view of the Mafia, then, not only from his Hell's Kitchen experience but from Valachi, either directly or through Barzini's explication (Don Corleone's biggest competitor is named Barzini). But if Valachi first introduced the notion of family crime, and Barzini explicated it, it was Puzo who made the symbol ubiquitous.

2. The preceding two quotations are from John G. Cawelti, *Adventure, Mystery, Romance: Formula Stories as Art and Popular Culture* (Chicago: Univ. of Chicago Press, 1976), 78. The tandem reappears in John Sutherland's *Bestsellers* and in essays by Fredric Jameson and Eric Hobsbawm. E. J. Hobsbawm, "Robin Hoodo: A Review of Mario Puzo's *The Sicilian," New York Review of Books,* Feb. 14, 1985, 12-17; Fredric Jameson, "Reification and Utopia in Mass Culture," *Social Text* 1 (1979), 130-48; John Sutherland, *Bestsellers: Popular Fiction of the 1970s* (London: Routledge & Kegan Paul, 1981), chap. 3.
3. Jameson, "Reification and Utopia," 146.
4. Puzo's own, scattered comments on the social realities behind *The Godfather* reveal little. In an interview, he emphasizes that the novel was meant to be not realistic but romantic: "To me *The Godfather* isn't an exposé; it's a romantic novel." As quoted by Tom Buckley, "The Mafia Tries a New Tune," *Harper's,* Aug. 1971. 54. In *The Godfather Papers,* Puzo claims to have written the novel "entirely from research," then testifies that actual manfiosi found his fictional depictions very true to life. Mario Puzo, *The Godfather Papers and Other Confessions* (New York: Putnam, 1972), 35.
5. Puzo's autobiographical novel, *The Fortunate Pilgrim* (1964), seems on its surface to exemplify the long-standing tradition of interpreting Italian-American familialism as a barrier to mobility. One reviewer wrote, "The writer renders with fidelity the life-style of an Italian-American community in which Old Country values of propriety, order and obedience to established authority collide with New World ambition, initiative, and disdain for tradition." Sheldon Grebstein, "Mama Remembered the Old Country," *Saturday Review,* Jan. 23, 1965,44. Yet, I would argue, the novel harbors a countervailing analysis, demonstrating how the Puzo family used traditional values to ensure a steadily progressive mobility, culminating in Mario's freedom to become a writer.
6. Herbert J. Guns, *Urban Villagers: Group and Class in the Life of Italian-Americans* (New York: Free Press, 1962); Virginia Yans-McLaughlin, *Family and Community: Italian Immigrants in Buffalo, 1880–1930* (Ithaca: Cornell Univ. Press, 1977); Thomas Kessner, *The Golden Door: Italian and Jewish Immigrant Mobility in New York City, 1880–1915* (New York: Oxford Univ. Press, 1977); Thomas Sowell, *Ethnic America* (New York: Basic, 1981).

Most Italian immigrants to the United States originated from the *Mezzogiorno,* the regions of Italy south and east of Naples, including Sicily. The traditional view of Italian-American ethnicity is extrapolated from several very well known, mid- to late-twentieth-century studies of southern Italy: Phyllis H. Williams, *South Italian Folkways in Europe and America: A Handbook for Social Workers, Visiting Nurses, Schoolteachers. and Physicians* (New Haven: Yale Univ. Press, 1938); Carlo Levi, *Christ Stopped at Eboli,* trans. Frances Frenaye (New York: Farrar, Straus & Giroux, 1947); Edward Banfield, *Moral Basis of a Backward Society* (New York: Free Press, 1958); and Ann Cornelisen, *Women of the Shadows* (New York: Dell, 1976). vThese essays prompted American social workers like Leonard Covello and scholars like Herbert Guns, Rudolph Vecoli, Thomas Sowell, Thomas Kessner, and Virginia Yans-McLaughlin to adopt a variant on the "culture of poverty" argument for blue-collar Italian Americans, although

Cornelisen, for one, warns against approaches based on "residual vestiges of peasant mentality. " Cornelisen, *Women of the Shadows,* 220.

For an overview of traditional scholarship on Italian-Americans, including an analysis of its limitations, see Micaela di Leonardo, *The Varities of Ethnic Experience: Kinship, Class, and Gender among Callfornia Italian-Americans* (Ithaca: Cornell Univ. Press, 1984), 17-25, 96–108.

7. Leonard Covello, "The Influence of Southern Italian Family Mores upon the School Situation in America," in Francesco Cordasco and Eugene Bucchioni, eds., *The Italians: Social Backgrounds of an American Group* (Clifton, N.J.: Kelley, 1974), 516. Covello's extremely influential essay was originally written as a dissertation in 1944 and finally published as *The Social Background of the Italo-American School Child: A Study of the Southern Italian Family Mores and Their Effect on the School Situation in Italy and America* (Totowa, N.J.: Rowman & Littlefield, 1972).

8. Francis A. J. Ianni, with Elizabeth Reuss-Ianni, *A Family Business: Kinship and Social Control in Organized Crime* (New York: Russell Sage Foundation, 1972), 55. Ianni notes that "the acculturation process works in crime as elsewhere" (61), but nonetheless traces the familial structure of the Luppollo syndicate back to Italy: "The origins of this familialism are Italian and not American" (155).

The urgency to place the Mafia along an Old World-New World continuum resurfaces in the work of the historian Humbert S. Nelli, who adopts the opposite position from Ianni's. Nelli concedes the "group unity" and "cooperative effort" of Italian-American mobs, but stresses almost entirely the individualism and "American way of life" of the gang leaders. See Humbert S. Nelli, *The Business of Crime: Italians and Syndicate Crime in the United States* (Chicago: Univ. of Chicago Press, 1976), 255-57.

Scholars of the Mafia in southern Italy also insist on the evolving interdependence of familial and/or fraternal organization and capitalist enterprise. The Italian Mafia in recent years is thought to have been restructured in imitation of the Italian-American Mafia. See Pino Arlacchi, *Mafia Business: The Mafia Ethic and the Spirit of Capitalism,* trans. Martin Ryle (New York: Schocken, 1986); Anton Blok, *The Mafia of a Sicilian Village, 1860-1960: A Study of Violent Peasant Entrepreneurs,* with a foreword by Charles Tilly (New York: Harper & Row, 1975); and E. J. Hobsbawm, *Primitive Rebels: Studies in Archaic Forms of Social Movement in the 19th and 20th Centuries,* 2d ed. (New York: Praeger, 1963), chap. 3.

9. Eli Zaretsky, *Capitalism, the Family, and Personal Life* (New York: Harper & Row, 1976). Zaretsky's small book, little known, is an extraordinarily lucid reappraisal, spanning several centuries, of the relation between Western family structure and capitalism.

10. For a review essay on what I am calling the new ethnic theory, consult Werner Sollors, "Theory of American Ethnicity, or:"? S ETHNIC?/TI AND AMERICAN/TI, DE OR UNITED (W) S TATES S SI AND THEOR?" *American Quarterly* 33 (Bibliography, 1981), 257-83. I am myself indebted to this article for bringing Abner Cohen, among others, to my attention.

The rise of the new ethnicity, as represented in the work of Michael Novak, Peter Schrag, Richard Gambino, even Glazer and Moynihan, has prompted severely critical responses, primarily from the political Left. Typically, the work of the ethnic demythologizers challenges the romance of ethnicity either by dismissing ethnic cultural difference altogether or by reducing difference to a variable entirely dependent upon *class.* In Stephen Steinberg's *The Ethnic Myth,* ethnicity is, for all explanatory purposes, entirely discounted. In Herbert Gans's very influential work, family values are interpreted as the product of working-class status and are hence "pan-ethnic," shared by blue-collar folk of all backgrounds, whereas the ethnicity of the middle class is what Gans calls "symbolic," meaning that it is private, a matter of individual identity and friendship without socioeconomic significance. Tellingly, Gans says middleclass ethnicity is "cost-free" without inquiring into its profitability; the middleclass family is implicated in capitalism, once again, only as a buffer or safety valve for the system. See Steinberg, *The Ethnic Myth: Race, Ethnicity, and Class in America* (New York: Atheneum, 1981); Gans, "Symbolic Ethnicity: The Future of Ethnic Groups and Cultures in America," in Herbert J. Gans et al., eds., *On the Making of Americans: Essays in Honor of David Riesman* (Philadelphia: Univ. of Pennsylvania Press, 1979); Gans, foreword to Neil C. Sandberg, *Ethnic Identity and Assimilation* (New York: Praeger, 1974).

11. The quote is from Abner Cohen, *Two-Dimensional Man: An Essay on the Anthropology of Power and Symbolism in Complex Society* (Berkeley: Univ. of California Press, 1974), 99. See also Abner Cohen, "Introduction" to *Urban Ethnicity,* ed. A . Cohen (London: Tavistock, 1974), ix-xxiv.

Major critical efforts to reconceive ethnic literature in the light of new ideas about ethnicity include William Boelhower, *Through a Glass Darkly: Ethnic Semiosis in American Literature* (Venice: Edizioni Helvetia, 1984) ; Jules Chametzky, *Our Decentralized Literature: Cultural Mediations in Selected Jewish and Southern Writers* (Amherst: Univ. of Massachusetts Press, 1986); Mary V. Dearborn, *Pocahontas's Daughters: Gender and Ethnicity in American Culture* (New York: Oxford Univ. Press, 1986); and Werner Sollors. *Beyond Ethnicity: Consent and Descent in American Culture* (New York: Oxford Univ. Press. 1986).

12. Rose Basile Green, *The Italian-American Novel: A Document of the In teraction of Two Cultures* (Rutherford, N. J. Fairleigh Dickinson Univ. Press, 1974), 355, 357, 364.

For a brief yet elegant discussion of *The Godfather,* in the context of an overview of Italian-American literature, see Robert Viscusi, *"De Vulgari Eloquentia:* An Approach to the Language of Italian American Fiction," *Yale Italian Studies* I (Winter 1981), 21-38. Implicitly challenging traditional accounts of ethnic literature, Viscusi acknowledges the inventive role of the imagination in the creation of a post-European ethnic culture. His language-oriented approach is itself calculated to invent terms in which we might appreciate a previously ignored literature. By emphasizing the linguistic savvy of Italian-American writing, Viscusi means to present this literature in the strongest possible light, given the bias toward language of the journal sponsoring his essay and, more important, of the critical community it represents. Whereas Viscusi's highly "literary" approach seems to have nothing whatsoever to do with business, is it a coincidence that the most important property he attributes to Italian-American literature is its ability to "be *diplomatic,* to *negotiate* the terms on which Italian America can exist " (emphasis mine)?

13. Mario Puzo, *The Godfather* (New York: Putnam, 1969), 216. Further references to this edition are given in parentheses in the text.
14. Cohen, "Introduction," xvii.
15. Peter Dobkin Hall, "Marital Selection and Business in Massachusetts Merchant Families 1700–1900" in Michael Gordon, ed., *The American Family in Social-Historical Perspective,* 2d ed. (New York: St. Martin's, 1978), 101–14.

For other discussions of ethnicity, economics, and ethnic businesses, see Ivan H. Light, *Ethnic Enterprise in America: Business and Welfare among Chinese, Japanese, and Blacks* (Berkeley: Univ. of California Press, 1972); John Bodnar, Roger Simon, and Michael P. Weber, *Lives of Their Own: Blacks, Italians, and Poles in Pittsburgh, 1900-1960 :* Thomas Sowell, *Race and Economics* (New York: McKay, 1975).

16. Ianni, *A Family Business,* 157.
17. Ibid., 64-65, 92, 116-18.
18. The don reminds Tom of his real background, less to take away from the meaning of Tom's initiation into the don's nuclear family than to highlight, by contrast, that meaning. Tom's marriage to an Italian-American, like his adoption by Don Corleone, constitutes a rebirth as an Italian-American on his wedding day.
19. There is much excess baggage in this sprawling, desperately populist novel : great detail on postures of war between the families, which Sutherland deviously and persuasively attributes to Puzo's reaction to World War II (*Bestsellers,* 45); well-stroked portrayals of the making of the Corleone soldiers, including Rocco Lampone, Luca Brasi, and the ex-cop Albert Neri; speculations in the *National Enquirer* vein into the activities, both private and public, of Frank Sinatra and friends; painfully unnecessary excursions into the sexual lives of Sonny, his mistress Lucy Mancini, and Dr. Jules Segal. In my experience teaching the novel, the reactions to these tangents vary. Sinatra merits a passing interest, the sex lives of Sonny and the doctor hardly any at all. The passages that chronicle the making of McCluskey the bad cop and Neri the enforcer are avidly read; similar chronicles become hallmarks of the Mafia genre subsequently. In *The Godfather,* the tangents do not so much detract from the main narrative as fill it out during its middle stretches, sustaining interest while holding final revelations in abeyance.
20. "The visual scheme is based on the most obvious life-and-death contrasts; the men meet and conduct their business in deep-toned, shuttered rooms, lighted by lamps even in the daytime, and the story moves back and forth between the hidden, nocturnal world and the sunshine that they share with the women and children." Pauline Kael, "Alchemy: A Review of Francis Ford Coppola's *The Godfather,*" *New Yorker,* March 18, 1972, 132.
21. "The novel is a tale of family succession, showing the rise of the true son and heir and reaching a climax with his acceptance of the power and responsibilities of Godfather. It tell show Michael Corleone comes to understand his father's character and destiny and then allows himself to be shaped by that same destiny." Cawelti, *Adventure, Mystery, Romance* 52-53.

In his review of the first *Godfather* film for *Commentary,* William S. Pechter was perhaps the first critic to emphasize that while the icon of "the Godfather" meant Don Vito Corleone, the narrative belonged to Michael:

> What is the family whose claims override all others in *The Godfather?* It is, for one thing, a patriarchy, and the story the film has to tell is basically not Don Corleone's but Michael's: a story of his initiation into the family by an act of murder, of the succession of the youngest, most assimilated son to the patriarchal powers and responsibilities and the ethnic mystique of his father.

Pechter, "Keeping Up with the Corleones," *Commentary* 54 (July 1972), 89.

22. "[The southern Italian peasant] despised as a *scomunicato* (pariah) anyone in any family who broke the ordine della famiglia or otherwise violated the *onore* (honor, solidarity, tradition, 'face') of the family." Richard Gambino, *Blood of My Blood: The Dilemma of the Italian-Americans* (Garden City, N.Y.: Doubleday, 1974), 4.
23. Mary Antin wrote in 1912, "I was born, I have lived, and I have been made over. . . . Did I not become the parent and they [her parents] the children, in those relations of teacher and learner?" Antin. *The Promised Land* (Boston: Houghton Mifflin, 1912), xii. In 1981, Richard Rodriguez echoed Antin's Emersonian image of self-birth, in an aside to "my parents—who are no longer my parents, in a cultural sense." Rodriguez, *Hunger of Memory: The Education of Richard Rodriguez* (Boston: Godine, 1981), 4.
24. Claude Brown reports that "godfather" ranks among the most popular handles, or nicknames, of black inner-city America. *New York Times Magazine,* Sept. 16, 1984, 38. I have a suspicion that *The Godfather* is also a secret vice for very different segments of American society. More than one professor of English has confessed that Puzo may, after all, have some considerable gifts. A black woman, also an English professor, told me she had read the novel five times and once saw the film at a theater three days in a row! I hope, by explaining my own fascination with the text, I do not deprive others of the mystique of a favorite vice.

It is also a wonderful fact, without being a coincidence, that Puzo's major project after *The Godfather* screenplays was scripting *Superman: The Movie* and *Superman II.* For what is the story of Superman if not a meta-narrative of immigration, about a refugee whose power derives from his dislocation, whose secret identity is hidden under a disabling Anglo-conformity (as Clark Kent), but whose true promise is revealed in his fight "for truth, justice, and the American way"? And who, conversely, is Don Corleone if not the latest in a continuing series of ethnic supermen? For a discussion of superman imagery in the context of American ethnicity, consult Sollars. *Beyond Ethnicity,* chap. 3.

25. "The Making of *The Godfather,*" *Time,* March 13, 1972. 61. By 1980, reports John Sutherland, *The Godfather's* publishers were claiming worldwide sales of fifteen million. The title

Sutherland gives the novel, "the bestseller of bestsellers," echoes nicely the Sicilian phrase for the boss of bosses, *capo di tutti capi.* Certainly, no other contemporary work has sold as well. How one compares a present-day popular novel with, say, *Gone with the Wind* or *Uncle Tom's Cabin* is no easy matter. Sutherland, *Bestsellers.* 38, 46.

26. For a review of the Mafia literature from 1969 to 1975, see Dwight C. Smith, Jr., "Sons of the Godfather: 'Mafia' in Contemporary Fiction," *Italian Americana* 2 (Spring 1976), 191-207; the statistical reference is from p. 192. A shorter bibliography appears in Cawelti. *Adventure, Mystery, Romance,* 304n .
27. In Jameson's view ("Reification and Utopia," 145), the butchery of the Corleones symbolizes the "wanton ecocidal and genocidal violence" of capitalism in America. Cawelti adds (*Adventure, Mystery, Romance,* 78), "I suspect there is a definite relation between the fascination with limitless criminal power. . . . and the public's reluctant awareness of the uncontrollable power of violence in the hands of the government."
28. Jameson, "Reification and Utopia," 146; Cawelti, *Adventure, Mystery, Romance,* 78.
29. "At a time when the disintegration of the dominant communities is persistently 'explained' in the (profoundly ideological) terms of the deterioration of the family, the growth of permissiveness and the loss of authority of the father, the ethnic group can seem to project an image of social reintegration by way of the patriarchal and authoritarian family of the past." Jameson, "Reification and Utopia," 146–47.
30. Well into the seventies, even after the rise of the new ethnicity, it was conventional to attribute the poor performance of Italian-Americans in the professions, the arts, the American Catholic church, politics, and big business to the tenacity of familial values and southern Italian culture. In the last few years, however, the conspicuous rise of Italian-Americans has reversed the age-old formula. Stephen S. Hall wrote in a 1983 cover story for the Sunday *New York Times Magazine:*

Is there a single thread that runs through all these [stories of successful Italian-Americans)? If anything, it is the unusual propensity to merge, rather than separate, the professional and the personal. Borrowing from a culture in which the extended family can easily include 30 to 40 "close" relatives, Italians thrive on community. They are accustomed to large numbers of people, and they seem to have developed an emotional facility in dealing with them. Even in large companies, they have a knack for keeping things on a human scale. "The professional community," explains one Italian-American psychotherapist, "becomes the next family."

Hall, "Italian-Americans: Coming Into Their Own," *New York Times Magazine,* May 15, 1983, 29.

31. It is amusing to speculate how Puzo's usage of ethnicity in his career as a writer parallels, broadly speaking, the usage of ethnicity depicted in his novels. Puzo began his career in the now venerable fashion of aspiring American literati, with a novelistic account of his years as an expatriate (in postwar Germany), *The Dark Arena* (1955). Only subsequently did he specialize in ethnic narrative and become known as a specifically Italian-American writer. With *The Fortunate Pilgrim* (1964), Puzo was able to promote himself as an earnest realist, little known but "serious," as if Italian-American writers toiled honestly on the margins of the American literary community just as their characters worked on the margins of the American economy. With *The Godfather* (1969) and its offspring, Puzo launched himself on a career as both a popular novelist and a Hollywood screenwriter, exploiting ethnic materials for power and profit, as if in faint imitation of the exploitation of family and ethnicity by his Mafia characters.
32. Jameson, "Reification and Utopia, " 145.
33. Pauline Kael, "Fathers and Sons," *New Yorker,* Dec. 23, 1974, 64.

Critical Thinking

1. In what respects do cultural studies and the lived experiences of cultures intersect and influence each other?
2. Has the ***The Godfather*** shaped negative and positive attitudes towards Italian Americans?

Create Central

www.mhhe.com/createcentral

Internet References

The International Center for Migration, Ethnicity, and Citizenship
www.newschool.edu/icmec

The National Italian American Foundation
www.niaf.org

Order of The Sons of Italy in America
www.osia.org

Unit 8

UNIT

Prepared by: John A. Kromkowski, *Catholic University of America*

Contemporary Dilemmas and Contentions: The Search for Convergent Issues and Common Values

Ethnic identity and recent concerns include a large range of convergent issues, language preservation, fair hearings for homeland interests, enclave neighborhoods, inclusion in ethnic studies, and all ethnic groups articulate agendas as historical American expressions of fairness and justice. An important aspect of interest among all ethnic groups is accurate data and information about their ethnic group.

The values of American ethnic groups are thoroughly patterned into their worldview and their appropriation of the expansive promise of the American icon—the Statue of Liberty. Ethnicity in America for immigrants and ethnics became a complex of identifications and loyalties that included sentimental attachment to home village, region, or nation; a certain religious affiliation; and the notion of being part of a distinct religious culture. But immigration and their ethnicity in America included loyalty to America and an identification with a particular city, district, or neighborhood in which they settled, membership in the local ethnic community and its institutional expressions. Ethnicity offers a sense of belonging to a certain class or distinct occupation. Thus ethnicity was essentially a local identity. The relative saliency of its components and each of these elements of ethnic and religious identity changed under the impact of events and with the passing generations.

Ethnicity is often associated with immigrants and with importation of culture, language, stories, and foods from foreign shores. Appalachian, Western, and other regional ethnicities are evidence of multigenerational ethnic cultural development within the American reality. The persistent, ongoing process of cultural formation and personal identity are expressed locally in unique and intriguing folkways, dialects, languages, myths, festivals, food displays, and other enduring monuments and visible signs of the past and of the public dimension of cultural consciousness that constitutes ethnicity. After all, it was this American promise that resonated in their hearts and minds in 1965 when a coalition of Mediterranean and eastern European Americans in the national government supported the 1965 Voting Rights Act that ensured fair elections for the disenfranchised in the South. This legislative coalition was accomplished through deliberative democracy. Along with Immigration Reform of the same year America instituted fundamental change that significantly altered the terms of race and ethnic relations. The massive migration of peoples during the past decades, which has included significantly large Mediterranean and eastern European populations, has reengaged the issue of immigration in American politics and the ethnic factor now reaches nearly all Americans. Should ethnic populations be denied their distinctiveness through absorption into the mass of modernity, or can their distinctiveness accompany them into mainstream modern America?

To address this question is to step into the search for a normative base for resolving dilemmas and contentions among groups. Significant clarification can be gained by defining ethnicity. What constitutes ethnic identity? Are ancestry and place of origin important? Are contextual factors such as other populations, ethnicities and economic, educational cultural and social dynamics as well as traditions determinative? Are the influences of such factors of ethnic groups and the manifestations of their presence in a metropolitan region firmly congealed? Certain lines of clarification to these introductory issues were drafted for a project sponsored by the National Center For Urban Ethnic Affairs for a project focused on the Detroit Metropolitan Region. The regional chair of this project Thaddeus Radzilowski, President of the Piast Institute, proposed the following deep description of the experience of American ethnicity:

> Ethnicity is one of the deepest and most enduring of human identities because it is based on language, religion, culture, family, common history and local community. It can have political salience and as such can play both negative and positive roles. However, political or public salience is not necessary for its survival. It can be the basis of community formation and a generous pluralism on the one hand, or divisiveness and prejudice on the other.
>
> Ethnicity in America is a creative adaptation to life in the New World by immigrants, both free and coerced. It was an attempt by newcomers to make themselves "at home" in a new place, often under difficult and challenging conditions. Out of the process came cultures that were

born out of preservation, adaptation, direct borrowing and invention, often reinforced by prejudice and interest. Successful ethnicities have kept the ability to change themselves to meet new conditions as well as to modify the dominant society in which they are embedded and to affect other ethnic cultures with whom they exist.

Ethnic adaptation to preserve core values and to mobilize group members in times of difficulty has happened with remarkable speed given the usual more leisurely pace of historical change. To be able to anticipate and use ethnicity in ways beneficial to the evolution of our society requires a clear understanding of recent history and current prospects if it is to succeed. . . . At this point it is not utopian to suggest the possibility of the re-polarization of ethnicity and its return as a vehicle to talk about civic values, community and multiculturalism. This discourse will require rethinking of multiculturalism at the same time. It's harder version, which postulates the incomprehensibility and irreconcilability of cultures to each other is useless for any civic dialog. Multiculturalism in its soft form is at this time too superficial and vapid to carry any meaningful concepts of community development. Neither has a language or a story out of which to fashion a political dialogue, nor are they, any more than is race, embedded in institutions in which people can act in the civic arena. . . . We should begin with pilot projects in a number of areas. Because of my own experience and because of the nature of the locale, I would clearly suggest my own Institute working with the University of Michigan in Detroit and Dearborn as one of the major sites for such activity.

The Detroit area has a large Polish-American population (600,000), the largest Arab-American population in the United States (300,000) a sizeable Italian-American group and a growing Hispanic, largely Mexican-American, population anchored by a city which has an 80% African-American population. The university has centers for the study of Arab and Hispanic population and a new endowment for a Polish chair and center. The area's fifth largest ethnic group is Italian-American. . . . We can prepare training materials drawn from the lessons of the pilot projects and assist groups in using them. The key will be to have groups reflect on their history and experience in America and the adaptation of their cultures to the American reality with an eye to learning how they can utilize that experience in shaping a generous and genuinely multicultural society and civic life. . . .

It is important to note as a caution that in so far as we espouse and practice multiculturalism and believe in a pluralist and open society, we are being quintessentially Western and especially American. It might ironically be even seen as one of our ethnocentricities given the fervor of our commitment. No other modern world culture has placed such a high neither premium on such ideas nor developed their theoretical underpinnings as well as we have. These are not transplanted concepts without roots in our culture. Thus, we have a greater certainty we can succeed at them, more than perhaps any other society in the world. We need to be able to take this fact into consideration in our preparation for the work we will do.

Article

Prepared by: John A. Kromkowski, *Catholic University of America*

Comparison on Ethnic Pride: Irish Catholic, Eastern European, Arab, Hispanic, Italian, Chinese, and other Mixed Ethnicities: The Zogby Center Polls 2000–2004

Learning Outcomes

After reading this article, you will be able to:

- Determine whether measures of public opinion are good indicators of values and behaviors. Under what conditions and about what sorts of issues?
- Discuss those findings that you found surprising and explain why you were surprised.

We compared the polling results on ethnic pride across seven ethnic groups within the populace of the United States: Arab, Hispanic, Italian, Chinese, Irish Catholic, Eastern European Catholic and Catholic with mixed ethnic background. Certain categories excluded one or more of these groups.

A. Ethnic Pride

Americans maintain a tremendous sense of recognition with regards to their ethnic origins and make-up. When we asked individuals in four of our seven groups to assess "How strong are your emotional ties to your family's country of origin?" over 70% of those polled said they maintained at least somewhat strong emotional ties. And while Chinese Americans appear to have the greatest connection with their country of origin at 40.1% (followed shortly thereafter by Arabs, Hispanics and lastly Italians), more than a third of each group claimed to have very strong emotional ties.

Table 1 Emotional Ties to Country of Origin

	Arab	Hispanic	Italian	Chinese
Very strong	39.7	36.8	34.3	40.1
Somewhat Strong	38.7	33.5	41.4	41.8
Not strong	21.5	29.1	23.8	18.1

As was reported in Zogby's 2000 Culture Poll entitled *What Ethnic Americans Really Think,* most Americans would appear to be very proud of their ethnic heritage, a fact that would seem to corroborate the strong emotional ties that many Ethnic Americans maintain with their country of origin. When asked, "On a scale of 1 to 5, with 1 being not at all and 5 being extremely, how proud are you of your ethnic heritage?" Between 70% and 90% of each one of our target

Table 2 Ethnic Pride

	Irish Catholic	Eastern European	Mixed	Arab	Hispanic	Italian	Chinese
Proud	81.6	80.7	70.4	85.5	90.0	90.7	85.2
Average pride	12.8	12.3	17.9	10.1	8.2	6.6	10.3
Not proud	5.2	6.6	10.9	3.8	1.4	2.4	3.0

groups expressed some degree of pride (4 or 5 on the scale) with regards to their ethnicity. Inversely, less than 11% of each respective group said they are not at all proud of their ethnic composition. Italian and Hispanic Americans are most likely to say that they are very proud of their origins at 90.7% and 90.0% respectively, while Catholics with mixed ethnic background are least likely to do so (70.4%).

When asked, "How important is your ethnic heritage in defining you as a person?" a majority of those polled responded that their ethnicity did in fact contribute in at least some way to their persona. This was especially true of Arab, Hispanic and Chinese-Americans, of whom over 50% went so far as to say that their ethnic heritage was very important in defining them as a person. Catholics with mixed ethnic background would seem to place the least amount of importance on ethnicity, with 40.5% claiming that their ethnic heritage is not at all important in defining them as a person. A large chunk of Eastern European Catholics (35.0%) and Irish Catholics (32.4%) also see their ethnic heritage as irrelevant to their self-definition.

B. Discrimination

While the majority of our respective target groups expressed a similar sense of recognition and pride regarding their ethnic heritage, responses were somewhat more polarizing as they pertained to discrimination. In response to the question "Have you personally experienced discrimination in the past because of your ethnicity/ancestral heritage?" an overwhelming majority of Irish Catholics, Eastern European Catholics, Catholics with mixed origins and Italian-Americans (88.6%, 91.6%, 90.8% and 79.1% respectively) said that they had never been victimized on account of their ethnic background. On the contrary, nearly half of those Hispanic and Chinese-American individuals polled (48.9% and 49.0%) respectively) claim to have been discriminated against.

When asked "How worried are you about the long-term effects of discrimination?" our results mirrored those of the previous question regarding the subject. As might be expected, for example, Hispanic and Chinese-Americans appear to be the most concerned by discrimination in the long-term, with 56.9% of the former and 46.3% of the latter at least somewhat worried. Italian-Americans are markedly less concerned, demonstrated by the fact that over 80% of those polled expressed no concern about the long-term effects of discrimination.

Arab-Americans would seem to be the most concerned about the contentious issue of discrimination, with an astonishing 25% very worried about the long-term effects of discriminatory behavior. This reality is perhaps less surprising in view of the political and social climate in the post-911 era. A significant majority of Arab Americans (60%) consider the events since September 11 to have negatively affected the public display of their heritage.

Table 3 Importance of Ethnic Heritage in Self-Definition

	Irish Catholic	Eastern European	Mixed	Arab	Hispanic	Italian	Chinese
Very important	24.5	25.0	20.1	55.6	55.6	48.1	54.0
Somewhat important	43.1	39.7	38.7	29.9	30.6	37.4	31.7
Not important	32.4	35.0	40.5	14.0	13.5	14.0	13.6

Table 4 Discrimination

	Irish Catholic	Eastern European	Mixed	Hispanic	Italian	Chinese
Yes	11.2	8.2	9.2	48.9	20.2	49.0
No	88.6	91.6	90.8	50.8	79.1	49.7

Table 5 Discrimination: Long-Term Effects

	Arab	Hispanic	Italian	Chinese
Very worried	25.0	15.4	3.8	5.4
Somewhat worried	34.6	41.5	14.3	40.9
Not worried	38.8	42.3	81.4	53.5

C. Taking a Closer Look at Ethnic Pride

1. Compared by Age

All of the groups we studied registered strong emotional ties to their land of heritage, regardless of the age of the respondent.

In general the strength of those ties decreased with age, with individuals aged 18 to 29 claiming to have the strongest emotional ties and those aged 65 and above having the weakest. The exception to the rule was the Chinese American population, where 18 to 29 year-olds actually recorded the weakest emotional ties (73.8%) and 50 to 64 year-olds the strongest (88.5%). Amongst Italian Americans 50 to 64 year-olds registered the weakest emotional ties (70.55%), although 18 to 29 year-olds maintained the strongest ties (83.0%).

Table 6 Emotional Ties

	Arab	Hispanic	Italian	Chinese
18–29	89.0	91.0	83.0	73.8
30–49	80.2	88.1	77.2	83.6
50–64	77.9	84.2	70.5	88.5
65+	70.6	81.0	75.1	79.6

Among Arab, Hispanic and Chinese Americans, younger generations appear to have the most pride in their ethnic heritage. For the three Catholic groups, the trend is reversed. It is those over 65 years old who seem to exhibit the most ethnic pride. The age gap is most remarkable in the case of Catholics with mixed background. Only 52.7% of its 18 to 29 year-olds claim to be proud of their ethnic heritage compared to 81.9% of those over 65 years old. For Italian Americans, the percentage of those proud of their ethnic heritage does not vary much across the age categories, although the older generations do seem to show slightly more pride than the younger ones.

For Arab, Hispanic and Chinese Americans, the relative importance of ethnic heritage decreases with age, with few exceptions. This is not the case with regards to the other four groups. In fact, quite to the contrary, those aged 65 and above were most concerned by the importance of their ethnic heritage among Eastern European Catholics, Catholics with mixed background and Italian Americans. For Irish Catholics, the age difference is not obvious among those over 30, although there is a significant dip for those aged 18 to 29.

2. Compared by Political Party Affiliation

There does not appear to be any generality to assess the relationship between political party affiliation and the emotional ties held to one's land of heritage. Amongst Hispanic and Italian Americans registered Democrats had the strongest emotional ties, while Republicans and/or independents had the strongest ties in the Arab and Chinese American communities. Emotional ties do not, however, vary extraordinarily with party affiliation, as evidenced by the fact that over 70% of all respondents supposedly maintain strong ties to their land of heritage.

Generally, registered democrats exhibit the greatest pride in their ethnic heritage within the groups that we examined. There are a few exceptions. First, among Arab Americans, a greater percentage of republicans and independents claim to be proud

Table 7 Pride in Ethnic Heritage

	Irish Catholic	Eastern European	Mixed	Arab	Hispanic	Italian	Chinese
18–29	72.0	61.7	52.7	94.0	91.6	90.0	90.2
30–49	83.8	83.1	65.5	84.2	91.1	87.7	83.7
50–64	77.0	77.4	74.5	81.5	90.8	93.0	83.0
65+	87.2	89.6	81.9	87.6	83.4	93.6	77.8

Table 8 Importance of Ethnic Heritage

	Irish Catholic	Eastern European	Mixed	Arab	Hispanic	Italian	Chinese
18–29	52	51.9	61.8	94.0	91.6	90.0	90.2
30–49	69.8	66.0	57.8	84.2	91.1	87.7	83.7
50–64	67.1	61.9	53.8	81.5	90.8	93.0	83.0
65+	69.4	73.4	66.9	87.6	83.4	93.6	77.8

Table 9 Emotional Ties

	Arab	Hispanic	Italian	Chinese
Democrat	73.3	88.9	80.1	78.4
Republican	75.5	82.1	72.9	80.0
Independent	84.3	83.3	72.9	81.3

Table 10 Pride in Ethnic Heritage

	Irish Catholic	Eastern European	Mixed	Arab	Hispanic	Italian	Chinese
Democrat	83.3	81.2	71.6	82.5	90.6	92.2	90.3
Republican	84.4	83.2	69.5	87.0	87.0	91.8	81.3
Independent	75.4	76.7	69.9	86.7	90.8	86.7	82.4

of their ethnic heritage. Then for Irish and Eastern European Catholics, it is also the republicans that lead. Democrats are slightly behind while independents are left at the bottom.

Different from the case with ethnic pride, democrats seem to lead in almost all groups in their emphasis on the importance of ethnic heritage. The only exception was Chinese Americans, where democrats lagged almost ten percent behind independent voters. Between the groups of democrats, Arab, Hispanic and Italian Americans were most likely to claim that their ethnic heritage was very important to them. The groups that are least likely to see the importance of ethnic heritage are independent Catholics with eastern European or mixed ethnic background (56.4% and 53.8% respectively).

Table 11 Importance of Ethnic Heritage

	Irish Catholic	Eastern European	Mixed	Arab	Hispanic	Italian	Chinese
Democrat	71.1	70.0	64.3	87.8	88.9	86.8	83.7
Republican	69.1	65.4	57.1	81.8	82.1	86.2	81.3
Independent	60.7	56.4	53.8	84.8	83.3	82.4	93.1

3. Compared bv Gender

With the exception of Chinese Americans, women appear to maintain stronger emotional ties with their country of origin than do men. With that said, the difference between the emphasis that men and women place on their emotional ties is negligible. Only Arab Americans exhibited any significant gap between male and female respondents, with 11.0% more females claiming to have strong emotional ties to their land of origin than men (83.9% and 72.9%) respectively).

Women appear slightly more likely to exhibit a tremendous sense of pride in their ethnic heritage than men do. Indeed, amongst all Catholic groups, Arab, Hispanic and Italian Americans, a greater percentage of females claimed that they are very proud of their ethnic background. On the contrary, Chinese American men are slightly more proud of their heritage than their female counterparts (87.7% and 82.9% respectively).

Table 12 Emotional Ties

	Arab	Hispanic	Italian	Chinese
Male	72.9	69.7	72.4	82.3
Female	83.9	70.9	78.7	81.5

Among 5 of the 7 groups, female respondents are more likely to view their ethnic heritage as important or somewhat important in defining themselves. The gender gap varies between 6% and 8.4%. One exception is the Catholics with mixed background where males lead females by 7.1%. There is little gender difference among eastern European Catholics. For both genders, the Catholic groups lag far behind the other four ethnic groups in their perceived importance of ethnic heritage.

4. Compared by Income

Income does not have a consistent impact upon the respondents' emotional ties to their country of origin. The Italians exhibit the least variation across the income groups. The group difference is less than 4.6%. Those with an annual income less than $50,000 exhibit the strongest emotional attachment. Within

Table 13 Pride in Ethnic Heritage

	Irish Catholic	Eastern European	Mixed	Arab	Hispanic	Italian	Chinese
Male	79.5	78.9	66.6	83.6	87.7	89.1	87.7
Female	83.6	82.4	73.9	87.4	91.8	92.1	82.9

Table 14 Importance of Ethnic Heritage

	Irish Catholic	Eastern European	Mixed	Arab	Hispanic	Italian	Chinese
Male	63.2	65.1	62.5	81.7	82.2	82.4	82.0
Female	71.0	64.4	55.4	89.3	89.6	88.4	89.5

the other three ethnic populations, the difference in emotional ties varies greatly across the income groups. For the *Hispanics,* those who earn less than $35,000 a year profess stronger attachment to their country of origin while those who have an annual income over $75,000 allege the least affection. Among the *Chinese Americans,* however, it is the lowest income group that claims weakest emotional ties to their motherland. As to the Arabs, those making between $50,000 and $75,000 a year are most estranged from their country of origin.

Table 15 Emotional Ties

	Arab	Hispanic	Italian	Chinese
>$35K	78.1	76.8	78.3	76.1
$35–50K	82.2	69.4	78.3	87.3
$50–75K	72.9	68.0	74.7	84.5
$75K+	78.7	62.7	73.7	87.3

The income group that shows the least pride in ethnic heritage are the Catholics with mixed background who earn more than $75,000 a year. Only 63.2% of this group claim to be proud of their ethnic heritage. On the other hand, those with an income of less than $35,000 see the highest percentage of respondents within this group taking pride in their ethnic background. Similarly, among eastern Europeans, those that exhibit the most pride in their ethnic heritage are also from the lowest income group. Irish Catholics, however, see a different pattern here. Almost all its income groups exhibit immense pride in their ethnic heritage except those making less than $35,000 per year. Those from the lowest income category lag behind other groups by more than 10% in terms of their ethnic pride.

Among the Arab Americans, the group that lags behind are those making between $50,000 and $75,000, which is consistent with our previous findings on emotional ties—this group also happens to be the one that exhibits the weakest emotional ties to their country of origin.

The same cannot be said for Hispanic Americans and Chinese Americans though. Among the Hispanic group, those with an annual income less than $35,000 exhibit the least pride in ethnic heritage while those making more than $75,000 per year show almost equally strong pride as the other two groups. However, as we show earlier, the same lowest-income group has the strongest emotional ties to their country of origin while the highest-income group has the weakest. It shows that emotional ties to the country of origin and pride in ethnic heritage do not always go hand in hand. Similarly, those Chinese Americans with an annual income under $35,000 show the least emotional attachment to China yet the most pride in ethnic heritage. On the whole, we do not see great variation across income groups among the Chinese Americans on their pride in ethnic heritage.

Among Italian Americans, income does not seem to have a strong impact upon their pride in ethnic heritage. All groups exhibit immense pride although the income group making between $50,000 and $75,000 per year falls slightly behind. The same group shows relatively weaker ties to their country of origin in our previous findings.

Table 16 Pride in Ethnic Heritage

	Irish Catholic	Eastern European	Mixed	Arab	Hispanic	Italian	Chinese
<$35K	69.1	86.5	79.3	78.1	86.3	93.1	86.9
$35–50K	83.8	74	78.8	82.2	91.7	91.6	86.1
$50–75K	86.6	75.7	66.0	72.9	92.5	89.2	83.2
$75K+	82.7	78.5	63.2	78.7	90.2	92.1	85.0

Income does not have a uniform impact upon the importance respondents attach to their ethnic heritage. Catholic groups, in general, attach much less importance to their ethnic heritage compared to other ethnic groups. Among the Catholics, the two groups that attach most importance to their ethnic heritage are those with Eastern European or mixed background and an annual income under $35,000 (74.9% and 71.4% respectively). Also for the Catholics with mixed background, one's income level and the importance of ethnic heritage are negatively correlated. In other words, the higher one's income is, the less likely it is for one to consider their ethnicity important in defining themselves. For Irish Catholics, the importance of their ethnic heritage does not vary much across income groups. The only exception is the group who make between $35,000 and $50,000 per year. This group tends to rate the importance of their ethnic heritage particularly low compared to others. Only 58.3% of this group believe that ethnic heritage plays an important role in their self-definition. As to east European Catholics, those with an income between $35,000 and $50,000 are least likely to acknowledge the importance of ethnic heritage.

For all income groups of Hispanic Americans, ethnic heritage plays an important role in their self-definition. The group that attaches the greatest importance to their ethnicity are those with an income between $35,000 and $50,000. Like their Hispanic counterparts, all groups of Italian Americans consider their ethnicity an important part of their self-definition. The group that lags behind slightly are those making between $50,000 and $75,000 a year—82.4% of them declare that ethnic heritage is important or somewhat important in defining themselves.

Among the Chinese Americans, those least likely to acknowledge the importance of ethnic heritage earn between $50,000 and $75,000. Only 76.4% of them claim that ethnic heritage is important for their self-definition. On the other hand, the group most likely to see the importance of their ethnic heritage are those with an income between $35,000 and $50,000.

emotional ties to China, compared to 80.9% of those who are not unionized.

The difference in ethnic pride between union members and nonunion members varies across the groups. For 4 of the 6 groups, the trend seems to be that the unionized respondents are more likely to be proud of their ethnic heritage than their non-unionized counterparts. Big gaps are found among Italian Americans and Catholics with mixed background. Among the former, 90.2% of their union members claim to be proud of their ethnicity compared to only 78.5% of their non-unionized counterparts who say so. For the latter, the percentages are 77.0% for union members as against 68.7% for non-union members. There is little difference between unionized eastern European Catholics and their non-unionized counterparts. For Irish Catholics, non-union members are slightly more likely to show pride in their ethnic heritage.

Tabe 18 Emotional Ties

	Hispanic	Italian	Chinese
Yes	70.0	77.4	86.4
No/NS	70.5	75.0	80.9

Table 17 Importance of Ethnic Heritage

	Irish Catholic	Eastern European	Mixed	Arab	Hispanic	Italian	Chinese
<$35K	68.1	74.9	71.4	78.2	86.8	87.9	83.3
$35–50K	58.3	52.6	65.2	83.3	90.5	89.2	90.3
$50–75K	66.4	56.9	60.4	84.7	85.4	82.4	76.4
$75K+	65.2	64.9	50.9	92.5	82.4	86.8	87.6

Table 19 Pride in Ethnic Heritage

	Irish Catholic	Eastern European	Mixed	Hispanic	Italian	Chinese
Yes	80.0	80.2	77.0	91.7	90.2	88.9
No/NS	82.1	82.1	80.9	68.7	89.2	84.2

5. Compared by Union Membership

Union membership does not seem to have an impact on Hispanic Americans' emotional affinity to their country of origin. For both union members and non-union members, about 70% of the respondents acknowledge strong or somewhat strong emotional ties.

Union membership has a minor effect upon Italian American's emotional ties. Those who are union members are slightly more likely to declare their emotional attachment, but the difference of merely 2.4% between the union members and the non-union member is almost negligible.

The gap between unionized Chinese Americans and their non-unionized counterparts is more pronounced. 86.4% of the unionized Chinese Americans claim strong or somewhat strong

For almost all ethnic groups, union members are somewhat more likely to acknowledge the importance of ethnic heritage in self-definition than non-union members. The difference varies from 1.0% to 15.5%. The greatest difference is found among Catholics with mixed ethnic background.

The only exception are the Hispanic Americans, among whom the non-union members are slightly more likely to declare the importance of their ethnic heritage than union members are.

Generally, within each ethnic group, union members are more likely to declare strong emotional ties to their country of

Table 20 Importance of Ethnic Heritage

	Irish Catholic	Eastern European	Mixed	Hispanic	Italian	Chinese
Yes	68.3	67.4	71.2	84.8	88.8	90.9
No/NS	67.3	63.9	55.7	86.7	84.1	84.6

origin; they are more likely to be proud of their ethnic heritage; they are more inclined to consider ethnic heritage important in their self-defmition.

6. Compared by Relationship Status

Relationship status seems to affect the ethnic groups' emotional ties differently. Among the Hispanics, those who are single, divorced, widowed or separated (D/S/W) are more likely to claim strong emotional ties to their country of origin. The Chinese Americans are just the opposite. Those who are married see the highest percentage of respondents with strong emotional ties.

86.1% of Chinese Americans in matrimony acknowledge their emotional attachment to China compared to 74.5% among the single and 74.6% among the D/W/S. We see a more homogeneous picture among the Italians with the singles slightly ahead of the other groups by 2 to 6 percent.

Among the Catholics and Chinese Americans, those who are on D/W/S status are most likely to take pride in their ethnic heritage. For the Hispanics, the group that shows least pride in their ethnic heritage are those who are single. The Italian Americans who are married are most likely to be proud of their ethnic heritage, followed closely by those who are on D/W/S status. The percentages are 91.8% and 90.4% respectively. Out of all the groups, those least likely to be proud of their ethnic heritage are Catholics with mixed ethnic background who are married or single.

Taken as a whole, Catholics do not see their ethnic heritage as important as Hispanic Americans, Italian Americans or Chinese Americans do. The group that deviates most are the single Irish Catholics. Less than half of this group believe that their ethnic heritage is important in defining themselves. Other groups that are unlikely to acknowledge the importance of their ethnic heritage are single/married Catholics with mixed ethnic background as well as single eastern European Catholics. The group with the highest percentage of respondents acknowledging the importance of their ethnicity are single Hispanic Americans. More than 90% of them consider their ethnicity an important part of their self-definition. Italian Americans do not see much of a variation across the groups. Whatever their relationship status is, Italian Americans tend to see their ethnic heritage an important part of their self-definition. Almost the same can be said about Chinese Americans with an exception of those who are on D/W/S status. 73.2% of Chinese Americans who are divorced, widowed or separated consider their ethnicity important, which is more than 10% lower than those who are married or single.

Table 21 Emotional Ties

	Hispanic	Italian	Chinese
Married	67.2	74.2	86.1
Single	78.3	80.2	74.5
D/W/S	74.2	75.4	74.6

Table 22 Pride in Ethnic Heritage

	Irish Catholic	Eastern European	Mixed	Hispanic	Italian	Chinese
Married	82.1	78.5	68.1	90.3	91.8	84.2
Single	76.5	86.6	68.6	80.0	86.5	85.9
D/W/S	86.3	90.7	81.4	88.5	90.4	88.8

Table23 Importance of Ethnic Heritage

	Irish Catholic	Eastern European	Mixed	Hispanic	Italian	Chinese
Married	71.6	64.7	57.2	85.3	85.7	86.7
Single	49.6	60.0	58.0	90.3	83.9	85.4
D/W/S	70.2	74.0	67.6	84.9	85.1	73.2

Critical Thinking

1. Are measures of public opinion good indicators of values and behaviors? Under what conditions and about what sorts of issues?
2. Discuss those findings that you found surprising. Why were you surprised?

Create Central

www.mhhe.com/createcentral

Internet References

The Ancient Order of Hibernians
www.aoh.org

The Anti Defamation League
www.ADC.org

The Chicago Jewish News Online
www.chicagojewishnews.org
www.polamcon.org

The International Center for Migration, Ethnicity, and Citizenship
www.newschool.edu/icmec

The Jewish American Committee
www.ajc.org

The Jewish American Congress
www.Ajcongress.org

League of United Latino Citizens
www.lulac.org

National Association of Arab Americans
www.naaa.org
www.aai.org

The National Italian American Foundation
www.niaf.org

National Urban League
www.nul.org

Order Sons of Italy in America
www.osia.org

Polish American Journal
www.polamioumal.com

Article

Prepared by: John A. Kromkowski, *Catholic University of America*

Changing Standards in Voting Rights Law

Frank R. Parker

Learning Outcomes

After reading this article, you will be able to:

- Identify the purposes of the Voting Rights Act of 1965.
- Explain the ongoing remedies for having free and fair elections in a democracy.

Black, Hispanic, Native American, and other minority citizens have used litigation in the federal courts to overcome discriminatory redistricting plans and to increase minority representation at all levels of government. . . . [L]egal challenges to state and local redistricting plans, while not the only means by which minority voters can influence the redistricting process, can be productive. Two of the newest black members of Congress—Rep. Mike Espy of Mississippi and Rep. John Lewis of Georgia—were elected after discriminatory plans were struck down under the Voting Rights Act and new congressional districts with black population majorities were created. Similarly, court suits filed by minority voters eliminated discriminatory multi-member legislative districts and produced dramatic increases in the number of black and Hispanic state legislators following the 1970 and 1980 Censuses.

For minority citizens to be effective participants in the redistricting process, either in state legislatures or local governing bodies, or in the courts, they must learn the rules of the game. What are the requirements of the "one-person, one-vote" rule? How great a deviation from population equality is constitutionally tolerable? What procedures are available for challenging racially discriminatory plans that dilute minority voting strength? What legal standards do the courts apply to strike down racially discriminatory plans?

The Legal Framework at the Beginning of the 1980s

The Supreme Court has ruled that neither the Constitution nor the Voting Rights Act give minority voters a federally guaranteed right to a redistricting plan that maximizes their influence in the electoral process. From a legal standpoint, then, the focus of any efforts to improve minority representation must focus on eliminating racial discrimination in any proposed or existing plan. This raises the question: what is the definition of racial discrimination? Does racial discrimination mean a plan that was adopted with discriminatory *intent,* or merely one that has a discriminatory *effect?*

Until 1980, the Supreme Court and lower federal courts had struck down voting laws and redistricting plans under the Constitution and the Voting Rights Act when they had a racially discriminatory *effect.* This meant that at-large election systems and gerrymandered redistricting plans were unconstitutional when they had the effect of denying minority voters an equal opportunity to elect candidates of their choice, regardless of the intent of the plans.

Then, in 1980 in *City of Mobile v. Bolden,* the Supreme Court adopted a new standard. The Court ruled that discriminatory methods of election were not illegal per se unless it could be proven that they had been adopted or maintained with the *intent* to discriminate. This meant, for example, that an at-large voting system that diluted minority votes and resulted in an all-white city council was not necessarily illegal unless minority voters could prove that the system had been adopted or maintained for the specific purpose of discriminating against minority voters. Further, the Court appeared to reject as proof of discriminatory intent the kinds of circumstantial evidence that the courts previously had accepted as proving voting discrimination (such as absence of any minorities in elective positions, a past history of discrimination, and electoral rules that disadvantaged minorities).

Two years later, the Supreme Court in *Rogers v. Lodge* retreated from the extreme position it had taken in the *Mobile* decision. The Court reaffirmed that proof of discriminatory intent was required, but held that proof could be circumstantial evidence showing that the challenged election system denied minority voters an equal opportunity to elect candidates of their choice. But further debate over the intent requirement was made moot when Congress in 1982 amended the Voting Rights Act in language that specifically instructed the Court that the standard of "intent" was unacceptable.

Section 2 of the Voting Rights Act, as amended in 1982, prohibits any voting practice or procedure, including any redistricting plan, which "results" in racial discrimination. This means that a challenged voting plan is unlawful if, "based on the totality of circumstances," minority voters "have less opportunity than other members of the electorate to participate in the political process and to elect the representatives of their choice."

In addition to Section 2 of the Voting Rights Act, two other legal principles have commonly been used in fighting racially discriminatory election systems; the one-person one-vote principle, and Section 5 of the Voting Rights Act. Each of these are discussed below.

The *one-person, one-vote principle* requires state legislatures and local governing bodies to create election districts of equal population so that each person's vote has equal weight. If one district has a small population and another (with the same number of representatives) a large population, each voter in the smaller district has more influence than each voter in the large district in determining who is elected.

This principle is important because districts that are unequal in population can result in discrimination against minority voters, particularly those living in heavily populated urban areas. The one-person, one-vote rule can be used to strike down racially discriminatory redistricting plans even when claims of racial discrimination otherwise can't be proven.

As stated by the Supreme Court in *Reynolds v. Sims* (1964), the one-person, one-vote rule requires "substantial equality of population among districts." What does "substantial equality" mean? The standard varies depending on what level of government is involved. By 1980 the Supreme Court had adopted different rules for judging the legality of congressional redistricting plans, state legislative redistricting plans, and local redistricting plans.

For congressional redistricting plans, all of a state's congressional districts must be equal in population, and no deviations from equal-sized districts are allowed unless they can be justified by state officials. Applying this test during the 1970s, the Supreme Court struck down congressional redistricting plans with deviations as small as 4.13 percent. During the 1980s, as described later in this section, the Supreme Court adopted even stricter standards on allowable deviations in congressional redistricting.

For state legislative redistricting plans, constitutionality depends upon the degree of deviation from equal-size districts and whether the deviations can be justified by some reasonable state interest. Deviations of less than 10 percent are not presumed to be unconstitutional and need not be explained or justified by state officials. However, plans with deviations of less than 10 percent are not immune from legal challenge if there is proof of discrimination or improper motives. Deviations between 10 percent and 16.4 percent are presumed to be unconstitutional and will not be upheld by the courts unless state officials can justify them on the basis of consistent and reasonable state policies. Deviations larger than 16.4 percent generally are unconstitutional per se and will be struck down.

Slightly larger deviations from equal-sized districts are tolerated in local redistricting plans. The Supreme Court upheld one county redistricting plan with a deviation of 11.9 percent, but indicated that a larger deviation probably would not be allowed.

Section 5 of the Voting Rights Act requires nine states and parts of seven others[1] to obtain prior approval ("preclearance") for all voting law changes—including all new redistricting plans—from either the Justice Department or the U.S. District Court for the District of Columbia. The states and localities covered by Section 5 are those that had literacy tests for voters and low levels of minority voter registration when the Voting Rights Act was enacted in 1965. Later amendments covered additional states and localities with substantial numbers of Hispanic or other language-minority citizens which conducted English-only elections.

Under Section 5, the burden of proving the legality of changes in voting laws is placed on the state or locality. The state or locality must convince the Justice Department or the D.C. District Court that a proposed change in its voting laws does not have a racially discriminatory purpose and will not have a discriminatory effect. Anyone can write a letter to the Justice Department complaining about discrimination in a plan submitted for Section 5 approval and giving reasons why the Justice Department should object to the plan. Further, if the state or locality files a suit in District Court in Washington, D.C., to obtain preclearance, affected minority citizens can file a motion to intervene in the lawsuit to protect their rights. If the Justice Department objects to a plan or the D.C. District Court denies approval, the change cannot be implemented.

Section 5 is the part of the Voting Rights Act most frequently used to prevent racial discrimination in elections. Since 1965, the Justice Department has used Section 5 to block more than 2,000 discriminatory voting law changes (see Table 1). Congressional, state, and local redistricting plans have all been rejected.

Table 1 Number of Changes Blocked by Justice Department Section 5 Objections, by Type of Change, 1965 to 1988

Type of Change	Number of Objections
Municipal annexations	1,088
Methods of election	472
Redistricting	248
Polling place changes	46
Changes in form of government	39
Special elections	39
Precinct changes	19
Candidate qualifications	13
Voter registration procedures	12
Governmental consolidations/ divisions of political units	12
Reregistration/voter purges	9
Bilingual procedures	9
Municipal incorporations	7
Voting methods	3
Miscellaneous	119
Total	2,167

Source: Voting Section, Civil Rights Division, U.S. Department of Justice

During the 1970s, the Supreme Court adopted a limited interpretation of the discriminatory "effect" standard of Section 5. The Court ruled that a new redistricting plan does not have a discriminatory effect prohibited by Section 5 unless, compared with the previous plan, it diminishes the voting strength of minority voters. This interpretation (called the "Section 5 retrogression standard") protects minority voters, but it also means that if a prior plan was discriminatory, and a new plan is equally discriminatory, the new system must be approved (unless it was adopted with a discriminatory intent) because minority voters are no worse off than they were before.

Changes in Law During the 1980s

During the 1980s, Congress and the Supreme Court altered the legal standards that were in effect in 1980 (see Box 1). The greatest change occurred in 1982 when Congress amended the Voting Rights Act to overrule the *Mobile* decision and to eliminate the requirement of proving discriminatory intent. The Supreme Court then interpreted the 1982 amendment *to* simplify even further the legal requirements for proving unlawful minority vote discrimination.

In amending Section 2 of the Voting Rights Act in 1982, Congress indicated that minority voters can prove discriminatory results based on a number of factors. For example, they can show the existence of racial bloc voting and a lack of minority representation. Other factors to be considered by the courts include a history of discrimination against minorities, the use of discriminatory election rules, discrimination in slating candidates for office, differences between minorities and whites in income, education, employment, and other socioeconomic characteristics, and racial campaigning.

Then, in *Thornburg v. Gingles,* decided in 1986, the Supreme Court made it even easier for minority voters to prove a violation of the Voting Rights Act. The *Gingles* case involved a challenge by black voters in North Carolina to at-large voting in multi-member and gerrymandered state legislative districts that, in effect, prevented black voters from electing candidates of their choice to the state legislature. The Supreme Court ruled that at-large election systems are illegal if:

(1) the minority population is geographically compact enough that a single-member district can be created where minorities are in the majority;
(2) minority voters tend to vote for the same candidates (i.e. bloc vote), indicating that they are "politically cohesive"; and
(3) except for special circumstances (such as minority candidates running unopposed), the candidates preferred by minority voters usually are defeated by white bloc voting.

This new standard, in effect, makes it illegal for a state or locality with racial bloc voting not to create a district in which minorities are in the majority if such a district can be created. This liberal standard is likely to have important ramifications after 1990, especially in parts of the country with substantial minority populations.

The Supreme Court's decision also makes it easier for minority voters to eliminate discriminatory multi-member legislative districts. Such districts were the principal focus of litigation in the South and Southwest during the 1970s and early 1980s, and most were eliminated. However, in some states that were untouched by this wave of litigation, multi-member districts remain.

The Justice Department estimates that more than 1,300 jurisdictions have changed their election systems since 1982 to comply with Section 2. Section 2 has been applied to strike down racially discriminatory congressional redistricting plans, state redistricting plans, at-large county and city election systems, at-large elections for state court judges, and voter registration procedures.

In two other Section 2 cases, the Chicago, Illinois, and Montgomery, Alabama, city council redistricting cases (*Ketchum v. Byrne* and *Buskey v. Oliver*), federal courts struck down plans that reduced the number of black districts (Chicago) and reduced the black percentage of a district (Montgomery). The courts applied a retrogression standard similar to the one applied to states covered by Section 5 of the Voting Rights Act. These decisions have important implications for redistricting after 1990. Section 2 of the VRA—which the courts applied in those cases—applies nationwide, and the court rulings in those cases can be used throughout the country after the 1990 Census to prevent the elimination of existing majority black congressional and state legislative districts that currently have black representatives.

Measuring Malapportionment

During the 1980s the Supreme Court also adopted stricter standards for congressional redistricting and, in a striking about-face, opened the door to challenges to legislative redistricting plans which have the purpose and effect of partisan political gerrymandering.

In *Karcher v. Daggett,* handed down in 1983, the Court held that a New Jersey congressional redistricting plan was unconstitutional even though the total deviation from districts of equal size was a mere 0.6984 percent. The Court ruled that such a deviation could have been avoided, given that the legislature had rejected a plan with a population deviation of only 0.4514 percent, and that the state had failed to show that the deviation in its approved plan was necessary to achieve a legitimate goal.

On the same day it handed down its decision in the New Jersey case, the Supreme Court in *Brown v. Thomson* upheld a Wyoming state legislative redistricting plan where the total deviation in one district was 89 percent—a deviation much higher than any previously approved by the Supreme Court. The Court accepted the state's argument that this degree of deviation from the ideal was necessary to permit one isolated county to retain the seat in the state legislature that it had been granted in 1913 and to preserve county boundaries in that one district. Two of the Court's five-member majority (Justices O'Connor and Stevens) stated that they agreed with the decision only because the 89 percent deviation applied to just one county. They wrote that they had "the gravest doubts that a statewide legislative plan with an 89 percent maximum deviation could survive constitutional scrutiny . . ."

One redistricting issue not conclusively decided during the 1970s was how population malapportionment should be measured in "mixed" plans where some representatives are elected districtwide and others are elected from subdistricts within the district. The Supreme Court resolved this issue early in 1989 in *Board of Estimate v. Morris,* a challenge to the system of electing members to the New York City Board of Estimate. The Board of Estimate was composed of three members elected citywide (the mayor, city council president, and city comptroller) and the five borough presidents, each of them elected from the five individual boroughs that constitute New York City. The boroughs vary greatly in population size, and the lower courts—looking only at differences in borough populations—held the election system unconstitutional for violating the one-person, one-vote rule. The Supreme Court held that in calculating the malapportionment in this mixed plan, the courts must consider the weight of citizens' votes for both the borough representatives and their proportional share of the vote for the citywide elected officials. This method of calculation reduced the overall deviation from 132 percent to 78 percent, but the Supreme Court ruled that even a deviation that high was constitutionally unacceptable. This decision settles the question of how malapportionment should be measured in mixed plans and indicates that despite the Wyoming case, the Supreme Court is not loosening the strict numerical standards for judging one-person, one-vote violations.

New Law Governing Partisan Political Gerrymandering

During the 1970s the Supreme Court refused to hear suits based on allegations that redistricting plans discriminated against candidates or voters of a particular political party. In 1986, however, in *Davis v. Bandemer,* the Supreme Court in a split decision ruled that claims of political gerrymandering could be litigated in federal court. Although the Indiana plan in question in that case created state legislative districts that were equal in population size, the plaintiffs charged that the Republican-controlled state legislature had gerrymandered the districts to maximize Republican voting strength and to minimize the number of Democratic districts. They contended that the legislature's plan discriminated against Democrats by packing more Democratic voters into districts which already had large Democratic majorities and by splitting up other Democratic districts, thus assuring a larger number of "safe" Republican seats.

While the Supreme Court agreed that intentional political gerrymandering violated the 14th Amendment, it ruled that the plaintiffs' claims had not been proven. The Court required evidence of "both intentional discrimination against an identifiable political group and an actual discriminatory effect on that group." Although discriminatory intent had been proven, said the Court, a sufficient discriminatory effect had not. Unconstitutional discrimination, the Court said, occurs only when a redistricting plan "will consistently degrade a voter's or a group of voters' influence on the political process as a whole."

What this means may be worked out in lawsuits brought after the 1990 Census. In a case involving California *(Badham v. Eu)* that was decided after the Indiana case, Republican plaintiffs argued that the Democrats had gerrymandered California's congressional districts to limit the number of Republican members of Congress. Although political commentators thought the Republicans had presented a strong case, the District Court dismissed their claims and the Supreme Court affirmed without opinion, three Justices dissenting. The results in these two cases suggest that litigants attempting to prove partisan political gerrymandering will have a difficult time convincing the courts to uphold their claims.

New Law Governing Section 5 of the Voting Rights Act

During the 1980s the Justice Department amended its Voting Rights Act regulations to broaden the types of discrimination that can be challenged under Section 5. Objections are now permitted when a voting law change is likely to have a discriminatory result that violates the Section 2 "results" standard. This means that a new redistricting plan can be blocked by a Justice Department objection if it has discriminatory results, regardless of its intent and regardless of whether it is retrogressive.

"Litigants attempting to prove partisan political gerrymandering will have a difficult time convincing the courts to uphold their claims."

The Supreme Court has continued to take a narrow view of the Section 5 "effect" standard. In *Lockhart v. United States,* decided in 1983, the Court overruled the Justice Department's objection to changes in a Texas city's election system. Under the proposed plan, a mayor and four city council members would be elected using numbered posts and staggered terms of office.[2] The Supreme Court noted that numbered posts and staggered terms generally are discriminatory because they prevent minority voters from single-shot voting. However, the Supreme Court added that the proposed changes would not diminish minority voting strength because minorities could not single-shot vote under the preexisting election system.

When the Justice Department adopted its new Section 5 regulations in 1987, it agreed that voting law changes should be objected to under Section 5 if they meet the new results test under Section 2. However, the Federal courts, in judicial preclearance proceedings under Section 5, have not yet ruled on the applicability of the Section 2 results standard to Section 5 preclearance proceedings.

Implications for the 1990s

Opportunities for minority voters and others to challenge redistricting plans and to gain increased representation have been expanded by legal developments during the 1980s. Minority voters need not prove discriminatory intent to challenge a redistricting plan that dilutes their votes; all they have to prove is discriminatory results. Further, the Supreme Court has said that the results test is satisfied if minority voters can prove two things: that a majority black, Hispanic, or other minority single-member district can be created, and that past racial bloc voting has prevented minority voters from electing candidates

Box 1

Important Supreme Court Decisions of the 1980s that will Affect Redistricting after the 1990 Census

City of Mobile v. Bolden, 446 U.S. 55 (1980).

In this challenge to at-large city council elections, a divided Supreme Court ruled that for cases alleging a dilution of minority voting strength, proof of discriminatory intent was necessary to establish a 14th Amendment violation. The Court also rejected as meeting this requirement the kinds of circumstantial evidence that courts in the past had accepted as proving voting discrimination (no blacks elected, discrimination in employment and municipal services, history of discrimination, discriminatory electoral rules).

Rogers v. Lodge, 458 U.S. 613 (1982).

The Supreme Court reaffirmed that proof of discriminatory intent was required to prove unconstitutional minority vote dilution. But in an aboutface from the Mobile decision, the Court ruled that direct evidence of intent was not necessary and that the intent standard could be satisfied by the kinds of circumstantial evidence courts had accepted in the past as proof of voting discrimination. (The impact of this decision, however, was superseded by congressional passage of the 1982 amendment to Section 2 of the Voting Rights Act, which eliminated the necessity of proving discriminatory intent.)

Karcher v.Daggett, 462 U.S. 725 (1983).

The Supreme Court found that a New Jersey congressional redistricting plan violated the one-person, one-vote requirement even though the total deviation from population equality was a mere 0.6984 percent because a better plan with a deviation of only 0.4514 percent had been rejected by the legislature. The Court reaffirmed the rule that "absolute population equality" is the "paramount objective" in congressional redistricting. Any deviation from equal-sized districts, no matter how small, shifts the burden to the state "to prove that the population deviations in its plan were necessary to achieve some legitimate state objective."

Brown v. Thomson, 462 U.S. 835 (1983).

In a 5-4 decision, the Supreme Court upheld an 89 percent population deviation affecting one county in the Wyoming state legislative reapportionment plan, based on the state's historic policy of preserving county boundaries. The majority made clear, however, that it was only ruling on one district, not the statewide plan. Justices O'Connor and Stevens, whose votes were necessary to the five-member majority, in a concurring opinion expressed "the gravest doubts that a statewide legislative plan with an 89 percent maximum deviation could survive constitutional scrutiny despite the presence of the State's strong interest in preserving county boundaries."

Thornburg v. Gingles, 478 U.S. 30 (1986).

The Supreme Court upheld Congress's 1982 amendment to Section 2 of the Voting Rights Act that eliminated the requirement of proving discriminatory intent in minority vote dilution cases and simplified the legal standards for proving a Section 2 violation under the new "results" test. The Court held that Section 2 focuses on "an inequality in the opportunities enjoyed by black and white voters to elect their preferred representatives." The Court stated that the critical elements of a Section 2 violation were whether a single-member district could be drawn in which minorities had a majority and whether there was racially polarized voting that resulted in the defeat of minority-preferred candidates.

Davis v. Bandemer, 478 U.S. 109 (1986).

For the first time, a Supreme Court majority held that claims of political gerrymandering were justiciable in federal court, but by a divided vote reversed the District Court decision which had found a constitutional violation. A plurality of the Court ruled that the Democrats challenging the plan had not proven "a sufficiently adverse effect" to demonstrate that they had been "unconstitutionally denied [their] chance to effectively influence the political process."

Board of Estimate v. Morris, 103 L.Ed.2d 717 (1989).

The Supreme Court unanimously held that the method of electing members of the New York City Board of Estimate, composed of three city officials elected citywide and five borough presidents elected from unequally populated boroughs, violated the one-person, one-vote rule because of population disparities among New York's five boroughs. The Court ruled that the votes of borough residents for the citywide elected officials must be included in calculating the degree of population malapportionment, which reduced the deviation percentage from 132 percent to 78 percent, but also found that this high deviation could not be justified. "We note that no case of ours has indicated that a deviation of some 78 percent could ever be justified," the Court stated.

of their choice. These developments provide minority groups with a legal basis for creating new districts in which minorities are in the majority in the redistricting process after the 1990 Census. In addition, there are now legal safeguards to assure that population shifts do not result in the elimination of existing majority black congressional and legislative districts currently represented by black legislators.

The stricter one-person, one-vote standard for congressional redistricting will make it easier for minority groups and others to challenge congressional redistricting plans, and the states will have to design congressional districts that are more precisely equal in population. And the more detailed census data that will be available after 1990 will allow the Supreme Court to adopt stricter population standards for state legislative districts as well.

The Supreme Court's decision to allow challenges to redistricting plans because of political gerrymandering may also cause an increase in redistricting litigation. Most redistricting plans involve some degree of political manipulation of boundary lines, and whether or not there is a violation of the new standard may depend on whether the political group claiming to be disadvantaged can convince the court that the plan would consistently degrade that party's votes over time or substantially negate its influence in the electoral process.The present constitutional standard is not one that can be easily applied, and further litigation will be necessary to establish precise guidelines on what constitutes unconstitutional political gerrymandering.

Since any revision of district lines may also have implications for racial representation, minority groups may have to follow these cases closely—or even become parties to the litigation to protect their interests if a court decides there is a constitutional violation and orders a new plan drawn up.

The Justice Department's revision of its Section 5 regulations may increase the number of objections to redistricting plans that have racial discriminatory results. Under the new standard, evidence that minorities will be worse off is no longer necessary for a Section 5 objection. During the Reagan administration, the Justice Department did not fully implement this new standard. Whether it will do so in the future will depend who is appointed Assistant Attorney General in charge of Department's Civil Rights Division and how willing he or she is to vigorously apply the new standard. In any case, though, thanks to court decisions in the 1980s, minority groups now have stronger legal safeguards to protect their rights.

Notes

1. The Section 5 preclearance requirement currently applies to all of Alabama, Alask Arizona, Georgia, Louisiana, Mississippi, South Carolina, Texas, and Virginia, and to parts California (four counties), Florida (five counties), Michigan (parts of two counties), New Hampshire (parts of seven counties), New York (Manhattan, Brooklyn, and the Bronx), North Carolina (40 counties), and South Dakota (two counties).
2. "Numbered Posts" means that each candidate must qualify and run for a particular post or place on the ballot (e.g. Post No. 1, Post No.2, etc). "Staggered terms" is an election system under which not all the offices are up for election at the same time. For example, when half the offices may be up for election one year and the other half up for election the next year. Both systems eliminate or minimize the opportunity for minority voters to elect candidates of their choice through "single-shot voting." Single-shot voting, a tactic sometimes successful employed by minority voters, is voting for less than the full number of positions to be filled. For example, if there are four positions to be filled and more than four candidates running and if white voters spread their votes out over four different candidates, minority voters may be able to elect a candidate of their choice by casting only one vote and concentrating the votes on one candidate. This is impossible when there is a post system, since voters have only one vote for each post, and may be ineffective under a staggered term system because a staggered term system reduces the number of seats to be filled at each election.

Critical Thinking

1. Explain the values contradiction found in voter exclusion and democratic, representative government.
2. Why did various state governments pass laws that excluded persons from voting?
3. Can the courts effectively assure free and fair elections?

Create Central

www.mhhe.com/createcentral

Internet References

American Civil Liberties Union (ACLU)
www.aclu.org

Human Rights We
www.hrweb.org

Frank R. Parker is Director of the Voting Rights Project of the Lawyers' Committee for Civil Rights Under Law in Washington, D.C. Mr. Parker has published numerous articles on minority voting rights, has been litigating voting rights cases on the behalf of minority plaintiffs for more than 20 years, and has been lead attorney in several landmark cases. Mr. Parker received his law degree from Harvard Law School.

U.S. Department of Justice, 1989.

Article

Prepared by: John A. Kromkowski, *Catholic University of America*

Veterans' Racial and Ethnic Composition and Place of Birth: 2011

Jason-Harold Lee and Julia B. Beckhusen

Learning Outcomes

After reading this article, you will be able to:

- Determine whether the composition of the U.S. military would be different if all Americans were required to serve.
- Write a race and ethnic profile of the U.S. military.

Introduction

In 2011, about 21.5 million (9.1 percent) civilians 18 years and older in the United States were veterans of past and current conflicts or have served during periods of peace. The American Community Survey (ACS) collects data on veterans in order to help government agencies, such as the Department of Veterans Affairs, to establish programs for job counseling, training, and placement of veterans. The Department of Labor uses these data to set standards to determine if government contractors fulfill contractual obligations prohibiting employment discrimination. State and local governments, in addition to private organizations, use these data to provide valuable veteran services, such as medical services and nursing home care. This brief highlights civilian veterans 18 years and older who currently reside in the United States, focusing on racial, ethnic, and regional diversity.

Racial and Ethnic Diversity

When analyzing the racial composition of civilian veterans in 2011, veterans as a whole were more likely to be non-Hispanic White compared to nonveterans.[1]

Reproduction of the Veteran Status Question From the 2011 American Community Survey.

Has this person ever served on active duty in the U.S. Armed Forces, military Reserves, or National Guard? *Active duty does not include training for the Reserves or National Guard, but DOES include activation, for example, for the Persian Gulf War.*

- Yes, now on active duty
- Yes, on active duty during the last 12 months, but not now
- Yes, on active duty in the past, but not during the last 12 months
- No training for Reserves or National Guard only → *SKIP to question 28a*
- No, never served in the military → *SKIP to question 29a*

The degree of racial and ethnic diversity among veterans decreased with age. Although older veterans were predominately non-Hispanic White, younger veterans reflect the increasing diversity in the military today.[2] Figure 1 shows the racial and ethnic distribution of the veteran population compared with that of the nonveteran population stratified by five age groups.

For the youngest age group, 18 to 34 years, 65.4 percent of veterans identified themselves as non-Hispanic White, compared with 56.9 percent of nonveterans. About 14.9 percent of veterans reported their race as Black or African American and

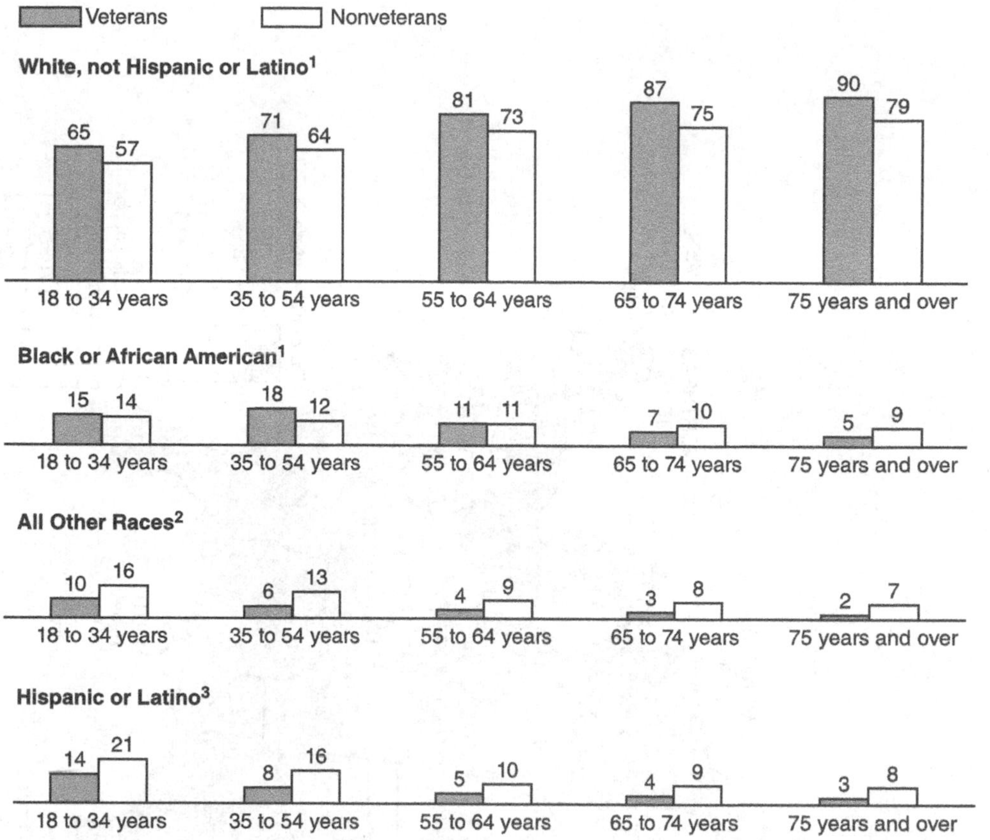

[1] The ACS gives the respondent the option of choosing more than one race. These categories include individual who chose only one race.
[2] Five categories make up this population: American Indian and Alska Native alone, Asian alone, Native Hawaiian and Other Pacific Islander alone, Some Other Race alone, and Two or More Races, where "alone" refers to respondents who chose only one race category.
[3] This includes individuals who reported a race other than "White." Adding race and hispanic origin categories may not sum to 100 percent.
Sources: U.S. Census Bureau, 2011 American Community Survey.

Figure 1 Race and Hispanic Origin by Veteran Status and Age for the Civilian Population 18 Years and Older (In percent. Data based on sample. For information on confidentiality protection, sampling error, nonsampling error, and definitions, see *www.census.gov/acs/www/*)

10.5 percent reported All Other Races. In addition, 13.6 percent of the veteran population between 18 and 34 years reported their ethnicity as Hispanic.[3] For each of the older age groups, the percentage of non-Hispanic White veterans and nonveterans increased significantly. The share of civilian veterans 75 years and older that was non-Hispanic White was 90.3 percent compared with 78.7 percent of nonveterans. For the remaining veteran population in the oldest age group, 5.1 percent reported their race as Black or African American, 2.5 percent as part of the All Other Races category, and 2.8 percent described their ethnicity as Hispanic.

Place of Birth

Figure 2 shows the geographical distribution of veterans born in the United States by their place of birth. In 2011, 95.5 percent of all veterans were born in 1 of the 50 states or in the District of Columbia. Just under one-third of the total U.S.-born veteran population came from six states: New York (8.0 percent), California (6.8 percent), Pennsylvania (6.6 percent), Texas (5.7 percent), Ohio (5.2 percent), and Illinois (5.0 percent). A smaller percentage of native-born veterans were born abroad to American parents (0.9 percent), born in Puerto Rico (0.5 percent), or born in the remaining Island Areas (0.1 percent).[4]

There were distinct regional differences in the birthplaces of U.S.-born veterans. About 9.0 million veterans, or 40.4 percent of all veterans born in the United States, were born in the South. In comparison, 4.8 million (22.3 percent) came from the West, 4.7 million (21.9 percent) came from the Midwest, and 3.3 million (15.4 percent) came from the Northeast.

The remaining veteran population was born outside the United States and its territories without U.S. citizenship.

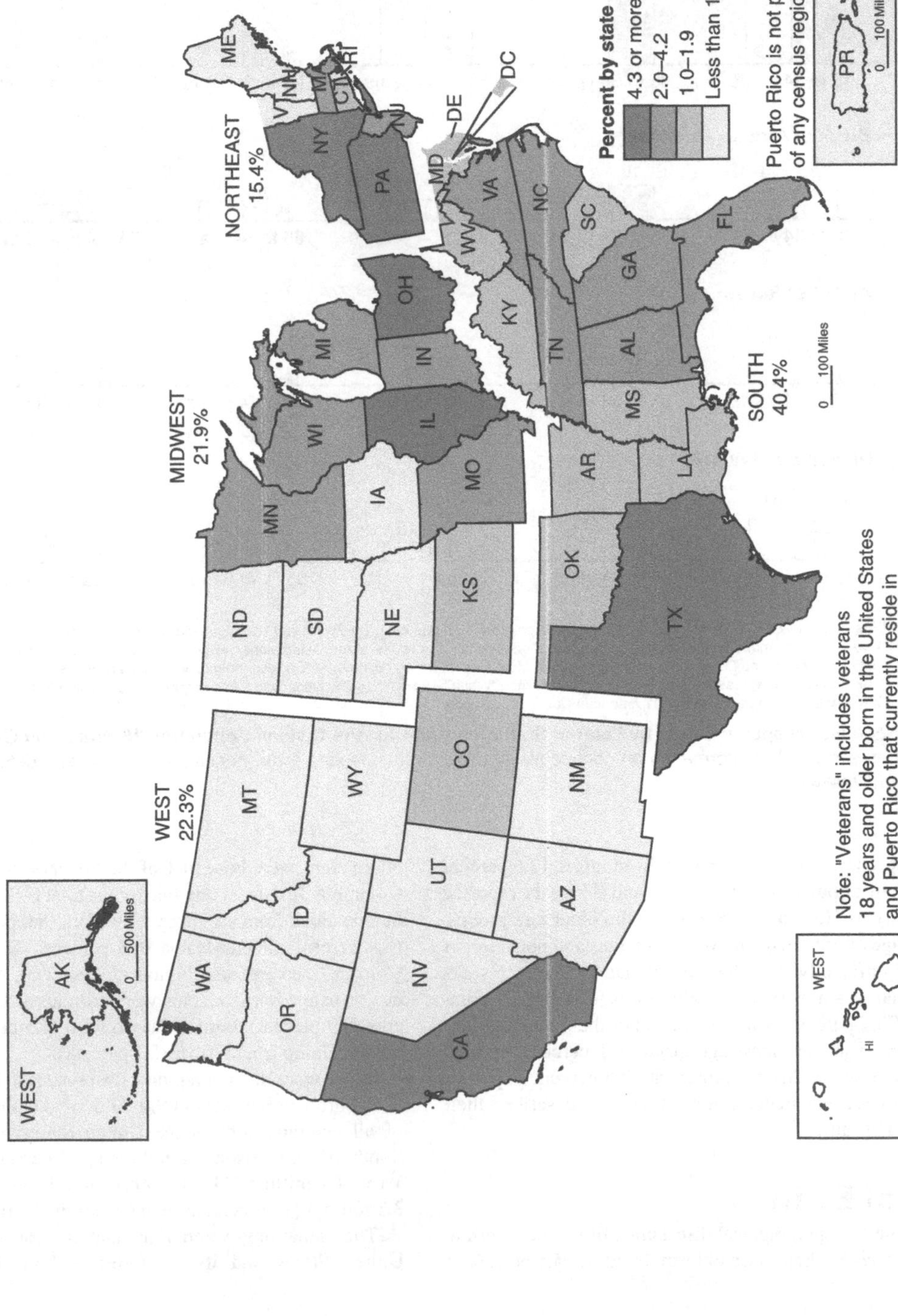

Note: "Veterans" includes veterans 18 years and older born in the United States and Puerto Rico that currently reside in 1 of the 50 states or the District of Columbia.

Source: U.S. Census Bureau, 2011 American Community Survey.

Figure 2 Place of Birth Distribution of Veterans Born in the United States: 2011

Table 3 Countries of Birth of Foreign-Born Veterans: 2011

(For information on confidentiality protection, sampling error, nonsampling error, and definitions, see *www.census.gov/acs/www*)

Country	Naturalized and noncitizens	Margin of error[1]	Percent	Percent margin of error[1]
Total	**636,128**	**14,943**	**636,128**	**0.1**
Mexico*	82,394	5,948	13.0	0.2
Philippines*	73,638	4,548	11.6	0.2
Germany*	51,140	3,105	8.0	0.1
Canada*	36,600	3,078	5.8	0.1
Italy	20,766	2,193	3.3	0.1
Jamaica	19,871	2,642	3.1	0.1
Korea	18,873	2,805	3.0	0.1
England	17,261	2,383	2.7	0.1
China	17,044	2,236	2.7	0.1
Vietnam	16,116	2,225	2.5	0.1
Cuba	15,516	2,474	2.4	0.1
All other	266,909	8,309	42.0	0.7

* The estimates for these countries are significantly different from the estimates for all other geographic areas at the 90 percent confidence level.

[1] Data are based on a sample and are subject to sampling variability. A margin of error is a measure of an estimate's variability. The larger the margin of error in relation to the size of the estimate, the less reliable the estimate. This number, when added to or subtracted from the estimate, forms the 90 percent confidence interval.

Note: Because of sampling variability, some of the estimates in this table may not be statistically different from estimates for other geographic areas both listed and not listed in the table.

Source: U.S. Census Bureau, 2011 American Community Survey.

Although the majority of individuals serving in the U.S. Armed Forces are U.S. citizens, citizenship is not a requirement to join the military. Lawful Permanent Residents (LPRs) of the United States have been eligible to enlist in the military since the Revolutionary War.[5] Special provisions of the Immigration and Nationality Act (INA) have made it possible for noncitizen members of the military to obtain U.S. citizenship.[6] In 2011, 2.9 percent of veterans were either naturalized citizens or noncitizens. Less than 1.0 percent (0.4 percent) of the total veteran population remained noncitizens after their military service ended. Over half (58.5 percent) of the foreign-born veteran population came from 11 countries.[7] Table 1 shows these 11 countries and the number of veterans born in each. The largest share (12.9 percent) was born in Mexico, followed by the Philippines (11.6 percent), Germany (8.0 percent), and Canada (5.8 percent).

What Is the American Community Survey?

The American Community Survey (ACS) is a nationwide survey designed to provide communities with reliable and timely demographic, social, economic, and housing data for the nation, states, congressional districts, counties, places, and other localities every year. It has an annual sample size of about 3.3 million addresses across the United States and Puerto Rico and includes both housing units and group quarters (e.g., nursing facilities and prisons). The ACS is conducted in every county throughout the nation, and every municipio in Puerto Rico, where it is called the Puerto Rico Community Survey. Beginning in 2006, ACS data for 2005 were released for geographic areas with populations of 65,000 and greater. For information on the ACS sample design and other topics, visit www.census.gov/acs/www.

Source and Accuracy

The data presented in this report are based on the ACS sample interviewed in 2011. The estimates based on this sample approximate the actual values and represent the entire household and group quarters population. Sampling error is the difference between an estimate based on a sample and the corresponding value that would be obtained if the estimate were based on the entire population (as from a census). Measures of the sampling errors are provided in the form of margins of error for all estimates included in this report. All comparative statements in this report have undergone statistical testing, and comparisons are significant at the 90 percent level unless otherwise noted. In addition to sampling error, nonsampling error may be introduced during any of the operations used to collect and process survey data such as editing, reviewing, or keying data from questionnaires. For more information on sampling and estimation methods, confidentiality protection, and sampling and nonsampling errors, please see the 2011 ACS Accuracy of the Data document located at www.census .gov/acs/www/Downloads/data_documentation/Accuracy/ ACS_Accuracy_of_Data_2011.pdf.

Notes

1. Federal surveys now give respondents the option of reporting more than one race. Therefore, two basic ways of defining a race group are possible. A group such as African American may be defined as those who reported Black or African American and no other race (the race-alone or the single-race concept) or as those who reported Black regardless of whether they also reported another race (the race-alone-or-in-combination concept). Hispanics may be any race. The U.S. Census Bureau uses a variety of approaches when analyzing race. In this report, the term "non-Hispanic White" refers to individuals who are not Hispanic or Latino and reported White and no other race (White, not Hispanic or Latino). "Black or African American" refers to individuals who may be Hispanic or Latino and reported Black or African American and no other race. "All Other Races" refers to individuals who may be Hispanic or Latino and reported Asian alone, Pacific Islander alone, American Indian alone, Alaskan Native alone, or multiple races. Race and ethnicity are defined throughout the report in terms of the following categories: (1) White, not Hispanic or Latino; (2) Black or African American; (3) All Other Races; and (4) Hispanic or Latino.
2. For more information on diversity in today's military, see http:// prhome.defense.gov/RFM/MPP/ACCESSION%20POLICY/ PopRep2010/summary/Sect_Il.pdf.
3. Adding race and Hispanic origin categories may not sum to 100 percent.
4. The U.S. Island Areas consist of American Samoa, the Commonwealth of the Northern Mariana Islands, Guam, and the U.S. Virgin Islands.
5. Approximately half of the Army enlistees in 1840 were immigrants, and between 1862 and 2000, more than 660,000 military veterans became citizens through naturalization. In 2005, roughly 35,000 noncitizens served in the military, and approximately 8,000 enlist each year. For more information, see Center for Naval Analyses: Non-Citizens in Today's Military: Final Report on the Internet at http://cna.org/sites/default/files/ research/D0011092.A2.pdf.
6. If the service occurred during peacetime, members qualify if they: (1) Served honorably in the U.S. Armed Forces for at least 1 year, (2) obtained lawful permanent resident status, and (3) filed an application while still in the service or within 6 months of separation. Noncitizens who served during periods of hostilities and whose service was honorable on or after September 11, 2001, and veterans of certain past wars and conflicts can immediately file for citizenship. Additionally, the Naturalization at Basic Training Initiative of August 2009 gives noncitizens the opportunity to naturalize when they graduate from basic training (Army and Navy). For more information, see "U.S. Citizenship and Immigration Services—Naturalization through Military Service," on the Internet at www.uscis.gov/portal/site/uscis/menuitem. 5af9bb95919f35e66f614176543f6dla/?vgnextoid= 26d805a25c4c4210VgnVCMl00000082ca60aRCRD&vgnextch annel=ce613e4d77d73210VgnVCM100000082ca60aRCRD.
7. Foreign-born persons include all people who indicated they were either a U.S. citizen by naturalization or they were not a citizen of the United States. Persons born abroad of American parents or born in Puerto Rico or other U.S. Island Areas are not considered foreign born.

Critical Thinking

1. Discuss the demographic disparity between the military and civilian population of America.
2. Is citizenship essential for military service?
3. Are military or other types of public service essential for democratic citizenship?

Create Central

www.mhhe.com/createcentral

Internet References

Diversity.com
www.diversity.com

Social Science Information Gateway
http://sosig.esrc.bris.ac.uk

Sociosite
www.sociosite.net

U. S. Bureau of Citizenship and Immigration Services
www.USCIS.gov/portaffsftefuscis

U.S. Census Bureau
www.census.gov

U.S Census Bureau, 2012.

Article

Prepared by: John A. Kromkowski, *Catholic University of America*

A Striking Racial Divide in Deaths by Firearms

A black-and-white split between prevalence of homicides and suicides

DAN KEATING

Learning Outcomes

After reading this article, you will be able to:

- Determine the core and central findings of this article.
- Relate these data to a search for remedies to gun violence.

Gun deaths are shaped by race in America. Whites are far more likely to shoot themselves, and African Americans are far more likely to be shot by someone else.

The statistical difference is dramatic, according to a Washington Post analysis of data from the U.S. Centers for Disease Control and Prevention. A white person is five times as likely to commit suicide with a gun as to be shot with a gun; for each African American who uses a gun to commit suicide, five are killed by other people with guns.

Where a person lives matters, too. Gun deaths in urban areas are much more likely to be homicides, while suicide is far and away the dominant form of gun death in rural areas. States with the most guns per capita, such as Montana and Wyoming, have the highest suicide rates; states with low gun ownership rates, such as Massachusetts and New York, have far fewer suicides per capita.

Suicides and homicides are highly charged human dramas. Both acts shatter families, friends and sometimes communities. But the reactions are as different as black and white, and those differences shape the nation's divided attitudes toward gun control.

For instance, African Americans tend to be stronger backers of tough gun controls than whites. A Washington Post-ABC News poll this month found that about three-quarters of blacks support stronger controls, compared with about half of whites. The poll also found that two-thirds of city dwellers support stronger gun controls, while only about a third of rural residents back them.

Suicide and homicide rates among Asian Americans and Hispanic Americans do not reflect the sharp differences seen among blacks and whites.

Gun homicides, especially mass shootings, tend to spark demands for change. Although suicides account for almost twice as many gun deaths as homicides nationwide, they tend to be quiet tragedies, unnoticed outside the confines of family and friends.

Suicide is "absent from the discussion of gun policy," said Daniel Webster, director of the Johns Hopkins Center for Gun-Policy and Research in Baltimore. "The availability of firearms does indeed increase the risk of suicide, but most people don't see it that way."

Opponents of gun control counter that some countries with high gun ownership rates, such as Israel, have few suicides and that countries such as Russia, where guns are scarce, have high rates of suicide. The reasoning is that determined people can find a way to kill themselves, although suicide experts say the prevalence of guns allows for impulse suicides that otherwise might not occur.

The most ardent advocate of gun rights, the National Rifle Association, casts the link between guns and suicide as something of a virtue. "Gun owners are notably self-reliant and exhibit a willingness to take definitive action when they believe it to be in their own self-interest," the NRA wrote in a fact sheet, "Suicide and Firearms," on the Web site for its lobbying arm. "Such action may include ending their own life when the time is deemed appropriate."

'A Different Mind-Set'

Janett Massolo, who is white, works at a suicide-prevention center in Reno, Nev. She provides training in suicide prevention and counsels families that have lost a member to suicide. She understands their grief—nearly 17 years ago her daughter Shannon killed herself.

Shannon was a 15-year-old high school student. Her behavior was sometimes erratic, but her mother put it down to teenage volatility. After Shannon's best friend shot herself to death, she told her mother that she was appalled. "How could anything get that bad?" she said.

Six months later, shortly before noon on a Saturday, Massolo told her daughter that she was running next door for a minute. Shannon said she was hopping into the shower. When Massolo returned to the house five minutes later, her daughter's body was on the floor in her parents' bedroom. At first, Massolo thought Shannon was searching for something under the bed. Then she saw the head wound.

Her father's handgun had been in an unlocked drawer; the bullets were elsewhere in the bedroom. Massolo said her daughter would not have had time to get the gun, find the bullets, load the gun and kill herself in the time she was next door. Massolo concluded that Shannon had planned her suicide.

Shannon knew how to handle the gun. Her parents had taught her and her sisters to fire weapons. They had gone to shooting ranges. "The mind-set out here is that we use guns for hunting, for target shooting, to keep the family safe," Massolo said. "If you want to keep the family safe and you have mental illness in the family, then lock your guns up for a while or give them away for a while. We're not saying give them away forever. We don't want to take the gun away."

The gun Shannon used to kill herself had been in the family for years. It was a gift to her father from his father-in-law, a former Reno police officer. Shannon had used it for target practice.

"That's something we've dealt with," Massolo said in a recent interview. "We taught her how to kill herself. But we were trying to teach her how to be safe. It's a different mindset out here about guns. I know the East Coast doesn't think that way."

Massolo said the weapon had sentimental value to her husband, so after the suicide inquiry, he got it back from the police. His wife won't look at it, but her husband won't part with it.

"The gun did not kill Shannon," she said. "Shannon killed Shannon. I tell him it was not his fault. It could have been any method. She killed herself. That was my way of relieving some of his guilt."

Shanda Smith, who is black, has a different view of guns and their place in society. Nearly 20 years ago, her two children were shot to death on their way to a church Christmas party in the Congress Heights neighborhood of Southeast Washington.

Smith, a single mother who never knew her parents, remembers the new Scrabble game her children had opened two days before the church party. "I remember one of the words was 'peril,'" she said in a recent interview. "They didn't know it. I told them it means danger."

Rodney Smith, 19, was home on break from the University of Kansas, where he had a football scholarship. He had borrowed a relative's beat-up Camaro Z28 and was driving his sister, Volante, 14, and two younger children to the party. Boo, as his sister was called, was in the passenger seat.

As the car approached the church on Martin Luther King Jr. Avenue, someone ran up to it and fired a handgun at Rodney and Boo. Smith's two children were in body bags being loaded into an ambulance when she got to the scene. It would turn out that the Smiths were killed in a case of mistaken identity.

"They were right where they needed to be," Smith said of her children, "but somebody had access to a gun, and he shot the wrong kids."

Smith channeled her grief into a group called Survivors of Homicide, where she works with others who have lost family members and close friends to shootings. Her favorite event is an annual Christmas party she hosts for children who have lost siblings or parents to shootings.

Smith's children were killed in 1993, when the District had one of the highest homicide rates in the nation. Even though rates have dropped sharply, Smith knows many families that have suffered from gun homicides. But she said they don't buy guns as a solution. "That's a difference in the African American community," she said. "We don't teach our kids to go hunting and shoot. We don't have guns in our homes."

'Missing the Point'

Contrasting life experiences, whether from a family member's suicide or the death of a relative in a homicide, drive the nation's split over an essential element of the gun debate: Would fewer guns save lives? Survivors of homicide victims consistently tell pollsters that the answer is yes, but the response to suicide is different.

"We have less empathy with those who take their own lives," said Sean Joe, an expert on suicide and violence at the University of Michigan. "So we don't have the same national outcry. The key argument for me is that increased access to firearms increases suicide and homicide."

Scholars say it is no coincidence that places in the United States with high suicide rates also have high gun ownership rates. By contrast, the states with the lowest gun ownership rates tend to have the lowest suicide rates.

Eleanor Hamm works at the statewide suicide hotline for Colorado, which has high rates of gun ownership and suicide. Her suicide-prevention program is accredited by the American Association of Suicidology, but her experience with guns, which started when she got her first at 6, puts her closer to the NRA.

"The Western region is the highest region in suicide," she said in an interview. "Out here, we own guns. You're not ever going to get the guns away from anybody. What we can do is a better job of mental health. That will make a difference."

Hamm, echoing the NRA position, said people without access to guns will kill themselves by other means. "It's easy for the passion of the day to look at gun control," she said. "It's missing the point of mental health and what is really, truly taking place."

But experts say the urge to commit suicide is neither unstoppable nor permanent. "I emphasize that suicide is preventable—treatment works," said Iliana Gilman, spokeswoman for a crisis hotline in Austin.

The impulse to commit suicide has been described as a trance, and the speed and lethality of a gun make it harder to interrupt that trance. Attempts at suicide are more than 20 times as likely to be fatal when a gun is used.

"They are blinded," said Lanny Berman, executive director of the American Association of Suicidology. "They are so focused and tunnel-visioned on 'I have to end the pain I'm in; I have to end it now.' . . . A firearm is an immediate end to the problem."

Some experts say mass shootings such as the one in which 20 first-graders and six adults were killed at Sandy Hook Elementary School in Newtown, Conn., in December can often be seen as extravagant suicides rather than homicidal rampages. And the young man behind that massacre killed himself before he could be apprehended. Preventing those deaths, experts say, requires better treatment of mental health problems and limiting access to weapons.

"If I had to choose one thing," said Joe, the Michigan professor, "I would try to reduce access and availability of firearms. The means matter more."

Critical Thinking

1. Explain the disparities reported in this article.
2. In light of gun violence evidence what remedies can be used to lower gun related deaths?

Create Central

www.mhhe.com/createcentral

Internet References

National Association for the Advancement of Colored People (NAACP)
www.naacp.org

National Urban League
www.nul.org

Sociosite
www.sociosite.net

Unit 9

UNIT

Prepared by: John A. Kromkowski, *Catholic University of America*

New Horizons and the Recovery of Insight: Understanding Cultural Pluralism

The words *race*, *religion*, and *ethnicity* have been used to describe a wide and sometimes ill-defined and contradictory set of experiences and identities. The apparent confusion arises because race and ethnicity are contextual; more a social process than a primordial, and fixed given of biology and origin. Their meanings change in each place with time and circumstances for each group. The discussion of race, religion, and ethnicity require attention to methodological approaches and interpretive categories that frame the current ferment in this field at the practical and theoretic levels. However, one finding is beyond doubt. Patterns of intersection of religion, race, and ethnicity are definitely specific to the locations and regimes within which they are embedded. Moreover, even the claims and efficacy of scientific knowledge and applications appear to be influenced by their history and most significantly by the privileging of certain ways and languages of knowing within respective power-fields established and maintained by regimes. In certain respects, race and ethnicity are both indigenous and transplanted social inventions that have become rooted in the social experience and fostered by regime development. The search for fresh insight into and consciousness of the social and symbolic formation of cultures is an important meta-descriptive challenge. The debate regarding the relationship of various ways of knowing invites us to search for understanding and particular skills, competencies, and rules for dialogue among religious, ethnic, and political traditions. Support of civilization and peaceful means of resolving differences are clearly imperative. While the situation of these issues is worldwide, understanding and action in this arena is nearly always local and specific.

The expansion of public and scholarly attention to race and ethnic relations suggest that new horizons and insights into the variety of situations related to ethnicity and race are required. Ethnicity seems to include the winds of war and political change in Africa and the Middle East and the attendant refugee crisis and the changes of regime. The ethnic factor is related to the new mobility, uncertainty, genocidal violence, problems with acculturation, and assimilation after the euphoric expectations of democracy and the expansion of open markets into Eastern and Central Europe. The Peoples Republic of China, once imaged as a country without ethnicities, is engaged in rapid urbanization and extension into the lives of hundreds of ethnicities and cultures that are different from the regime's leadership. These aforementioned and many more situations reveal the saliency of ethnicity and its function in reviving the spirited particularities and varied cultural textures of communal passion and violence in group relations. The idea of a universal, modern humanity and the expectation that reasonable utilities could be easily discerned appear to be withering. The confidence of modernity has turned into an array of post-modern preferential claims and the proliferation of critical theories of reality that argue for and against popular excitations of nostalgia and new options for the end to oppression. In many respects ethnic and race relations in the United States seems to be immune to the most turbulent features of the breakdown and has taken another pathway and constructed another pattern of continuity and change to the reality of ethnicity and race. Perhaps this is the case, because ongoing affinities to race and ethnicity are not as vigorously spirited. Also, ethnic affinities are expressed in more subtle ways and other objects have filled the social imaginations toward peacefulness. The turn toward a fresh understanding of race and ethnicity requires the reconsideration of their origins as dimensions of human sociality. This perspective reengages currently disparate academic disciplines and invites them to fashion fuller explanations and deeper insight into the pluralistic fundamental aspects of the human condition. Social theory grounded in shallow philosophical anthropology and data driven accounts have often avoided, neglected, and ignored fundamental problems and thus reduced analysis of race and ethnicity to measurements and correlations. The Humanities and philosophical religious approaches to race and ethnicity have deepened the intellectual deficit. Their single-minded attention to texts and traditions as canons of literary artifacts has diminished the existence of tradition as embedded in lived communities and as constitutive of the valued variants of forms of being. This proposed research agenda includes a synthesis of data driven understandings race and ethnicity and the recovery of access to the substantive and essential aspects of social realties. Such multi-disciplinary understandings of existential, local communities would yield fresh and deeper insight into the human condition, the mystery of human variety, the variety of value articulations and finally a locus for serious reflection on the luminosity of social existence. Thus the search for new horizons invites nothing less that re-uniting the social sciences with the humanities and the scientific study of reality. The reader is invited to trust the experiences discovered in manifestations of spiritedness associated with the symbols and behavior through which race and ethnicity enter our awareness. The first step on this pathway and enormous adventure toward understanding is the recognition that it is past time to move beyond description in the analysis of race and ethnic relations. The transmission of ethnic tradition through music, an avenue of expression with the particular capacity to mediate stirrings of the spirit, suggests linkages between religion and ethnicity. The interaction of ethnicity and religion is curiously exposed in the etymology of the Greek word *ethnikos* (i.e., the rural, Gentile, or pagan people of the ancient Mediterranean world). Though such philological roots no longer drive our principal understanding of ethnicity, the experience of social affinity and cultural affiliation elaborated in the following articles about ethnics deepens our awareness and understanding of ethnicity—a changing yet persistent aspect of human identity and social cohesiveness. As Eric Voegelin noted, the self-interpretation of a society does not wait for the social scientist. Societies in historical existence are not merely facts and events and external locations; they are "little worlds of meaning, *cosmions,* illuminated with meaning from within by human beings who continuously create and bear it as the mode and condition of their self-realization . . . relations between its members and groups of members, as well as its existence as a whole, transparent for the mystery of human existence . . . members of a society experience it more than as an accident or a convenience; they experience it as of their human essence."

Understanding race and ethnic relations can be taken by considering the comparative intensities of ethnic and race identities of large immigrant receiving countries and small counties. The affiliation of people to places and senses of rootedness in profound ways to a place even to exclude the desire and prospect of ever leaving kith and kin are clear markers of ethnic intensity. Another approach to different levels of affinity to a group is to estimate the costs and benefits that accrue to various expressions of group affiliation and affinity. Yet another perspective becomes obvious when an ethnic group is not self-defined, but constrained. Labeled and constrained by boundaries and coercion imposed and from which escape and self-determination is difficult if allowed at all. An alternative ramp toward personal and group freedom is articulated by the total denial of group status and reality which attempts to transcend the notion of membership through the claim and production of autonomous individualism The preceding thought experiments have variable levels of applicability, but the purpose of this exercise is to reveal the problem with both the modern claim of a universal humanity based on nearly common genetic structure and post-modern playfulness of totally imaginary options for socialities. The scientific claim misses the right question. The post modern misses the enormity of the gulf between text and statement and the production and construction of the human cultures and the revelation of the human constant in the existence of meaning giving articulation in time tested and experience, outcome and evidence based traditions and symbolization of order embedded in human consciousness and the practices of socialities in specific places based on the deep insight to the human condition. The articulations of human consciousness into patterns of explanation and shared bonds of union are ongoing human expressions. They are transmitted through socialization and in detailed useful, sustaining forms of knowledge about four central aspects of existence and reality. These are the self, others, nature (the world and universe) and finally as well as initially the mystery of being that transcends the mundane and invites human consciousness to participate and to co-create our selves and our relations with others, nature and existence self in whatever ways we wish.

Ethnicity and Modernity: Expression and Articulations

The formation of an ethnic identity and the extension of ethnic identity is a complex process that includes: various forms of communication and the elaboration of imaginative accounts as well as historically, demographically and sociologically accurate and verifiable production of accessible knowledge, information, the evocation of spirited sentiment. These characteristics have widened, deepened and perhaps utterly changed our understandings of ethnicity as a cultural phenomenon and as a topic of academic exploration. Ethnicity was initially explored by anthropology and sociology. Given the intellectual grounding of their theories and ideologies of economic and social change which included the drivers of historical development measured by the transition from rural to urban society and from primitive to modern human development, the waning and withering of ethnicity as a meaningful phenomena was an expected outcome. This hopeful march of history toward universalism and modernity did not occur at the rate expected. The complexities of social change, the migration of people, the uses of race and nationalism as ideological cudgels and the persistence and reconfiguration of race and ethnicity as interpretative canons have prompted a fundamental rethinking of ethnicity in various academic and applied fields: social sciences, the humanities and literature, philosophical and the natural biological sciences as well as new horizons in the relationships of ethnicity to religious and theological dimensions of reality.

Today historians, social workers, social psychologists and political scientists are fully entered into this field and added their considerable disciplines to the discourse and the application of ethnicity. Such intellectual production has spilled-over into nearly all forms of popular communication, education at all levels and in the common currency of social political mentalities that define social reality. The ethnic and race factor can be seen throughout all large-scale forms of human organization. The outcomes and consequences of large-scale organizations are uncertain and owing to the pace and extent of globalization, technological change, and mobility the exploration of race and ethnic relations and the attendant aspects of pluralism and diversity reveal the rugged-edges of voices in public ferment that champion and challenge the group claims.

What is none the less certain is that public discussion, personal preferences and private attitudes about the relationships between and among the variety of other cultural phenomena have become more clearly visible. The horizon of global diversity and the stunning and ongoing pluralism of humankind affect more and more persons and groups as they negotiate relationships within larger arenas of commerce and political order and the mini-world of workplace and neighborhood. The study of such forms of human activity initially employed class and citizenship to describe and explain behavior. Today the recognition for identity politics and the claimed collapse of class-based causes for change, conflict and continuity are producing new ideologies. Such ways of action and explanation argue for the efficacy of human agency and the meaning of epochal events and imagination and magical-thinking to alter the range of truth-values that can be discerned as forces within large and complex societies as well as the final horizon of globalization as a limit of pluralism in the human condition.

Even the hardened position of power analysis and the possession of authoritative uses of violence gave way to the persistence capacity of humans to articulate their self and group expression of personal and group meaning through the discovery, recovery, and invention of ethnic/religious identities, affinities and animosities. Thus ethnicity emerged as a modern form of symbolization and displaced the sciences and ideologies of linear universal human development, which can be called the historical and cultural turn of the social creation of human organization and its attendant re-definition of an epoch of human development as post-modern. This shift in perspective suggests that new attention to the ways and modalities of explaining social order and its foundation in human imagination must be added to the discussion of race and ethnic relations. The relationship between personal consciousness and one's participation in shared consciousness as a group are oftentimes mediated through ethnic symbolizations grounded in the meaning providing evocation of ethnicities that are derived from historical and imagined ethic experiences and traditions.

Article

Prepared by: John A. Kromkowski, *Catholic University of America*

The Geometer of Race

In the eighteenth century a disastrous shift occurred in the way Westerners perceived races. The man responsible was Johann Friedrich Blumenbach, one of the least racist thinkers of his day.

STEPHEN JAY GOULD

Learning Outcomes

After reading this article, you will be able to:

- Explain what scientific claims are.
- Determine the relationship between science, popular culture, and public discourse.

Interesting stories often lie encoded in names that seem either capricious or misconstrued. Why, for example, are political radicals called "left" and their conservative counterparts "right"? In many European legislatures;the most distinguished members sat at the chairman's right, following a custom of courtesy as old as our prejudices for favoring the dominant hand of most people. (These biases run deep, extending well beyond can openers and scissors to language itself, where *dexterous* stems from the Latin for "right," and *sinister* from the word for "left.") Since these distinguished nobles and moguls tended to espouse conservative views, the right and left wings of the legislature came to define a geometry of political views.

Among such apparently capricious names in my own field of biology and evolution, none seems more curious, and none elicits more questions after lectures, than the official designation of light-skinned people in Europe, western Asia, and North Africa as Caucasian. Why should the most common racial group of the Western world be named for a mountain range that straddles Russia and Georgia? Johann Friedrich Blumenbach (1752–1840), the German anatomist and naturalist who established the most influential of all racial classifications, invented this name in 1795, in the third edition of his seminal work, *De Generis Humani Varietate Nativa* (On the Natural Variety of Mankind). Blumenbach's definition cites two reasons for his choice—the maximal beauty of people from this small region, and the probability that humans were first created in this area.

> *Caucasian variety.* I have taken the name of this variety from Mount Caucasus, both because its neighborhood, and especially its southern slope, produces the most beautiful race of men, I mean the Georgian; and because . . . in that region, if anywhere, it seems we ought with the greatest probability to place the autochthones [original forms] of mankind.

Blumenbach, one of the greatest and most honored scientists of the Enlightenment, spent his entire career as a professor at the University of Göttingen in Germany. He first presented *De Generis Humani Varietate Nativa* as a doctoral dissertation to the medical faculty of Gottingen in 1775, as the minutemen of Lexington and Concord began the American Revolution. He then republished the text for general distribution in 1776, as a fateful meeting in Philadelphia proclaimed our independence. The coincidence of three great documents in 1776—Jefferson's Declaration of Independence (on the politics of liberty), Adam Smith's *Wealth of Nations* (on the economics of individualism), and Blumenbach's treatise on racial classification (on the science human diversity)—records the social ferment of these decades and sets the wider context that makes Blumenbach's taxonomy and his subsequent decision to call the European race Caucasian so important for our history and current concerns.

The solution to big puzzles often hinges upon tiny curiosities, easy to miss or to pass over. I suggest that the key to under standing Blumenbach's classification, the foundation of much that continues to influence and disturb us today, lies in the peculiar criterion he used to name the European race Caucasian—the supposed superior beauty of people from this region. Why first of all, should a scientist attach such importance to an evidently subjective assessment; and why, secondly, should a aesthetic criterion become the basis of a scientific judgment about place of origin? To answer these questions, we must compare Blumenbach's original 1775 text with the later edition 1795, when Caucasians received their name.

Blumenbach' s final taxonomy of 1795 divided all humans into five groups, defined both by geography and appearance—in his order, the Caucasian variety, for the light-skinned people of Europe and adjacent parts of Asia and Africa; the Mongolian variety, for most other inhabitants of Asia, including China and Japan; the Ethiopian variety, for the dark-skinned people of Africa; the American variety, for most native populations of the New World; and the Malay variety, for the Polynesians and Melanesians of the Pacific and for the aborigines of Australia. But Blumenbach's original classification of 1775 recognized only the first four of these five, and united members of the Malay variety with the other people of Asia whom Blumenbach came to name Mongolian.

We now encounter the paradox of Blumenbach's reputation as the inventor of modern racial classification. The original four-race system, as I shall illustrate in a moment, did not arise from Blumenbach's observations but only represents, as Blumenbach readily admits, the classification promoted by his guru Carolus Linnaeus in the founding document of taxonomy, the *Systema Naturae* of 1758. Therefore, Blumenbach's only original contribution to racial classification lies in the later addition of a Malay variety for some Pacific peoples first included in a broader Asian group.

This change seems so minor. Why, then, do we credit Blumenbach, rather than Linnaeus, as the founder of racial classification? (One might prefer to say "discredit," as the enterprise does not, for good reason, enjoy high repute these days.) But Blumenbach's apparently small change actually records a theoretical shift that could not have been broader, or more portentous, in scope. This change has been missed or misconstrued because later scientists have not grasped the vital historical and philosophical principle that theories are models subject to visual representation, usually in clearly definable geometric terms.

By moving from the Linnaean four-race system to his own five-race scheme, Blumenbach radically changed the geometry of human order from a geographically based model without explicit ranking to a hierarchy of worth, oddly based upon perceived beauty, and fanning out in two directions from a Caucasian ideal. The addition of a Malay category was crucial to this geometric reformulation—and therefore becomes the key to the conceptual transformation rather than a simple refinement of factual information within an old scheme. (For the insight that scientific revolutions embody such geometric shifts, I am grateful to my friend Rhonda Roland Shearer, who portrays these themes in [her] book, *The Flatland Hypothesis.*)

BLUMENBACH IDOLIZED his teacher Linnaeus and acknowledged him as the source of his original fourfold racial classification: "I have followed Linnaeus in the number, but have defined my varieties by other boundaries" (1775 edition). Later, in adding his Malay variety, Blumenbach identified his change as a departure from his old mentor in the most respectful terms: "It became very clear that the Linnaean division of mankind could no longer be adhered to; for which reason I, in this little work, ceased like others to follow that illustrious man."

Linnaeus divided the species *Homo sapiens* into four basic varieties, defined primarily by geography and, interestingly, not in the ranked order favored by most Europeans in the racist tradition—*Americanus, Europaeus, Asiaticus,* and *Afer,* or African. (He also alluded to two other fanciful categories: *ferus* for "wild boys," occasionally discovered in the woods and possibly raised by animals—most turned out to be retarded or mentally ill youngsters abandoned by their parents—and *monstrosus* for hairy men with tails, and other travelers' confabulations.) In so doing, Linnaeus presented nothing original; he merely mapped humans onto the four geographic regions of conventional cartography.

Linnaeus then characterized each of these groups by noting color, humor, and posture, in that order. Again, none of these categories explicitly implies ranking by worth. Once again, Linnaeus was simply bowing to classical taxonomic theories in making these decisions. For example, his use of the four humors reflects the ancient and medieval theory that a person's temperament arises from a balance of four fluids (*humor* is Latin for "moisture")—blood, phlegm, choler (yellow bile), and melancholy (black bile). Depending on which of the four substances dominated, a person would be sanguine (the cheerful realm of blood), phlegmatic (sluggish), choleric (prone to anger), or melancholic (sad). Four geographic regions, four humors, four races.

For the American variety, Linnaeus wrote *"ritfus, cholericus, rectus"* (red, choleric, upright); for the European, *"albus, sanguineus, torosus"* (white, sanguine, muscular); for the Asian, *"luridus, melancholicus, rigidus"* (pale yellow, melancholy, stiff); and for the African, *"niger, phlegmaticus, laxus"* (black, phlegmatic, relaxed).

I don't mean to deny that Linnaeus held conventional beliefs about the superiority of his own European variety over others. Being a sanguine, muscular European surely sounds better than being a melancholy, stiff Asian. Indeed, Linnaeus ended each group's description with a more overtly racist label, an attempt to epitomize behavior in just two words. Thus the American was *regitur consuetudine* (ruled by habit); the European, *regitur ritibus* (ruled by custom); the Asian, *regitur opiniohibus* (ruled by belief); and the African, *regitur arbitrio* (ruled by caprice). Surely regulation by established and considered custom beats the unthinking rule of habit or belief, and all of these are superior to caprice—thus leading to the implied and conventional racist ranking of Europeans first, Asians and Americans in the middle, and Africans at the bottom.

Nonetheless, and despite these implications, the overt geometry of Linnaeus's model is not linear or hierarchical. When we visualize his scheme as an essential picture in our mind, we see a map of the world divided into four regions, with the people in each region characterized by a list of different traits. In short, Linnaeus's primary ordering principle is cartographic; if he had wished to push hierarchy as the essential picture of human variety, he would surely have listed Europeans first and Africans last, but he started with native Americans instead.

The shift from a geographic to a hierarchical ordering of human diversity must stand as one of the most fateful transitions in the history of Western science—for what, short of railroads and nuclear bombs, has had more practical impact, in this case almost entirely negative, upon our collective lives? Ironically, Blumenbach is the focus of this shift, for his five-race scheme became canonical and changed the geometry of human order from Linnaeari cartography to linear ranking—in short, to a system based on putative worth.

I say ironic because Blumenbach was the least racist and most genial of all Enlightenment thinkers. How peculiar that the man most committed to human unity, and to inconsequential moral and intellectual differences among groups, should have changed the mental geometry of human order to a scheme that has served racism ever since. Yet on second thought, this situation is really not so odd—for most scientists have been quite unaware of the mental machinery, and particularly of the visual or geometric implications, lying behind all their theorizing.

Scientists assume that their own shifts in interpretation record only their better understanding of newly discovered facts. They tend to be unaware of their own mental impositions upon the world's messy and ambiguous factuality.

An old tradition in science proclaims that changes in the theory must be driven by observation. Since most scientists believe this simplistic formula, they assume that their own shifts in interpretation record only their better understanding of newly discovered facts. Scientists therefore tend to be unaware of their own mental impositions upon the world's messy and ambiguous factuality. Such mental impositions arise from a variety of sources, including psychological predisposition and social context. Blumenbach lived in an age when ideas of progress, and the cultural superiority of European ways, dominated political and social life. Implicit, loosely formulated, or even unconscious notions of racial ranking fit well with such a worldview—indeed, almost any other organizational scheme would have seemed anomalous. I doubt that Blumenbach was actively encouraging racism by redrawing the mental diagram of human groups. He was only, and largely passively, recording the social view of his time. But ideas have consequences, whatever the motives or intentions of their promoters.

Blumenbach certainly thought that his switch from the Linnaean four-race system to his own five-race scheme arose only from his improved understanding of nature's factuality. He said as much when he announced his change in the second (1781) edition of his treatise: "Formerly in the first edition of this work, I divided all mankind into four varieties; but after I had more actively investigated the different nations of Eastern Asia and America, and, so to speak, looked at them more closely, I was compelled to give up that division, and to place in its stead the following five varieties, as more consonant to nature." And in the preface to the third edition, of 1795, Blumenbach states that he gave up the Linnaean scheme in order to arrange "the varieties of man according to the truth of nature." When scientists adopt the myth that theories arise solely from observation, and do not grasp the personal and social influences acting on their thinking, they not only miss the causes of their changed opinions; they may even fail to comprehend the deep mental shift encoded by the new theory.

Blumenbach upheld the unity of the human species against an alternative view, then growing in popularity (and surely more conducive to conventional racism), that each race had been separately created.

Blumenbach strongly upheld the unity of the human species against an alternative view, then growing in popularity (and surely more conducive to conventional forms of racism), that each major race had been separately created. He ended his third edition by writing: "No doubt can any longer remain but that we are with great probability right in referring all. . . varieties of man. . . to one and the same species."

AS HIS MAJOR ARGUMENT for unity, Blumenbach noted that all supposed racial characteristics grade continuously from one people to another and cannot define any separate and bounded group. "For although there seems to be so great a difference between widely separate nations, that you might easily take the inhabitants of the Cape of Good Hope, the Greenlanders, and the Circassians for so many different species of man, yet when the matter is thoroughly considered, you see that all do so run into one another, and that one variety of mankind does so sensibly pass into the other, that you cannot mark out the limits between them." He particularly refuted the common racist claim that black Africans bore unique features of their inferiority: "There is no single character so peculiar and so universal among the Ethiopians, but what it may be observed on the one hand everywhere in other varieties of men."

Blumenbach, writing 80 years before Darwin, believed that *Homo sapiens* had been created in a single region and had then spread over the globe. Our racial diversity, he then argued, arose as a result of this spread to other climates and topographies, and to our adoption of different modes of life in these various regions. Following the terminology of his time, Blumenbach referred to these changes as "degenerations"—not intending the modem sense of deterioration, but the literal meaning of departure from an initial form of humanity at the creation (*de* means "from," and *genus* refers to our original stock).

Most of these degenerations, Blumenbach argued, arose directly from differences in climate and habitat—ranging from such broad patterns as the correlation of dark skin with tropical environments, to more particular (and fanciful) attributions, including a speculation that the narrow eye slits of some Australian aborigines may have arisen in response to "constant clouds of gnats . . . contracting the natural face of the inhabitants." Other changes, he maintained, arose as a consequence of customs adopted in different regions. For example, nations that compressed the heads of babies by swaddling boards or papoose carriers ended up with relatively long skulls. Blumenbach held that "almost all the diversity of the form of the head in different nations is to be attributed to the mode of life and to art."

Blumenbach believed that such changes, promoted over many generations, could eventually become hereditary. "With the progress of time," Blumenbach wrote, "art may degenerate into a second nature." But he also argued that most racial variations, as superficial impositions of climate and custom, could be easily altered or reversed by moving to a new region or by adopting new behavior. White Europeans living for generations in the tropics could become dark-skinned, while Africans transported as slaves to high latitudes could eventually become white: "Color, whatever be its cause, be it bile, or the influence of the sun, the air, or the climate, is, at all events, an adventitious and easily changeable thing, and can never constitute a diversity of species," he wrote.

Convinced of the superficiality of racial variation, Blumenbach defended the mental and moral unity of all peoples. He held particularly strong opinions on the equal status of black Africans and white Europeans. He may have been patronizing in praising "the good disposition and faculties of these our black brethren," but better paternalism than malign contempt. He campaigned for the abolition of slavery and asserted the moral superiority of slaves to their captors, speaking of a "natural tenderness of heart, which has never been benumbed or extirpated on board the transport vessels or on the West India sugar plantations by the brutality of their white executioners."

Blumenbach established a special library in his house devoted exclusively to black authors, singling out for special praise the poetry of Phillis Wheatley, a Boston slave whose writings have only recently been rediscovered: "I possess English, Dutch, and Latin poems by several [black authors], amongst which however above all, those of Phillis Wheatley of Boston, who is justly famous for them, deserves mention here." Finally, Blumenbach noted that many Caucasian nations could not boast so fine a set of authors and scholars as black Africa has produced under the most depressing circumstances of prejudice and slavery: "It would not be difficult to mention entire well-known provinces of Europe, from out of which you would not easily expect to obtain off-hand such good authors, poets, philosophers, and correspondents of the Paris Academy."

Nonetheless, when Blumenbach presented his mental picture of human diversity in his fateful shift away from Linnaean geography, he singled out a particular group as closest to the created ideal and then characterized all other groups by relative degrees of departure from this archetypal standard. He ended up with a system that placed a single race at the pinnacle, and then envisioned two symmetrical lines of departure away from this ideal toward greater and greater degeneration.

WE MAY NOW RETURN to the riddle of the name Caucasian, and to the significance of Blumenbach's addition of a fifth race, the Malay variety. Blumenbach chose to regard his own European variety as closest to the created ideal and then searched for the subset of Europeans with greatest perfection—the highest of the high, so to speak. As we have seen, he identified the people around Mount Caucasus as the closest embodiments of the original ideal and proceeded to name the entire European race for its finest representatives.

But Blumenbach now faced a dilemma. He had already affirmed the mental and moral equality of all peoples. He therefore could not use these conventional criteria of racist ranking to establish degrees of relative departure from the Caucasian ideal. Instead, and however subjective (and even risible) we view the criterion today, Blumenbach chose physical beauty as his guide to ranking. He simply affirmed that Europeans were most beautiful, with Caucasians as the most comely of all. This explains why Blumenbach, in the fist quote cited in this article, linked the maximal beauty of the Caucasians to the place of human origin. Blumenbach viewed all subsequent variation as departures from the originally created ideal—therefore, the most beautiful people must live closest to our primal home.

Blumenbach's descriptions are pervaded by his subjective sense of relative beauty, presented as though he were discussing an objective and quantifiable property, not subject to doubt or disagreement. He describes a Georgian female skull (found close to Mount Caucasus) as "really the most beautiful form of skull which. . . always of itself attracts every eye, however little observant." He then defends his European standard on aesthetic grounds: "In the first place, that stock displays. . . the most beautiful form of the skull, from which, as from a mean and primeval type, the others diverge by most easy gradations. . .. Besides, it is white in color, which we may fairly assume to have been the primitive color of mankind, since. . . it is very easy for that to degenerate into brown, but very much more difficult for dark to become white."

Blumenbach then presented all human variety on two lines of successive departure from this Caucasian ideal, ending in the two most degenerate (least attractive, not least morally unworthy or mentally obtuse) forms of humanity—Asians on one side, and Africans on the other. But Blumenbach also wanted to designate intermediary forms between ideal and most degenerate, especially since even gradation formed his primary argument for human unity. In his original four-race system, he could identify native Americans as intermediary between Europeans and Asians, but who would serve as the transitional form between Europeans and Africans?

The four-race system contained no appropriate group. But inventing a fifth racial category as an intermediary between Europeans and Africans would complete the new symmetrical geometry. Blumenbach therefore added the Malay race, not as a minor, factual refinement but as a device for reformulatint? an entire theory of human diversity. With this one stroke, he produced the geometric transformation from Linnaeus's unranked geographic model to the conventional hierarchy of implied worth that has fostered so much social grief ever since.

> I have allotted the first place to the Caucasian. . . which makes me esteem it the primeval one. This diverges in both directions into two, most remote and very different from each other; on the one side, namely, into the Ethiopian, and on the other into the Mongolian. The remaining two occupy the intermediate positions between that primeval one and these two extreme varieties; that is, the American between the Caucasian and Mongolian; the Malay between the same Caucasian and Ethiopian. [From Blumenbach's third edition.]

Scholars often think that academic ideas must remain at worst, harmless, and at best, mildly amusing or even instructive. But ideas do not reside in the ivory tower of our usual metaphor about academic irrelevance. We are, as Pascal said, a thinking reed, and ideas motivate human history. Where would Hitler have been without racism, Jefferson without liberty? Blumenbach lived as a cloistered professor all his life, but his ideas have reverberated in ways that he never could have anticipated, through our wars, our social upheavals, our sufferings, and our hopes.

I therefore end by returning once more to the extraordinary coincidences of 1776—as Jefferson wrote the Declaration of Independence while Blumenbach was publishing the first edition of his treatise in Latin. We should remember the words of the nineteenth-century British historian and moralist Lord Acton, on the power of ideas to propel history:

> It was from America that. . . ideas long locked in the breast of solitary thinkers, and hidden among Latin folios, burst forth like a conqueror upon the world they were destined to transform, under the title of the Rights of Man.

For Further Reading

Daughters of Africa. Margaret Busby, editor. Pantheon, 1992. A comprehensive anthology of prose and poetry written by women of African descent, from ancient Egyptian love songs to the work of contemporary Americans. The collection features the work of Phillis Wheatley, the first black to publish a book of poetry in the United States.

Critical Thinking

1. What does the history of science contribute to our understanding of culture?
2. Discuss the ways in which popular common sense language and scientific language intersect.

Create Central

www.mhhe.com/createcentral

Internet References

Sociosite

www.sociosite.net

Stephen Jay Gould, a contributing editor a *Discover,* is a professor of zoology at Harvard who also teaches geology, biology, and the history of science. His writing on evolution has won many prizes, including a National Book Award, a National Magazine Award, and the Phi Beta Kappa Science Award. For *Discover's* November 1993 special section on ten great science museums, Gould wrote about the glass flowers at Harvard's Botanical Museum.

Article

Prepared by: John A. Kromkowski, *Catholic University of America*

Racism Isn't What it Used to Be

But Not Everyone has Noticed

ED MARCINIAK

Learning Outcomes

After reading this article, you will be able to:

- Identify the core elements of Marciniak's argument.
- Identify the core elements of Wycliff's argument.

A new vocabulary is surfacing to assess the state of race relations in the United States. The operative words and approaches signal remarkable changes.

In the 1960s our racial language was dominated by "civil rights," "integration," "desegregation," "prejudice," "discrimination," "colored," and "Negroes." Nowadays, the comparable words and ideas have become: "racism," "diversity," "hate crimes," "racial profiling," "redlining," "reparations," "blacks," and "African Americans."

We are in transition, striving to find a racial vocabulary appropriate to today's society and culture. This is a touchy, controversial endeavor.

The 1960s, furthermore, emphasized equality of treatment—in employment, voting, housing, and government services. In the new millennium the stress has shifted to equality of results. Now the assumption of some is that ethnic and racial groups should be proportionately represented in occupations, incomes, wealth, college graduations, achievements, and failures. On the other hand, black athletes now dominate the nation's sports, such as track, basketball, football, and baseball (almost). Inequality is not the same as inequity.

The variations in language reflect the notable developments in race relations since 1963 when Martin Luther King Jr. gave his "I Have a Dream" speech to two hundred thousand people, culminating the March on Washington. Or since 1964 when Congress enacted the U.S. Civil Rights Act. Consider only a few of the changes:

In 1966, 42 percent of American blacks had incomes below the official poverty line. Recently, the U.S. Census Bureau reported that 24 percent of the nation's blacks were under that poverty line. At the same time, the poverty rate for whites was 8 percent.

Nationwide, the count of black elected officials zoomed from some 100 in the 1960s to 9,000 in the new millennium. In political jurisdictions where the voting majority is of one race, candidates of another continue to gain office.

We now have a national holiday in January honoring a black minister who preached and practiced nonviolence. And it can no longer be claimed that 11 A.M. on Sunday is the nation's most segregated hour of the week.

Affirmative-action programs originally intended for blacks now embrace Hispanics, Asians, women, and/or gays. Some university affirmative-action programs give priority to students in poverty.

The reading public has come to realize that Toni Morrison is black and a writer. But she is not a black writer.

Hispanics will soon overtake blacks as the largest "minority." Meanwhile, efforts to create ongoing coalitions among blacks, Hispanics, and Asians have not been successful.

A growing number of blacks who have "made it" want to be seen as having arrived there by their own ability rather than affirmative action. In California, Florida, Michigan, and Texas, for example, affirmative-action programs based on race in college admissions have been challenged by whites, and also by some blacks.

These racial changes since the 1960s—and others too numerous to highlight—have encouraged a new generation of black leaders to recommend that priority also be given to those social problems that only tortuously can be linked solely to racism. They point, for example, to the prevalence of black-on-black crime, absentee fathers, the disproportion of AIDS among blacks compared to whites, the large number of single-parent black households in public-housing projects, and the poorly performing public schools in those neighborhoods. The victims of black crime are predominantly black.

That is why in Chicago last year, U.S. Representative Bobby Rush (D-Ill.) convened a summit on black-on-black crime and asked the attendees to "find alternatives to the culture of gun violence. It is critical we teach by example the true method of conflict resolution..." At about the same time, James T. Meeks, vice president of Jesse Jackson's Rainbow/Push coalition, appealed to fellow blacks: "Let's stop blaming everybody else for the problems of black men and start doing something for ourselves. Yes, white folks have treated us wrong. Yes, there is an injustice, but we're doing a whole lot of stuff to ourselves. To black America, if you want to help, we've got to start in our own house."

Several years ago, the need for such self-scrutiny was dramatically summarized in the *Economist* (March 7, 1998):

> *Black unemployment in desperate ghettos is not obviously the result of racism. Most of the worst-stricken cities are run by black mayors, after all; and social services that might once have ignored the plight of blacks are also run by blacks. Black entrepreneurs as well as white ones have fled the inner cites for the suburbs.... A bigger cause of black poverty is that 70 percent of all black children are born out of wedlock.... During the Depression, poverty was acute but families were more cohesive.*

In spite of an era of high prosperity, the persistence of child poverty among blacks (and whites), can be attributed, in the main, to the decline in marriage and to the tide of single-parent households. Statistics for 1999 from the U.S. Census Bureau confirmed this conclusion: 50 percent of black children under six in families without a father lived in poverty, while only 9 percent of those in a two-parent family were poor.

While the new black leaders may echo the *Economist*'s devastating overview, they do not deny that racism exists. For them, however, racism as *the* reason for the durability of black poverty has become more difficult to substantiate. Consequently, they search for new ways to eradicate disparities in income, seeking additional means of uprooting black poverty. They struggle to have their voices heard and their proposals implemented. In doing so, they play down white guilt and black helplessness.

On the other hand, the racial gains since the 1960s, the disturbing social conditions within some black communities, and the calls for self-help initiatives have put traditional civil-rights leaders on the defensive. Disinclined to air "dirty linen" in public, they continue viewing the world through the prism of race. As a result, the civil-rights establishment now strives even harder to keep racism high on the nation's agenda and conscience. How? By shunning the more favorable data about black achievement. They publicize instead anecdotal data about racism's presence to garner support for their contention that the nation's 34 million blacks are still the victims and that racism is omnipresent.

In their eagerness, hyperbole often suffuses their arguments. Alabama's Southern Poverty Law Center recently claimed in a fund-raising letter: "I'm sure that you are well aware that our schools are racked with racial strife and intolerance against those who are different. Some call it a national crisis. Our communities are seething with racial violence. African Americans, Hispanics, and Asian Americans are assaulting each other."

In their tug of war with the venerable civil-rights establishment, new—and increasingly influential—black leaders no longer seek to divide (victimizers vs. victims). Instead, they hope to unite blacks and whites so that together they will address the serious social problems that beset inner-city neighborhoods. Their first priority goes to reducing urban poverty. In the new millennium, a new civil-rights agenda is being fashioned to promote two-parent families, curb street violence, improve public schools, reduce dependency on drugs, and uproot poverty. These objectives may prove to be more difficult to achieve than the equal-opportunity goals of the civil-rights movement in the 1960s, but they are no less worthy of pursuit.

Don Wycliff

Ed Marciniak is absolutely right when he says we are struggling for a new way to talk intelligently and usefully about race. But what inhibits such conversation, I think, is less the lack of a new vocabulary than the persistence of an old one: the vocabulary of racial guilt and innocence. Our whole racial "dialogue" has become a contest to establish or escape guilt, and, as a result, is shot through with dishonesty.

Most white people—or what appears to me to be most—seem intent mainly on establishing their personal innocence: innocence of racial bias, of discrimination, of any connection to or benefit from slavery. Not only is this beside the point, it's also impossible. One cannot escape the personal implications of membership in a society, no matter how personally blameless one may be. Where race in America is concerned, there are no innocents.

For their part, black people—or at least black leaders—seem more intent than ever on pressing the issue of white personal guilt: for slavery, for segregation, for lingering discrimination, for whatever deficits African Americans still suffer. More than three decades into the nation's effort to pay off that promissory note Martin Luther King Jr. spoke of in his "I Have a Dream" speech, black leaders seem intent on denying that anything at all has changed, determined not to "let the white man off the hook." As a black man, a Christian, and a person who has required the forgiveness and forbearance of others more than once in his life, I am deeply troubled by this particular gambit. The notion of acting as moral prosecutor and judge of a fellow human being strikes me as odious. I take seriously the scriptural admonition against judging others, "for the measure by which you measure is the measure by which you will be measured." There is nothing more foolish and unbecoming, it seems to me, than to go about peering into the eyes of others in search of motes.

(I am reminded in this connection of an e-mail sent me by a black friend of about my age, fifty-four, after the recent deadly school shooting in San Diego. It was a newspaper column in which the writer, a white man, urged other whites to face up to the fact that this kind of behavior was a white kid's malady. My friend underscored that point in his accompanying note. I didn't reply to him, but if I had I would have told him you could bet that, before this terrible phenomenon runs its course, there'll be a black kid somewhere who will do the same thing. There is no racial immunity to the sort of demons that possess children and propel them to such murderous lunacy. To think such immunity exists is to succumb to the pride that goes before a fall—and an embarrassment.)

Not only is such moral prosecution foolish and unbecoming, it's ineffective. Increasingly over the last two decades, white people have given evidence that they have hardened to this sort of thing, that they're through feeling racial guilt—whether they ought to be or not. Obviously, not all take this attitude, but a growing number that now seem to be a majority do. This refusal of guilt first manifested itself in the election of Ronald Reagan and has continued ever since—even through the two Clinton administrations. Paralleling this change has been another: the loss by blacks of the moral high ground that goes along with victim status. Frankly, given the very real and dramatic progress African Americans have made over the last three and one-half decades, it is hard to sustain the argument that we remain, as a group, victims of a relentless and unyielding societal racism. To be sure, racism persists and continues to distort lives. Probably in no area is its effect greater than in law enforcement and criminal justice. The ruinous rates of black unwed motherhood to which Marciniak refers are not unrelated to the depressing rates of arrest and incarceration of black men, so many of whom are thereby rendered "unmarriageable."

But to contend, as some black spokesmen do, that racism remains the defining fact of black life in this country, that "a black man just can't get ahead," is simply, demonstrably false. There are too many exceptions, too many success stories, for that to be true. Such exceptions are now, arguably, the rule. But it wasn't just a general perception of steadily increasing black progress that eroded the notion of blacks as victims and changed the moral equation on race. Had that been the case, I don't think there would be the raw edginess to race relations that is so much in evidence now. No, there was one very specific and singular event that, I believe, sealed the change. That event was the trial of O.J. Simpson and the reaction of black people to it.

It appeared to many whites—and I hear this every time a hot racial issue is aired in the newspaper—that a black man got away with murder in this high-profile case by portraying himself as a victim of police racism. Not only did blacks on the Simpson jury let him get away, but the black community at large applauded it, demonstrating thereby that racial solidarity was more important than justice. Or so the thinking goes. I don't think it was fully appreciated at the time what a watershed in race relations the Simpson verdict was. Indeed, grotesque as the idea may seem, the Simpson case is emblematic of what many white and black conservative critics consider the grievous defect of affirmative action and other programs of racial redress: a black man escaped responsibility for the killing of two white persons so that society could make redress for his supposed victimization by a social institution, the police. Take away the homicidal element and these critics see the same principle at work in, for example, the University of Michigan affirmative-action cases: In an attempt to redress historical social wrongs, less-deserving minority applicants are favored over more-deserving white ones. It's an argument that, it appears, the Supreme Court is ready to buy.

So if there is unfinished business in the area of racial equality and the old vocabulary of racial guilt and innocence have become impediments, what's to be done? We could do far worse, I think, than go back to Martin Luther King Jr. for instruction and example. King and his "dream" are invoked so frequently and wantonly nowadays that I have almost grown tired of them. I know that's heresy, but there is a treacly quality to so much of the talk about King and his dream that it is like an overdose of candy. However, the fact is that King preached hard truths and he was not a man to take the easy road. He entered by the narrow gate—the gate of nonviolent direct action. You almost never hear anyone talk about that anymore. The genius of his approach was manifold. It involved direct action, an active challenge to injustice. But it was nonviolent, a refusal to use what he considered immoral means to achieve a moral end. It put the onus on those maintaining the system of injustice to respond—and to live with themselves afterward. It forced them to confront their consciences, not to listen to moral harangues.

That last fact is critical, especially in our over-the-top, in-your-face, finger-wagging age, when nobody feels any compunction about calling attention to the faults and failures of others. King had the grace and the good sense not to go about acting as moral prosecutor of his fellow humans—even if he may privately have considered them monsters. That may have been a tactical decision—like leaving room in a diplomatic negotiation for one's rival to gracefully back down, to save face. I like to think his belief in nonviolence was an expression of real grace, the result of King's having received forgiveness for his sins and thereby being inclined to forgive others. But whether King's attitude was tactical or something more—or something else entirely—I don't see any contemporary black leader who behaves that way. And that's a real loss because King's approach is the only way whites can be rendered receptive again to the need to exert themselves to rectify what remains of racism in American society.

We in the United States have made an amazing racial revolution over the last three and one-half decades. There may be another nation that has done as much, but if there is, I don't know of it. We must tell our people—black, white, brown, red, yellow—all about that revolution. We need to give ourselves a big round of applause. Then we must challenge ourselves—without condemning—to finish the job. And we must do it in terms that will cause people to nod "yes" instead of turning away in disgust. I personally am fond of those words from the preamble to the Constitution, the ones about creating "a more perfect union." Where is the Martin Luther King of our age, or the Abraham Lincoln, or the Lyndon Johnson, or the Cesar Chavez, who can speak those words in a way that will move us to the next stage of the struggle for American union?

Critical Thinking

1. What are the central elements of Marciniak's notion of racism?
2. What are the central elements of Wycliff's notion of racism?

Create Central

www.mhhe.com/createcentral

Internet References

The Council for Research in Values and Philosophy
www.crvp.org

Diversity.com
www.diversity.com

National Catholic Bishops Conference
www.USCCB.org

Sociosite
www.sociosite.net

Ed Marciniak *is president of the Institute of Urban Life at Loyola University, Chicago.*

Article

Prepared by: John A. Kromkowski, *Catholic University of America*

Race in America

A Discussion of Cathy J. Cohen's Democracy Remixed: Black Youth and the Future of American Politics

Both the plight of African American young people and their feelings and thoughts about this plight are major issues of concern in U.S. politics. In 2003, the Black Youth Project was launched, with funding by the Ford Foundation and the Robert Wood Johnson Foundation, to promote both social scientific analysis and public understanding of these issues (the project has an innovative and engaging Website that can be accessed at www.blaekyouthproject.com/). Cathy J. Cohen is the principal investigator of the project and, in *Democracy Remixed,* she draws upon a new national survey of black youth to offer a mixed-method empirical description and theoretical analysis of "black youth and the future of American politics." In this symposium, a diverse group of political and social scientists have been asked to critically assess the book's account and to comment more broadly on the importance of black youth to the future of American politics.—Jeffrey C. Isaac, Editor

YVETTE M. ALEX–ASSENSOH, TAEKU LEE AND MARK R. WARREN

Learning Outcomes

After reading this article, you will be able to:

- Identify the central obstacles to youth development and citizenship.
- Explain what can be done about youth violence.

In her book, Cathy Cohen sets out to jump-start a conversation about the second-class citizenship of black urban youth in the United States. Indeed, she does just that. In many respects, the themes that the author purposefully explores are not necessarily new. But they remain highly salient for blacks and for America at large. It is, for example, widely acknowledged in political science and public discourse that blacks are treated as second-class citizens. The statistics showing that black youth rank at or near the bottom of every important social and economic indicator of mobility are persistently evident in highbrow scholarship, as well as everyday media reports. Furthermore, the findings that black youth harbor a distrust of government, which they view as an agent of their being used and abused, has been chronicled in historical and contemporary studies of political socialization and black urban life. Yet, as Cohen demonstrates, good conversations are not only about new themes. In fact, at times, the most provocative conversations consider conventional topics in unconventional ways, framed with interesting twists, sounded with new urgency, and articulated in ways that engage multiple audiences.

This is what Cohen does in her book. She sheds new light on the theme of racism, and ends with provocative questions about black urban youth and the future of black politics, in an effort to remind all of us that the welfare, viability, and connectedness of black urban youth are inextricably linked to the overall welfare of American democracy.

Interesting Twists

Like many good conversationalists, Cohen begins *Democracy Remixed* by telling a story of a young black man whose unexpected life trajectory exemplifies the complexity of black urban youth in general. In this case, the young man was born into a hard-working two-parent household where education was valued and prioritized. The expectation was that he would benefit from a good education, earn a college degree, and go on to realize the American Dream. Those expectations have not materialized due, in part, to the substandard educational opportunities that are commonplace in urban areas, as well as to some poor personal choices that he made along the way. Her point in retelling the story is not merely to use it as a basis for depicting the larger structural issues that many black urban youth contend with daily, but also to highlight the role of politics, individual decision making, elected officials, and policymaking in facilitating the marginalizarion of black youth. To do that, Cohen does not merely utilize the normal definition of politics; instead, she contends that the definition of politics is and should always be in dispute, especially as she widens the traditional circle of black politics beyond incorporation, immigration, electoral politics, and discrimination to focus squarely on aspects of morality.

For instance, Chapter 2 explores the demonization of black youth by celebrities like Don Imus, but with particular emphasis on how black elites like Bill Cosby, as well as older generations of blacks, are condemning black youth for what they see as moral lapses that undermine the respectability of the black community. Cohen employs the concept of moral panic in an attempt to explore the harsh critiques of black elites like Wynton Marsalis, Oprah Winfrey, and Barack Obama, in addition to Cosby, who sometimes use their access to the dominant media to publically excoriate black youth. According to Cohen, these elites have exaggerated several aspects of the behaviors of black youth in ways that lead to increased marginalizarion of black youth in their own communities.

Cohen effectively argues that moral panics validate dominant norms of discrimination, which in turn lead to more policing and criminalization that have not been good for young black men and the urban communities in which they reside. Toward these ends, Cohen contends that moral panic and secondary marginalization undermine the efficacy and self-worth of black youth and affect negatively their membership in the American political community. While there are no data to show the actual link among moral panic, secondary marginalization, and a sense of alienation from the political process, Cohen's argument provides a compelling theoretical framework for subsequent analysis.

Another provocative twist is Cohen's operationalization of moral politics to explore topics that are usually deemed taboo in the black community and, therefore, are frequently unanalyzed in black politics: sex, abortion, and rap music. Her findings, inter alia, show that black youth acknowledge the lack of concurrence between some of their ideals about morality and their lived experiences. This is especially evident in terms of the ideal of marriage, which is often constrained by the sheer unavailability of eligible black men as marriage partners. When it comes to issues like rap music, the findings clearly show that many black urban youth are critical of the way sex and violence are offensively portrayed among black women and men.

Additionally, readers are offered useful information from discussions with black urban youth about sexual intimacy that are peppered with black youths' understanding of norms of personal responsibility and the existence of such norms in the black community. Yet, Cohen argues, moral issues among black youth do not occur in a vacuum; they must be assessed within the contexts of the disadvantaged environments that do not necessarily allow many black youth to achieve their ideals. Similar to the contents of the previous chapter, Cohen's arguments, in this regard, depend heavily on the sociological-cum-psychological literature. However, a major benefit is her ability to deftly expand the boundary of blackness in ways that cover new theoretical ground in black politics, with specific emphasis on black youth.

A third twist that Cohen introduces is what she calls a "groundbreaking" national survey that focuses on black youth. While her book does not include much information on the data set, the appendix suggests that it is a mix of standard political science variables–which include socioeconomic status, religiosity, and education—as well as other indicators on rap music, beliefs about sexuality, abortion, and sexual practices. The data set includes information about black youth, but also white and Latino/a youth, and it also includes rich information from focus groups that help to round out the data. The empirical material that Cohen provides should greatly enrich political inquiry for years to come.

A Sense of Urgency

Cohen underscores a sense of urgency about the plight of black youth and the discursive options that are available to them. What she says about parenting is true in general: "[I]f we do not create the opportunity or space to talk about, for example, single mothers raising our children, then we cannot develop effective policies that will empower those families" (p. 98). At least for Cohen, part of the solution to this moral dilemma for black urban youth is to "intervene in the discourse and change it from a rhetoric of striving to have two-parent households, striving to be heterosexual—to a discourse that highlights the true norms of family life in black communities with a focus on acceptance and empowerment" (p. 98).

I agree with the author that it is important to recognize the context in which most black urban families live, and to advocate as well as plan accordingly in terms of policy discussions and programmatic interventions. However, I am skeptical about any interventions that suggest an either/or approach to the empowerment of black urban youth, especially when the "true norms" of single-parent households are often the by-products of structural problems and discrimination. Any interventions that take place in urban areas must adopt a balanced approach of recognizing the current reality while also providing the discourse, as well as the resources, to move black urban youth individually and collectively to more advantaged positions.

Meanwhile, data from Cohen's groundbreaking national study also demonstrate that black youth are at a political crossroad. On the one hand, there is a clear sense of alienation. On the other hand, there is hope for the promise of opportunity that is evident in the lives of successful black entertainment moguls, as well as in the fortunes of President Obama. For example, black youth reversed previous trends of lower participation to engage in the 2008 Obama presidential campaign, and in focus groups they revealed that his presidency made them feel more connected to government. At the same time, black youth repeatedly confirm that one black president cannot change things alone and that the contemporary racial order continues to stack the deck against their odds of success. That is why Cohen says that we as a society must work to make sure that black youth are acknowledged and treated as equal and full members of the larger political community. While that plea is certainly rational, she does not provide a clear sense of how to make that happen, and so others are clearly needed to continue the conversation and offer explicit steps toward that end.

Multiple Audiences

A clear strength of Cohen's book is the extent to which it is clearly written to speak to multiple audiences. In some sections, it reads like the work of a public intellectual, in which the author is advocating for a particular group of policy objectives, ranging from accessibility to post-secondary education to ending violence and promoting civic engagement. In other instances, as she explains how her theories comport with, as well as depart from, conventional scholarly approaches, Cohen is clearly addressing the audience of professional political scientists. In still other instances, she appears to be speaking to the youth that she writes about, in an effort to convince them that others care about them and their future.

Yet the multiple audiences that are reflected in the book are also a metaphor for the multiple audiences that comprise black urban youth. Unlike the past, when the most noticeable differences among blacks were regional, partisan, or socioeconomic, the new immigration has resulted in intraracial differences in terms of ethnicity and religion, which scholars are increasingly assessing. Also important is the rise of multiracial identification. Yet while Cohen's analysis does allow for some parsing of differences among blacks in the analytical sections of the book, she tends to discuss black youth without clarifying significant variations among them. This is especially important in light of her concern that current discourse is limiting and exclusive in ways that undermine the political attachments of black youth. For if the goal is to enhance their political incorporation, then it is crucial to properly capture the complexity of this group.

Black Youth and the Future of Black Politics

One of the most important questions posed by Cohen concerns the role and future of black politics and whether or not the new generation of black politicians sees themselves as accountable to black youth and the black community. The question emerges as a result of the so-called success that some blacks have attained personally, policy gains in certain areas, and the election of Obama as the first African American president. Ironically, Cohen suggests—and the literature supports her in this regard—that many black politicians are attempting to live in a postracial society where they do not address race directly, which leaves the field open for racial conservatives to define an increasingly regressive racial agenda. The lives, hopes, and opportunities of black urban youth hang in the balance. According to the author, the first step in that regard is to match our democratic principles with our democratic practices in ways that allow for the full citizenship of black youth. Such words are fundamental not only to the political integration of black youth but also to the political integrity of our country

In a nutshell, *Democracy Remixed* is a *cri de couer* that is focused on the plight of black youth and America's obligation to integrate them into the fold as equal and meaningful members of the general American society. Like all good work, it raises more questions than it can possibly answer. To a large extent, it provides a solid theoretical framework and a good foundation of data for future researchers of the subject matter to mine and, indeed, build upon.

Taeku Lee

The statistics on what it means to be young and black in America never cease to roil and rankle, nor should they. An African American male born today will grow up trying to defy the one-in-three odds of spending time in jail at some point in his life. Black teens, who represent one of every six teenagers in the United States, represented more than two-thirds of newly diagnosed AIDS cases in 2009. Black youth are more than three times likelier to grow up in poverty than their white counterparts and, in the wake of the Great Recession, unemployment rates for 16–19-year-old African Americans in the labor market hit nearly 50% in November 2009. And it continues.

Alongside these staggering numbers are focal moments that command Americans of all stripes who advocate for a politics of postracialism and color blindness to open their eyes, their minds, and their hearts and ponder (however briefly) W. E. B. Du Bois' defining question, "How does it feel to be a problem?" As I write this essay, the current flashpoint is set in Sanford, Florida, where 17-year-old Trayvon Martin was killed by gunfire while returning to his father's home from a convenience store. But Martin's senseless death is connected by a lamentable thread of history to Oscar Grant, Derrion Albert, Sean Bell, the Jena 6, Emmett Till, Sam Hose, and beyond.

Such indicia of racial inequality and injustice confronting black youth ought to pose a serious challenge—perhaps even an existential threat—to concepts at the heart of the study of politics like democracy, consent, legitimacy, representation, citizenship, and power. Yet for the most part, youth of color amidst our *demoi* are politely ignored by political science. Political theorists and philosophers, to be sure, give some heed to the moral arbitrariness and ambiguous agency of "children" as a category of personhood, but to my knowledge only in terms irrespective of race (e.g., Archard and Macleod 2007; Schapiro 1999; Shrag 2004). Similarly, there is a rich and reemerging literature on the political socialization of preadults that is focused mainly on the confluence of social environment and familial influence on political learning, again in terms largely irrespective of race (e.g., Jennings and Niemi 1968; Jennings, Stoker, and Bowers 2009; see also Levine 2007; Niemi and Junn 2005).

Cathy Cohen's *Democracy Remixed* is—in its conception, construction, and consequences—a radical rethinking of what is political and whose material circumstances and subjective states of mind and aspiration merit the attention of political science. Ostensibly, the book concerns the emergent political identities and understandings of African American youth. For Cohen, however, politics is not just about active citizenship in the electoral sphere, or about its antecedents in attitudes about government, or even about what black youth feel about Barack Obama's election to the White House. These elements of politics are present in the book, to be sure. But Cohen is not prone to the sort of reflexive approach that a typical political scientist might take to the animating topic of this work: namely, to take established questions about political attitudes and behavior (à la the American National Election Studies) and see what 18-to-25-year-old African Americans have to say about them. This book is, instead, a *remix.* Cohen's more inclusive, disruptive view of politics stretches from the ballot to the bedroom, encompassing practices and perspectives in private spheres of interaction like intimate sexual relations, the allegedly corrupting influence of gangsta rap, and everyday discourses of respectability.

This move will likely raise some eyebrows, or possibly even invite smirks. Yet Cohen's theoretical and analytic commitments hold the promise of remaking political science inquiry itself. Lest this ring hyperbolic, consider the disruptive force of insisting on the relevance of our everyday understandings of sexuality and cultural consumption to political analysis. The thread that ties politics as observed in acts of schoolyard bullying or unprotected sex in the bedroom to politics as observed in acts of voting, contacting officials, buycotting, and the like is power—the imposition and, at times, insinuation of authority against will and regulation over freedom. Where better to see how power relations are negotiated than among our younglings, especially those who are constantly reminded, from early childhood on, of their alterity, their Otherness? By putting black youth at the front of the bus, Cohen not only studies their empowerment but also empowers them.

As a remix, the book is thus notable for the voices that are sampled into the narrative. While public figures like Bill Cosby, Don Imus, Kwame Kilpatrick, Tyler Perry, and Barack and Michelle Obama play a role here and there, the recurrent themes throughout are composed from the voices of ordinary youth themselves, as they see the world around them and the role of politics in it. Thus, the main findings are set into an empirical foundation made of several unique data sources: a 2003 nationally representative survey of young blacks, Latinos, and whites; a 2006 companion of 40 follow-up in-depth interviews of black youth respondents to the 2003 survey; a two-wave survey of young blacks, Latinos, Asians, and whites conducted in 2008 and 2009; and four qualitative focus-group interviews of youth of varying race and sexual orientation in Chicago conducted in 2004 and 2009. The 2003 survey, 2004 focus groups, and 2006 in-depth interviews comprise the Black Youth Project, and the 2008 survey and 2009 focus group comprise the Mobilization, Change, and Political and Civic Engagement Study.

Nearly eight years in the making from the initial raw data to its publication, *Democracy Remixed* has been well worth the wait. Cohen's writing is beautiful, her analysis lucid, and the substantive body of the book is chock-full of compelling findings and probative arguments. She starts by adapting the concept of "moral panics"—the social processes and institutional mechanisms that result in "irrational and inflated reactions to lesser events." One consequence of moral panics is that a person or group (e.g., "black youth") comes to be feared as "folk devils" disproportionate to that person or group's actual threat. Transposed to the context of African American youth, Cohen observes the dynamic of "secondary marginalization" that she first described in *Boundaries of Blackness* (1999). It is elite African Americans like Cosby who themselves do the "targeting, blaming, and shaming" of black youth, branding them for their purportedly deviant behavior. They do so, moreover, by foregrounding narratives of personal responsibility and keeping mum on structural narratives of class mobility, institutional racism, and the like.

One of many striking findings is how black youth respond to this policing and marginalization from within and without. Data from the Black Youth Project show high rates of sexual activity and direct experience with pregnancies and abortions. Yet far from normalizing or touting these acts of alleged deviance, a large majority of black youth are willing to publicly denounce their peers' "wrong morals about important things like sex and work." African American youth, in comparison to young Latinos and whites, are also the most likely to espouse patriarchy, take a dim view of premarital sex, and oppose abortion. Similarly, African American youth are likelier than others to describe rap music as violent, hypersexual, misogynist, and too apolitical.

These findings are especially notable because Cohen elsewhere (2004) suggests that acts of seeming deviance among African Americans might instead be acts of purposive resistance. Here is one of several points in the book-where her voice of prepotent courage and relevance sings resonantly. Rather than diminuendo from the obvious contradiction that this represents, Cohen amps up a forceful defense of a third possibility other than shaming African American youth for their "deviance" or rhapsodizing about their "resistance." She candidly considers what it would mean to interpret this gap between revealed choices and avowed beliefs as acts of "defiance"—oppositional gestures constrained by an ever-shrinking counterpublic sphere and the ever-expanding reach of neoliberal discourses of personal responsibility. The withering social critique here of the role that Obama's heteronormativity plays in shrinking this space for defiant discourse—both in his own words and deeds and in the mainstream public's construction of the First Family—is a *coup de maître.*

Through the author's reworking of the dialectics of deviance and defiance—and their relation to moral panics and secondary marginalization—a key underlying element of the book becomes her insistence that the seemingly self-defeating and deviant decisions and discourses of African American youth are rational and prudent in light of the structures and standpoints before them that constrain free choice. This is not a new argument (see, e.g., Shelby 2007), but in Cohen's deft hands they have a fresh moral and political urgency. This is an account of street smarts as *phronesis,* if you will, and recurs as a theme that tethers her analysis of the politics of hip-hop, sexuality, and respect in early chapters with her ensuing analysis of the more "mainstream" meat-and-potatoes of political behavior and racial/ethnic politics in ensuing chapters.

Thus, not only does Chapter 4 show that an alarming number of black youth have tuned out of politics and see government as racially exclusionary and unresponsive; it also presents a forceful account of why this is evidence that black youth are not guileless. Importantly, for Cohen it is equally critical that these same youth continue to espouse and find some hope in the American creed, rather than descend into the sort of nihilism and "full-blown political alienation" foretold by Cornel West in

Race Matters (1994). Similarly, Chapter 5 not only laments the yawning gap in turnout rates between young voters and more mature citizens but also shows that youth (especially youth of color) can be mobilized to act when there is a glaring absence of accountability (as in 2004) and when there is an opportunity to make racial history (as in 2008). True to Cohen's form, however, the story of the 2008 election in her book is not a Panglossian embrace of postracial politics. While black youth are buoyed by Obama's election, they do not see this achievement as transforming their relationship to the state or altering the defining role of race and racism in their lives.

There are, to be frank, faltering moments and bits here and there to quibble about. Two in particular bear brief mention. The first is on the inclusion of data and analysis on Latino and Asian American youth. In itself, this is a key innovation and intervention into existing research practice. Given the social processes of racial sorting that result in the resegregation of youth of color in public schools, it is clearly no longer self-evident that white youth should be the default group to compare to young African Americans. Yet the integration of these up-and-coming groups into the narrative flow is at times uneven. Perhaps more pressingly, some findings on Latino and Asian youth are presented somewhat routinely, leaving this reader begging for more time and deeper analysis. Some of these findings are eye-popping. The "politics of invisibility" that Cohen discusses in Chapter 5, for instance, describes roughly 12% of African Americans in 2008, but fully 41% of Latinos and 35% of Asian Americans. This shortfall in the book, however, seems an unavoidable consequence of the fact that the author's theoretical and empirical sights are set first and foremost on African American youth. In this context, the expeditious availability of raw data from the Black Youth Project and the Mobilization, Change, and Political and Civic Engagement Study is laudable, and hopefully future scholarship will pick up where Cohen leaves off on other youth of color.

Another complaint on a minor register regards the balance between the aims of social criticism and empirical rigor found in the book. These aims, of course, need not work against one another. In fact, much of the strength of this work lies in bringing cold, hard facts to the table of public discourse riven by speculation and ideology, and parsing these facts to adjudicate competing claims. All of this is done with virtuoso precision. The quibble arises with what at times reads like a sequential recital of predicted probabilities in the presentation of multivariate analysis. To this reader, there is sometimes an insufficient differentiation between curio and crux, with the effect of interrupting the exegetical arc of a chapter.

This is a small, perhaps idiosyncratic, cavil. I should note that a more forcefully put variation on this negative theme might be cast against this work. Namely, not everyone will be convinced by parts of the empirical analysis. The wellspring of data and statistical analysis will not unmoor some critics from the clutches of attributing the unequal outcomes and opportunities that black youth find to their poor individual decision making or the pathological culture of the groups to which they belong. Yet other critics might raise the banner of causal inference and question Cohen's success at executing an explanatory mode of social science inquiry. To my reading, these sorts of well-practiced modes of scholarly and political criticism are diversions from the great triumph in *Democracy Remixed.* Standing astride the polemics of racial discourse and the dialectics of explanation and interpretation, it achieves the uncommon aspirational and transformative aims of social science research.

On a very personal note, the net result is that Cohen pulls off something uncommon at the hands of a scholar (especially a political scientist): her work evokes emotions. I do not mean here the eruptions of ire, petulance, and provocation that often result when one academic finds the work of another to be inept, polemical, or mean-spirited. Rather, in reading the book, one cannot help but feel the sense of hope and despair, anger and pride that comes from kindling the bonds of human connection. Cohen achieves this by being unafraid of making a mess: She willingly mixed the politics of her personal convictions with the science in her data analysis; she looks for agency where others might be content to find only structure; she sees in the dimly lit margins shadows of seldom heard, yet at times luminous, voices. In short, she brilliantly performs the dictates of a remix: to breath new life into a tune by sampling fresh beats and, by doing so, extending that tune's relevance and improving the fidelity of its original aspirations.

References

Archard, David, and Colin Macleod. 2007, *The Moral and Political Status of Children.* Oxford: Oxford University Press.

Cohen, Cathy. 1999. *Boundaries of Blackness.* Chicago: University of Chicago Press.

——. 2004. "Deviance as Resistance: A New Research Agenda for the Study of Black Politics." *Du Bois Review* 1(1): 27–45.

Jennings, M. Kent, and Richard Niemi. 1968. "The Transmission of Political Values from Parent to Child." *APSR* 62: 169–84.

Jennings, M. Kent, Laura Stoker, and Jake Bowers. 2009. "Politics Across Generations: Family Transmission Reexamined." *Journal of Politics* 71(3): 782–99.

Levine, Peter. 2007. *The Future of Democracy.* Medford, MA: Tufts University Press.

Niemi, Richard, and Jane Junn. 2005. *Civic Education.* New Haven: Yale University Press.

Schapiro, Tamar. 1999. "What Is a Child?" *Ethics* 109(July): 715–38.

Shelby, Tommie. 2007. "Justice, Deviance, and the Dark Ghetto." *Philosophy and Public Affairs* 35(2): 126–160.

Shrag, Francis. 2004. "Children and Democracy." *Politics, Philosophy, and Economics* 3(3): 365–79.

West, Cornel. 1994. *Race Matters.* New York: Vintage.

Mark R. Warren

"Wynton Marsalis stated that he does not listen to rap or hip-hop because it is ignorant." (p. 44)

In her new book, Cathy Cohen refuses the demonization but also the victimization of black youth. Her project aims to reclaim black youth as political and moral agents in their own lives and within American democracy. In order to do so, Cohen explains what young black people think about sexual, cultural, and political issues, as well as their understandings of the situations they face and the choices they make in their lives. The result is a richly nuanced account that offers a powerful direction out of the structure/culture trap that has stymied efforts to understand black youth and address their conditions.

It might be surprising that a study of the political views of young black people spends so much time on moral (sexual) and cultural (hip-hop) issues. However, moral concerns lie at the heart of *Democracy Remixed* in part because the "immorality" of black youth is widely condemned by the larger society—and by significant portions of the black community as well. From the dominant perspective, black youth listen to rap and hip-hop apparently because they are "ignorant" and cannot appreciate "better" musical forms. Moreover, this ignorant, violent, and oversexualized music is symbolic of the moral degradation of black youth.

Let me clarify that Cohen is no blind supporter of hip-hop culture. She critiques the commercialization of much of rap music, its stereotypical portrayals of black men and women, its violence, and its misogyny. Yet she also shows that rap music, as distorted by commercialization as it is, nevertheless remains highly relevant to the lives of young black people. Rap music contains strains that critique the systemic racial discrimination experienced by many young blacks and that address the real-life situation facing black youth, especially those who are poor—nearly 40% of all black youth.

We social scientists are so used to reading statistics that it may be hard to grasp the human reality of that percentage. Nearly 50 years after the historic gains of the Civil Rights movement that opened up opportunities to many black people, and in a polity that elected an African American as president, half of all black children grow up in or near poverty. Poverty, poor education, and mass incarceration have combined in such a way that low-income black youth face a human and social justice crisis of dire proportions. Michelle Alexander's recent book, *The New Jim Crow,* reports that 70% of black men in the North Lawndale neighborhood of Chicago are ex-offenders, mostly for drug offenses, and will suffer legally sanctioned discrimination for the rest of their lives for their criminal records.[1]

Hip-hop culture is one arena in which black youth struggle to make sense of this situation and of their lives. And this meaning making is at the heart of Cohen's concern and at the center of her contributions to a different understanding of black youth morality and politics. Cohen draws from surveys designed to measure what black youth think and do, and she also incorporates material from in-depth interviews and focus groups. In other words, rather than relying upon what others tell us about black youth, an approach that can demonize or victimize, she reports what many black youth themselves think as they struggle to be authentic agents in their own lives.

Structural Constraint and Personal Responsibility

These findings are complex and revealing, and certainly rebut popular stereotypes of black youth as ignorant and immoral. Cohen reports that black youth grasp very well the structural oppression they face—growing up in poor and often violent neighborhoods, attending underfunded and often dysfunctional schools, and being harassed at the hands of local police. Yet they also see that many blacks have "made it." Even in the context of tremendous structural barriers, young black people don't give up. They hold themselves and other black youth accountable for their personal choices. I interpret this claim of personal responsibility as the fundamentally human drive for respect and liberation. Liberation cannot be given; it must be achieved through personal and collective action. Black youth perhaps know that if they do not take responsibility for their actions, they cannot achieve their full humanity—no matter what the larger society thinks of them or how it treats them, positively or negatively.

One of Cohen's most revealing findings concerns the disconnection between beliefs and actions. Black youth want to be responsible for their moral choices, yet they face situations that strongly constrain them. Cohen reports that the large majority of black youth—80%—think that too many young blacks have the wrong morals about sex and work. Yet 70% report that they themselves have had sexual intercourse; indeed, 42% of people in the 15–17 age group report sexual intercourse, while 43% of the whole youth cohort report having been or gotten someone pregnant. The author helps us understand why this might occur, when barriers to participation in mainstream American life are so large.

Cohen also suggests a more supportive public policy response. If 50% of children born to women under the age of 30 (80% for black children) are being born out of wedlock, then we would do better to develop programs that support the "true norm" of single parents and their children than continue to condemn the situation as deviant—an approach, she asserts, that can lead to "acceptance and empowerment" (p. 98).

The constraints facing black youth are not just structural, however; they are also profoundly cultural. One of the difficulties black youth face in realizing their personal agency is the larger moralizing and stereotyping of them by the larger society. Another one of Cohen's fascinating findings is that older black people often share the moral condemnation of black youth. Drawing from theories of moral panic, she offers us some understanding of why that might be, that is, as a way to protect their status in a racially stigmatizing society.

Whatever the reasons, however, what this means is that black youth remain structurally constrained and morally condemned by both the larger society and its institutions and by many black adults who could help provide guidance. Cohen calls for the creation of honest discourse about the conditions facing black youth that can help them make reasonable and healthy moral decisions. Indeed, she powerfully reveals just how much black youth are struggling to find themselves and navigate responsibly throughout their lives. She reports, for example, that although black youth have sexual intercourse at higher rates than whites, they are also more likely to use protection against pregnancy and sexually transmitted diseases.

Resolving the Structural/Cultural Trap

Cohen's project is essential because she seeks to recover the political agency of black youth. They are not defenseless victims but authentic actors in community and political life. She reports that fully a quarter of black youth in one survey report participating in "buycotts," that is, making consumer decisions on the basis of political values. Indeed, many young black people consider listening to rap music in and of itself to be a political act. To be fair, Cohen points out that relatively few black youth participate in political protests and other forms of activism—perhaps around 8% do so. However, a much larger proportion, around 40%, participates in a broader category of civic engagement that includes volunteer activity but also possibly more politically oriented forms of community engagement.

At the end of the book, Cohen argues that civic and political engagement on the part of black youth is necessary so that they can demand the resources they need to advance their situation. In other words, mobilization addresses structural discrimination. I would like to suggest, going further, that collective action can also provide the honest spaces where black youth can address their moral concerns and take responsibility for their lives. In other words, it is through participation in groups that undertake collective action that black youth can resolve the structure/culture trap.

Youth Organizing: Personal and Collective Agency

One form of political community engagement, called youth organizing, has grown rapidly across the country, particularly among youth of color in urban communities. In youth organizing groups, young blacks discuss the conditions they face in their lives, identify problems, and develop action campaigns around solutions they design—usually supported by, and in alliance with, adults in the community.[2] For example, youth organizing groups have campaigned to open community centers, expand mass transit service and summer job opportunities, fight gang violence and police abuse, limit tobacco and alcohol advertising in urban neighborhoods, establish restorative justice discipline policies to combat the "school-to-prison" pipeline, and open new high schools oriented to community leadership and social justice, among many other issues.[3] In this way, black youth work for structural change.

These groups, however, also provide "free spaces" in which young people can discuss the wide range of issues they face in their lives and develop a sense of political *and* personal efficacy.[4] In other words, these are precisely the kinds of moral spaces for honest discourse that Cohen argues we so desperately need. Youth organizing groups typically include mentoring of individual young people as part of the collective process. Hip-hop culture and debates about the morals and politics of hip-hop culture feature prominently as young people work to build a positive community. Mentoring and community building help young people navigate a direction through personal and educational processes.

The victories that young people achieve—the opening of a community center, the changes in school disciplinary procedures—make a real difference in their lives, even if they appear small in relation to larger structural challenges. Moreover, when young people achieve victories through organizing campaigns, they gain tremendous confidence in themselves and develop respect for each other and their community. They become responsible actors in their own lives and in the community. They gain hope.

Youth organizing is moral politics because, like all politics, it concerns both interests and values—how black youth can improve the material reality of their situation, but also how can they demand respect. In these groups, young people can begin to construct a sense of how they want to live their lives.[5] Cohen convincingly shows that black youth want to live a moral life—achieving in school, getting a good job, avoiding early sexual activity—but they face structural contexts in which other behavior makes a certain sense. Through organizing, black youth have the opportunity to integrate thought and action. More broadly, they can break out of the structural/cultural bind and offer social scientists and the broader public a way to resolve it. They can develop actions that meet their moral values.

In dominant discourse, the structure/agency duality results in a polarized stalemate: Either we work to address structural racism or black youth are expected to pull themselves up by their bootstraps, à la Barack Obama. Agency in youth organizing is different because individual choice and behavior are connected to collective discourse and action. Youth organizing seeks to transform individual lives through efforts to change communities and structures.

Youth organizations remain fairly small and localized efforts at this point—although their ability to work with young people as they connect to one another in local communities and schools is a necessary part of their contribution. Yet I believe Cohen's book reveals the possibilities for a broader potential. She shows us that black youth are not passive victims of discrimination. Nor do most want to accept anti- or asocial behavior. Indeed, young black people are searching for ways to take responsibility for their lives in the context of limited choices and persistent stereotyping.

Black youth cannot be expected to solve their problems on their own. Cohen demonstrates that black youth, far from being a problem for American democracy, form a critical part of the solution to the problems we face. If adults—social scientists and the broader public including older black people as well—would approach them as intelligent and caring moral agents, we could begin to work together for greater racial equality and a more inclusive democracy.

Notes

1. Alexander 2010, 191.
2. For a description of this emerging field, see Warren, Mira, and Nikundiwe 2008 and also Warren and Mapp 2011.
3. See Checkoway et al. 2003 as one source.
4. For a more detailed discussion of this process, see Ginwright 2009; on free spaces more generally, see Evans and Boyte 1992.
5. The pursuit of moral meaning in political action is treated more broadly by Taylor 1989.

References

Alexander, Michelle. 2010. *The New Jim Crow: Mass Incarceration in the Age of Colorblindness.* New York: New Press.

Checkoway, Barry, et al. 2003. "Young People as Competent Citizens." *Community Development Journal* 38(4): 298–309.

Evans, Sara M., and Harry C. Boyte. 1992. *Free Spaces: The Sources of Democratic Change in America.* Chicago: University of Chicago Press.

Ginwright, Sean. 2009. *Black Youth Rising: Activism and Radical Healing in Urban America.* New York: Teachers College Press.

Taylor, Charles. 1989. *Source, of Self: The Making of Modern Identity.* Cambridge. MA: Harvard University Press.

Warren, Mark R., and Karen L. Mapp. 2011. *A Match on Dry Grass: Community Organizing as a Catalyst for School Reform.* New York: Oxford University Press.

Warren, Mark R., Meredith Mira, and Thomas Nikundiwe. 2008. "Youth Organizing: From Youth Development to School Reform." *New Directions in Youth Development* 117(Spring): 27–42.

Critical Thinking

1. Explain the process of civil education and moral development.
2. Describe the various aspects of youth violence and approaches to curb violence among armed and unarmed young persons.

Create Central

www.mhhe.com/createcentral

Internet References

American Civil Liberties Union (ACLU)
www.aclu.org

Center for Research in Ethnic Relations
www.warwickac.ukllaclsoc/CRER_RC

The International Center for Migration, Ethnicity, and Citizenship
www.newschool.edu/icmec

National Association for the Advancement of Colored People (NAACP)
www.naacp.org

Sociosite
www.sociosite.net

Yvette M. Alex-Assensoh is Vice President for Equity and Inclusion, and professor of Political Science at the University of Oregon.

Taeku Lee is Professor of both Law and Political Science, and Chair of the Political Science Department at the University of California at Berkeley.

Mark R. Warren is Associate Professor of Public Policy and Public Affairs at the McCormick Graduate School at the University of Massachusetts-Boston.

Article

Prepared by: John A. Kromkowski, *Catholic University of America*

A Promised Land, A Devil's Highway: The Crossroads of the Undocumented Immigrant

DANIEL G. GROODY

Learning Outcomes

After reading this article, you will be able to:

- Describe the condition of immigrants at the border.
- Explain the motivation and values of religious organizations who work with immigrants in need.

The great legacy of Archbishop Oscar Romero's life was his identification with the crucified Christ. While his witness to the God of life reached its ultimate expression during his last liturgy, the sacrifice of his own life on the altar of God was the culmination of his solidarity with those who suffer on the altar of the world. Among the many poor people for whom he laid down his life are those who eventually emigrated from his country in search of more dignified lives. As we reflect on the contribution of Oscar Romero's life, I would like to do so in light of what Ignacio Ellacuría calls "the people crucified in history." In particular, I would like to look at the physical, spiritual, and theological terrain of the undocumented immigrant coming across the Mexican-American border today.

The context of Romero's death leaves much room for reflection, but in the very least, it prompts us to consider the integral relationship that his faith expressed at liturgy and that his commitment to the poor expressed in the struggle for justice. As a starting point, I would like to look at the relationship between the Eucharist and immigration. While, on the surface, there does not appear to be an obvious connection between what happens at Mass and what happens on the border, the correlation became clearer the first time I attended a Eucharistic celebration in El Paso, Texas, where Mexico meets the United States. We celebrated Mass outside on November 1, in the open air, in the dry, rugged, and sun-scorched terrain where the two countries meet. In this liturgy, we remembered all the saints and the souls who had gone before us. We also remembered the thousands of Mexican immigrants who died at the crossroads of the border in recent years. Like other liturgies, a large crowd gathered to pray and worship. Unlike at other liturgies, however, a sixteen foot iron fence divided this coummunity in half, with one side in Mexico and the other side in the United States.

To give expression to our common solidarity as a people of God beyond our political constructions, we joined altars on both sides of the wall. Even while border patrol agents and helicopters surrounded us and kept a strict vigilance—lest any Mexicans cross over—we sang, we worshiped, and we prayed. We prayed for our governments. We prayed for those who died. And we prayed to understand better our interconnectedness to each other. I remember in particular the sign of peace, when one normally shakes a hand or shares a hug with one's neighbor. Unable to touch my Mexican neighbor except through some small holes in the fence, I became acutely aware of the unity that we celebrated but also the divisions that we experience. Even while this Eucharist testified to our unity in Christ, the wall between us revealed the dividedness of our current reality, for no other reason than that we were born on different sides of the fence.

A Faith Perspective on a Complex Reality

For the last few decades, I have been talking to immigrants, border patrol agents, *coyote smugglers* (those who transport people across), ranchers, vigilante groups, educators, congresspersons, medical personnel, social workers, human rights advocates, and others involved in this immigration drama. Ranchers have seen their property trashed by immigrants who parade through their land and leave behind water jugs, litter, and discarded clothing. Educators and hospital administrators have felt increasing financial pressure from the influx of newly arrived immigrants. Border patrol agents have told stories of being pinned down by gunfire from drug smugglers of cocaine and marijuana. Congressional leaders have felt pressure, especially since September 11, to establish policies that aim at safeguarding a stable economy and protecting the common good. Coyote smugglers have talked about guiding people across the treacherous terrain along the border and gaining a profit while doing so. But most of all, migrants have shared what it is like to break from home, cross the border, and enter the United States as undocumented immigrants. In the process, they have revealed not only much about the physical terrain of the immigrant journey but also the spiritual terrain of their faith lives.

In speaking with these different groups along the border, I have learned that each constituency believes that it has certain rights. Each group has a point to make, a truth to defend. These include the rights to private property, jobs, national security, civil law and order, and other such rights. The legitimacy of each claim makes it clear that immigration is a complex reality and that it is not easy to untangle a web of competing interests. Yet, it is here that theology can offer some important reflection about what it means to be human before God and what it means to live together in society.

From a theological perspective, while every truth claim merits its consideration, not every claim has equal authority. Christian theology asserts that as a starting point, those who suffer the most deserve the greatest hearing (Matthew 25:31–46), even though, ironically, the voice of the "least" is often the last one to be heard, if it is heard at all. Oscar Romero learned throughout his life that the poor themselves not only deserve to be heard but are key to gaining an accurate grasp of reality, without which wise choices cannot be made. In the context of immigration, this is where the stories of the immigrants themselves are particularly important. As some of the most vulnerable members of society, immigrants clarify that whatever "rights" are at stake in this debate, one of the most neglected is the right to a more dignified life. These rights become clearer when one listens to the stories as they emerge from various crisis points along the border, including detention centers, hospitals, shelters, train stations, deserts, mountains, and along rivers and highways and other areas. Their stories have made me look at the immigration issue differently. They have helped me see that the journey of an undocumented immigrant is not a camping trip through a scenic part of the American Southwest but a descent into the vast expanses of hell; their journey toward a promised land" takes place on what Luis Alberto Urrea calls "a devil's highway."

The Evolution of the Mexican-American Border

The pathways of this highway have been carved out slowly over time. The Mexican-American border has undergone a complex evolution, especially over the last century. Up until the end of the Mexican-American War in 1848, when Mexico ceded what is now much of the Southwestern United States, people moved freely and cyclically throughout the current border states and Mexico. The border area remained relatively porous, and enforcement was relatively light through most of the nineteenth and twentieth centuries, except for a vigilante organization in 1880 that tried to keep the Chinese out. In 1924, the U.S. Border Patrol began tightening the border through more systematic enforcement efforts. In time, stricter border policies emerged, especially in the 1980s when President Reagan declared a "war on drugs." This "war" made the border an increasingly militarized zone as American drug enforcement entities battled against wealthy, organized drug cartels for superiority in firepower and surveillance.

An important development for the border was the devaluation of the Mexican peso in 1983, which triggered an explosion of foreign-owned factories along the Mexican side of the border. U.S. companies took advantage of the exchange rate by moving their assembly plants from the states to Mexico in pursuit of cheap labor. Hundreds of thousands of Mexican citizens, many of whom had lost their land because of Mexican agricultural policies, came north to work in *maquiladoras*. In the last few years, however, more than a quarter of these plants have closed down as companies have discovered even cheaper labor in Asia. Consequently, hundreds of thousands of jobs along the border have disappeared, digging the Mexican economy into a deeper hole and making unemployment and underemployment more the norm than the exception.

In the 1990s, the Clinton administration, fueled by much anti-immigrant sentiment that was brewing in California such as that reflected in proposition 187, further intensified border control with policies such as Operation Hold the Line, in El Paso, and Operation Gatekeeper, in San Diego, and later, other similar initiatives. By erecting walls and fences, by stationing border patrol agents every quarter mile along the border in the major urban areas, and by the increased use of military technology, including drone planes, infrared technology, motion sensors, and other such instruments, crossing outside of normal ports of entry became much more difficult, which, by design, has significantly raised the stakes of migrating illegally. To avoid detection, immigrants are pushed to the most remote areas of the border where surveillance is thin.

While policies such as Operation Gatekeeper in 1994 and similar initiatives along the border were meant to deter immigrants from crossing illegally, they have not changed the flows at all but merely redirected migrants into more life-threatening territory, such as waterless deserts and mountains. With temperatures exceeding 120 degrees in the shade, many have to walk fifty miles or longer in treacherous conditions. In such surroundings, one's body cooks like an egg, which causes heat stroke, brain damage, and even death. Because it is physically impossible to carry the food and water necessary for this type of trek, many do not make it. I realized how extreme this journey was when one day, a coyote offered me a "ride-along scholarship" so that I could see what the journey was like. Instead of paying the going rate of $1,800 to take me across the border, he said he was going to "teach" me what it was like, for free. His words were as follows:

> *We'll walk for three or four days, and all you will have with you are a few tortillas, some sardines, and water. The food is so bad you won't want to eat, and you will get so tired you won't think you are going to make it. If you push on, you can do it, but if you fall behind, we will leave you behind. And*

> *you should wear high heel, leather boots, because we come across rattlesnakes in the desert at night, but if you have the right boots on, the snake's teeth won't penetrate your skin and you'll be okay.*

Because of such dangers, every day, immigrants dehydrate in deserts, drown in canals, freeze in mountains, and suffocate in tractor trailers. As a result, the death toll has increased 1,000 percent in some places. When asked what he thought about the dangers, an immigrant named Mario said,

> *Sure, I think about the dangers. I think about them all the time. But I have no choice if I am going to move forward with my life. The fact is, amidst the poverty in Mexico, I am already dead. Crossing the desert gives me the hope of living, even if I die.*

If they make it across the border, most immigrants will work at low-paying jobs that no one else wants except the most desperate. They will debone chickens in poultry plants, pick crops in fields, and build houses in construction. As one person noted, "it looks like entering the U.S. through the desert as undocumented immigrants do is some kind of employment screening test administered by the U.S. government for the hospitality, construction, and recreation industries." Willing to work at the most dangerous jobs, an immigrant a day will die in the workplace, even while for others, the workplace has become safer over the last decade. Immigrants die cutting North Carolina tobacco and Nebraska beef, chopping down trees in Colorado, welding a balcony in Florida, trimming grass at a Las Vegas golf course, and falling from scaffolding in Georgia.

With an economic gun at their backs, they leave their homes because hunger and poverty push them to cross the border. Mario told me in an immigration detention center,

> *Sometimes my kids come to me and say, "Daddy, I'm hungry." And I don't have enough money to buy them food. And I can't tell them I don't have any money, but I don't. I can barely put beans, potatoes, and tortillas on the table with what I make. But I feel so bad that I sometimes will go into a store, even if it is two or three blocks away, or even three or four kilometers away, or even another country in order to get food for my family. I feel awful, but nothing is worse than seeing your hungry child look you in the eyes, knowing you don't have enough food to give them.*

Immigrants are pushed by economic poverty, pulled by the hope of a better life in the United States, and blocked by an iron wall at the border. At this border, where the ideals of freedom in America are safeguarded, many immigrants clash with a form of slavery embedded in the contemporary American imagination.

Crossing the Borders of our Own Mind

While many Americans hailed the crumbling of the Berlin Wall in 1989 and mourned the death of sixty-eight people who died trying to cross it over a period of twenty-eight years, many of us have stood idle as we have constructed a new wall between Mexico and the United States. Since 1994, more than 4,000 undocumented immigrants have died trying to find their way into America. The tragic loss of life along the Mexican-American border is a challenge to the national consciences of Mexico, the United States, and, indeed, the global community. While it raises serious questions about structural injustice, it challenges all of us to reflect on how we regard those labeled as "different" by mainstream society.

Despite the obstacles that immigrants face in crossing the border, perhaps the more difficult borders to cross today are the borders of our own minds, especially, those that guard our deep-seated biases and prejudices and those we put up when we encounter someone who we consider to be totally "other" than we are. Mexican immigrants bear some of the worst stereotypes in today's society and are some of the first to be typecast in a negative light. Not infrequently in mainstream media, they are typecast as illegal, nontaxpaying "leaches" who suck dry the funds of local communities while selling drugs, committing crimes, and taking jobs away from Americans. Some even lump immigrants into the same category as terrorists, as an unwelcome threat, without ever realizing that the terrorists of September 11 came into the country with legal visas. Nonetheless, in the popular mind, immigrants are perceived as a menace to the common good and the preservation of U.S. culture. Absurdly, some—apparently unaware of the last battle against indigenous Americans at Wounded Knee—argue that immigrants are taking away "Native American" culture.

Whatever one's perceptions about these popular impressions, sadly, many of the immigrants themselves begin to believe the stereotypes spread about them. Often looked at as uneducated, lazy, and inferior, they begin to internalize many of these labels. Such stereotypes have their origin from the time of the Spanish conquest in the early sixteenth century. Unfortunately, many immigrants come to believe some of the ways that contemporary society typecasts them. Perhaps, one of the more challenging roads to conversion for them is not only believing in God but believing in themselves. Lydia comments,

> *We are constantly reminded that we are less than everybody else, that we are poor, that we don't have an education, that we don't speak right, that we are lesser human beings in one way or another. Sometimes, we even begin to wonder whether God thinks that way about us too.*

The more challenging road to conversion for many Americans often means unlearning the negative stereotypes and seeing more clearly the inner worth, dignity, and respective contributions that immigrants bring to this country.

A Day without a Mexican

Despite the tide of anti-immigrant sentiment, the economic undercurrent is such that immigrants are an essential and vital part of our current economic reality. We have effectively walled off the truth about the role that immigrants play in sustaining the infrastructure of America. As Pastor Robin Hoover of

Humane Borders says, "our nation virtually posts two signs on its southern border: 'Help Wanted: Inquire Within' and 'Do Not Trespass.'" Without the help of immigrant labor, the U.S. economy would virtually collapse. We want and need cheap immigrant labor, but we do not want the immigrants.

A few years ago an interesting documentary came out called *A Day without a Mexican.* It attempted to show what the American economy would look like if there were no Mexicans working here anymore. There would be no maids in hotels. No people to wash dishes in restaurants. No landscapers to mow grass. No cheap hands to do construction. No people to pick vegetables in the fields. As a result, lettuce would cost more than eight dollars a head; industries would shut down; various sectors of the economy would be paralyzed. Even though the U.S. economy needs these immigrants and even though multinational corporations profit from their labor, immigrants today are not afforded the same opportunities or open doors that immigrants experienced in previous generations. In fact, the opposite is true. Instead of receiving hospitality and openness, many immigrants find scapegoating and rejections, hostility and fear.

Today, some immigrants are greeted by vigilante groups and civilian border patrols who hunt them down, treat them like animals, and even threaten to kill them. In parts of the Southwest, racist violence runs deep in groups such as the Civil Homeland Defense, Ranch Rescue, and American Border Patrol (not to be confused with the U.S. Border Patrol). "If I had my way," one rancher reportedly bellowed at a meeting with U.S. Border Patrol officials, "I'd shoot every single one of 'em." The fact is that most immigrants are not stealing jobs from Americans; they are doing work that most Americans do not want to do. Moreover, not only are immigrants not a drain on the U.S. economy, but they also contribute with direct and indirect taxes. Even though immigrants collectively pay more than $90 billion in taxes, many are afraid to use social services for fear that it will expose their undocumented status.

Nonetheless, like previous immigrants from Ireland, Italy, Germany, Eastern Europe, China, and Japan, these Mexican immigrants, as Jorge Bustamante notes, are often valued for their cheap labor but are not afforded the human rights due to them as contributing members of society. They become a "disposable commodity" when they are no longer useful. It is here in particular that the Scriptures and Catholic social teaching have something important to say.

The Relationship of Immigration to Revelation

According to the Judeo-Christian Scriptures, immigration is not simply a sociological fact but also a theological event. In the process of immigrating, God revealed his covenant to his people. This covenant was a gift and a responsibility; it reflected God's goodness to them, but it also called them to respond to newcomers in the same way that Yahweh responded to them when they were in slavery: "So you too must befriend the alien, for you were once aliens yourselves in the land of Egypt" (Deuteronomy 10:19).

Building on this same foundation, Catholic social teaching has reiterated that the true moral worth of any society is how it treats its most vulnerable members. John Paul II consistently underscored the moral responsibility of richer nations to help poor nations, particularly with regard to more open immigration policies. While some in America claim that these undocumented immigrants have no right to be here, the church believes that a person's true homeland is that which provides the person with bread.

When Moisés reached Tijuana, he said that the reason why he wanted to come to the United States was that he could barely put food on the table with what he earned. He said that his ambition was simply to provide "bread" for his family. On this same day, a few miles away on the other side of the border near a very popular resort hotel on Coronado Island, a woman said that she had come to the area because she was looking for a "specialty bread," a delicacy that she could not find anywhere else. The contradictions of the moment were striking: two people can live in the same geographical place but live in two totally different worlds. These two lives are microcosms of a larger contrast between Mexico and the United States, between the First World and the Third World.

While the church recognizes the right of a nation to control its borders, it does not see this right as an absolute right, nor does it see sovereign rights as having priority over basic human rights. It acknowledges that the ideal is that people find work in their home countries; however, it also teaches that if their countries of birth do not afford the conditions necessary to lead a fully human life, then those persons have a right to emigrate. While border reform does not mean naively opening our borders to everyone, as if there were no need to take into account other political and socioeconomic factors, the church makes every effort to put human life at the forefront of the discussion. It critically asks why barriers have been steadily lowered when it comes to commerce but have steadily risen when it comes to labor. If Oscar Romero were alive today, he would likely challenge those unjust social structures that benefit the elite at the expense of the poor or that calculate financial costs but ignore the human costs of economic systems and political policies. He would indict a society that values goods and money more than it does human beings and human rights, which directly contradicts the biblical narrative. While some Americans and some Christians may see our privileged life in the United States as a divine right, a scriptural reading of reality offers an entirely different perspective.

The gospel vision challenges the prevailing consumerist mentality of American culture, which seeks meaning through a seemingly endless accumulation of goods, even while the rest of the world suffers for want of basic needs. Jesus, in his life and ministry, went beyond borders of all sorts, including those defined by the authorities of his own day, such as clean/unclean, saintly/sinful, and rich/poor. In doing so, he called into being a community of magnanimity and generosity that would reflect God's unlimited love for all people (Acts 2). He called people "blest," not when they have received the most, but when they have shared the most and needed the least. Christians, as such, distinguish themselves not by the quantity of their possessions but the quality of their heart, which expresses itself in service. Above all, this quality of the heart is measured by the extent to which one loves the least significant among us.

In many respects, immigrants sit at America's door like Lazarus sat at the gate of the rich man (Luke 16:19–31), hoping for scraps to fall from the American table of prosperity. While there are many texts through which to analyze today's reality along the border, the Judgment of the Nations (Matthew 25: 31–46) is a particularly challenging text through which to read the issue of immigration. In this passage, Jesus says, "I was hungry and you gave me food, I was thirsty and you gave me drink, a stranger and you welcomed me, naked and you clothed me, ill and you cared for me, in prison and you visited me." The corollaries to the immigrant experience are striking. Hungry in their homelands, thirsty in the treacherous deserts in which they cross, naked after being robbed at gunpoint by *bandito* gangs, sick in the hospitals from heat-related illnesses, imprisoned in immigration detention centers, and, finally, if they make it across, estranged in a new land, they bear many of the marks of the crucified Christ in our world today.

Migrants undergo a way of the cross every day. They experience an economic crucifixion when they realize that they can no longer subsist in their homeland. They experience a social crucifixion when they have to leave their families and friends behind. They undergo a cultural crucifixion when they leave behind the familiar and come into a new and strange land. They experience a legal crucifixion when they cross the border and become "illegal aliens." For those who die in the deserts and mountains, they experience an actual crucifixion, dying some of the most horrible deaths imaginable. And they even experience a religious crucifixion of sorts when they experience themselves as strangers, outsiders, and even threats to church communities, if they are welcomed there. As an archbishop, Romero was one that welcomed the excluded and put them at the center of his pastoral attention and ministry. His own spirituality and identification with the crucified Christ compelled him to go the poor as his response of love to the God of love.

Spirituality and theology are built into the struggles of immigration, particularly, migrants, even if the situation does not look that way on the surface. John Paul II notes,

> *The immediate reasons for the complex reality of human migration differ widely; its ultimate source, however, is the longing for a transcendent horizon of justice, freedom and peace. In short, it testifies to an anxiety which, however indirectly, refers to God, in whom alone humans can find the full satisfaction of all his expectations ("Message for World Migration Day," no. 1).*

What appears to be simply a sociological, political, and economic phenomenon has a deep theological current under the surface. Theology, above all, engages the hopes and struggles of the human heart, and from there, it seeks to find God's revelation in the midst of everyday life, even and especially in those "godless" areas where God seems disturbingly absent. Theology takes flesh in the ordinariness of life, and because it is rooted in everyday life, it is also rooted in the everyday sufferings of people.

Theology, as it is disclosed in history, has always evolved in this way. While Christians today regard the cross as the one symbol that summarizes God's redemptive love for the world, at the time of Jesus, it held no initial theological significance. In biblical times, the cross was a form of capital punishment, which, in the Old Testament, reflected more of God's curse than his blessing (Deuteronomy 21:23). However, upon deeper reflection, a theological truth emerged about the cross, symbolizing God's self-giving love to God's people. In a similar way, migration, like the cross, has deep theological dimensions. Immigrants hold much potential to be bearers of new life. In response to the challenge of immigration, the U.S. bishops, as expressed in their pastoral letter *Strangers No Longer: Together on the Journey of Hope,* have sought "to awaken our peoples to the mysterious presence of the crucified and risen Lord in the person of the migrant and to renew in them the values of the Kingdom of God that he proclaimed" (Catholic Bishops of Mexico and the United States, no. 3). Building on this similar spirit, Romero not only reached out to those on the edge of society but realized that the church is born on the margins, where those who are crucified live and suffer today.

Amid such difficult conditions, many immigrants offer a surprising but compelling witness of faith. When María came north from Guatemala, she wanted to work in the United States for only two years, then return home to her family. I met her on the Mexican side of the border, just before her third attempt to cross. In the previous ten days, she had tried twice to cross the border through a remote route in southern Arizona. On her first attempt, she was mugged at the border by a *bandito* gang. Though bruised and beaten, she continued her journey through the desert and ran out of food. Just before she reached the road, she was apprehended by the border patrol and put into an immigration detention center. A few days later, she tried again. This time, her coyote smuggler tried to rape her, but she managed to free herself and push her way through the desert once again. After four days of walking, she ran out of food, water, and even strength. After almost dying in the desert, the border patrol found her, helped her, and then sent her back to Mexico.

After chronicling her story to me for a long time and after telling me about her suffering in detail, I was curious about how she dealt with these trials before God, so I asked her, "If you had fifteen minutes to speak to God, what would you say to Him?" Thinking that she would have given Him a long litany of complaints, María surprised me when she said,

> *First of all, I do not have fifteen minutes to speak to God. I am always conversing with Him, and I feel His presence with me always. Yet, if I saw God face to face, the first thing I would do is thank Him, because He has been so good to me and has blest me so abundantly.*

It is extraordinary to ponder that thousands of years ago, Israel's strongest affirmations about God's faithfulness often came in the midst of its own exile in Babylon, not in the midst of prosperity. Given that many immigrants live as exiles in the United States, it is striking to witness such faith amid such adversity and to see such revelation in unsuspected places.

Migration as a Journey of Hope

Archbishop Romero understood that salvation was intimately intertwined with a commitment to the crucified peoples of today. He testified to the mercy of God in a merciless world. "In my life," he said, "I have only been a poem of the love of God, and I have become in Him what He has wanted me to be." Standing in solidarity with Christ on the altar and through Christ as crucified with the poor, Romero came to be known as an *entregado,* one who not only gives one's life for his people but also reveals through faithful witness the life of the Savior, known in Spanish as *El Salvador.* He also understood that following this Savior led him to a migration of hope, even and especially when his labors for justice took place amid a seemingly hopeless situation.

As immigrants such as those from Mexico and other parts of Latin America fight for more dignified lives, it is helpful to remember that the term *immigrant* is built into the church's very self-definition. It sees itself as comprising a "pilgrim people" moving from sin to grace, from cross to resurrection, and from this world to the next. In the Eucharist, the church protests against the walls and barriers that we set up between ourselves, and it affirms again and again that we are one body in Christ. It realizes that, this side of heaven, we all live in the same country; we all live on the same side of the fence. To the church, death is the ultimate border; the journey of faith is the ultimate migration; and God is the ultimate promised land. Christ teaches that we will be able to cross over this final border to the extent that we have been able to cross over the smaller borders in this life and see our interconnectedness to each other (Luke 16:19–31). In the very least, we need a new imagination to bring about a new immigration policy.

Life itself, if we live it well, is a process of endless migration. Movement toward the promised land inevitably calls us to cross borders of every sort, and it makes us vulnerable in the process. As undocumented immigrants remind us, this journey is not a road for the fainthearted. Each day, God calls us out of our comfort zones as we move from the known to the unknown, from the secure to the insecure, from the land of our physical birth to the land of our spiritual birth. It is only when we choose not to migrate, when we stagnate, when we seek to save our lives rather than lose them in God, that we spiritually die. If "migration" is worked into the self-definition of all peoples, then we might find those who come to us as immigrants less threatening than we often do. And we might see not only a reflection of ourselves but that of God, who, even when we were lost, did not abandon us to die. Rather, in love, God "migrated" to us in the Incarnation so that, through Him, we might migrate with Him across all borders into the fullness of God's loving embrace and find our true homeland in God's Kingdom.

Discussion Questions

1. Given the complexity of the immigration question, why do you think that the church has taken the stance of defending the immigrant—even the undocumented immigrant? Since most Americans are the offspring of immigrants, why do you think the anti-immigration sentiment is so strong?
2. Discuss: Have you had personal or business dealings with undocumented immigrants? Do they work hard? If legislation were passed that prohibited helping undocumented immigrants, would you be willing to break the law and still help them? Why? Why not?
3. How is the Eucharist a sign that breaks down walls and barriers? Discuss Father Groody's point that the term *immigrant* is "built into the church's very self-definition."

Resources and Further Study

Catholic Bishops of Mexico and the United States. *Strangers No Longer: Together on the Journey of Hope.* Washington D.C.: United States Conference of Catholic Bishops, 2003. www.usccb.org/mrs/stranger.shtml (accessed May 2, 2007).

Elizondo, Virgil. *Galilean Journey.* Maryknoll, N.Y.: Orbis Books, 1983.

Groody, Daniel G. *Border of Death, Valley of Life: An Immigrant Journey of Heart and Spirit.* Lanham, Md.: Rowman & Littlefield, 2002.

———, prod. *Dying to Live: A Migrant's Journey.* Video/DVD. Notre Dame, Ind.: University of Notre Dame, 2005.

———. *Globalization, Spirituality, and Justice: Navigating the Path to Peace.* Maryknoll, N.Y.: Orbis Books, 2007.

———, ed. *The Option for the Poor in Christian Theology.* Notre Dame, Ind.: University of Notre Dame Press, 2007.

Groody, Daniel G., and Gioacchino Campese, eds. *A Promised Land, a Perilous Journey: Theological Perspectives on Migration.* Notre Dame, Ind.: University of Notre Dame Press, 2007.

John Paul II. "Message for World Migration Day." United States Conference of Catholic Bishops, November 21, 1999. www.usccb.org/pope/wmde.htm (accessed May 2, 2007).

Skylstad, William. "Comprehensive Immigration Reform." United States Conference of Catholic Bishops, January 15, 2006. www.usccb.org/bishops/immigrationreform.shtml (accessed May 2, 2007).

Critical Thinking

1. Describe conditions of migrants near the border?
2. Why are religious organizations engaged in this situation?

Create Central

www.mhhe.com/createcentral

Internet References

The Council for Research in Values and Philosophy
www.crvp.org

Diversity.com
www.diversity.com

The International Center for Migration, Ethnicity, and Citizenship
www.newschool.edu/icmec